Ordnance Survey of Ireland

GW00418682

Dubl Street Guide

City and District

General Travel Information

Travel Services and Local Radio Stations	I
Motoring Information	II
Dart and Suburban Rail Lines	III
Dublin Bus Services	IV
Route Planner	V

Index and Legend to Map Pages — VI
Dublin City and District Maps — 1
City Centre Maps — 59

Tourist Information

The Story of Dublin	64
Places to Visit	65
Churches and Cathedrals	72
Libraries	74
Art Galleries	75
Museums	76
Some Famous Dublin People	77
Dublin's Parks and Gardens	79
Dublin as a Sporting Centre	81
Dublin Alive Alive Oh!	82
Embassies	83
Dublin Bus Information	84

Industrial Estates and Business Parks	88
Index to Street Names	89
Index to Hospitals	121

2nd EDITION   SPECIAL THANKS TO BORD FÁILTE AND OFFICE OF PUBLIC WORKS.

TRAVEL SERVICES

AIR

DUBLIN AIRPORT	7056705
Aer Lingus	
Information	705 6705
Reservations	705 3333
Air France	844 5633
British Airways	1 800 626 747
British Midlands	283 8833
City Jet	844 5566
Delta Airlines	676 8080
Lufthansa	844 5544
Ryanair	609 7800
Swissair	677 8173
Virgin Atlantic	873 3388

CORK AIRPORT	
(0715-2300 HOURS)	(021)313131
(2300-0700 HOURS)	(021)313288

SHANNON AIRPORT	
	(061) 471444
	(061) 471666

SEA

STENA SEALINK	
DUBLIN	204 7777
DÚN LAOGHAIRE	204 7700
CORK	(021) 272965
ROSSLARE	(053) 33115
IRISH FERRIES	
DUBLIN	661 0511
CORK	(021) 551995
ROSSLARE	(053) 33158
BRITTANY FERRIES	
CORK	(021) 277801
SWANSEA / CORK FERRIES	
CORK	(021) 271166

RAIL

IARNRÓD ÉIREANN	
IRISH RAIL	
INCLUDING DART SUBURBAN RAIL	836 6222

BUS

BUS ÁTHA CLIATH	
DUBLIN BUS	873 4222
BUS ÉIREANN	
IRISH BUS	836 6111

ROAD

A.A. RESCUE	
FREEPHONE	1 800 667788
R.A.C. RESCUE	
FREEPHONE	1 800 535005

LOCAL RADIO STATIONS
NATIONAL AND LOCAL WEATHER AND ROAD INFORMATION
ARE BROADCAST FERQUENTLY ON THE FOLLOWING WAVELENGTHS.

RTE

RADIO 1	FM 88.5 89.1MHz
2FM	FM 90.7 91.3MHz
	MW 1278 kHz
RAIDIO NA GAELTACHTA	
	FM 92.9 93.5MHz
FM3	FM 92.9 93.5MHz

INDEPENDENT RADIO

ANNA LIVIA	103.8FM
ATLANTIC 252	LW 252 kHz 1190 m
98FM	98.1FM
EAST COAST RADIO	94.9FM
	102.9FM
RADIO NA LIFE	102.2FM
CKR CARLOW	97.3FM
	97.6FM
FM 104	104.4FM
RADIO IRELAND	100.3FM

RTE HAS IMPLEMENTED AN AUTOMATIC TUNING SYSTEM (RDS) ON ITS THREE NATIONAL FM NETWORKS. AN RDS RECEIVER CONTINUALLY SCANS FOR THE BEST SIGNAL, GIVING OPTIMUM RECEPTION AT ALL TIMES.

DRIVING IS ON THE LEFT THROUGHOUT IRELAND.
SEAT BELTS must be worn by drivers and passengers.
CRASH HELMETS must be worn by motorcyclists and pillion passengers.

WARNING SIGNS

The following are examples of the principal signs.

TWO-WAY TRAFFIC

Dangerous Corner or Bend Ahead

Series of Dangerous Corners or Bends Ahead

Slippery Stretch of Road Ahead

Sharp Rise Ahead

Sharp Depression Ahead

Series of Bumps or Hollows Ahead

Junction Ahead With Road or Roads of Equal Importance.

Steep Ascent Ahead

Steep Descent Ahead

Road Narrows Dangerously

Roundabout Ahead

Junction Ahead With Roads of Less Importance. (minor roads shown by thin arms)

Unprotected Quay, Canal or River

Road Works Ahead

Children Sign (School etc.)

Traffic Lights Ahead

Junctions Ahead With Roads of Equal Importance

With Roads of Less Importance

Advanced Warning of a Major Road Ahead

12' 6"
Low Bridge Ahead

Level Crossing Ahead guarded by gates.

Level Crossing Ahead Unguarded.

End of Dual Carriageway.

EMERGENCIES

☎ **999 112**

Police

Ambulance

Fire Brigade

Life Boat

Coastal Rescue

REGULATORY SIGNS

These signs implement road regulations and show the course to follow etc.

STOP

Parking

Traffic **must** proceed in the direction of the arrow.

Keep to Left Carriagway

Traffic may **not** proceed in the direction of the arrow.

Parking Permitted

Clearway Stopping or Parking Prohibited (except Buses and Taxis)

Parking Prohibited

TAXI RANK Parking for taxis only.

Give Way

YIELD RIGHT OF WAY

SPEED LIMITS

MOTORWAY
70 mph/112 kph.

NATIONAL LIMIT
60 mph/96 kph

OTHER LIMITS MAY APPLY IN TOWNS, BUILT-UP AREAS AND SOME ROADS AS INDICATED.

(30) (40) (∕)
End of Speed Limit

INFORMATION SIGNS

These signs will give information regarding direction, distance, place etc.
Amenities of particular interest to tourists are displayed on a brown background in white.

↑ Loch Garman WEXFORD
N11

← Bré BRAY

Motorway ahead
NO L-drivers,
Vehicles under 50 c.c.,
Slow vehicles (under 30 mph),
Invalid-carriages,
Pedal-cycles,
Pedestrians,
Animals.
Motorway ahead

↑ N 11
N 7

← N 81

M50
Entry to Motorway

Motorway Regulations no longer apply →

500m
Approaching end of Motorway

◄ 2 Bré BRAY

N 4 →

← N 11

Cearnóg Mhuirfean
Merrion Square 2

← An Nás NAAS
4 km

2 km

ⓘ Eolas do Thurasoiri TOURIST INFORMATION

Slí na Bóinne BOYNE DRIVE

III DART and Suburban Rail Network

Western Suburban Service. Runs from Connolly Station to Mullingar.

Northern Suburban Service. Runs from Pearse Station to Dundalk.

DART Service. Runs from Howth to Bray

Leixlip
Leixlip Confey
Clonsilla
Coolmine
Blanchardstown/Castleknock
Ashtown
Broombridge

City Centre

Malahide
Portmarnock
Howth Junction
Bayside
Sutton
HOWTH

Kilbarrack
Raheny
Harmonstown
Killester

Hazelhatch/Celbridge
Clondalkin
Cherry Orchard
HEUSTON STN.

CONNOLLY STN.
TARA STREET
PEARSE STN.

Lansdowne Road
Sandymount
Sydney Parade
Booterstown
Blackrock
Seapoint
Salthill/Monkstown
DÚN LAOGHAIRE
Sandycove/Glasthule
Glenageary
Dalkey
Killiney
Shankill
BRAY

South Western Suburban Service. Runs from Heuston Station to Kildare Town

South Eastern Suburban Service. Runs from Connolly Station to Arklow.

 iarnród éireann AND **DART**

For further information: (01) 836 6222

 FEEDER BUS

DUBLIN BUS
CHANGING WITH THE CITY

Route Network

Dublin Bus operates the bus network in the greater Dublin area. This network extends from Balbriggan in North County Dublin to Kilcoole in County Wicklow and westwards as far as Kilcock, County Kildare.

For information on all Dublin Bus services, telephone our customer service bureau at 873 4222

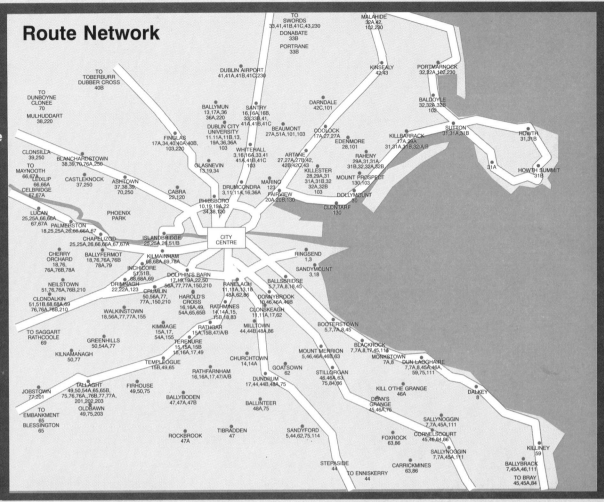

NITELINK

EXPRESS BUS FROM CITY CENTRE EVERY THURSDAY, FRIDAY & SATURDAY 12 midnight 1am, 2am, 3am.

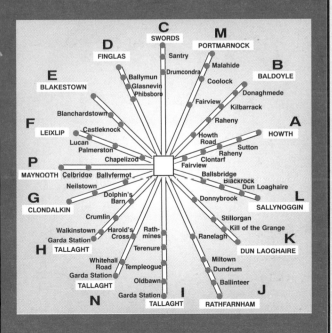

AIRLINK

EXPRESS COACH

CONNECTING DUBLIN AIRPORT

CITY CENTRE

NATIONAL BUS AND RAIL STATION.

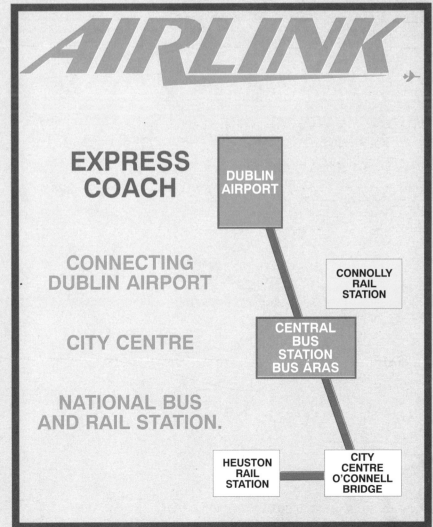

INDEX TO MAP PAGES

The map pages that follow are outlined below.
Please note that the yellow areas will appear
on more than one page e.g.
Sutton appears on both pages 24 and 25.
Ringsend appears on both pages 37 and 61.

*CITY CENTRE MAP IS AVAILABLE
ON PAGES 59 TO 62 AT
A SCALE OF 1:10 000
SEE INDEX BELOW.*

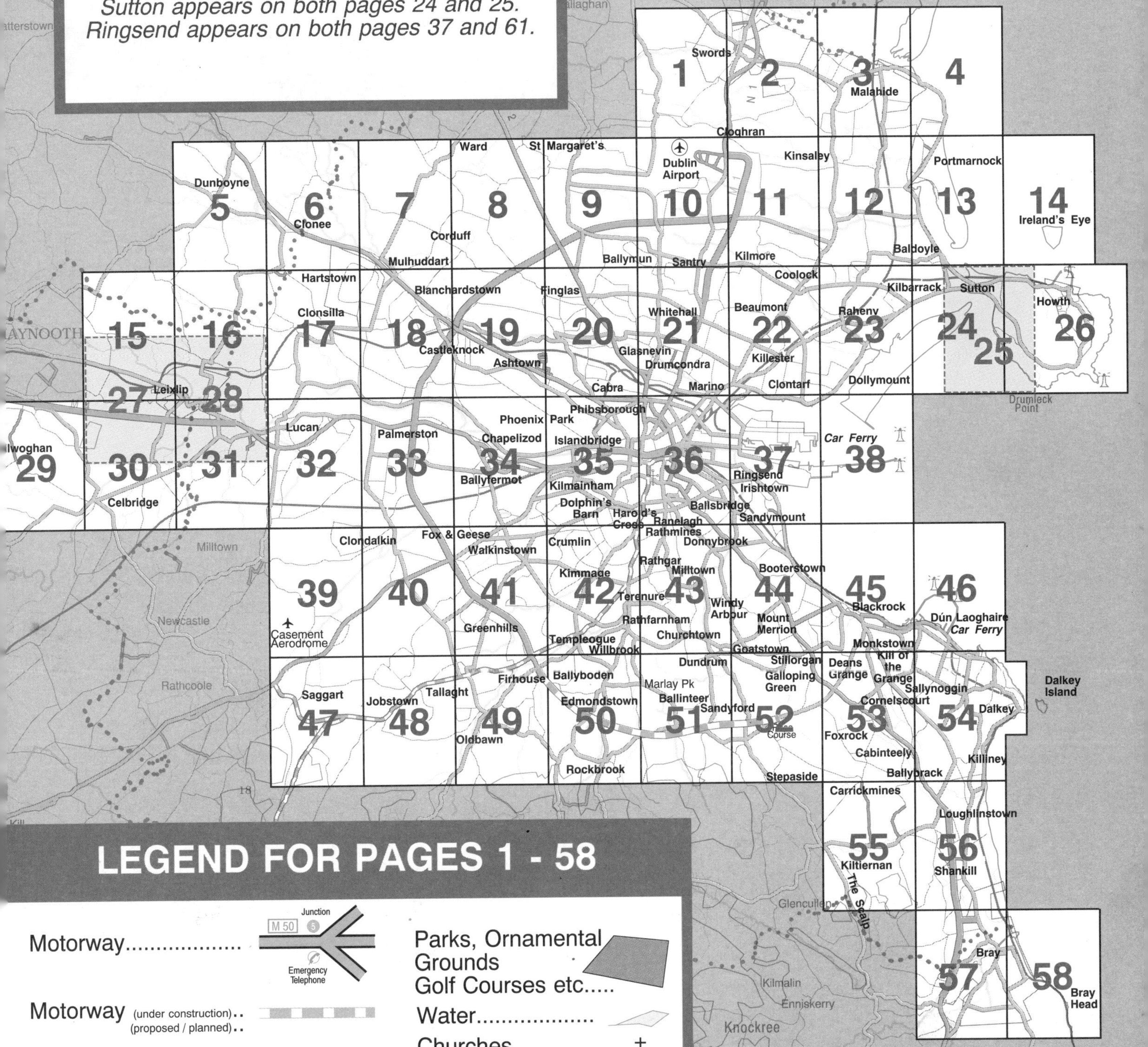

Map index grid (with place names):

- 1 Swords
- 2
- 3 Malahide
- 4
- Cloghran
- Ward, St Margaret's
- Dublin Airport, Kinsaley, Portmarnock
- 5 Dunboyne
- 6 Cfonee
- 7
- 8
- 9
- 10
- 11 Ballymun, Santry, Kilmore
- 12
- 13
- 14 Ireland's Eye
- Corduff, Mulhuddart, Baldoyle
- Hartstown, Blanchardstown, Finglas, Coolock, Kilbarrack, Sutton
- 15 MAYNOOTH
- 16
- 17 Clonsilla
- 18
- 19 Castleknock, Ashtown
- 20
- 21 Whitehall, Glasnevin, Drumcondra
- 22 Beaumont, Killester
- 23 Raheny
- 24
- 25
- 26 Howth
- Cabra, Marino, Clontarf, Dollymount, Killiney
- 27 Leixlip
- 28
- Phibsborough
- 29
- 30 Celbridge
- 31
- 32 Lucan
- 33 Palmerston
- 34 Chapelizod, Ballyfermot
- 35 Phoenix Park, Islandbridge, Kilmainham, Dolphin's Barn
- 36
- 37 Ringsend, Irishtown, Ballsbridge, Sandymount
- 38 Car Ferry
- Harold's Cross, Ranelagh, Rathmines, Donnybrook
- 39 Newcastle, Casement Aerodrome
- 40 Clondalkin, Fox & Geese, Walkinstown
- 41 Greenhills
- 42 Crumlin, Kimmage, Terenure
- 43 Rathgar, Rathfarnham, Churchtown, Milltown, Windy Arbour
- 44 Mount Merrion, Goatstown
- 45 Blackrock, Monkstown
- 46 Dún Laoghaire Car Ferry, Stillorgan
- 47 Saggart
- 48 Jobstown, Tallaght
- 49 Oldbawn, Firhouse
- 50 Ballyboden, Edmondstown, Rockbrook, Templeogue, Willbrook
- 51 Marlay Pk, Ballinteer, Sandyford, Dundrum
- 52 Galloping Green, Deans Grange, Stepaside
- 53 Foxrock, Cornelscourt, Cabinteely, Kill of the Grange, Sallynoggin
- 54 Dalkey
- Dalkey Island
- 55 Kiltiernan
- 56 Shankill, Ballybrack, Loughlinstown, Carrickmines
- 57 Bray
- 58 Bray Head
- The Scalp, Glencullen, Kilmalin, Enniskerry, Knockree

LEGEND FOR PAGES 1 - 58

Motorway	M 50, Junction 5, Emergency Telephone
Motorway (under construction)	
(proposed / planned)	
Main Roads/Streets	
Other Roads	ELTON PARK
Other Roads (unnamed)	7
Public Buildings	
Built-up Areas	
Post Office	PO
Parks, Ornamental Grounds Golf Courses etc	
Water	
Churches	†
Garda Síochána Stations	★
Rail Stations	
Bus Routes	
Route Numbers	31B
Termini	31
Industrial Estates	31

SCALE: 1:15 000 (1cm = 150m) — 0 m, 250 m, 500 m, 750 m, 1 km

CITY CENTRE

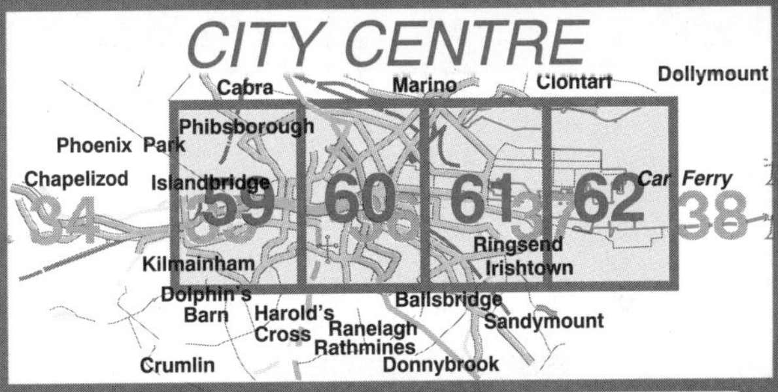

Cabra, Marino, Clontarf, Dollymount
Phibsborough
Phoenix Park
Chapelizod, Islandbridge — 34, 59, 60, 61, 62, 38
Kilmainham
Dolphin's Barn, Harold's Cross, Ballsbridge, Sandymount
Cross, Ranelagh, Rathmines, Donnybrook
Crumlin, Ringsend, Irishtown, Car Ferry

SCALE: 1:10 000 (1cm = 100m) — 0 m, 100 m, 200 m, 300 m

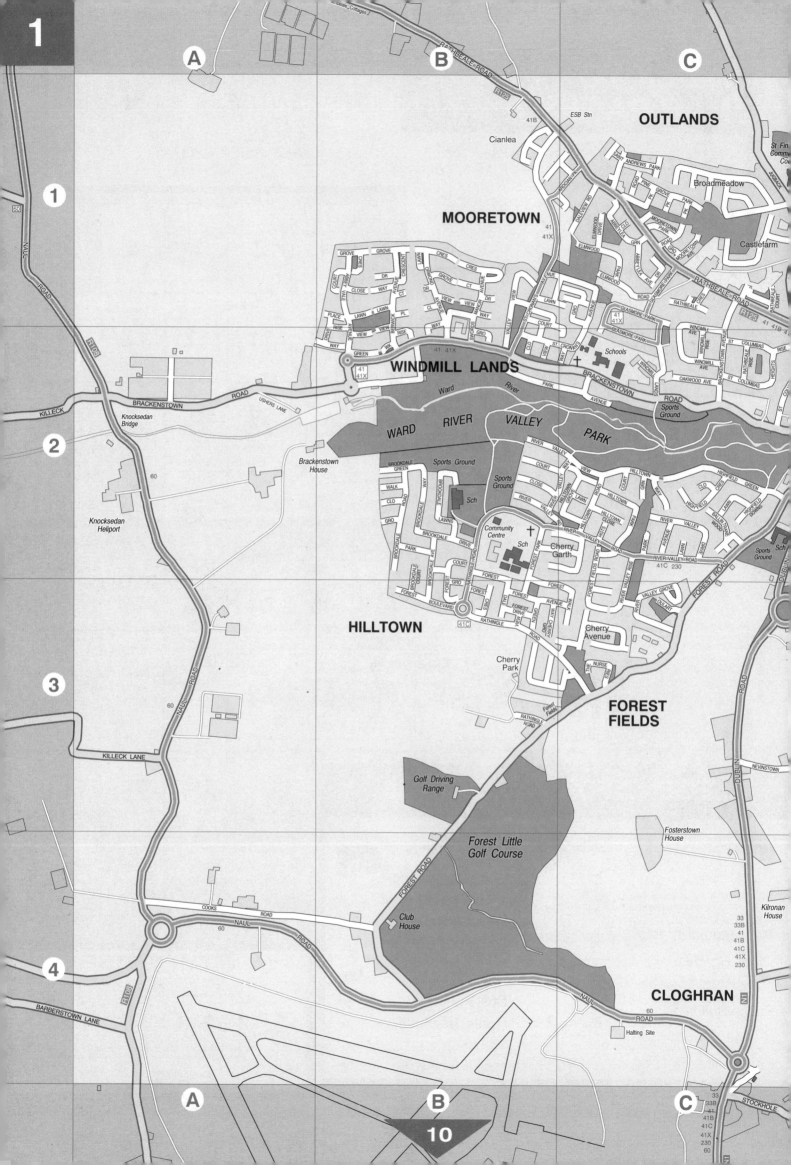

A   B   C

1

The Island Golf Links

2

ROAD COVERED BY HIGH TIDE

Malahide Point

Malahide Marina

Marina Village

OLD YELLOW WALLS ROAD

Milford

School

Grave Yard

CAVE'S STRAND

BISSET'S STRAND

Sonesta

SEABURY DR

CASTLE COVE

SEABURY

GREEN CRESCENT

Fire Stn.

GAS YARD

32A

Jetty

YELLOW WALLS ROAD

SEA ROAD

Inhir Ide Drive

Inhir ide

TALBOT COURT

MILLVIEW COURT

Fairhaven

STRAND STREET

NEW STREET

Tenne Ground

THE GREEN LANE

TOWNYARD LANE

230 32A 42 102

Car Park

GD CROFT

CASTLE DOWN RD

CASTLE CLOSE

DOWNS

WALK

102
230

102

230

YELLOW WALLS

CHALFONT

CHALFONT PLACE

CHALFONT PARK

THE RAVEN

O'DWYONS LANE

ST IVES

SEAPARK COURT

Malahide Station

Casino

102

Malahide Railway Ave

OLD STREET

THE MALLS

COAST ROAD

MAYFAIR

Car Park

R106 ROAD

Island View

42

Ard na Mara

MILLVIEW

MILLVIEW LAWNS

Burial Ground

School

230

CASTLE TCE

KILLEEN TCE

KILLEEN MEWS

BATH

THE RISE

GROVE ROAD

THE MOORINGS

MULDOWNEY COURT

Martello Tower

leen ares

PLACE

CLOSE

ARD NA MARA CRES.

42

102

R106

DUBLIN ROAD

Cricket Ground

Car Park

ST MARGARET'S AVE

CARLISLE TCE

WINDSOR TCE

Sch

ST ANDREW'S GROVE

GROVE ROAD

GROVE AVE

GROVE LAWNS

GROVE LAWN

The Golf Links

Seapark

MALAHIDE

Talbot

SWORDS ROAD

R108

102

Castleview Park

42

GATEBROOK LAWNS

LARKSON SPRINGS

3

Golf Course

ST MARGARET'S ROAD

ST MARGARET'S PARK

Grave Yard

CHURCH RD

School

R124

SEAPARK HILL

Bisc

Auburn Grove

Auburn House

Sports Ground

Malahide Castle

Car Park

Playground

ASHLEIGH LAWN

PARNELL COTTAGES

THE HILL

Golf Course

Reservoir

Conv.

MALAHIDE DEMESNE

Sports Ground

ST. SYLVESTER VILLAS

42

THE BAWN

THE BAWN GROVE

HILL DRIVE

SEAMOUNT

HEIGHTS

DRIVE

ROAD

DUBLIN ROAD

BACK ROAD

CAS TLEFIELD

MANOR

BROOMFIELD

Car Park

CAREY'S LANE

R107

42

Streamstown House

KINSALEY LANE

CONNOLLY AVENUE

Community School

School

R124

THE HILL

42

Dal Ríada

Sch

4

FELTRIM ROAD

R107

42
43

43

42
43

FELTRIM

Telecom Eireann

Sports Ground GAA

BLACKWOOD LANE

Wheatfield Stud

Leisure Centre

Sports Gd

32X
102
230

CARRICK HILL ROAD

Portmarnock Stud

Community School

Club House

Sports Ground

A   B   C

12

Corballis Golf Links

Strand

IRISH

SEA

iscayne

COAST ROAD

Sports Ground

Castle

R105

32A

102

230

MONKS MEADOW

32
32X

ELMER COURT

LIMETREE

AVENUE

PINE LODGE

ROAD

WHITFIELD

WALK

BRAEMEN DRIVE

BRIAR

ASHLEY

RISE

KELVIN CLOSE

WALK

HEATHER GARDENS

Martello
Tower

230 102 32X

WENDELL AVE

BLACKTHORN CLOSE

DEWBERRY PARK

HEATHER WALK

ELLO COURT

WENDELL AVE

STRAND ROAD

32
32A

CARRICKHILL

PORTMARNOCK

PARK

TILMOBARG

RISE

BROAD

CRESCENT

WALK

KHILL RISE

BEA

WALK

PARKVIEW

AVE

JRTMARNOCK

RISE

DRIVE

CARRICKHILL HEIGHTS

102
230

BURROW

A

B

C

1

Normans Grove
House

70X

M3

29

R157

R156

Newtown
Bridge

Sports
Ground

62

70X

Gunnocks
House

Kilbrina

The
Paddocks

Temple Manor

Tolka River

2

ST PETER'S PARK

COURTHILL DRIVE

ST PATRICK'S PARK

MEADOW VIEW

Sadleir
Hall

Sports
Ground

DUNBOYNE

School

PO

School

M3

Grave
Yard

70

School

Tennis
Court

College

Millfarm

Newtown

R157

Community
Centre

Castleview

Convent

RIVERCOURT

70
70X

R156

70 70X

3

R157

Woodview

Castlefarm House

Congress
Hall

Beechdale

Dunboyne
Athletic
Club

St Peter's
Dunboyne GAA

Sports Ground

Chestnut
Grove

4

Cemetery

Stirling
House

Stirling
Stud

A

The Cottage

B

C

Sunny Bank

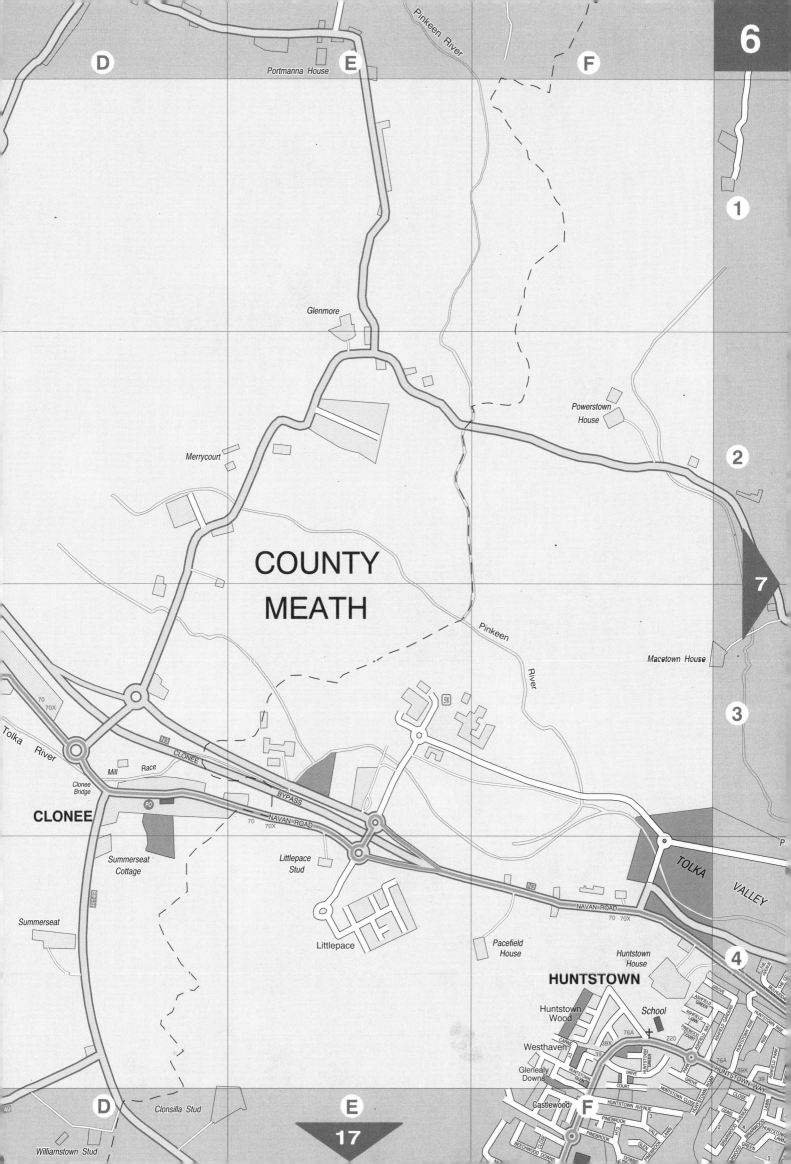

D

E Portmanna House

F

1

Pinkeen River

Glenmore

Powerstown House

2

Merrycourt

COUNTY
MEATH

7

Pinkeen

Macetown House

River

3

70 70X

58

Tolka River

CLONEE

N3

Mill Race

Clonee Bridge

PO

BYPASS

CLONEE

70

NAVAN ROAD

70X

TOLKA

P

Littlepace Stud

N3

VALLEY

Summerseat Cottage

NAVAN ROAD

70 70X

4

R149

Littlepace

Pacefield House

Huntstown House

Summerseat

Huntstown Wood

School

HUNTSTOWN

THE VENUE

MELHILL

ASHFIELD GREEN

HUNTSTOWN RISE

GROVE

ASHFIELD GARDENS

Westhaven

76A

CARNE CT

39X

PINEWOOD COURT

ASHFIELD LAWN

ASHFIELD WAY

HUNTSTOWN RISE

HUNTSTOWN WAY

Glenealy Downs

39

220

HUNTSTOWN ROAD

76A

39X

HUNTSTOWN PARK

39

A9

D

Clonsilla Stud

E

17

Castlewood

HUNTSTOWN GLEN

DRIVE

HUNTSTOWN GREEN

PARK

COURT

GROVE

HUNTSTOWN CLOSE

F

HUNTSTOWN AVENUE

PINEBROOK HTS

GDNS

CLOSE

BRIARWOOD

BRIARWOOD AVENUE

HUNTSTOWN LAWN

Williamstown Stud

PINEBROOK VALE

PINEBROOK LAWN

GLEN

BRIARWOOD GREEN

BEECHWOOD DOWNS

A　　　　　B　　　　　C

BELCREE LANE

Larch Grove

Kilmartin House

RATOATH ROAD

Grave Yard

Hollywoodrath

R121

1

Dublin County Golf Course

HOLLYSTOWN

R121

2

6

Tyrrelstown House

Golf Range and Par 3 Golf Course

Cruiserath House

Pitch and Putt

Macetown House

R121

3

Grave Yard

Reservoir (Covered)

Allotments

Mountain View

ST BERNA PETE'S PARK

238

PARLICKSTOWN GARDENS

GREEN PARK GROVE AVENUE

CRESCENT

WELLVIEW

LADY'S WELL PARK

238 220

COURT COURT GREEN

Parslickstown House

CT PARSLICKSTOWN AVE

LADY'S WELL ROAD

DROMHEATH AVE

26

TOLKA

38 220

238

Sch

GARDENS

GROVE

CHURCH ROAD

DROMHEATH DR

238 220

VALLEY

N3

PARK

Buzzardstown House

238 220

4

38

238

School

38 220

Warrenstown

SHEEPHILL PARK GREEN

WESTWAY CLOSE

ASHFIELD GREEN

THE AVENUE THE COURT

MULHUDDART WOOD

THE GROVE THE HILL

College

WESTWAY PARK

238

ASHFIELD LAWN

HUNTSTOWN RISE

THE GREEN

SHEEPHILL AVE

PINEWOOD COURT

ASHFIELD CAMBRIDGE

MULHUDDART

BLACKCOURT ROAD

WAY 220

SNUGBORO

ROAD

220

ASHFIELD PARK

BLAKESTOWN ROAD

Tolka

Village Heights

Sch

R121

38 220

70 70X

Schs

WESTWAY

HUNTSTOWN GREEN 220

HUNTSTOWN WAY

76A

39

BLANCHARDSTOWN ROAD NORTH

CORDUFF GROVE

VALE

HUNTSTOWN CLOSE CLOSE

Coolmine Cottages

Tolka River

38 238

CORDUFF PARK

BROOKWAY

GREEN

AVENUE

A

WHITESTOWN

Whitestown

3

B

18

TOLKA

BROWN PARK

BLACKCOURT ROAD

CORDUFF PARK

C

238

CORDUFF

Driving Range

Broghan New Bridge

Cherryhound

D

E

F

Broghan House

Pitch and Putt
Course

1

Dunsoghly
Castle

Newtown Cottag

NORTH ROAD N2

Kilmore House

Woodlands

Kilshane
House

2

Newtown
House

9

Op n Golf Cen

(Golf Course

Burial
Gr

Huntstown
House

Sand &
Gravel Pit

3

Cloghran House

13

133

Grange House

CAPPAGH ROAD

Kildonan House

Electricity
Station

4

38

220

BALLYCOOLIN ROAD

Veterinary Research
Laboratory
(A.I. Station)

Northway
Estate

38

Cappoge
Cottages

D

E

F

220

NEW ROAD

19

40A

Sports Groun

CAPPAGH AVENUE

BARRY DRIVE

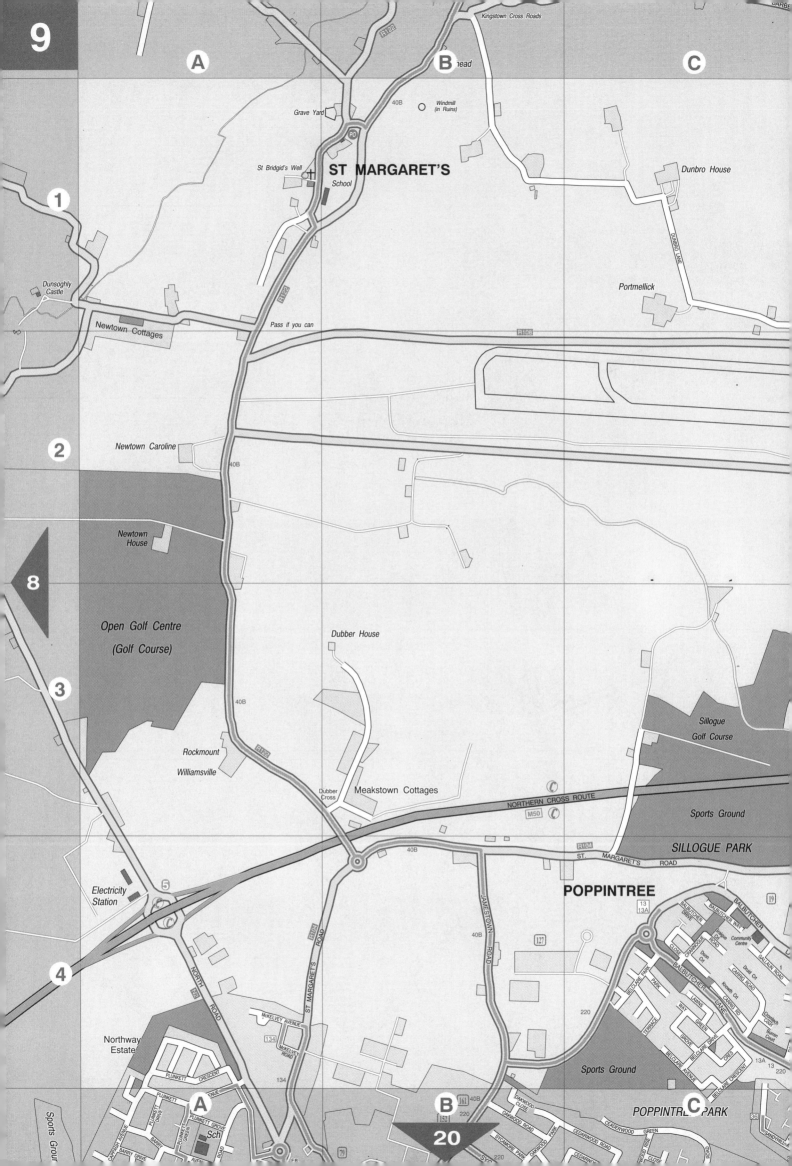

A B C

Kingstown Cross Roads

...head

Windmill
(in Ruins)

Grave Yard

40B

PO

Dunbro House

St Bridgid's Well

ST MARGARET'S

School

Portmellick

1

Dunsoghly
Castle

R122

Newtown Cottages

Pass if you can

R108

Newtown Caroline

40B

2

Newtown
House

8

Open Golf Centre
(Golf Course)

Dubber House

Sillogue
Golf Course

3

Rockmount

R122

Williamsville

40B

Dubber
Cross

Meakstown Cottages

NORTHERN CROSS ROUTE

Sports Ground

M50

SILLOGUE PARK

Electricity
Station

5

ST. MARGARET'S ROAD

R104

POPPINTREE

13
13A

19

4

NORTH ROAD

ST MARGARETS ROAD

JAMESTOWN ROAD

40B

127

220

BALBUTCHER WAY

Community
Centre

McKELVEY AVENUE

134

McKELVEY ROAD

Northway
Estate

220

PLUNKETT CRESCENT

134

PLUNKETT GROVE

Sports Ground

BELCARE

Sch

A B C

POPPINTREE PARK

A   B   C

2

1

Cloghran
Stud Farm

M1
41X

ESB
Sub Stn

41X

R132

Sports
Complex

2

Sports Ground

10

Edendale

M1

Edenville

CLONSHAUGH ROAD

3

3

TURNAPIN
GROVE

41X

Woodlands

CLONSHAUGH ROAD

Belcamp

Sports Ground

BELCAMP PARK

Cara Park

SWIFTS GROVE

47

Sch

CLONSHAUGH HEIGHTS

MEADOW

CLONSHAUGH CLOSE

CLONSHAUGH PARK

CLONSHAUGH WALK

Priorswood
Estate

PO

School

MOATVIEW COURT

CLONSHAUGH DRIVE

MOATVIEW DRIVE

BELCAMP GARDENS

DARNDALE PARK

DARNDALE

88

CLONSHAUGH CRES

CLONSHAUGH AVENUE

CLONSHAUGH GREEN

1

MOATVIEW AVENUE

MOATVIEW GARDENS

BELCAMP GREEN

BELCAMP CRESCENT

Tulip Court

Sch

Primrose
Grove

Snowdrop
Walk

NEWBURY GROVE

PARK DRIVE

LAWNS

GUN PARK

FERRYCARRIG DRIVE

BELCAMP GROVE

BELCAMP AVENUE

BUTTERCUP CRES

PK DR

SQ

Buttercup CLO

Santry
PARK

COURT

WALK

AVENUE

EW CLOSE

WAY

River

Larch
Hill

GUN CRES

GRO

27

FERRYCARRIG PARK

101

Marigold
GRO

PK

CT

Sports Ground

RIVERSIDE AVENUE

RIVERSIDE PARK GROVE

TH GROVE

RIVERSIDE CRESCENT

RIVERSIDE ROAD

GUN DRIVE

GUN AVE

FERRYCARRIG ROAD

FERRY CARRIG AVE

PRIORSWOOD ROAD

27
101

4

Sports
Gd

KILMORE

17A

A

17A

PO

Subway

BARRYSCOURT ROAD

MACROOM AVENUE

Schs

GREENCASTLE PK

MACROOM ROAD

GREENCASTLE DR

GREENCASTLE CRESCENT

GREENCASTLE AVENUE

STARDUST MEMORIAL ROAD

B

22

GREENCASTLE PARADE

117

BLUNDEN

R107

NEWTOWN DRIVE

SLADEMORE

GT

AYREFIELD PLACE

C

Sch

ADARE AVENUE

ADARE DRIVE

ADARE PK

ADARE GREEN

LANE

CASTLETIMON RD

KILBARRON DRIVE

TINAHELY

PARK

GREEN

LANE

Sch

101

27

Abbeville

Baskin
Cottages

BASKIN LANE

Baskin Hill

Emsworth

Middletown House

Spring Hill

Lime Hill

St
Doolagh

Cemetery

Sports
Gd

Belcamp
Hutchinson

Belcamp
College

BELCAMP LANE

GROVE LANE

42

27

43

FELTR. **D**

KINSALEY

Kinsaley Bridge

Kinsaley House

Agricultural Institute

Sch

42
43

BALGRIFFIN

St Doolagh's Park

Balgriffin Cottages

Balgriffin Park

Cemetery

BALGRIFFIN

Sports Ground

42
43

Clare Hall

Woodlawns

New Grove Estate

FATHER COLLINS PARK

Sports Grounds

School

The Grange

Grangemore

DONAGHMEDE

Grange Abbey Drive

DONAGHMEDE PARK

Sch

D

E

Kinsaley Hall

Hazelbrook

Sheilmartin

Drumnigh House

MAYNE ROAD

Moyne Lodge

Mayne River

E

Telecom Eireann

Sports Ground GAA

Portmarnock Bridge

Trotting Track

Church (Disused)
Grave Yard

Golf Driving Range

OLD ROAD

STATION ROAD

Portmarnock Station

230

Malahide Golf Course

Club House

Community School

Sports Ground

Portmarnock Stud

F

Leisure Centre

Sports Gd

BLACKWOOD LANE

Ardilaun

Carrick Court

Sch

The

St ANNE'S SQUARE

HAZEL GROVE

STRAND ROAD

PO

Murragh

230

Stapolin Estate

Castlerosse

School

F

BALDOYLE

Brookstone

Sch

CARRICKHILL ROAD UPR

WOODLANDS

PINE CT

BEACH PARK

WALK

DRIVE

BLACK BERRY LANE

32X

1

2

13

3

4

The Steer
Tower

Ireland's
Eye

Rowan Rocks

Carrigeen Bay

Thulla

Lighthouse

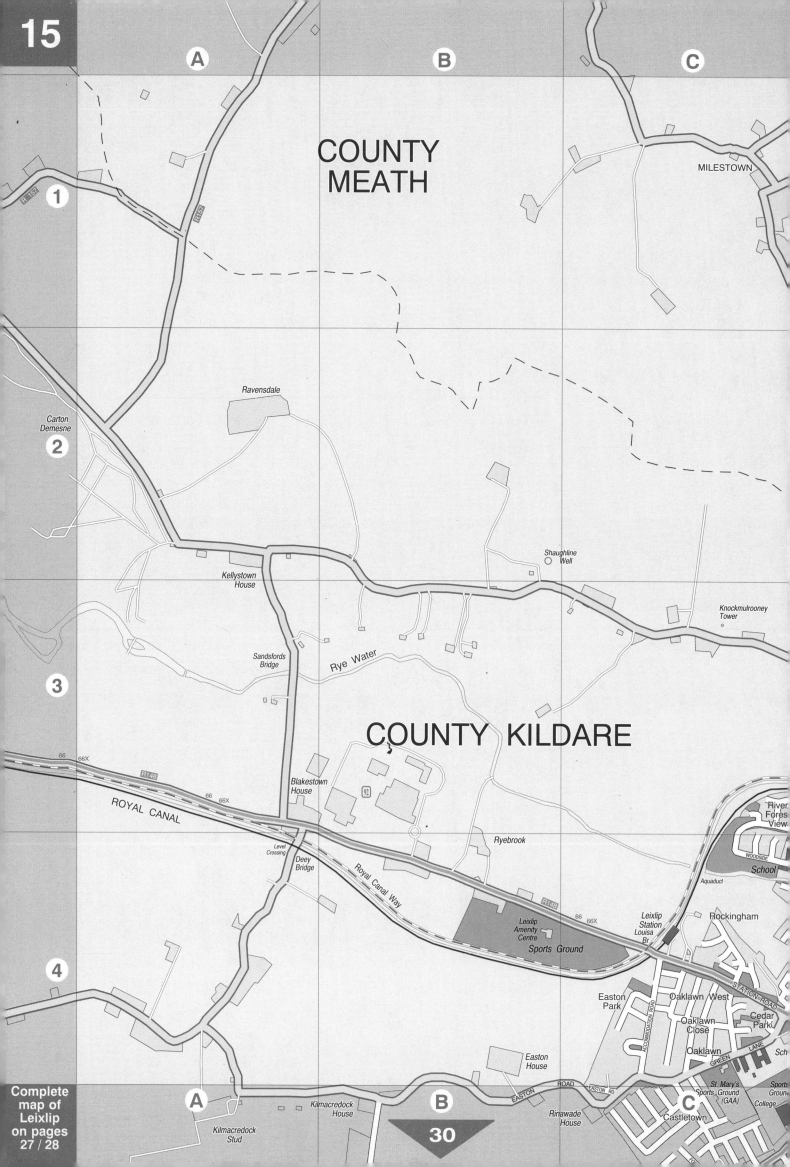

A   B   C

COUNTY
MEATH

MILESTOWN

1   R 157

Carton
Demesne
2

Ravensdale

Shaughline
Well

Kellystown
House

Knockmulrooney
Tower

Sandsfords
Bridge

Rye Water

3

COUNTY KILDARE

66   66X

R 148

ROYAL CANAL

66   66X

Blakestown
House

92

Ryebrook

Royal Canal Way

R 148

Level
Crossing

Deey
Bridge

River
Fores
View

WOODSIDE

School

Aquaduct

Leixlip
Amenity
Centre   66   66X   Leixlip
Station
Louisa
Br   Rockingham

Sports Ground

4

STATION ROAD

Easton
Park   Oaklawn West

ACCOMMODATION ROAD   Oaklawn
Close   Cedar
Park

Oaklawn

Easton
House   GREEN   LANE

A   B   C

Kilmacredock
House   EASTON   ROAD   EASTON RD   St. Mary's
Sports Ground
(GAA)   Sports
Groun

30

Kilmacredock
Stud   Rinawade
House   Castletown   College

COUNTY
MEATH

COUNTY
KILDARE

COUNTY
DUBLIN

Stirling House

Stirling Stud

Sunny Bank

William

R149

Hilltown House

Confey Abbey

Mount Thunder

Leavalley

Allenswood House

Cemetery

Confey House

Leixlip Confey Station

Cope Bridge

Confey GAA Club

Royal Canal Way

R149

ROYAL CANAL

R149

Collins Bridge

River Forest

River Forest

Library

Glendale

River Forest

NEWTOWN GLENDALE

ST CATHERINE'S VIEW

Glendale Meadows

Rye Water

Sch

Newtown Park

Ryevale House

Ryevale Lawns

CONFEY

Mandalay

Avondale

Ryevale Lawns

St Mary's Park

St Catherines

Sports Ground

Schs

Riverdale

St Catherines Park

Highfield Park

The Mall

Health Centre

Ralph Square

Fire Station

MILL LANE

THE BLACK AVENUE

LEIXLIP

RIVER

Sports Ground

Rye Bridge

Castlepark

Leixlip Bridge

Reservoir

66A 66X

66

66B 66X

66X

66B

66A 66X

6

A   B

R148

Clonsilla Stud

Williamstown Stud

1

Ongar Stud

R149

HARTSTOWN

Wood

Westhaven

Gleneally Downs

Castlewood

76A
89X

C

HUNTSTOWN GLEN
HUNTSTOWN GREEN

CARNE

COURT

PINEBROOK

HUNTSTOWN AVENUE

Sch

39
39X
76A
220

Blakesfield

HARTSTOWN PARK

BEECHWOOD CLOSE
MEADOW COPSE
MEADOW DRIVE

CHERRYFIELD VIEW
CHERRYFIELD CLOSE
CHERRYFIELD COURT

MEADOW WAY
MEADOW GREEN

Sch

CHERRYFIELD LAWN

ELMWOOD

HAZELWOOD AVENUE
OAKVIEW AVENUE

WOODVALE CRESCENT
WOODVALE DRIVE

HARTSTOWN ROAD

2

Barnhill

St Joseph's Hospital

Windermere

39
39X

Aldemere

Stonebridge

WILLOW WOOD PARK
WILLOW WOOD CLOSE
WILLOW WOOD GREEN
WILLOW WOOD DRIVE
WILLOW WOOD GROVE
WILLOWS DRIVE
WILLOWS GREEN

STONEBRIDGE ROAD

INGLEWOOD DRIVE

Lohunda Park

LOHUNDA RD

SHELERIN ROAD

39
39X

Portersgate

HEIGHTS
RISE
WAY
AVE
DRIVE
CLO
COURT
GREEN
CRES
VIEW

16

Royal   Canal   Way

CLONSILLA

R121

ROYAL CANAL

R149

LEVEL CROSSING

Barberstown House

Beech Park House

Clonsilla Station

LEVEL CROSSING

CLONSILLA ROAD

LARCH GROVE

LAMBOURNE AVENUE
LAMBOURNE RD

Weavers Row

PO

LAMBOURNE PARK

The Villa

3

Sports Centre

R121

Green Mount

239

Westmanstown Golf Course

Luttrellstown Golf Course

Luttrellstown

The Gables Stud

Club House

239

4

LOWER   LUCAN   ROAD

R109

RIVER   LIFFEY

A

Clanaboy House

R109

LIFFEY ROAD

St. Edmondsbury House

B

32

C

Club House

Hermitage Golf Course

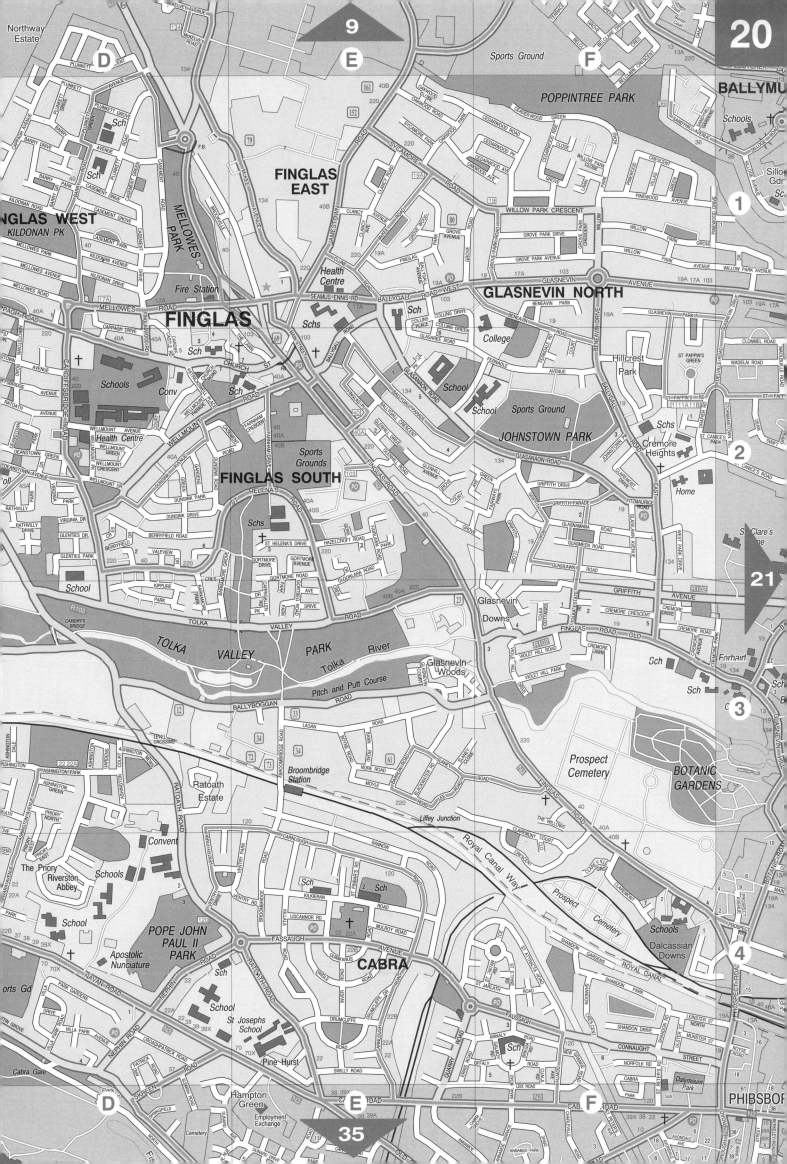

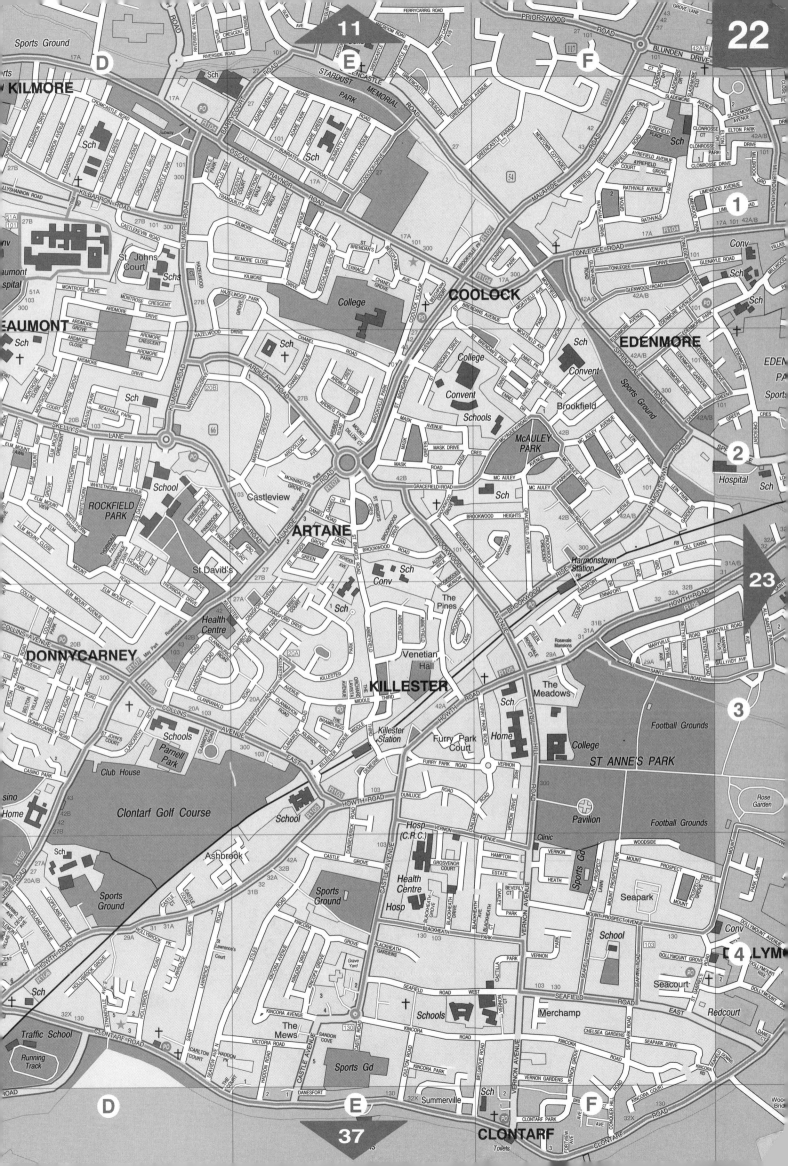

ADMIRAL

Georgian
Hamlet

WILLIE NOLAN

HOOKSTONE

Sch

COLLEGE STREET

MAIN STREET

DUBLIN ROAD

D

Tuscany Park

Turnberry

Meadowbrook
Estate

Sch

PO

31A
31B
32B
32X
102

31B
32
32A

STRAND ROAD

4

WARRENHOUSE ROAD

WARREN GREEN

31B

32B

102

BURROWFIELD

ROAD

1

R106

Cush Park
Club
House

E

Sutton

Golf

Links

F

BURROW ROAD

2

1

CLAREMONT ROAD

31

PARKVALE

MEADOWBROOK LAWN

PARKVALE

MOYCLARE PARK

DRIVE

School

MOYCLARE ROAD

MOYCLARE CLOSE

32

32A

32B

Sutton Station

32
32A
32B

LEVEL
CROSSING

Sutton
Station

St. Domhnach's
Well

Bayside Station

SUTTON

RAILWAY AVE

BALDOYLE ROAD

32X

SUTTON
PARK

SUTTON

PARK

LAWNS

Sutton Park

2

Kilbarrack
Cemetery

32

32A

DOWNS

PARK

1

31B

31A

Binn
Eadair
View

THE CREST

THE COURT

3

Tramway
Court

School

STATION ROAD

102

LAUDERS LANE

LEVEL
CROSSING

R105

PO

31

31B

32B

2

SUTTON

DUBLIN ROAD

R105

31 31A

31A

Sailing
Club

Sutton

Strand

31B

School

Sutton
LTC

CHURCH ROAD

HOWTH ROAD

GREENFIELD ROAD

R105

Sutton

Creek

School

Glencarraig

Convent

Santa Sabina
Manor

31B
31A

ROAD

Offington
Manor

OFFINGTON PARK

OFFINGTON DRIVE

OFFINGTON LAWN

OFFINGTON AVENUE

OFFINGTON

OFFINGTON COURT

CARRICKBRACK ROAD

1

31

2

Deer Park

STRAND ROAD

CARRICKBRACK HEATH

Duncarraig

CARRICKBRACK HILL

LA VISTA AVENUE

31A

CARRICKBRACK LAWN

CARRICKBRACK HILL

Sch

St. Fintans
Cemetery

CRESCENT

ST FINTANS PARK

ST FINTAN'S CRESCENT

OLDCASTLE AVENUE

31B

Sports
Gd

Sch

BEACH

25

STRAND ROAD

31A

GROVE ST

ST FINTAN'S

SHEILMARTIN DRIVE

ROAD

31A

SHEILMARTIN

2

1

South
Hill

R105

3

Sutton
House

Tower

Cliff

Walk

4

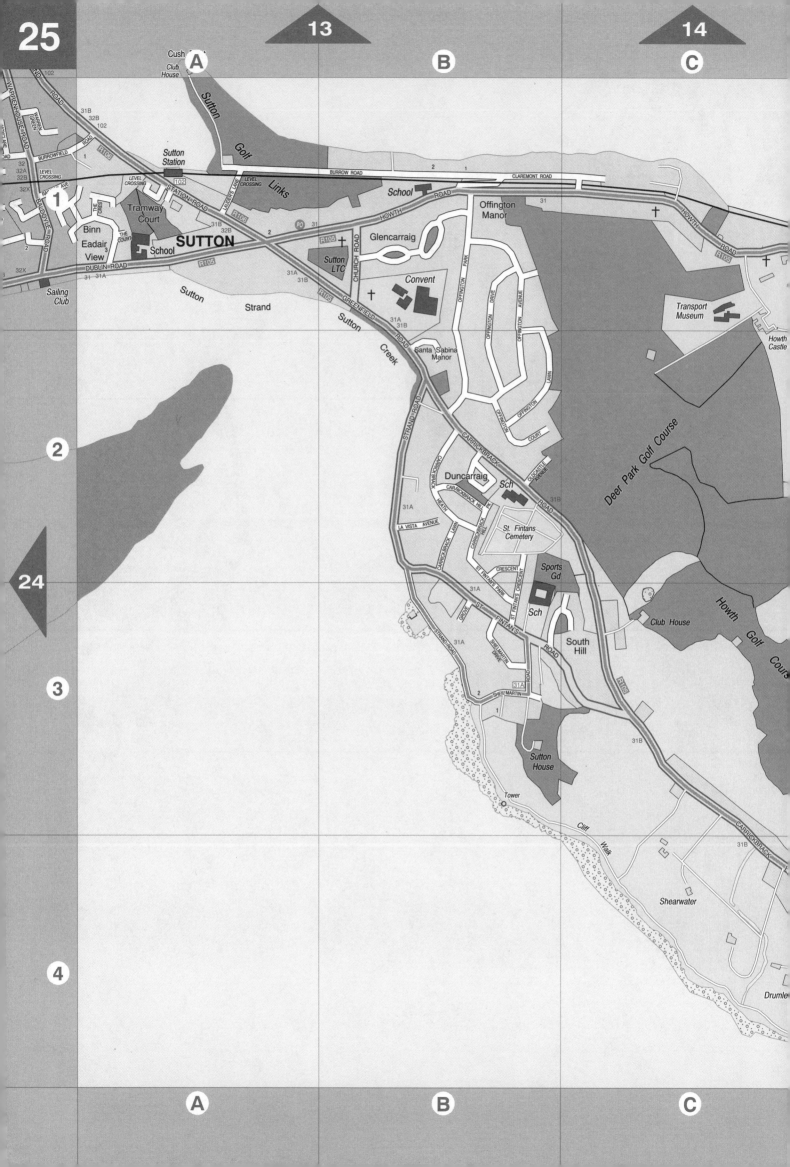

A **B** **C**

Cush
Club
House

Sutton

Golf

WARRENHOUSE ROAD

31B
32B
102

BURROWFIELD

LEVEL
CROSSING

32
32A
32B

BALDOYLE ROAD

RAHENY AVE

Links

Sutton
Station

LEVEL
CROSSING

STATION ROAD

102

LADER'S LANE

LEVEL
CROSSING

BURROW ROAD

2

1

CLAREMONT ROAD

School

HOWTH ROAD

Offington
Manor

31

Tramway
Court

THE CREST

THE COURT

Binn
Eadair
View

School

SUTTON

31B

R106

R106

2

PO

31

HOWTH ROAD

Glencarraig

OFFINGTON PARK

31

DUBLIN ROAD

R105

31 31A

31A
31B

Sutton
LTC

CHURCH ROAD

Convent

Santa Sabina
Manor

OFFINGTON DRIVE

OFFINGTON AVENUE

Transport
Museum

Sailing
Club

2

Sutton   Strand

GREENFIELD ROAD

31A
31B

OFFINGTON LAWN

OFFINGTON COURT

Howth
Castle

1

Sutton

Creek

STRAND ROAD

CARRICKBRACK

OLDCASTLE AVENUE

Deer Park Golf Course

2

CROSSBRACK

Duncarraig

Sch

CARRICKBRACK ROAD

31B

24

CARRICKBRACK HEATH

CARRICKBRACK HILL PK

31A

LA VISTA AVENUE

CARRICKBRACK LAWN

St. Fintans
Cemetery

CRESCENT

Sports
Gd

Club House

Howth Golf Cours

3

ST FINTAN'S PARK

ST FINTAN'S CRESCENT

Sch

South
Hill

GROVE

31A

ST FINTAN'S ROAD

SHIELMARTIN DRIVE

2

SHIELMARTIN

R105

31B

STRAND ROAD

31A

Sutton
House

31A

1

Tower

Cliff   Walk

CARRICKBRACK

31B

4

Shearwater

Drumle

A **B** **C**

D   E   F

1

Lighthouse

WEST PIER
HARBOUR
EAST PIER

31B
Howth
Station

Balscadden Bay

Puck's Rocks

HARBOUR   ROAD
Tower
4   CHURCH   ST
1   5 PO   Car Park
EVORA   3   2
PARK   6   ABBEY STREET   BALSCADDEN   ROAD
LAWRENCE   ROAD
GRACE O'MALLEY ROAD   KILROCK ROAD   Nose of Howth
HOWTH   ASGARD PARK
Sch   TUCKETT'S LANE   3   31   NASHVILLE PARK   Car Park
MAIN   4
5   NASHVILLE ROAD   Kilrock
ST PETERS   9   2   7
TERRACE   6
GRACE O'MALLEY   GOATSBROOK
DRIVE   3   ASGARD ROAD
BALGLASS   8   CONBOOTEN LANE
Balglass   RD   31
Estate   31D
BALKILL PARK   THORMANBY
2

Sports   LAWNS   MARINERS
Ground   ROAD   COVE
DUNGRIFFAN   Cliff
Reservoir   GREY'S LANE   WOODCLIFF   CASANA   VIEW   Casana Rock
HEIGHTS   THORMANBY
BALKILL ROAD   Woodside   Thormanby   Thormanby   Walk
Woods   Lodge

Park   Golf   Course

Ben   R105
of   WINDGATE   BALKILL ROAD   31
Howth   31B   Piper's Gut
KITESTOWN
RD
SOAD   NEW   RD
WINDGATE   RISE   PO   31   Fox Hole
3
The
Summit   BAILEY
GN
RD   Car Park

Car
Park
31B

R105

Gaskin's Leap

31B   Whitewater Brook
CARRICKBRACK
R105   Earls-   ROAD   THORMANBY   Webb's Castle Rock
cliffe   Convent
CEANCHOR ROAD   The Great
Cliff   Walk   Baily
4

Doldrum Bay   Lion's Head

Baily Lighthouse

Drumleck Point

COUNTY KILDARE

COUNTY KILDARE

Shaughline Well

Knockmulrooney Tower

Kellystown House

Sandsfords Bridge

Rye Water

Blakestown House

Ryebrook

66 66X

R148

ROYAL CANAL

66 66X

Level Crossing

Deey Bridge

Royal Canal Way

R148

66 66X

Leixlip Amenity Centre

Sports Ground

River Fore View

WOODSIDE

School

Aquaduct

Leixlip Station

Louisa Br

Rockingham

Easton Park

Oaklawn West

STATION ROAD

ACCOMMODATION ROAD

Oaklawn Close

Oaklawn

GREEN LANE

Cedar Park

Sc

Easton House

EASTON ROAD

Easton Rd

St Mary's Sports Ground (GAA)

College

Spor Grou

Kilmacredock House

Rinawade House

Castletown

Kilmacredock Stud

FOREST PARK

R404

Elton Court

Leixlip P

66B

Wonderful Barn

Leixlip Gate

M4

Barnhall

KILCOCK

MAYNOOTH

LEIXLIP

BYPASS

ROAD

CELBRIDGE

R404

Sports Ground

67 67A 67X

ports round

Crodaun Forest Park

Crodaun Forest Park

Sewage Works

Alensgrove

AVENUE

PARK

COURT

CLO

FB

HAWTHORN VIEW

Reservoir

Ashgrove School

Sports Ground

The Walled Gardens

Castletown House

Boat Club

New Bridge

Sports Ground

Beatty Grove

OWBROOK

PARK

LODGE

THE CASTLETOWN GROVE

THE DRIVE

THE ELMS

THE CROFT

WOOD VIEW

CEDARWOOD

THE AVENUE

THE WOODLANDS

CASTLETOWN LAWN

3

THE COPPINS

THE OAKS

THE WILLOWS

67

Beatty Park

LIFFEY

Weir

Convent

R403

COUNTY
DUBLIN

Allenswood
House

Mount
Thunder

Confey
Abbey

Leavalley

Cemetery

Confey
House

Leixlip
Confey
Station

Cope
Bridge

Confey
GAA Club

Royal Canal Way

R149

ROYAL CANAL

R149

Collins
Bridge

River Forest

River Forest

Library

Glendale

NEWTOWN
GLENDALE

ST CATHERINE'S
VIEW

Glendale
Meadows

St Catherines

Rye Water

Ryevale
Lawns

Ryevale
House

66A
66X

River Forest

Newtown Park

Avondale

CONFEY

Ryevale
Lawns

Mandalay

66X

DISTILLER LANE

CAPTAINS HILL

R149

SKEAGHAN LANE

LANE

St Mary's
Park

Riverdale

St Catherines
Park

St Catherines

Sch

GROVE

CRESCENT

66A
66X

Sports
Ground

Schs

66B

XAULN

66B

Highfield
Park

66 66
66B 66B
66X

66B

Sports
Ground

PK RIVER CLO

PYE

AVENUE MALL

BECKETS LANE

POUND

Fire
Station

MILL LANE

BLACK

AVENUE

RIVER

THE

Weir

PO

The
Mall

MAIN STREET

Health
Centre

Ralph
Square

Grave
Yard

Castlepark

LEIXLIP

LIFFEY

Rye
Bridge

Reservoir

Leixlip Bridge

Leixlip
Castle

Weir

Power Station

Leixlip Golf Course

66 66A 66B 66X

LEIXLIP ROAD

R149

Cooldrinagh
Terrace

COOLDRINAGH LANE

FB

River

LIFFEY

Weir

Dunavarra

R109

MAIN

R407

Lucan
House

Grave
Yard

M4

KILCOCK MAYNOOTH

LEIXLIP

BYPASS

Cooldrinagh
House

FB

Pitch
And
Putt
Course

COOLDRINAGH LANE

Weston Park

N4

LEIXLIP ROAD

25 25A
66A 66B
207 66 67A 67X
67

66X

25A

Woodview

LUCAN

Mount
Zion

RIVER

LIFFEY

Weston
Aerodrome

R403

Club
House

Lucan Golf Course

WESTON LAWN

WESTON CLOSE

KEW PARK CRESCENT

KEW PARK

KEW PARK AVE

The
Crescent

WESTFIELD AVENUE

WESTON DRIVE

WESTON COURT

WESTON GREEN

WESTON MEADOW

WESTON HEIGHTS

WESTON WAY

Sally
House

WESTON

CELBRIDGE ROAD

COLD

CORNMILL ROAD

MILLSTREAM ROAD

HILLSTREAM ROAD

FB

ARDEEN

ANDERSON DRIVE

PRIMROSE LANE

N4

Lucan Golf Course

Woodview
Heights

School

207

66X

Woodview

CHERRY LAWNS

HILLCREST CLOSE

HILLCREST VIEW

WESTBROOK PARK

HILLCREST GREEN

HILLCREST AVENUE

HILLCREST WALK

HILLCREST

HILLCREST DRIVE

ADAMSTOWN ROAD

N4

207

25

TUBBER LANE

AIRLIE HEIGHTS

Sports
Ground

Dodsboro
Cottages

HILLSBORO ROAD

PO

GREENPARK ROAD

MEADOWVIEW GROVE

HILLCREST HEIGHTS

HILLCREST COURT

LAUDS

HILLCREST PARK

HILLCREST GRO

NEWCASTLE ROAD

Sports
Ground

Sch

67
67A
67X

Backweston Farm
Dept of Agriculture and Food

Tubbermaclugg
House

Somerton
House

Westbury
Court

FOX
WOOD

ROCK

ROAD

Atw
T

A   To Galway/Sligo   B   C

M4

3

67A

R405

OBELISK

Electricity Station

Reservoir

67A

M4

R405

Ballygoran Park

Ballygoran Stud

Sports Ground

67
67X

Salesian College

67
67A
67X

Sports Ground

1

FB

WAY
LAWNS
WOODS
CRESCENT
CASTLE
DRIVE
AVENUE
RISE
WALK
PARK
COURT
CLO

Corbally Stud

GREEN LANE

Thornhill Meadows

Ballygorten

Ashgrove
School

Thornhill Gardens

Griffinrath House

Thornhill Heights

Sports Ground

WILLOWBROOK PARK
WILLOWBROOK CLOSE
WILLOWBROOK GROVE

2

St Judes

Willowbrook Lawns

Electricity Sta

Oldtown House

Vanessa Lawns

Spor
Grou

3

Oldtown Cottages

School

VANESSA CLOSE

CHURCH ROAD

Pickering Forest

Cemetery

St Raphael's

Grattan Court

Oakleigh

Springfield

Killadoon Park

Hotel

Roselawn

CLANE ROAD

Ballymakealy Grove

Celbridge Abbey

THE LAWNS
THE GROVE
THE LANE
THE PARK
THE GREEN
THE DRIVE
THE COURT
RIVER LAWN

R405

Abbeyfarm

4

St. Patricks

R403

Fairlawn

Weir

Chelmsfo
Estate

A   B   C

D
St. Edmondsbury House
F
Club House

Clanaboy House

Hermitage Golf Course

Weirview
LOWER
LUCAN
RIVER LIFFEY
Sch
25

LUCAN
ROAD
25 25A 86 66A 66B 66X 67 67A 67X

BARNHILL CROSS ROADS
Lucan Bridge
83
Old Rectory
Sch
67X
67A
67

Hermitage Park
Sports Gd
Ballyowen Park

THE MALL
MAIN
STREET
7
THE OLD HILL ROAD
Sch
66X

St Loman's Hospital
Sch

PO
Sarsfield Park
Health Centre
LUCAN HEIGHTS
CHALET GARDENS
ROSELAWN
BALLYDOWD
LAWN
GROVE
CLO
AVENUE
WOODVILLE
ESKER LANE
GROVE
DRIVE
GREEN
MANOR
PL
CRES
GRO
BALLYOWEN GREEN
VIEW
CRES

Esker Lawns
Sch
Sports Ground
WOODVILLE
GREEN
FB

Beech Park
Beech Grove
66X
Willsbrook Park
207
25A

LUCAN
Cemetery
NEWLANDS ROAD
LUCAN ROAD
CHERBURY
PARK ROAD
PARK ROAD AVENUE
ESKER
207
LANE
CLO
WILLSBROOK VIEW
GREEN
DRIVE

LUCAN
Griffeen Park
Vesey Park
Griffeen River
BYPASS
ESKER
FB
ESKER GLEBE
VIEW
AVENUE
CLO
Elmbrook
ELMBROOK WALK
LAWN
CT
GRO
NEW
WAY
FOXFORD
LANE
Huntington Glen

Beaumount Cottages
66X
The Glebe
Esker Lodge
BURIAL GROUND
Esker Woods
ESKER WOOD DRIVE
25A
207

COLD HURST
COLDHURST
PARK
GDNS
CRESCENT
Rochfort Park

HILLCREST
HILLCREST GRO
CT
ROAD
NEWCASTLE ROAD
207
Sch
ST FINNIANS CRESCENT
CAMBRIDGE PARK
FIVE COURT
CLOSE
ST. FINNIANS AVENUE
LYNCHE'S LANE
25A
207
25A
WAY
MEWS
COLDHURST GREEN
Rochfort Downs

College
Sch
207
ESKER DRIVE
Sports Centre
BALLYOWEN
CLO
ROAD
AVENUE
RISE

stbury Court
Athletic Track
Sports Ground
Arthur Griffith Park
ESKER SOUTH
25A
Abbeywood Court
The Oaks
ABBEYWOOD
CLO
CRES
GDNS
WAY
CLO
Earlsfort

33

25A 207
ESKER ROAD
LUCAN
NEWLANDS
ROAD
25A
207
BALLYOWEN PARK

FOX WOOD
ROCK WOOD
ROCK FIELD
Finnstown Abbey
Sports Ground
GRIFFEEN VALLEY PARK
AVENUE
DRIVE
PARK
FOXBOROUGH ROAD
207
Rosewood Grove
Training and Education Centre
Sch
FODENE PARK
GREEN
GARDENS

3

LOCK
ROAD
FOXPARK
FOXFIELD
HAYDEN'S LANE
Foxborough
207
FODENE
GREEN
AVENUE
FODENE PARK
DRIVE
GROVE
ST RONAN'S GARDENS
78A

RONANST

4

Pitch and Putt Course
Cappagh Villa

GRAND CANAL
Grand Canal Way

Grange Cottage

KILCRONAN
GROVE
CRESCENT
COURT
CLOSE
AVENUE
DEANSRATH AVE
DEANSRATH LAWN
MELROSE LAWN
GREEN
MELROSE GROVE
AVE
LINDISFARNE PARK
GREEN
DRIVE
LINDISFARNE WALK
ASHWOOD DRIVE
51B 210
DEANSRATH
CRES
PARK
ROAD
GREEN
WAY
LAWN
DRIVE
CRES
AVENUE
MELROSE PARK
CRESCENT
MELROSE GREEN
LINDISFARNE VALE
LINDISFARNE AVENUE
CLOSE
AVE
ASHWOOD WAY
PARK
LAWNS
GROVE
Sports Ground
H

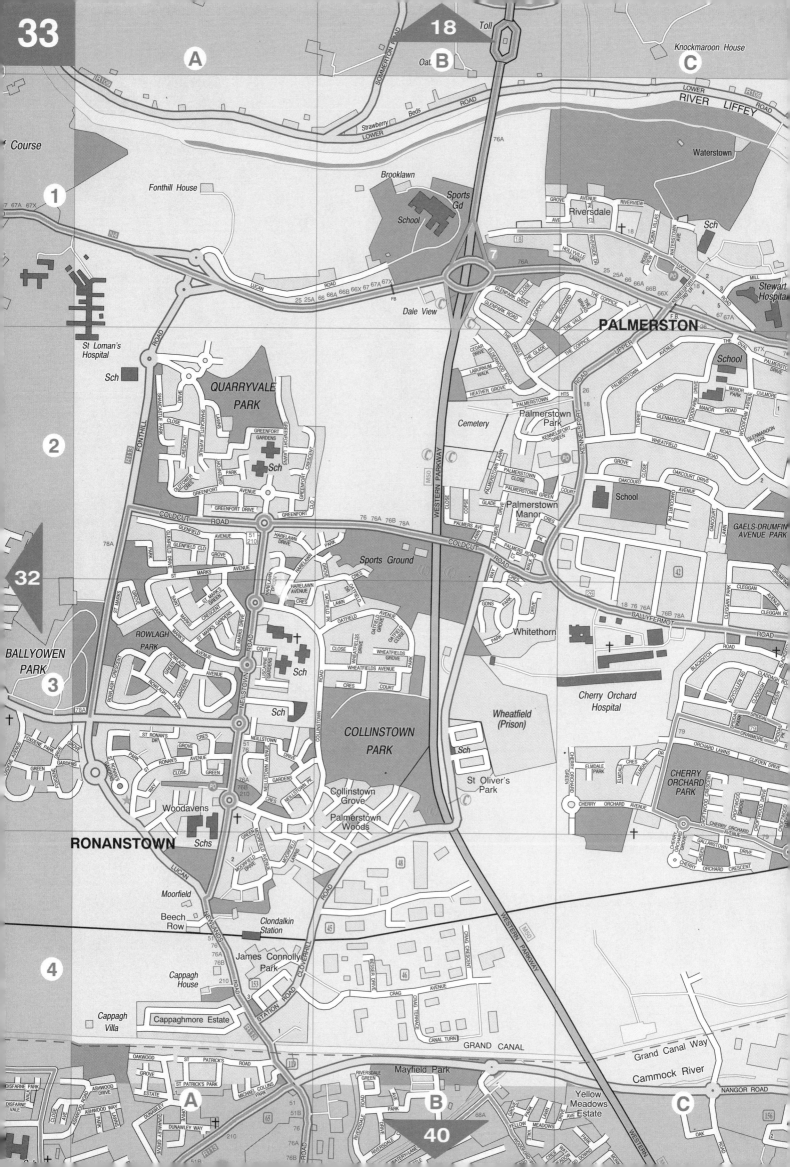

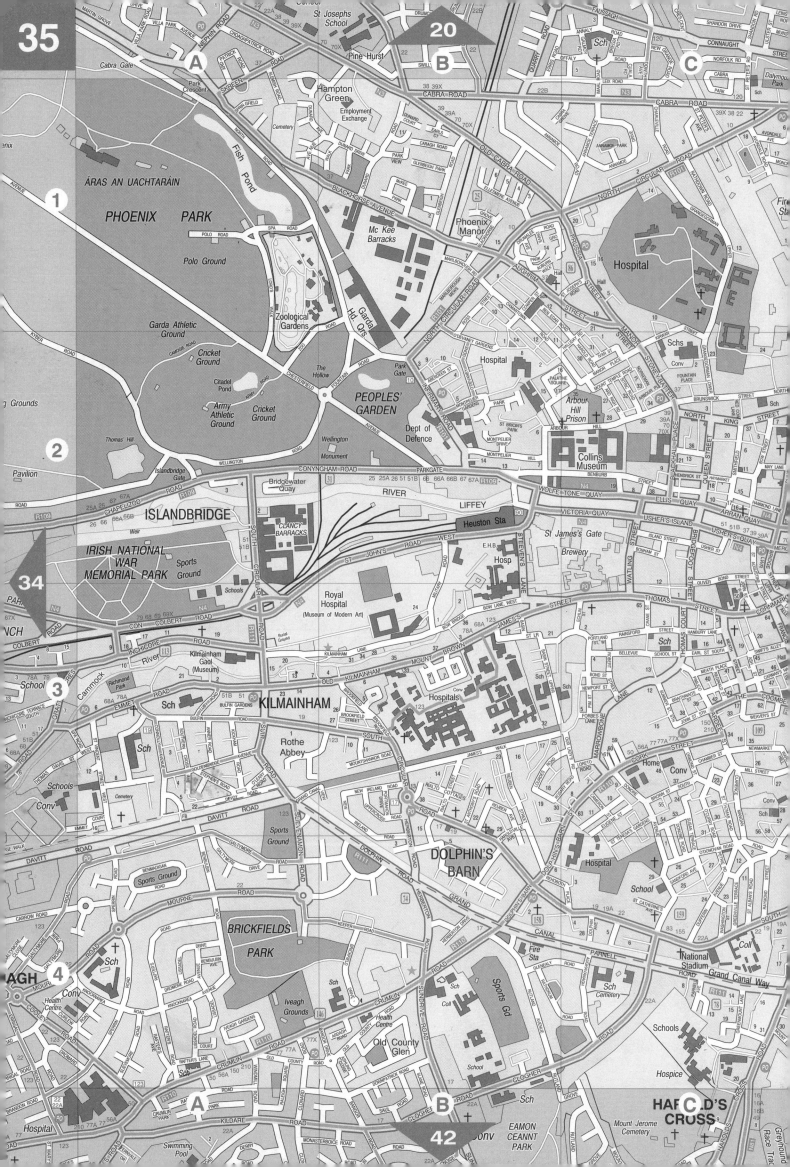

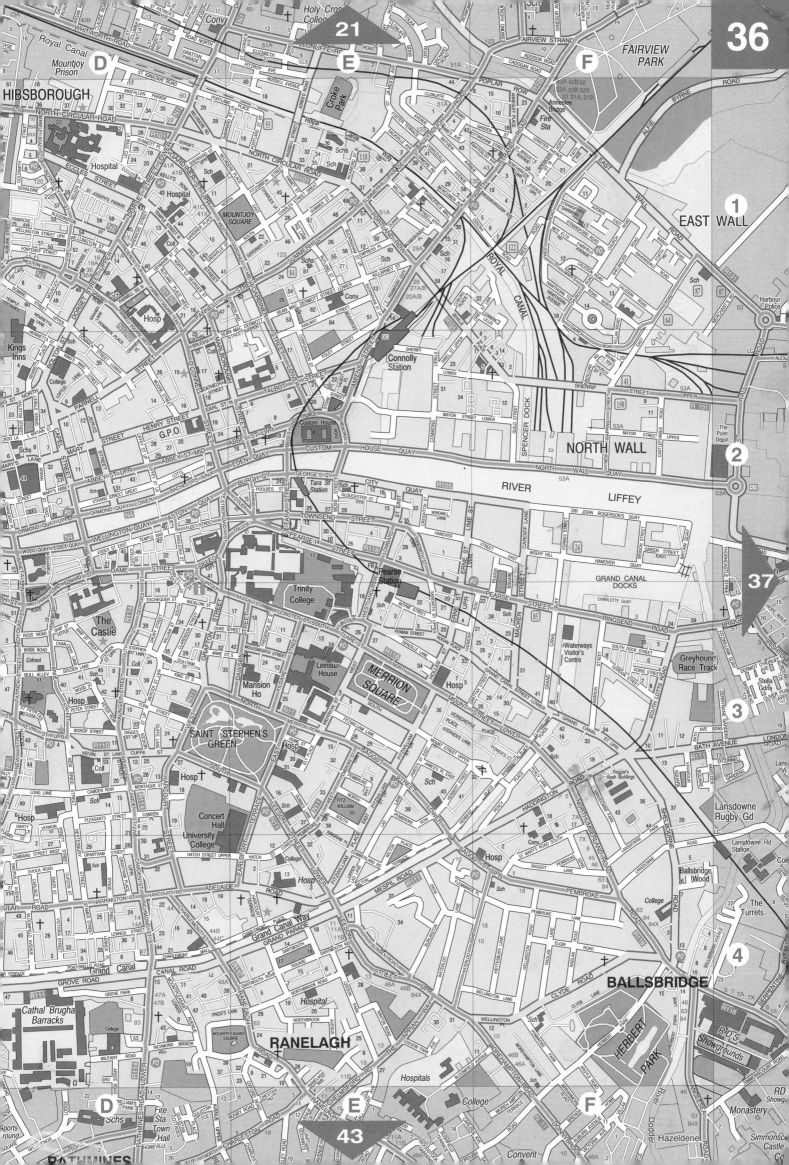

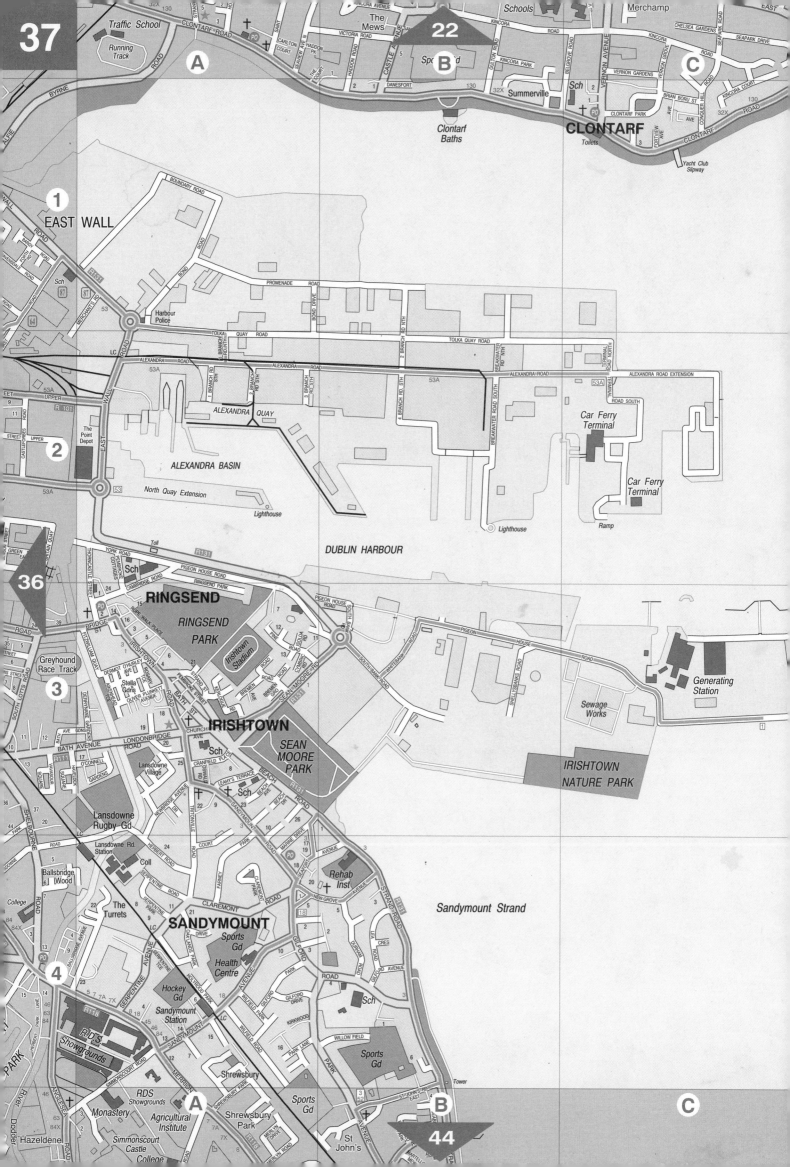

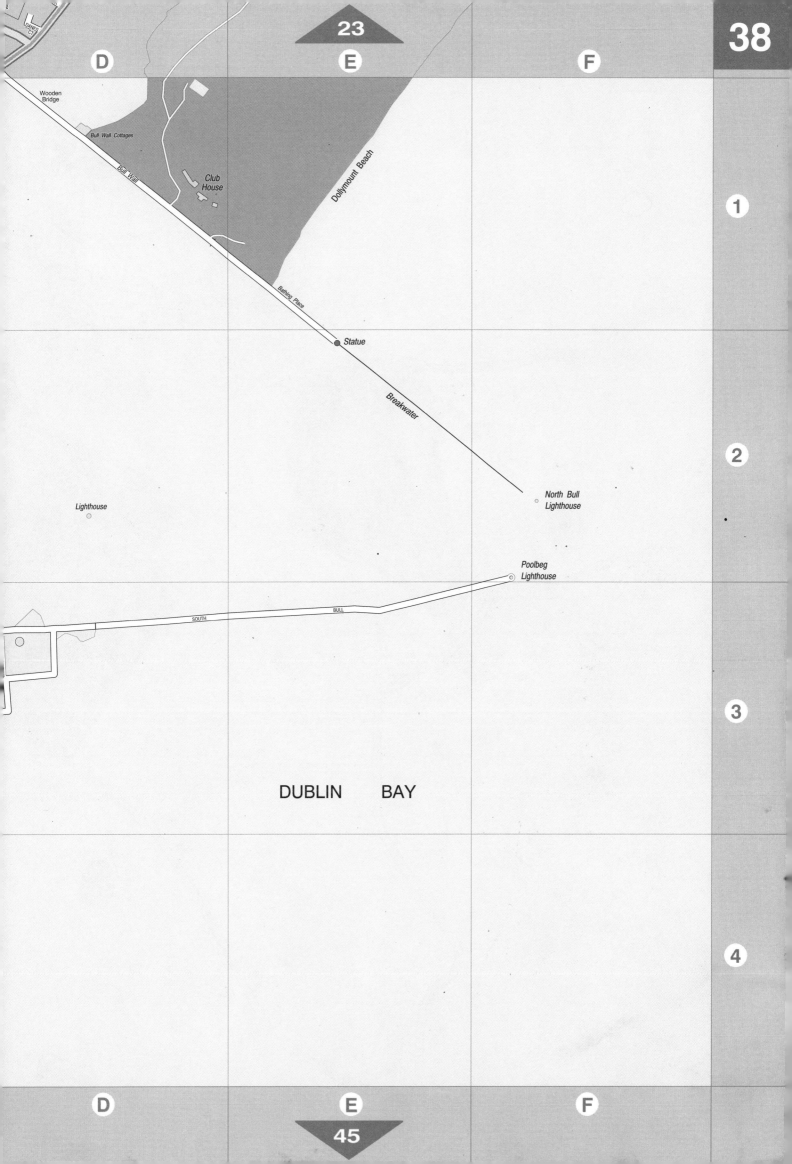

Wooden
Bridge

Bull Wall Cottages

Bull Wall

Club
House

Dollymount Beach

Bathing Place

Statue

Breakwater

North Bull
Lighthouse

Poolbeg
Lighthouse

Lighthouse

SOUTH   BULL

DUBLIN   BAY

DANES CT

1

2

3

4

GRAND CANAL

G r a n d   C a n a l

A

B

C

Grange Cottage

51B 210

CLOSE

KILCRONAN AVENUE

COURT

GROVE

DEANSRATH GREEN

MELROSE LAWN

MELROSE AVE

GREEN

LINDISFARNE PARK

CRES

WAY

KILMAHUDDRICK

DEANSRATH AVE

MELROSE

DEANSRATH ROAD

DEANSRATH GREEN

MELROSE CRESCENT

LINDISFARNE VALE

LINDISFARNE AVENUE

DRIVE

AVENUE

CT

MELROSE GROVE

LAWNS

DEANSRATH PARK

DEANSRATH ROAD

GROVE

LINDISFARNE

GREEN

GRO

CRES

CLOSE

WALK

MELROSE PARK

1

Sports Ground

210

H

Sch

OLD COTTS DRIVE

School

GREEN

LEALAND

LELAND ROAD

PO

†

Westbourne Court

WALK

GDNS

Sch

51B

LEYLAND CLOSE

LEALAND AVENUE

Westbourne Manor

CRES

GROVE

DRI

210

Halting Site

Westbourne Castle

LEALAND

1

68

Cherry D

OLDCHURCH

CRES

CHER

CHERRYWOOD CRESCENT

Sch

68A

OLDCHURCH WALK

OLDCHURCH AVE

Cherrywood Park

S

NANGOR ROAD

68

210

68

DRIVE

CHERRYWOOD LAWN

2

68

Kilcarbery House

Cammock River

Sewage Works

CORKAGH DEMESNE

Burial Ground

68

3

Baldonnell Orchard

Camac Valley Tourist Caravan and Camping Park

Casement Aerodrome and Military Camp

Baldonnell House

69

69X

4

Sports Ground

Moneen Cottage

Citywest Bridge

44

N7

A

B

C

NAAS ROAD

69   69X

N7

R120

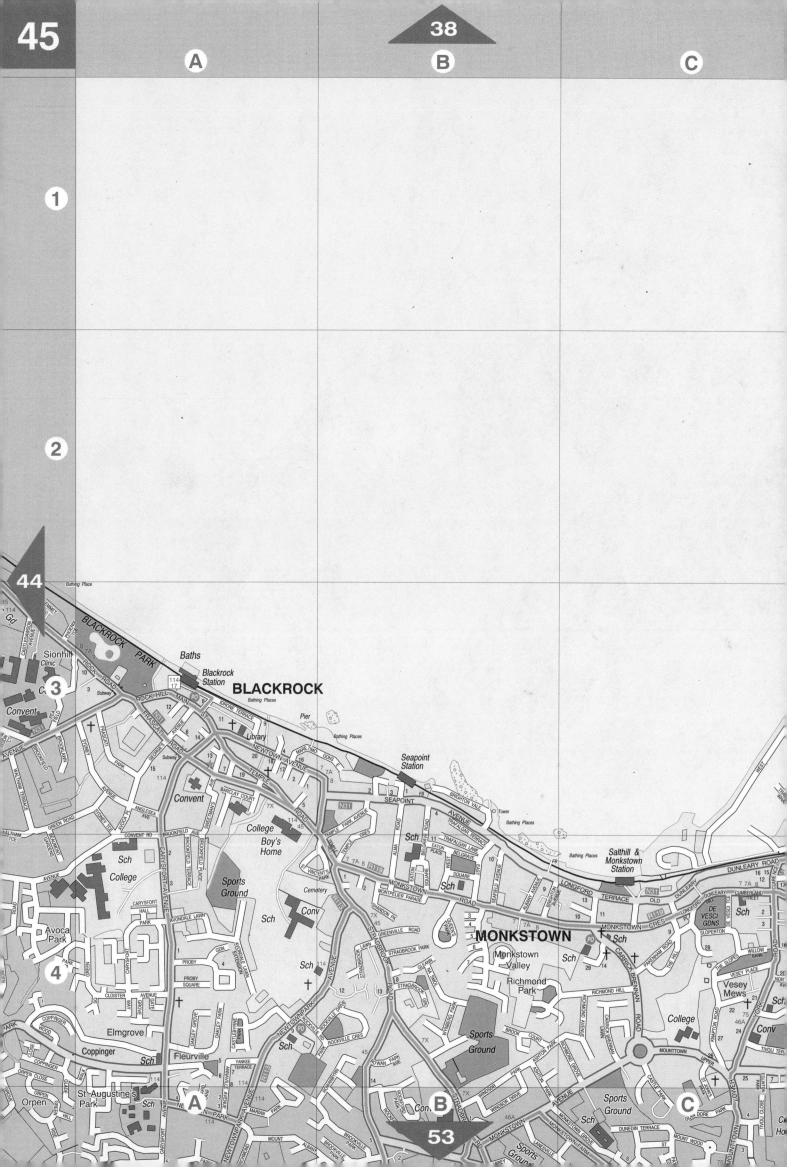

Bathing Place

Gd

Sionhill
Clinic

BLACKROCK PARK

ROCK ROAD

Baths

Blackrock
Station

BLACKROCK

Convent

3

Subway

ROCK HILL   MAIN ST   IDRONE TERRACE   Bathing Places

FRASCATI ROAD

GEORGES AVENUE   NEWTOWN AVENUE

Library

Subway

Convent

Barclay Court

College

Boy's
Home

Sports
Ground

Sch

Cemetery

Conv

Sch

Convent

Pier

Bathing Places

MARE TMO GDNS

TEMPLE ROAD

TEMPLE

Seapoint
Station

Brighton Vale

Tower

Bathing Places

SEAPOINT AVENUE

Sch

EATON SQUARE

BELGRAVE SQUARE

WEST

Sch

TRAFALGAR TERRACE

TRAFALGAR LANE

EATON PLACE

BELGRAVE

SEAFIELD AVENUE

ALBANY AVENUE

Salthill &
Monkstown Station

LONGFORD TERRACE

BRIGHTON AVENUE

DUNLEARY ROAD

OLD

DUNLEARY

MONKSTOWN CRES

De VESCI GDNS

Sch

Sloperton

WILLOW BANK

Vesey Place

The Slopes

Convent

College

WALTHAM TERRACE

SEAMOUNT GARDENS

GREEN ROAD

BROOKLAWN

BROOKFIELD

SYDNEY AVENUE

SYDNEY TCE

AVOCA PL

ANGLESEA AVE

CONVENT RD

Sch

College

Avoca
Park

4

CARYSFORT AVENUE

CARYSFORT

HALL

PARK

BROOKFIELD PLACE

BROOKFIELD TERRACE

AVONDALE LAWN

PROBY
SQUARE

AVONDALE LAWN EXTENSION

ST VINCENTS PARK

MONKSTOWN

Montpelier Parade

SHANDON PK

Queen's Park

MONKSTOWN

Monkstown
Valley

Richmond
Park

Sch

RICHMOND HILL

RICHMOND AVENUE

CARRICK BRENNAN LAWN

PAKENHAM ROAD

THE HILL

MONKSTOWN ROAD

CARRICK BRENNAN ROAD

College

Conv

YORK ROAD

Sch

Elmgrove

Coppinger

Sch

Fleurville

COPPINGER CLOSE

ORPEN CLOSE

COPPINGER WALK

COPPINGER GLADE

Orpen

St Augustine's
Park

Sch

OAKLEY GROVE

OAKLEY PARK

CASTLEBYRNE PARK

YANKEE TERRACE

NEWTOWNPARK AVENUE

NEWTOWNPARK

Sch

ROCKVILLE PARK

ROCKVILLE DRIVE

ROCKVILLE CRES

ROWAN PARK AVE

STRADBROOK ROAD

STRADBROOK PARK

GREENVILLE ROAD

Sch

Sch

Sports
Ground

WYNBERG PARK

WINDSOR DRIVE

MONKSTOWN GROVE

MONKSTOWN FARM

Conv

Sch

Sports
Ground

DUNEDIN TERRACE

MOUNTWOOD

MOUNTTOWN

TIVOLI TER

Vesey Mews

CASTLE PARK

GLEN DORE PARK

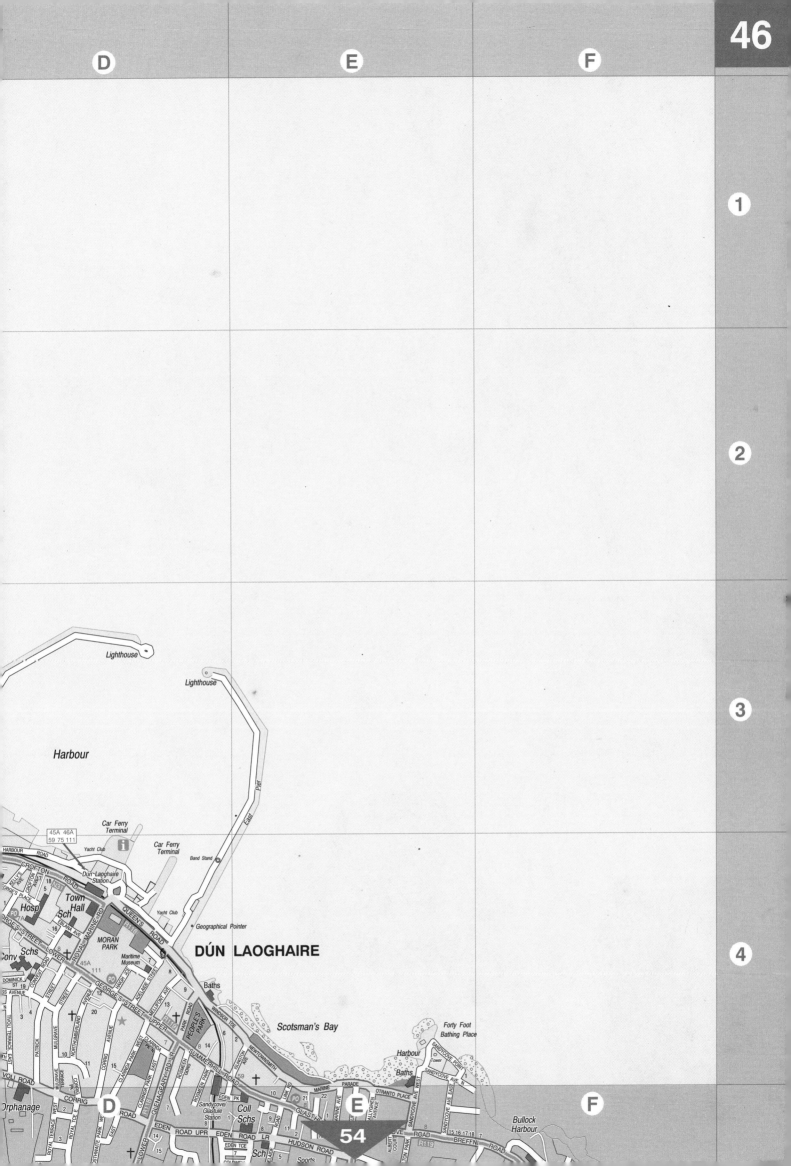

Lighthouse

Lighthouse

East Pier

Harbour

Car Ferry
Terminal

Yacht Club

Car Ferry
Terminal

Band Stand

45A 46A
59 75 111

HARBOUR ROAD

CROFTON ROAD

Dún Laoghaire
Station

GEORGE'S PLACE

Town
Hall

Hosp

Schs

QUEEN'S ROAD

Yacht Club

Geographical Pointer

4

GEORGE'S STREET

Conv

Schs

MORAN
PARK

ROYAL MARINE RD

Maritime
Museum

DÚN LAOGHAIRE

45A

111

DOMINICK
ST

Baths

GEORGE'S STREET UPPER

PEOPLE'S
PARK

Scotsman's Bay

Forty Foot
Bathing Place

Harbour

Baths

Tower

SANDYCOVE POINT

SANDYCOVE AVE WEST

SANDYCOVE AVE EAST N.

TIVOLI TERRACE EAST

PATRICK STREET

MULGRAVE STREET

NORTHUMBERLAND AVENUE

CORRIG AVENUE

CLARINDA PARK EAST

CLARINDA PARK WEST

WINDSOR TCE

SUMMERHILL ROAD

NEWTOWNSMITH

SUTTON AVE

MARINE PARADE

OTRANTO PLACE

ALBERT
COURT

ALBERT
PARK

BREFFNI ROAD

Bullock
Harbour

Orphanage

ROYAL TERRACE WEST

TIVOLI ROAD

CORRIG

ROSMEEN PARK

ROSMEEN GDNS

GLENAGEARY RD LR

EDEN ROAD UPR

EDEN ROAD LR

EDEN TCE

Sandycove/
Glasthule
Station

Coll
Schs

LINK RD

HUDSON ROAD

ALLYQUIN AVENUE

MARINE AVE

GLASTHULE ROAD

R119

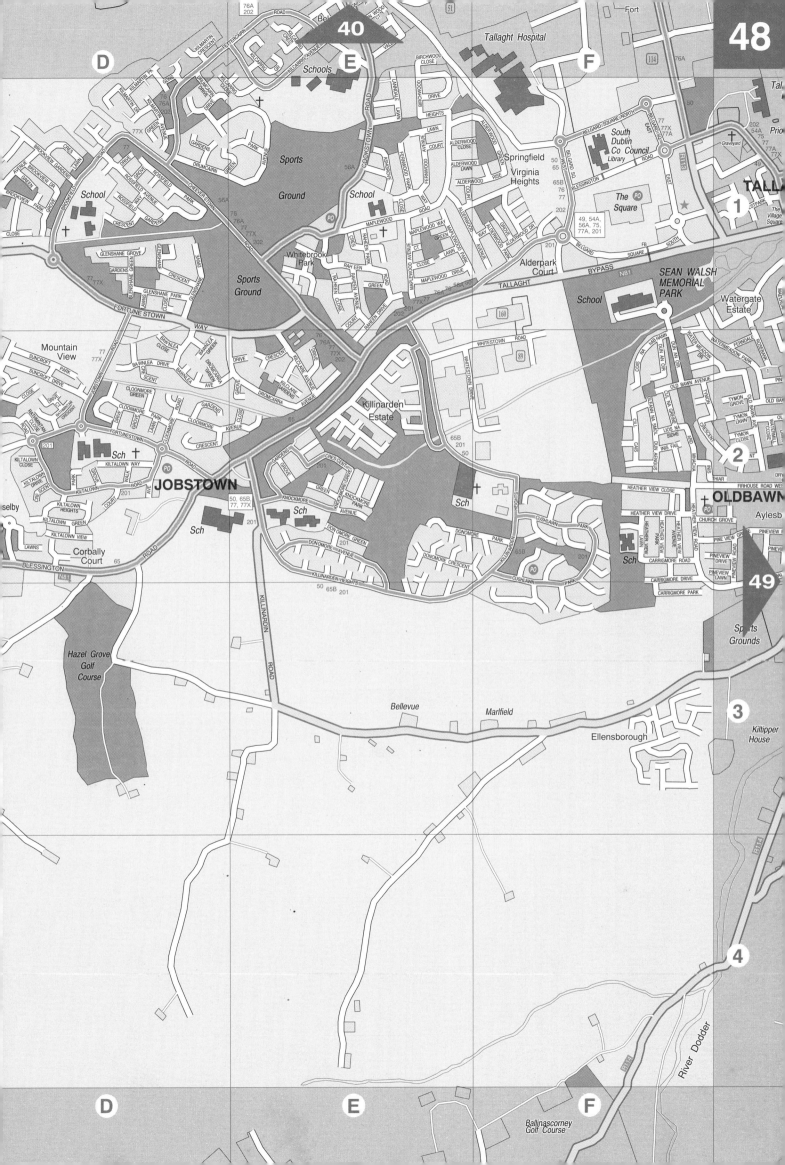

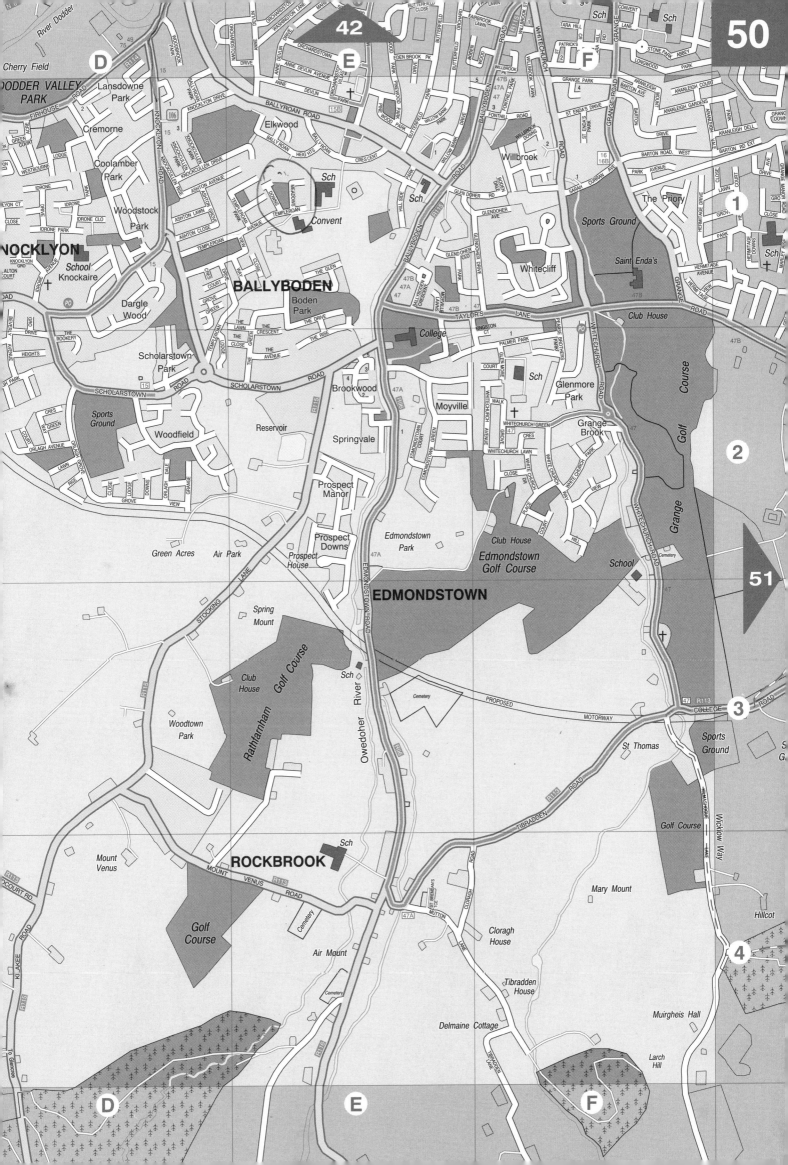

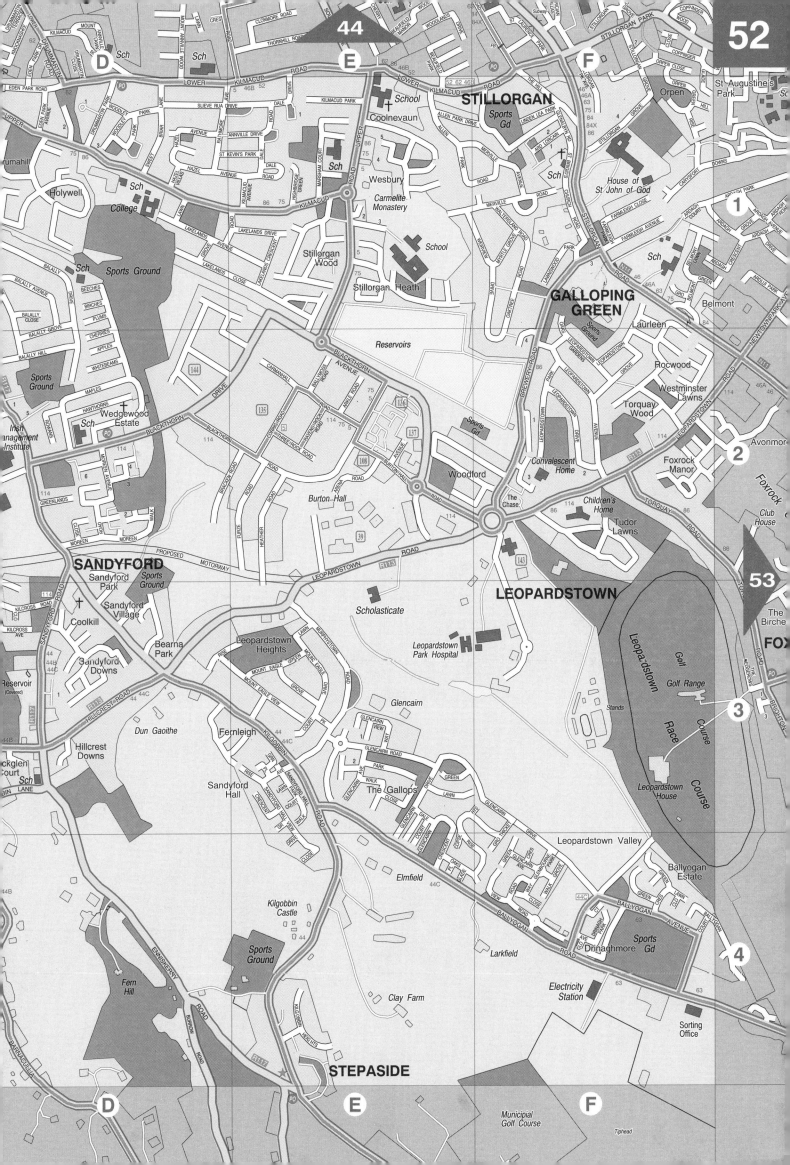

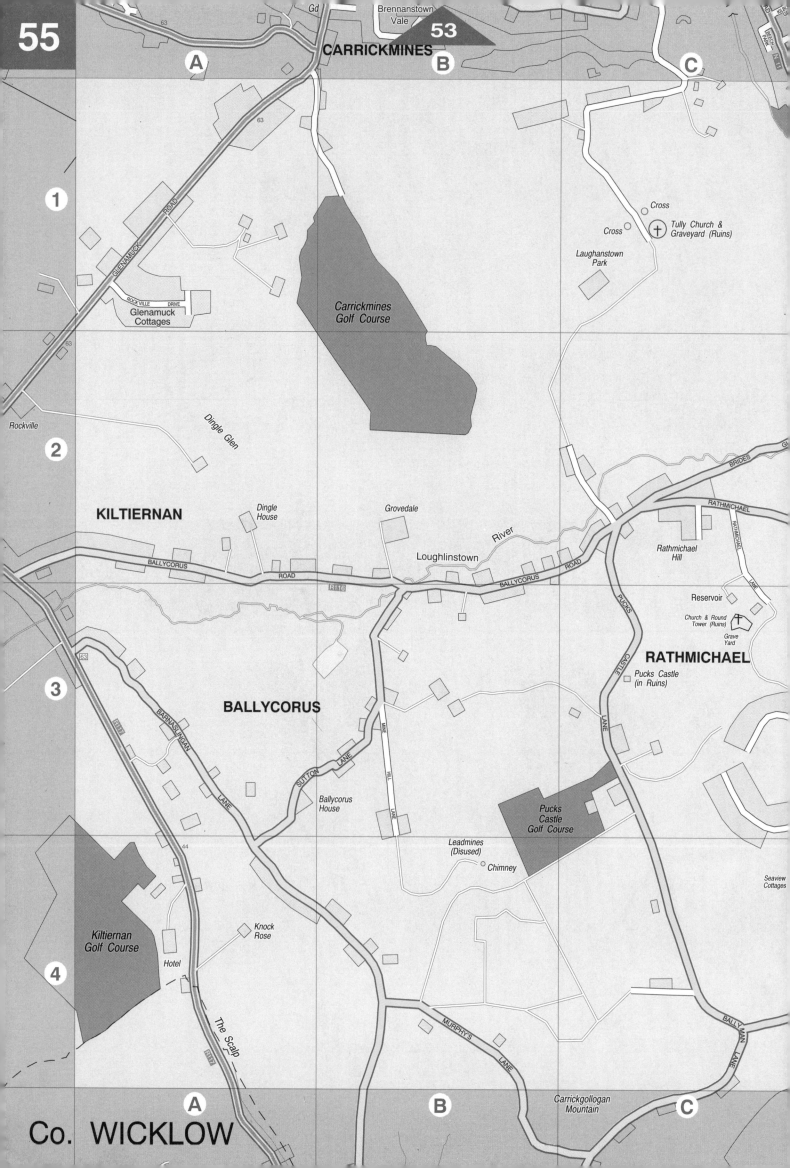

A   CARRICKMINES   53   B   C

63

Gd   Brennanstown Vale

1

Cross

Cross   Cross   ✝ Tully Church & Graveyard (Ruins)

Laughanstown Park

63   GLENAMUCK ROAD

ROCKVILLE DRIVE
Glenamuck Cottages

63

Rockville

2   Dingle Glen

Carrickmines Golf Course

KILTIERNAN   Dingle House   Grovedale   River   BRIDES GI

Loughlinstown   RATHMICHAEL

BALLYCORUS   ROAD   BALLYCORUS   ROAD   Rathmichael Hill   RATHMICHAEL LANE

R116   Reservoir

63   PUCKS   Church & Round Tower (Ruins)   Grave Yard

3   BARNASLINGAN LANE   R117   BALLYCORUS   RATHMICHAEL   Pucks Castle (in Ruins)

SUTTON LANE   MINE HILL LANE   CASTLE LANE

Ballycorus House

44   Pucks Castle Golf Course   Seaview Cottages

Leadmines (Disused)   ○ Chimney

Knock Rose

Kiltiernan Golf Course

Hotel

4

The Scalp   R117

MURPHY'S LANE   BALLYMAN LANE

A   B   Carrickgollagan Mountain   C

Co. WICKLOW

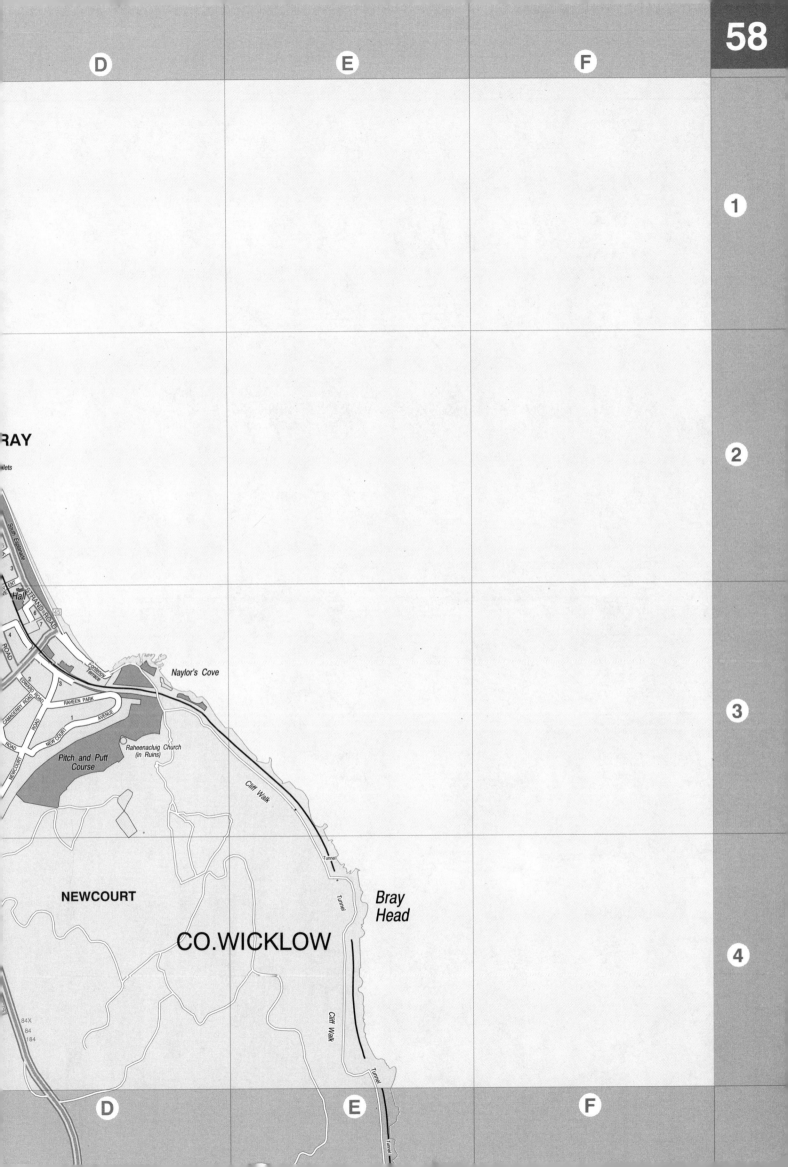

D

E

F

1

2

3

4

RAY

South Esplanade

Hall

STRAND ROAD

ROAD

Fonteboy Terrace

Naylor's Cove

EDWARD ROAD

RAHEEN PARK

NEW COURT AVENUE

CAMADERRY ROAD

ROAD

NEWCOURT ROAD

Pitch and Putt Course

Raheenacluig Church (in Ruins)

Cliff Walk

NEWCOURT

Tunnel

Tunnel

Bray Head

CO.WICKLOW

84X
84
184

Cliff Walk

Tunnel

Tunnel

D

E

F

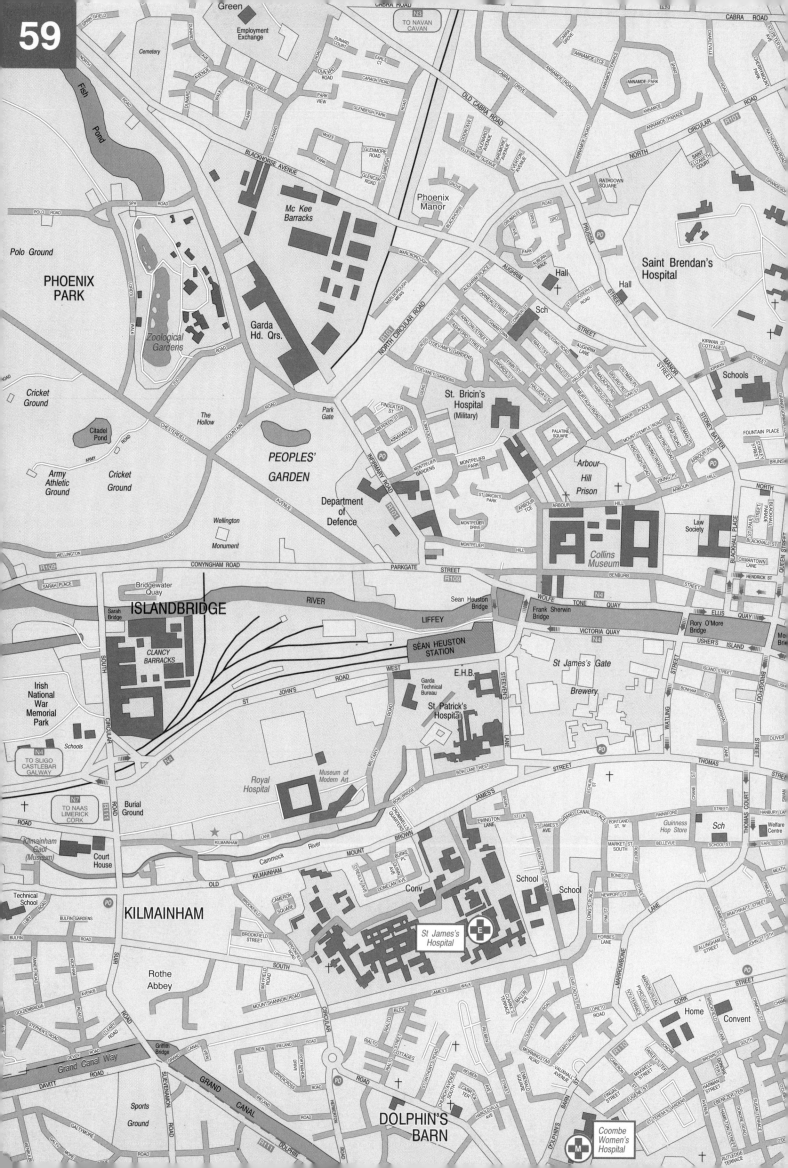

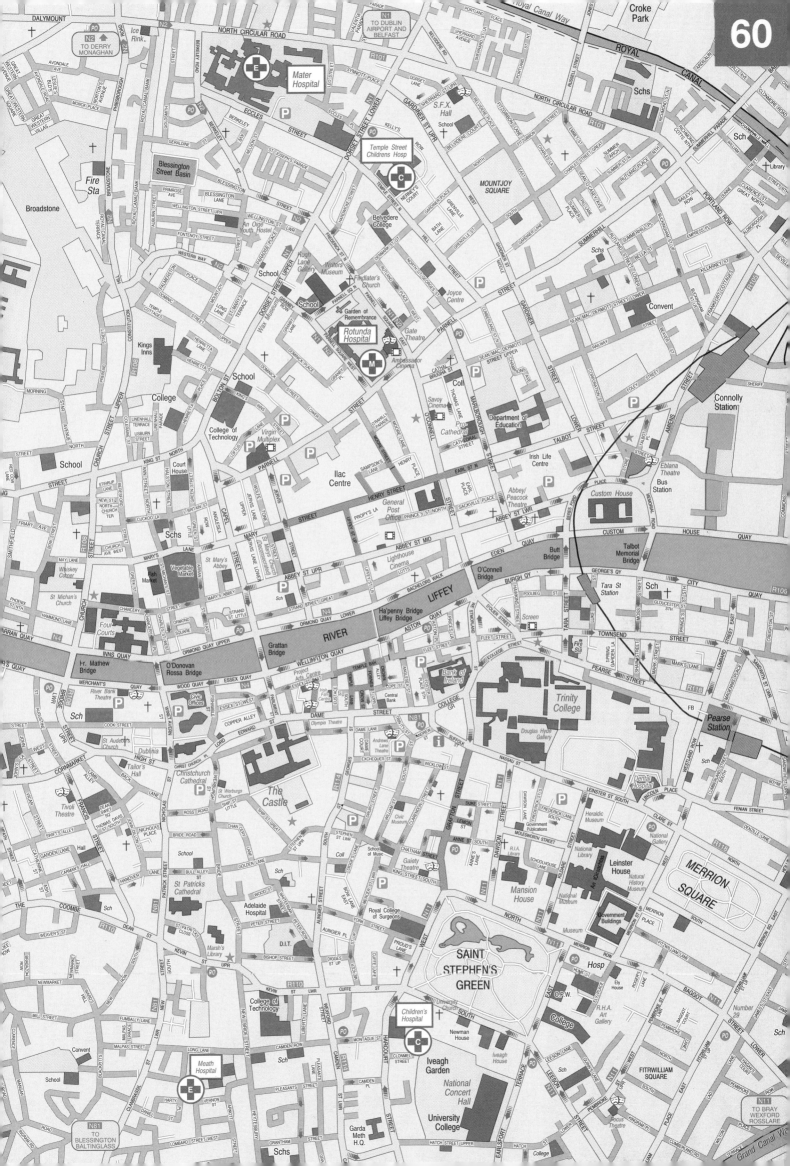

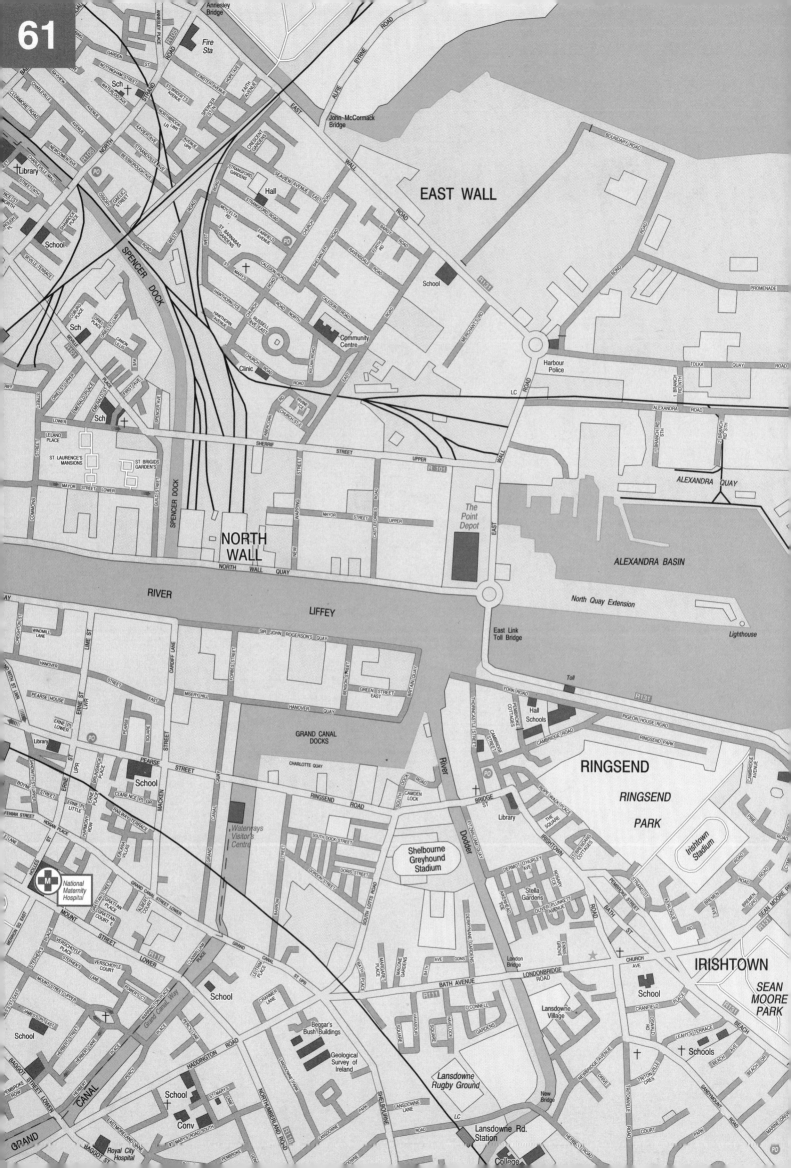

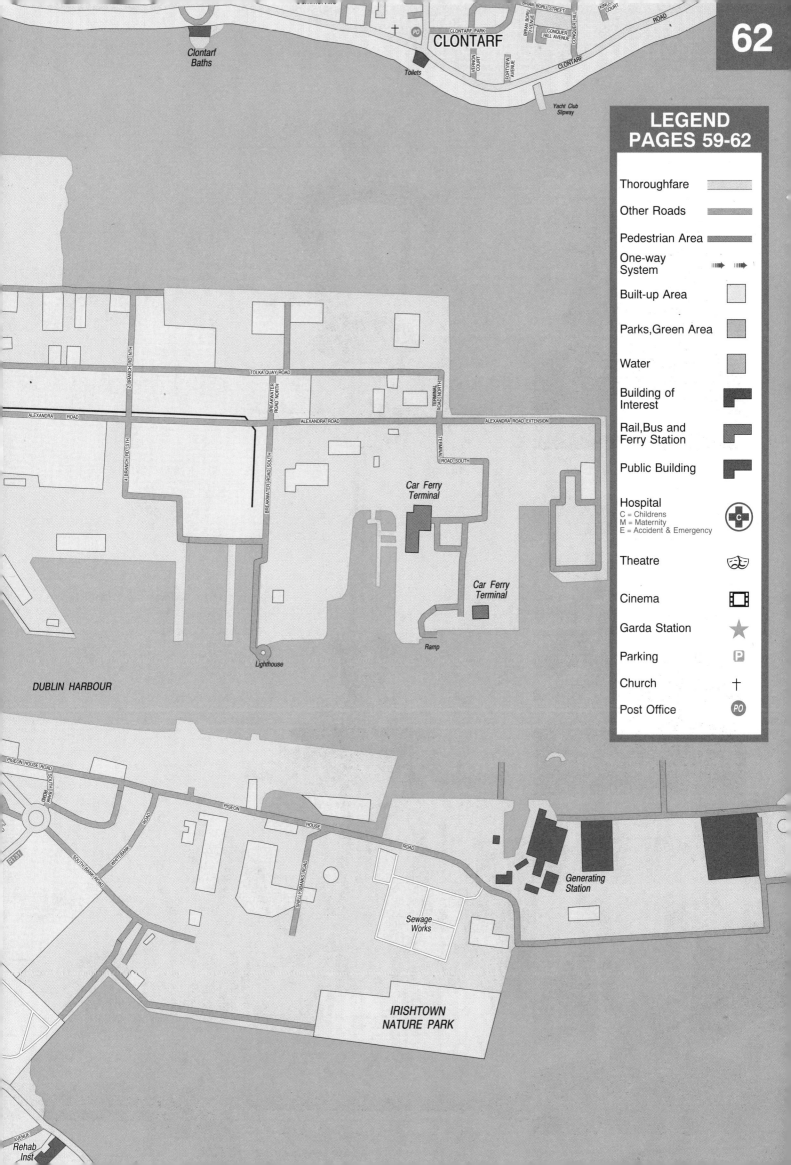

CLONTARF

Clontarf
Baths

Toilets

Yacht Club
Slipway

**LEGEND
PAGES 59-62**

Thoroughfare

Other Roads

Pedestrian Area

One-way
System

Built-up Area

Parks, Green Area

Water

Building of
Interest

Rail, Bus and
Ferry Station

Public Building

Hospital
C = Childrens
M = Maternity
E = Accident & Emergency

Theatre

Cinema

Garda Station

Parking

Church

Post Office

CLONTARF PARK

BRIAN BORU STREET

CONQUER HILL AVENUE

BRIAN BORU AVENUE

KINGS COURT

CLONTARF ROAD

VERNON COURT

FORTVIEW AVENUE

CONQUER HILL

CLONTARF ROAD

TOLKA QUAY ROAD

BREAKWATER ROAD NORTH

TERMINAL ROAD NORTH

ALEXANDRA ROAD

ALEXANDRA ROAD

ALEXANDRA ROAD EXTENSION

2 BRANCH RD NTH

4 BRANCH RD STH

BREAKWATER ROAD SOUTH

TERMINAL ROAD SOUTH

Car Ferry
Terminal

Car Ferry
Terminal

Ramp

Lighthouse

DUBLIN HARBOUR

PIGEON HOUSE ROAD

SOUTH BANK ROAD

SOUTH BANK ROAD

WHITEBANK ROAD

SHELLYBANKS ROAD

PIGEON HOUSE ROAD

Generating
Station

Sewage
Works

IRISHTOWN
NATURE PARK

AVENUE

Rehab
Inst

THE STORY OF DUBLIN

There is evidence of human settlement in the area of present-day Dublin dating back to remote prehistoric times. Ptolemy referred to Dublin as Eblana in A.D. 140 and a number of churches and monasteries existed in the vicinity in the early historic period. Saint Patrick is said to have visited Dublin in A.D. 448 where he made many converts to Christianity.

The history of Dublin as a city starts in A.D. 841, when Norse Vikings established a naval base by the Black Pool or Duibhlinn, which in turn became known by the Norse name of Dyfflin. The present name derives from the early English name of Divelin. Originally the site was below a hurdled ford or 'ath cliath' which is the origin of the current Irish name of Baile Atha Cliath – Town of the Hurdle Ford. An ancient highway south from the capital of Tara crossed the River Liffey at this point, which is now spanned by Father Mathew Bridge.

In A.D. 852-3 the Dublin settlement was the arrival point of further Norse settlers, under the leadership of Olaf the White. The construction of a fortified town followed, being situated on a steep ridge where Christ Church Cathedral and Dublin Castle now stand.

Ivarr the Boneless succeeded Olaf as king of Dublin in A.D. 871. During the following century Dublin became the capital of a small Norse trading and pirate kingdom called Dyfflinarskiri or Dublinshire. There was continual warfare between the Irish and the Danes over the following years. Outstanding events included the Battle of Dublin in A.D. 919 – a disastrous attempt to rid Dublin of its Scandinavian invaders. Niall Blackknee, king of Tara was killed in this battle, which was fought at Cell Mo-Shamhog or Islandbridge. In A.D. 999 Dublin joined in an unsuccessful attempt by the rulers of Leinster to overthrow Brian Boru. Danish power was finally broken when their Dublin/Leinster army, complete with overseas reinforcements, was crushed by the Irish under the leadership of Brian Boru at the Battle of Clontarf in 1014.

After Clontarf, Dublin continued under Danish rule and gained in prosperity, although it remained a small walled town for the following three centuries. When the half-Irish, half-Danish Sigtryggr Silkenbeard died, his dynasty died with him and Danish power began to wane.

Dublin became the seat of King Dermot I of Leinster for a while, and later, at the beginning of the twelfth century, came under the influence of Munster's Turloch Mor O'Brien and other Irish high kings, including the infamous Dermot McMurrough of Leinster. At this time the immediate Norse rulers of Dublin ranked merely as Earls, being subject to Irish rule.

Rory O'Connor, High King of Connacht assumed authority over Dublin in 1166. Under his direction Dermot McMurrough was driven overseas. McMurrough's return shortly afterwards signalled a new chapter in Dublin and Ireland's history, when he brought about the Anglo-Norman invasion of 1169.

McMurrough's son-in-law Richard Strongbow took control of Dublin and Leinster after the king's death. He was later defeated by Henry II of England who arrived in Dublin in 1171, establishing English authority in Ireland and making Dublin the headquarters of England's fluctuating power in Ireland for more than seven centuries. Under Henry II, Dublin received its first charter. Before he left, in 1172, he granted the city as a barony to the citizens of Bristol.

At this stage of Dublin's history the Norse influence and culture had become slight, as their descendants became absorbed into the native population. Whatever survivors were left had settled at Austmannabyr or Ostmaneby. This place later became known as Oxmanstown and was located north of the Liffey in the vicinity of St. Michan's Parish Church.

The Middle Ages saw little change, although the city walls were extended north of the Liffey in 1312. Among the buildings located within the city walls at this time were Dublin Castle, built between 1213 and 1228, Christ Church Cathedral and the churches of St.

Nicholas, St. Werburgh, St. John the Evangelist, St. Michael and St. Mary le Dam. North of the city walls were St. Mary's Abbey, the Dominican friary and the church of St. Michan, which was founded in 1096 by Bishop Samuel O'Hanly. To the south was St. Patrick's Cathedral, St. Bride's Church, the Franciscan friary, the archepiscopal palace of St. Sepulchre, the Carmelite friary, St. Stephen's Leper Hospital and the almshouse of St. Michael de Pole. In the eastern suburbs were St. Andrew's Parish Church, the Augustinian priory of All Hallows and the Augustinian nunnery of St. Mary de Hogge. Outside the western boundaries were St. Lawrence's Leper House, The Augustinian abbey of St. Thomas the Martyr, the hospital of St. John the Baptist, the Crutched friary and the hospital and priory of the Knights of St. John. A visit to the present-day Liberties region of Dublin will recall many associations with those ancient settlements, although much of Dublin's medieval heritage disappeared during the succeeding wartorn centuries.

THE CASTLE

The next era of Dublin's history saw an invasion by Edward and Robert Bruce in 1317, a disastrous Black Death which killed 14,000 in 1348, the 1437 crowning of Lambert Simnel as Edward VI of England in Christ Church Cathedral and the rebellion of Silken Thomas Fitzgerald in 1534. Following these events was the siege of Dublin by Owen Roe O'Neill in 1646 and the surrender of the city to the Parliamentarians by Royalist Ormonde in 1647 – a move designed to prevent Dublin falling into Confederate Catholic hands. Cromwell arrived in 1649 and by the end of the Cromwellian period the city was reduced to ruins, while the population had dwindled to a mere 9,000.

But the eighteenth century brought about a dramatic change under the new Protestant ascendancy. Dublin rapidly became one of Europe's most beautiful capital cities, as it spread out in all directions. This Georgian era was a period of architectural greatness, manifested in the noble squares and thoroughfares which were the setting for hundreds of magnificent private houses and superb public buildings such as the Parliament House in College Green. The arts also found ready encouragement from the wealthy society of the metropolis, who embellished their homes with the work of master stone carvers, painters, glassmakers, silversmiths and continental stucco workers.

A short-lived autonomy was conceded to the Irish Parliament by England in 1783, but this ended in 1800 with the Act of Union which united Ireland and Great Britain. The political unrest of the era culminated in the unsuccessful rising of 1798. A further insurrection by Robert Emmet in 1803 began and ended in failure on the streets of Dublin.

Towards the end of the last century Ireland's capital became the centre of two great cultural movements – the Gaelic League (Conradh na Gaeilge) founded in 1893 in an effort to restore the Irish language and the Irish Literary Renaissance which was dominated by the writings of Yeats and the founding of the Abbey Theatre.

The 1916 Rising, influenced greatly by the Gaelic League movement, was another major milestone. Three years later came the Declaration of Independence adopted in Dublin. The subsequent Anglo-Irish war ended in the Treaty of 1921. Following the setting up of the Irish Free State in 1922 came the tragic Civil War. Dublin once again became a shattered city but eventually recovered and the building of a modern European capital city began in earnest.

PLACES TO VISIT

Ashtown Castle Visitor Centre

Located in the Phoenix Park, 5kms from the City Centre. The Tower House possibly dates from the 17th Century, and nearby is the visitor centre. There are exhibitions, a film show, and visitors can view a colourful and realistic historical interpretation of the past.

Visiting times:

Nov.- Mid March	9.30am –	4.30pm	Sat. - Sun.
Mid March- end of March	9.30am –	5.00pm	Daily
April - May	9.30am –	5.30pm	Daily
June - Sept	9.30am –	6.30pm	Daily
Oct - Nov	9.30am –	5.00pm	Daily

Last admission 45 minutes before closing.

19 C4

Castletown House

Located in Celbridge, Co. Kildare. Castletown House, designed by Italian architect Alessandro Galilei and Irish architect Sir Edward Lovett Pearce for the speaker of the Irish House of Commons, William Conolly.

Building commenced in 1722, and Castletown House was continuously used by the Conolly family until 1965 when the house and lands were sold.

Castletown House came into state ownership in 1979 under the management of the Office of Public Works.

Visiting times:

DUE TO RESTORATION WORK
PLEASE PHONE 628 8252
FOR VISITING TIMES.

30 D2

Ashtown Castle Visitor Centre

Bank of Ireland

Bank of Ireland: (former Parliament House)
College Green.

Origins: Built between 1729 and 1739.

Designed by Sir Edward Lovatt Pearce (1699-1733) and enlarged by James Gandon and Robert Parke between 1785 and 1794.

The Bank of Ireland took over this building in 1804. It had been the scene of many dramatic events in Irish politics up to the passing of the Act of Union in 1800.

Visiting times: Monday, Tuesday, Wednesday, Friday
10 a.m. – 4 p.m.
Thursday 10 a.m. – 5 p.m.

36 D2

Celbridge Abbey

Located 12 miles from Dublin, Celbridge Abbey was built by Bartholomew Van Homrigh, Lord Mayor of Dublin in 1697.

The Abbey grounds contain many colourful attractions and are open to the public at the following times.

Visiting times:

Monday to Saturday	10 a.m. –	6 p.m.
Sunday/Bank Holidays	12 noon –	6 p.m.

29 C4

Castletown House

Custom House

Custom House
Custom House Quay
Origins: Designed by James Gandon and built between 1781 and 1791.
The building was reduced to a shell when it was gutted by fire during the War of Independence. It was restored by the Office of Public Works after the Irish Free State was established.   *36 E2*

Casino Marino

Casino Marino
Malahide Road.
Located just 4kms from the city centre, off the Malahide Road, Dublin 3.

The Casino, has been described as one of the finest 18th century classical buildings in Ireland. Access is by Guided Tour only.
Visiting times: June-Sept. 9:30 a.m. – 6:30 p.m. Daily
             Oct-May   10a.m. - 5 p.m. Daily
             Nov.   12noon - 4 p.m. Wed & Sun
             Feb.- April 12noon - 4 p.m. Wed & Sun
             Dec.-Jan. Closed   *22 D3*

City Hall
Lord Edward Street.
Origins: Formerly the Royal Exchange, designed by Thomas Cooley (1740 – 1784) and completed between 1769 and 1779.
This is the headquarters of Dublin's municipal government. Archives dating back to the twelfth century are stored in the Muniment Room. It also houses the mace and sword of the city, along with 102 Royal Charters, including the original charter of 1171 by which Dublin was granted to the men of Bristol by Henry II   *36 D2*

Dublinia – Christ Church,
St. Michael's Hill, Dublin 8.
The realistic and novel exhibition that is Dublinia is situated in the old Synod Hall on St. Michael's Hill, alongside of Christ Church Cathedral, to which it is connected by an ornate pedestrian archway over St. Michael's Hill.
The exhibition heralds the arrival of the Anglo-Normans in 1170 through a broad spectrum of Dublin life to the closure of the Monasteries in 1540.
Visiting times: Summer: 10 a.m. – 5 p.m. every day
              Winter: (Oct 1st – March 31st).
              Monday – Saturday 11 a.m. – 4 p.m.
              Sunday 10 a.m. – 4.30 p.m.
                            36 D3

Dublin Castle

The main entrance is located at the junction of Cork Hill and Castle Street. Dating from the 13th Century, the site, once a Viking stronghold, has served as a military fortress, prison, courts of law, and the core of British Administration in Ireland until 1922. Dublin Castle is now used for State functions. Guided tours of State Apartments, Chapel Royal and Undercroft.

Dublin Castle

St. Patrick's Hall

Dublin Castle

Visiting times: Monday/Friday   10 a.m. - 5 p.m.
Saturday/Sunday/
Public Holidays   2 p.m. – 5 p.m.

36 D3

The Throne Room

Dublin Castle

Dunsink Observatory
Dunsink Lane, near Castleknock.
Origins: Founded in 1783, this is one of the world's oldest observatories. It formerly belonged to Trinity College but is now the centre of the school of Astronomical Physics of the Dublin Institute for Advanced Studies.
Visiting times: Open to the public on the first and third Saturday of each month from September to March, between 8 and 10 p.m. Admission free on written application to the secretary enclosing stamp-addressed envelope.

19 B2

General Post Office
O'Connell Street.
Origins: Designed by Francis Johnston and built between 1814 and 1818.
The GPO became the focal point of the 1916 Insurrection and the Proclamation of the Irish Republic took place there. Destroyed by fire, it was restored in 1929. In the public office is a noteworthy statue representing the Death of Cuchulainn, the work of Oliver Sheppard R.H.A.

36 D2

Kilmainham Jail
Inchicore Road, Dublin 8.
One of the largest decommissioned jails in Europe, it played its part in some of the most patriotic and tragic episodes, that light the path of Ireland's journey to modern nationhood, from the 1780's to 1924. Featuring many exhibitions and a multi-lingual audio-visual show. Access by guided tour only.
Visiting times: Oct - April Mon - Sat. 9.30 a.m. – 6 p.m.
                                          Sunday   10.00 a.m. – 6 p.m.
                        April - Sept Daily   9.30 a.m. – 6 p.m.

35 A3

Kilmainham Jail

General Post Office

Leinster House

Four Courts
Inns Quay.

Origins: Designed by James Gandon and built between 1785 and 1802. This building, dominated by a great domed central mass, is one of Gandon's masterpieces. The Irish Law Courts and Law Library are housed here. Like the Custom House, Gandon's other great building, it was also destroyed by fire during the struggle for Irish independence. Although significantly altered, the building was completely restored by 1932.

36 D2

Leinster House
Kildare Street.

Origins: Designed by Richard Cassells, building commenced on this fine Georgian mansion in 1745. Originally the residence of the Duke of Leinster, the building became the property of the Royal Dublin Society in 1815. In 1922 it was purchased by the first Irish Free State Government to serve as a Parliament House. Presently it is the meeting place of the Dail (Chamber of Deputies) and Seanad (Senate).

36 E3

Waterways Visitor Centre
Grand Canal Quay, Dublin 2
Located at Grand Canal Docks, beside McMahon Bridge, Pearse Street.

The centre houses an exhibition outlining the history of Ireland's Inland Waterways and the activities and experiences currently available.

Featuring an audio-visual show and working models of various engineering features.

Visiting times: Oct. - May 12.30p.m. - 5.00p.m. Wed.- Sun.
                June - Sept. 9:30 a.m. – 6:30 p.m. daily
                Last admission 45 minutes before closing.

36 F3

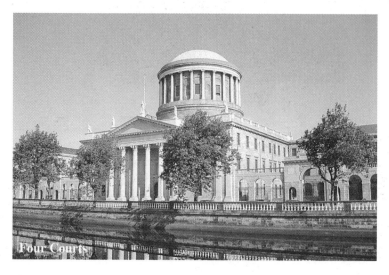

Four Courts

Royal Hospital and Irish Museum of Modern Art

Royal Hospital and Irish Museum of Modern Art
Military Road, Kilmainham.
The most important 17th century building in Ireland has been restored.
Guided tours available of the Master's Quarters, the Great Hall with
the portrait collection, and the chapel which contains outstanding
woodcarving by Tabary and a magnificent Baroque ceiling.
Visiting times: Tues – Sat 10 a.m. – 5:30 p.m.
                    Sun 12 noon – 5:30 p.m.
                    Closed Monday.   *35 B3*

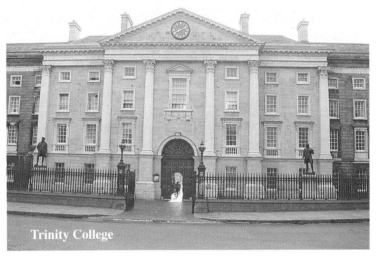

Trinity College

Mansion House

Mansion House
Dawson Street.
Origins: This Queen Anne house was built in 1705, the round room
having been added in 1821 as the venue for a function to honour King
George IV. Built in brick, the building underwent changes during the
Victorian era.
Since 1715 the Mansion House has been the residence of Dublin's
Lord Mayor. In 1919 the Declaration of Independence was adopted
here and here also was signed the truce which ended Anglo-Irish
hostilities in 1921.   *36 E3*

Trinity College
Main entrance, College Green.
Origins: Trinity College is the sole college of the University of
Dublin. Founded by Queen Elizabeth I in 1592, it is built on the site of
the Augustinian priory of All Hallows which was founded by Dermot
McMurrough. The oldest buildings now surviving are the Rubrics, a
range of brick apartments dating from 1700. The Palladian facade was
added in 1759. In the same year the Provost's house (facing the
northern end of Grafton Street) was built. This is the only great
Georgian house in Dublin still being used for its original purpose.
Many world-famous men have attended this college over the centuries.
See also 'Trinity College Library'.   *36 E2*

SWORDS

Swords is located 12.9 kms north of Dublin City Centre and is situated on the Ward River. Accessible by way of the N1, Swords Town has many features such as St. Colmcille's Well, the Old Constabulary Barracks, St. Columba's Church, Belfry, and Round Tower, and Swords Castle.

Swords Castle

Built in 1183 as a summer palace for the first Norman Archbishop of Dublin, Swords Castle was designed both as a residence and as a place of defence. In 1324 Archbishop de Bicknor left Swords and the castle fell into disrepair. Despite many attempts at renovation over the centuries, it has remained so. Currently in the ownership of Fingal Council, who intend to refurbish the castle in the near future.

2 D2

MALAHIDE

Malahide is a lively, picturesque small town, nestling on the south shore of the Broadmeadow Estuary , in North County Dublin. Located 14.5 kms from Dublin City Centre, it is accessible by the N1, R106, R107 and by direct rail link.
Malahide has many places of note, such as St. Sylvesters Well, Hicks Tower, The Arches, Casino, Robswalls, the most noted of all being Malahide Castle.

Malahide Castle

Built by Sir Richard de Talbot about 1200 and developed over the centuries into the imposing architectural achievement that it is today. The castle houses part of the National Portrait Collection in the Great Hall.

The extensive grounds incorporate the 20 acre Talbot Botanic Garden, which is open to all 9 a.m. to 9 p.m. daily.
Visiting times: April-Sept. Monday – Friday 10 a.m. – 5 p.m.
Saturday 11 a.m. – 6 p.m.
Sunday 11.00 a.m. – 6 p.m.
Closed 12:45 – 2 p.m. daily.
Nov.- March Sat., Sun. and Bank holidays 2 p.m. - 5 p.m.

Also included is the Fry Model Railway Museum, which contains a unique collection of hand-made models showing the history of Irish railways from its inception to the modern day period.

3 A3

Malahide Castle

Howth Castle

The great English architect Sir Edwin Lutyens restyled this 14th century castle overlooking Dublin Bay. The grounds are also noted for its wild rhododendron gardens. The grounds are open daily from 8 a.m. to sunset.

25 C1

Howth Transport Museum

This Museum is located in the grounds of Howth Castle. It features lorries, trucks, fire engines and tractors. Also exhibited is the restored Hill of Howth No.9 Tram. Open Saturday, Sunday and Bank Holidays: 2 - 6 p.m. Summer and 2 - 5 p.m. Winter.

25 C1

BRAY

This is one of Ireland's largest and oldest east coast seaside resorts, accommodating business, residential needs and tourist amenities, under the ever dominant Bray Head.

Bray

The Courthouse: located on Main Street between Quinsborough Road and Seapoint Road, this building was designed by William Murray, and built in 1841. It is now the location of Bray Heritage Museum, and Bray Tourist Office. Visitors 10 a.m. – 6 p.m. daily.
57 C2

The Town Hall: located on Main Street at the junction of Killarney Road and Vevay Road is the jewel in Bray's architectural crown. Designed by Edward G. Dawber for architects Thomas Newenham Deane & Son, it was built in 1884 at the request of Lord and Lady Brabazon for the people of Bray. Currently the seat of Bray Urban District Council.
57 C2

Other notable features include Oldcourt Castle, The Promenade and on the eastern side of Bray Head, the Cliff Walk fringes along a 5km feast of cliff face and sea views into Greystones.

LEIXLIP

What was once the village of Leixlip is now Kildare's youngest and most populous town. Situated on the river Liffey and the river Rye, the Salmon Leap (from which Leixlip gets its name) is overlooked by the 12th century Leixlip Castle. The river Liffey joins the river Rye in the heart of the old village and a lake formed by a hydroelectric dam offers a great opportunity for the angler and water sport enthusiast. The internationally renowned Liffey Descent canoeing event takes place here in September every year.

CHURCHES AND CATHEDRALS

Christ Church Cathedral
Main entrance, Christchurch Place.
Origins: The original church was built about 1030 by Sigtryggr Silkenbeard, Norse King of Dublin. A new church was built in 1173 by Strongbow. The present structure dates mainly from the nineteenth century, although the wonderful medieval crypt still remains. Christ Church contains many interesting historical remains.
Visiting times:
                10:00 a.m. to 5 p.m. daily

36 D3

St. Audoen's Church
High Street
Origins: St. Audoen's dates from medieval times and is the oldest of Dublin's parish churches. The tower houses Ireland's three most ancient bells, dating from 1423. There's a font in the nave dating from 1124. St. Audoen's Arch stands nearby. This is Dublin's only surviving city gate. Built in 1240 it originally led to a strand on the River Liffey.
35 C3

St. Mary's Church
Mary Street.
Origins: Dating from 1627, this was the first Dublin church to be built with galleries. Theobald Wolfe Tone was baptised here in 1763 and Sean O'Casey the playwright in 1880. The Church is now a retail outlet.

36 D2

St. Michan's Church
Church Street
Origins: Founded by the Norse in 1096, the present building dates from 1685-6, having been much restored in 1828. The Church's Harris organ is said to have been used by Handel during his visit to Dublin. Dry magnesium limestone vaults beneath the church contain mummified corpses which may be seen by the public.
Visiting times: Church and Vaults:
          April - Oct.   Monday - Friday   10 a.m. - 5 p.m.
          Nov. - March   Mon. - Friday 12.30 a.m. - 3.30 p.m.
          Saturday   10 a.m. - 1 p.m.
          Vaults closed on Sundays.   *35 C2*

St. Mary's Pro-Cathedral
Marlboro Street.
Origins: Designed by John Sweetman and built between 1815 and 1825. Originally intended for O'Connell Street but erected on this less suitable site to satisfy Protestant opposition at the time. The interior reveals the inspiration of Chalgin's Church of St. Philippe de Roule, Paris. Some interesting monuments may be seen inside. The metropolitan church of the diocese, it is used for State functions. A Latin Mass is sung each Sunday at 11 a.m. by the Palestrina Choir of which the famous tenor John McCormack was once a member.

36 D2

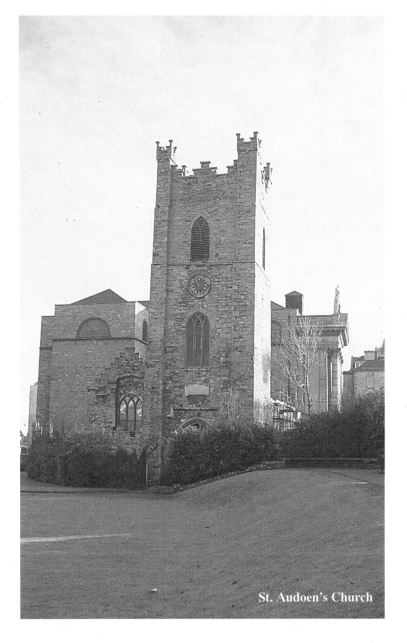
St. Audoen's Church

St. Werburgh's Church
Werburgh Street, off Christchurch Place.
Origins: Erected in 1715 on the site of the medieval successor to pre-Norman St. Werburgh's. Destroyed by fire in 1754, the church was re-opened in 1759. A spire was added in 1768 but removed in the early nineteenth century by the fearful authorities of Dublin castle, which it overlooked. Until 1790 St. Werburgh's was the Chapel Royal. In the vaults beneath is buried Lord Edward Fitzgerald. His captor Town Major Sirr, is buried in the nearby churchyard.
This fine Georgian building, now well restored, contains many interesting features including an attractive pulpit designed by Francis Johnston and carved by Richard Stewart, as well as a sixteenth-century Fitzgerald tomb located in the porch.
Visiting times: By appointment only. Tel. (01) 4783710
                Monday to Friday   10 a.m. – 4 p.m.
Entrance: North Door, 8 Castle Street. Main Sunday Service: 10:30 a.m.

36 D3

St. Patrick's Cathedral

St. Patrick's Cathedral
Patrick Street.

Origins: St. Patrick's, Ireland's largest church, was built on the site of the pre-Norman parish church of St. Patrick. The church was rebuilt in 1191 by Archbishop Comyn. In 1213 it gained cathedral status, but later, in 1300 a papal decree gave Christ Church precedence. At the Reformation it became a parish church, but under the Catholic restoration of Philip and Mary it once again became a cathedral.

A university was established there in 1320 but was suppressed later by Henry VIII. The square tower dates from the fourteenth century.

During the wars of the seventeenth century the Cromwellians used the ruinous cathedral as a stable for their horses. But the future saw a great improvement in the fabric of the building. A spire was added by the architect John Semple in 1749 and a general restoration was undertaken between 1844 and 1869 being financed by Sir Benjamin Lee Guinness. Jonathan Swift was Dean of St. Patrick's from 1713 to 1745. His pulpit may still be seen and his tomb, with its famous epitaph is in the south aisle. Buried nearby is Esther (Stella) Johnston one of Swift's two great lovers.

Visiting times:

Monday - Friday 9 a.m. - 6 p.m.
Saturday   9 a.m. - 5 p.m.(4p.m. Nov. - Mar.)
Sunday
Sept. - Mid June 10 - 11a.m. and 12.45 - 3p.m.
Mid June - Aug. 9.30 - 11a.m., 12.45 - 3p.m. and 4.15p.m. - 5p.m.

36 D3

LIBRARIES

Chester Beatty Library
20 Shrewsbury Road.
One of the world's most valuable private collections of oriental manuscripts and miniatures can be seen here. There are manuscripts of the New Testament, Manichean papyri and Eastern miniatures, as well as picture scrolls, albums and jades from the Far East.
Visiting times: Tuesday to Friday   10 a.m. to 5 p.m.
                   Saturday   2 to 5 p.m.
                   Guided Tours Wed. and Sat. from 2.30p.m.
                   Closed Mondays.
                   Admission free.
                   44 D1

Trinity College Library

Trinity College Library
Main entrance to college from College Green.
Dating from the late sixteenth century, Trinity College Library is Ireland's oldest library. It contains over 1,000,000 volumes and Ireland's most extensive collection of manuscripts and early printed books. Its greatest treasure is the Book of Kells (probably eighth century). This is considered to be the most beautiful illuminated manuscript in existence today. Manuscripts in the library include State letters of Queen Elizabeth I, diaries of Wolfe Tone and manuscripts of the Irish dramatist, John Millington Synge.
The library is housed in two buildings – the Old Library (completed in 1732) and the New Library (1967). Trinity College Library has the right to a copy of any book printed in Ireland or Britain.
Visiting hours: Monday to Saturday 9:30 a.m. to 5:30 p.m.
                 Sunday October-May 12noon to 4.30 p.m.
                 Sunday June-September 9:30 a.m. to 4.30 p.m.
                 36 E2

Royal Irish Academy Library
19 Dawson Street.
A very extensive collection of ancient Irish manuscripts can be seen in this library. These include the 'Book of the Dun Cow', the 'Book of Ballymote', the 'Speckled Book' and the 'Stowe Missal'. Also to be seen is the Cathach or Battle Book, believed to be the actual copy of the Psalms made in the sixth century by St. Colmcille. An autograph copy of the Annals of the Four Masters made in Donegal between 1632 and 1636 is also there.
Visiting hours: Monday to Friday 10:30 a.m. to 5:00 p.m.
                 Closed bank holidays and during the last
                 three weeks of August.
                 Admission free.
                   36 E3

Marsh's Library
St. Patrick's Close.
This is Ireland's oldest public library, founded in 1701 by Archbishop Narcissus Marsh. The collection consists mainly of theological, medical, ancient historical, Hebrew, Syriac, Greek, French and Latin literature. Still to be seen are the original carved bookcases and the cages into which readers were locked to prevent theft.
Visiting Hours: Weekdays 10 a.m. to 12:45 p.m. – 2 to 5 p.m.
                 Saturday 10:30 a.m. to 12:45 p.m.
                 Closed Tuesdays and bank holidays.
                   36 D3

National Library
Kildare Street.
Founded in 1877, the National Library is the largest public library in Ireland. Over 500,000 books as well as maps, prints and manuscripts are housed there. Its huge newspaper collection provides a rich source of historical reference. An extensive collection of historical and literary manuscripts relating to Ireland and microfilms of documents from overseas libraries and archives are available for reference. The public service counter is manned by helpful officials.
Visiting hours: Mon. 10 a.m. – 9 p.m.
                 Tues/Wed 2 p.m.- 9 p.m.
                 Thu/Fri 10 a.m. – 5 p.m.
                 Sat 10 a.m. – 1 p.m.
                   36 E3

National Library

Dublin City Libraries
There are twenty-eight public libraries maintained by the Corporation of Dublin.
The administrative headquarters for the Dublin Public Libraries is at Pearse Street. It houses special reference collections, including the Gilbert Library of manuscripts and books relating to Dublin. And there are extensive collections of books on Ireland. A collection of W. B. Yeats material contains a full edition of Mosada.

Other Dublin Libraries
Other libraries of note are the King's Inn Library, Henrietta Street; University College Library, Belfield; the Worth Library, Steeven's Hospital; the Franciscan Library, Franciscan House of Studies, Killiney; the Central Catholic Library at 74 Merrion Square; the Royal Dublin Society's Library at Ballsbridge and the library in the Ilac Centre, Henry Street.

ART GALLERIES

Hugh Lane Municipal Gallery of Modern Art.
Charlemont House, Parnell Square.
This building, dating from 1762, was formerly the residence of Lord Charlemont. The collection was originally housed in Harcourt Street, the present gallery dating from 1908. It was Sir Hugh Lane who contributed the nucleus of this collection of pictures. Lane was drowned in the sinking of the Lusitania in 1915. Before his death he left his continental collection to the National Gallery in London but had stipulated in his will that they should return to Dublin. Unfortunately an unwitnessed codicil of his will caused complications and his intentions were declared invalid.
After many years it was agreed in 1959 to divide the pictures between Dublin and London in two groups. The two groups are exchanged every five years. This gallery has an interesting collection of works by nineteenth and twentieth-century artists.

National Gallery
Merrion Lawn, Merrion Square West.
The gallery was officially opened in 1864. It then consisted of only 100 pictures donated by William Dargan and George Mulvany. Dargan was a railway entrepreneur who died in 1867. His statue may be seen on the lawn outside the gallery.
There are now over 2000 pictures in the gallery, representing all the European schools. Donors of pictures include Lady Milltown, Sir Hugh Lane, Edward Martyn, the Friends of the National Collections and Sir Alfred Chester Beatty. Famous works by Poussin, Goya and Gainsborough, may be seen. Irish artists are well represented, in a comprehensive collection which includes works by Ashford, Barry, Barrett, John Butler Yeats, Hone, Osborne, Lavery and Orpen. Part of the National Portrait Gallery provides an interesting survey of personalities spanning 300 years. This is housed under the same roof.

National Gallery

Hugh Lane Municipal Gallery of Modern Art.

Visiting times: Monday to Saturday: 10 a.m. – 5:15 p.m.
Sunday: 2 – 5 p.m.
Thursday open till 8:15 p.m.
Restaurant open during gallery hours.

Art Reference Library open Monday to Friday: 10 a.m. – 5:15 p.m. Free public lectures Sundays: 3 p.m. winter only and Tuesdays 10:30 a.m. Conducted tours of gallery on Sundays at: 2:30 p.m. 3 p.m. 3:30 p.m. and 4 p.m. Admission free.

36 E3

Royal Hospital and Irish Museum of Modern Art
Military Road, Kilmainham.
The Irish Museum of Modern Art was established in 1991 and exhibits Irish and International Art of the 20th century

Visiting times: Tues – Sat 10 a.m. – 5:30 p.m.
Sun – 12 noon – 5:30 p.m.
Closed Monday.

Visiting times: Tuesday to Friday   9.30 a.m. to 6 p.m.
Thursday   open until 8 p.m. (summer only)
Saturday   9.30 a.m. to 5 p.m.
Sunday   11 a.m. to 5 p.m.
Closed Monday.   Admission free.

36 D1

35 B3

MUSEUMS

National Museum
Kildare Street/Merrion Street.
The contents of this museum comes under three headings – Irish Antiquities, Art and Industrial and Natural History. The Irish antiquities division holds one of Europe's most impressive collections of antiquities. Items displayed cover every age from the Stone Age to medieval times. Gold lunulae, torques and fibulae from the Bronze Age are of particular interest, as well as famous items like the Tara Brooch, the Cross of Cong and the Ardagh Chalice from the early Christian period.
The main entrance is from Kildare Street but part of the natural history division is approached from Merrion Street.
Visiting times: Tuesday to Saturday   10 a.m. to 5 p.m.
Sunday 2 to 5 p.m.
Closed Monday.   *36 E3*

Dublin Civic Museum
South William Street.
Occupying the former City Assembly House, this museum was opened in 1953. It contains a permanent collection of exhibits of antiquarian and historical interest, pertaining to Dublin city. Newspapers and cuttings, as well as maps, prints, and various unique items provide a vivid record of Dublin's past.
Visiting times: Tuesday to Friday   10 a.m. to 5:30 p.m.
Sunday   11 a.m. to 2 p.m.
Saturday   10 a.m. – 5 p.m.
Closed Monday
Admission free.   *36 D3*

The Writer's Museum
18/19 Parnell Square North.
Opened in 1991 in two restored Georgian houses. It features a display of paintings, photographs, manuscripts and other memorabilia relating to Irish writers such as Shaw, Yeats, Beckett, Wilde, O'Casey, Joyce, Behan and Swift. Opening hours:
June/ July /August Monday to Friday 10 a.m. - 7 p.m.
The rest of the year Monday to Saturday 10 a.m. - 5 p.m.
Sundays and Bank Holidays 2 p.m. - 6 p.m.   *36 D1*

Genealogical Office and Heraldic Museum
2 Kildare St. Dublin 2.
Visit the oldest office of state in Ireland - founded 1552. See the unique Heraldic Museum with its colourful display of coats of arms, banners and facility.
Avail of the Consultancy Service on ancestry tracing designed to enable you to undertake on your own the task of uncovering your Irish roots.
Hours of opening: 10 a.m. - 12.30 p.m.
2 p.m. - 4.30 p.m. Monday - Friday.
36 E3

Genealogical Office and Heraldic Museum

National Print Museum
Garrison Chapel, Beggars Bush, Dublin 4.

This Museum houses a unique collection of implements, artefacts and machines from all sectors of the printing industry in Ireland. Many of them are still in full working order.

Visiting times: May - Sept.
Mon. - Fri.   10.00 - 12.30a.m.and 2.30 - 5p.m.
Sat., Sun. and Bank Holidays   2.30 - 5p.m.
Last Tour 4.30p.m.   *36 F3*

National Wax Museum
Granby Row.
On display are life-size figures of prominent Irish historical, political, theatrical, literary and sporting personalities. Taped narrations on each scene, guide one along. The Chamber of Horrors is a must for all the family.
Visiting times: Monday – Saturday   10 a.m. – 5:30 p.m.
Sunday   1 p.m. – 6 p.m.
36 D1

SOME FAMOUS DUBLIN PEOPLE

Dublin has produced an amazing number of well-known writers, scientists and scholars. Many of these personalities not only distinguished themselves in their native city, but through their work, established their names world-wide.

The following is a brief guide to some of the most famous people who were born in Dublin and/or lived there for a considerable period of time.

THE WORLD OF LETTERS

Samuel Beckett, (1906-1989). Novelist and dramatist, born in Dublin. Novels include 'Murphy','Mollag and Malone Dies'. Plays include 'Waiting for Godot', 'Va et Vient', and 'Silence'. Awarded the Nobel Prize for Literature in 1969.

Brendan Behan,(1923-1964). Dublin-born dramatist. Plays include 'The Quare Fellow' and 'The Hostage'.

Edmund Burke, (1729-1797). Son of a Dublin attorney. Orator, political philosopher and champion of American liberties.

James Joyce, (1882-1941). Poet and writer, born and educated in Dublin. Works include 'A Portrait of the Artist as a Young Man', 'Ulysses' and 'Finnegan's Wake'. The Martello Tower where Joyce lived outside Dublin is now a museum in his memory.

William E.H. Lecky (1838-1903). Famous Dublin-born historian.

Joseph Sheridan Le Fanu, (1814-1873). Nineteenth-century Dublin novelist, author of 'The House by the Churchyard', among others.

Charles Jones Lever, (1806-1872). A native of Dublin. His novels include 'Harry Lorrequer' and 'Charles O'Malley'.

Edmund Malone, (1741-1812). This great scholar specialised in the study of Shakespeare.

James Clarence Mangan,(1803-1849). Son of a Dublin grocer. His poetry includes 'Dark Rosaleen', 'O'Hussey's Ode to the Maguire' and the autobiographic ballad 'The Nameless One'.

James Joyce

Thomas Moore, (1779-1852). Like Mangan this poet was also a grocer's son. He distinguished himself as an adaptor of traditional airs and as a writer of biographies. Works include 'Moore's Melodies', 'The Twopenny Post Bag' and 'Lalla Rookh'.

Sean O'Casey (1880-1964). Originally a labourer, O'Casey became one of Ireland's most famous dramatists. Plays include 'The Shadow of a Gunman', 'Juno and the Paycock', 'The Plough and the Stars', 'The Silver Tassie' and 'Purple Dust'.

Birthplace, G.B.Shaw.

George Bernard Shaw, (1866-1950). Shaw, a world-famous playwright and wit spent the first twenty years of his life in Dublin, his birthplace. Works include 'John's Bull's Other Island', 'Candida', 'The Doctor's Dilemma', 'Man and Superman', 'Pygmalion', 'Heartbreak House' and 'Saint Joan'. In 1925 he won the Nobel Prize for Literature.

Richard Brinsley Sheridan, (1751-1816). Dramatist and distinguished parliamentary orator. Born in Upper Dorset Street. His three great comedies were 'The Rivals', 'The School for Scandal' and 'The Critic'.

James Stephens, (1882-1950). Novelist and poet. His novels include 'The Crock of Gold', 'The Charwoman's Daughter', 'The Demigods' and 'In the Land of Youth'. Poems include 'The Goat Paths' and 'The Snare'.

Jonathan Swift, (1667-1745). Known mainly as a satirist. Became Dean of St. Patrick's in 1713. Probably best known for 'The Tale of a Tub', the 'Drapier's Letters' and 'Gulliver's Travels'.

John Millington Synge, (1871-1909). Although a Dubliner, this dramatist's first love was the West of Ireland. This is reflected in his work. Best known are 'Playboy of the Western World', 'Riders to the Sea' and 'Deirdre of the Sorrows'.

Sir James Ware, (1594-1666). As an historian and antiquary, Ware is one of Dublin's most distinguished great scholars.

Oscar Wilde, (1854-1900). Born in Dublin and educated at Trinity College, Wilde moved to London when he was twenty-five. His outstanding works are the novel 'The Picture of Dorian Gray', and 'The Importance of being Earnest', his dramatic masterpiece. Also of note is his long letter 'De Profundis' and 'The Ballad of Reading Gaol'.

William Butler Yeats, (1865-1939). Born in London and educated in Dublin, Yeats contributed much to the cultural life of Dublin. He was awarded the Nobel Prize for Literature in 1923. Published works include 'Responsibilities', 'The Tower' and 'The Winding Stair'. This great literary personality played a major part in the establishment of the Abbey Theatre in 1904.

THE WORLD OF MUSIC

Michael William Balfe, (1808-1870). Balfe was famous as a conductor and composer of operas. Works include 'The Bohemian Girl' and 'Il Talismano'.

John Field, (1782-1837). Outstanding as a pianist and romantic composer. His nocturnes are said to have inspired Chopin. Glinka, founder of the Russian school, was taught by Field.

Sir Charles Villiers Stanford, (1852-1924). Composer of opera, songs, symphonies and chamber music.

THE WORLD OF PAINTING

George Barrett, (1732-1784). A founder member of the Royal Academy and landscape painter of note.

Robert Carver, (1750-1791). Carver's work portrays some of the best Irish landscapes of the eighteenth century.

Patrick Vincent Duffy, (1836-1909). Well known for his vivid landscapes.

Nathaniel Hone I., (1718-1784). Portrait painter and a founder member of the Royal Academy, London.

Nathaniel Hone II., (1831-1917). Painter of landscapes and seascapes. Hone II was a member of the Barbizon Group. He was also a founder of the modern school of Irish painting.

Edward Lutterell, (1650-1710). As well as being a painter, Luttrell goes down in the history of Irish art as being one of the earliest exponents of mezzotint engraving.

James Arthur O'Connor, (1791-1841). Landscape painter.

Sir. William Orpen, (1870-1931). Orpen specialised in portrait painting.

Walter Frederick Osborne, (1859-1903). A clear insight into field and street life is made available through the work of Osborne.

Sir Martin Archer Shee (1869-1950). The work of this portrait artist provides, through his subjects, a unique historical record.

William Sadler, (1782-1839). One of several outstanding landscape painters of the early nineteenth century.

Jack Butler Yeats, (1871-1957). This modern artist painted in a highly original style, his work distinguished by a heavy, unmistakeable texture. His brother was William Butler Yeats.

John Butler Yeats, (1839-1922). Well known as a portrait painter. Father of Jack and William Butler Yeats.

THE WORLD OF MEDICINE AND SCIENCE

Sir Robert Stawell Ball, (1840-1913). Noted astronomer and mathematician.

Abraham Colles, (1773-1843). In the medical world Colles is remembered for 'Colles' Law', 'Colles' fracture' and 'Colles' Fuchsia'.

Sir Dominic Corrigan, (1802-1880). Corrigan specialised in diseases of the aorta. Remembered for 'Corrigan's Disease', 'Corrigan's Pulse'. He also invented 'Corrigan's Button'.

Sir Philip Crampton, (1778-1858). This famous Dublin surgeon played an important role in establishing the fame of the Dublin medical school in the early nineteenth century. He was co-author of a book on bedside teaching with Robert Graves.

George Francis Fitzgerald, (1851-1901). Fitzgerald made a valuable contribution to the study of physics.

Robert Graves, (1796-1853). The concept of bedside teaching was introduced in medical education by Robert Graves. His book 'Clinical Lectures' became an international textbook for medical students.

Sir William Rowan Hamilton, (1805-1865). Hamilton was the discoverer of quaternions. Through his pioneering work he achieved international fame by foreshadowing the quantum theory and later important discoveries in nuclear physics.

Richard Kirwan, (1735-1812). The first systematic textbook in English on mineralogy was written by Kirwan.

Francis Rynd, (1801-1861). A major contribution was made to medical science by Rynd, through his invention of the hypodermic syringe.

George Salmon, (1819-1904). Dublin-born mathematician.

William Stokes, (1804-1878). Stokes is remembered for 'Stokes-Adams Syndrome' and 'Cheyne-Stokes Respiration'. He was the author of 'Diseases of the Chest and Diseases of the Heart and Aorta'.

Sir William Wilde, (1815 – 1876). Wilde was noted as an ophthalmologist, otologist, and archaeologist. In the medical field he is associated with 'Wilde's Incision' and 'Wilde's Cord'. He was Oscar Wilde's father.

THE WORLD OF STAINED GLASS AND SCULPTURE

Stained glass:
Harry Clarke, (1889-1931).
Michael Healy (1873-1941).
Evie Hone, (1894-1955).

Sculpture:
John Henry Foley, (1818-1874).
Thomas Kirk, (1777-1845).
Andrew O'Connor, (1874-1941).
Edward Smyth, (1749-1812).

Detail from panel, St. Michan's Church.

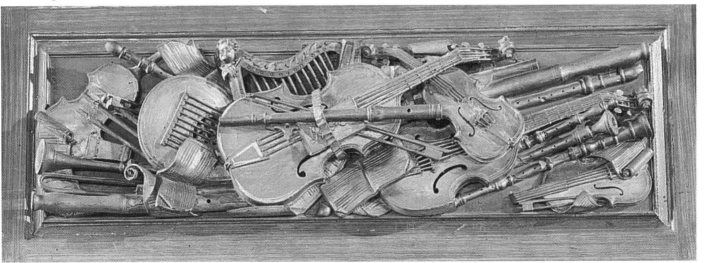

DUBLIN'S PARKS AND GARDENS

Garden of Remembrance
Parnell Square East Dublin 1.
The Garden of Remembrance was designed by Daithí Hanly and is dedicated to the memory of those who died in the cause of Irish freedom. The central theme is peaceful remembrance and reflection, and the sculpture by Oisen Kelly, "Children of Lir" reflects this. The garden is open daily during daylight hours.
36 D1

St. Anne's Park and Gardens
Mount Prospect Avenue, Clontarf.
In a pleasant setting adjacent to Dollymount Strand, the rose gardens in this park cover over three acres alone. The Park and Gardens are open all year round. Admission free. Entrance Howth Road/All Saints Road .
23 A3

Marlay Park
Rathfarnham.
This is the largest park on the south side of the Dublin. It covers three hundred acres in a highly picturesque setting at the foot of the Dublin mountains which is the starting point of the 'Wicklow Way' long distance signposted walk. A craft centre, including workshops, is situated within the area of the park.
51 A2

Merrion Square Park
Merrion Square.
Formerly only for the use of the residents of Merrion Square, this public park is surrounded on all sides by some of Dublin's finest Georgian architecture.
36 E3

National Botanic Gardens

National Botanic Gardens
Botanic Road, Glasnevin.
Covering 19.5 hectares, these beautiful gardens contain a huge assortment of trees, plants and shrubs. Rare blooms and palms are housed in the huge Victorian conservatories. These gardens were founded in 1795 when the estate, on which the gardens now stand, was purchased from the Ticknell family by the Royal Dublin Society.
Visiting times: Weekdays: 9 a.m. – 6 p.m. in summer.
                                                10 a.m. – 4:30 p.m. in winter.
                          Sundays: 11 a.m. – 6 p.m. in summer.
                                                11 a.m. – 4:30 p.m. in winter.
Greenhouses not open before 2 p.m. on Sundays.
Admission free.
21 A3

Herbert Park
Ballsbridge.
A charming mature park, well laid out with interesting trees, shrubs and flower beds. An attractive feature is the large pond on the eastern side of the park.
36 F4

St. Enda's Park

St. Enda's Park
Grange Road, Rathfarnham.
One of Dublin's most attractive suburban public parks. The park occupies the grounds of St. Enda's, the former school where the patriot Padraic Pearse once taught. The well-restored estate house has been opened as a museum to Pearse's memory.
Visiting hours:

Nov. - Jan.:	10 a.m. – 1 p.m. 2 p.m. – 4 p.m.
Feb.- March - April	10 a.m. – 1 p.m. 2 p.m. – 5:00 p.m.
May - Aug.	10 a.m. – 1 p.m. 2 p.m. – 5:30 p.m.
Sept. - Oct.	10 a.m. – 1 p.m. 2 p.m. – 5 p.m.

50 F1

St. Stephen's Green
Covering twenty-two acres at the top of Grafton Street, St. Stephen's Green is right in the heart of the city. The varied landscaping of this delightful park includes trees, flower beds, a waterfall and an artificial lake. Several notable monuments and sculptures may also be seen.
Visiting Times: During daylight hours. Monday to Saturday and from 10 a.m. on Sundays and Bank Holidays.
36 D3

Irish National War Memorial Park.
Islandbridge.
Designed by the English architect Sir Edward Lutyens, these gardens are dedicated to the memory of 49,400 Irish soldiers who died in the First World War. The Gardens are open every day all year round during daylight hours.
35 A2

National War Memorial Gardens.

Phoenix Park

North-western edge of city.

Acknowledged as one of the largest enclosed urban parks in the world, it covers 1,760 acres, with a circumference of seven miles.

Close to the main entrance at Parkgate Street are the People's Gardens and the Zoological Gardens (see separate entry). Within the park are the residence of the President of Ireland (Aras an Uachtarain), the American Ambassador's residence and the Ordnance Survey Office.

In the south-western part of the park is 'The Fifteen Acres', an area of playing fields actually covering two hundred acres. In eighteenth-century Dublin this was used as a duelling ground. During the visit of Pope John Paul II in 1979 it was the site of an outdoor Mass.

Visiting times: Phoenix Park is open to the public at all times but the People's Gardens have their own opening times. These are Monday to Saturday 10:30 a.m.; Sunday 10 a.m. Closing times range between 4 p.m. in December and January and 9:30 p.m. in June and July. Parkgate entrance.

35 B2

Zoological Gardens

Phoenix Park

In these outstanding attractive gardens may be seen a large collection of wild animals and birds from all over the world. Spacious houses and outdoor enclosures add to the total effect. Lion breeding has a long and distinguished history at Dublin Zoo. Two natural lakes house pelicans, flamingoes, ducks and geese.

Visiting hours: Weekdays   9.30 a.m. – 6 p.m.
            Sundays   10.30 a.m. – 6 p.m.
            Gardens close at sunset in winter.

35 A1

Other public parks

Most notable are Corkagh Demesne in Clondalkin, Palmerston Park Dartry, Bushy Park, Terenure, Mountjoy Square Park, Griffeen Valley Park in Lucan and Ward River Valley Park, Swords.

Furry Glen, Phoenix Park

Phoenix Monument, Phoenix Park

DUBLIN AS A SPORTING CENTRE

Dublin has facilities for an amazing variety of sports within a comparatively small area. Outstanding events among the city's sporting events are the Dublin Horse Show, held in August, the national hurling and Gaelic football finals in September in Croke Park and the international rugby games held between January and March in Lansdowne Road, while soccer takes place in Dalymount and Tolka Parks.

The following is a brief guide to the main facilities in city and suburban areas:

For angling enthusiasts: There is fresh water fishing on the River Liffey for salmon, trout, pike and perch. Trout fishing also available on the Rivers Tolka and Dodder.
Sea fishing is available at Dun Laoghaire to the south and at Howth to the north of the city. Fishing permits and bait for sea fishing are obtainable from Dublin fishing tackle shops.

For bowling enthusiasts: There are bowling greens at Herbert Park, Ballsbridge and Willie Pearse Memorial Park, Crumlin. Open 10 a.m. to dusk Monday to Sunday. Nominal fee. Bowling shoes essential. Facilities also at Clontarf Golf Club and Moran Park, Dun Laoghaire.

For golfers: Golfers are well catered for with over 25 G.U.I. affiliated courses (including the internationally renowned Portmarnock links) within a short distance of the city centre. A number of both private and municipal courses also exist. It is advisable to check in advance with the course as green fees and availability of tee time can vary. Generally mid-week is best for visitors. Some clubs have golf clubs and equipment for hire. There are also a number of both par 3 golf and pitch and putt courses throughout Dublin City and district.

For greyhound racing enthusiasts: Racing is held at Shelbourne Greyhound Stadium, Ringsend, on Wednesday, Thursday and Saturday at 8p.m.. Also at Harold's Cross Stadium on Monday, Tuesday and Friday at 8 p.m.

For rowing enthusiasts: The headquarters of most Dublin rowing clubs is at Islandbridge on the River Liffey. This is north of Kilmainham.

For swimmers: Just outside the city area there are beaches at Dollymount to the north and at Sandymount and Merrion to the south. There are numerous bathing places and public baths along the coast.
A number of indoor swimming pools and sauna baths are open to the public in the Dublin area. Full details can be obtained from the Dublin tourist information offices.

For tennis players: In return for a nominal fee there are ample facilities on offer at tennis clubs and public courts around Dublin.
Public courts are open at Herbert Park, Ballsbridge; Bushy Park, Terenure; Ellenfield Park, Whitehall; St. Anne's Estate, Dollymount and Johnstown Park, Finglas. Racket hire is not available at these centres.

DUBLIN *ALIVE ALIVE OH!*

Cabaret fans: A varied programme of cabaret entertainment is available at several Dublin locations. Details from Dublin tourist information offices.

Cinema-goers: Dubliners are well-known as regular cinema-goers, so the city is well-provided with cinemas. O'Connell Street has the Savoy Cinemas 1 to 6. The Lighthouse Cinema is in Middle Abbey Street, the Screen Cinema in Townsend Street and a Multiscreen cinema in Parnell Street. More cinemas are located in the suburbs. Full details are published in the evening newspapers.

Night-time revellers: Ballad singing, jazz, dancing and a host of other musical entertainment is available in pubs, restaurants, hotels and night clubs. Details are published in the evening newspapers.

Outdoor types: During July and August there are special concerts with an Irish flavour in St. Stephen's Green, as well as regular band recitals in other city parks. Detailed guides to what's on in Dublin are obtainable from Dublin tourist information office in O'Connell Street.

Theatre-goers: There's a wide choice of theatrical entertainment. The Abbey and the Peacock Theatres are in Lower Abbey Street, the Gaiety Theatre is in South King Street, the Eblana Theatre is located under the Central Bus Station at Store Street, the Gate Theatre is in Parnell Square, the Olympia Theatre is in Dame Street and the Project Arts Centre is located in East Essex Street. Andrews Lane Theatre, Andrews Lane, Tivoli Theatre, Francis St. Also National Concert Hall, Earlsfort Terrace.

Banking Hours: Monday to Friday 10a.m. - 4p.m.
Most Dublin branches are open until 5p.m. on Thursday. Closed Saturdays,Sundays and Public Holidays.
Dublin Airport Bank open every day for foreign exchange.
Departures: April to October 6a.m. - 8p.m.
             April to October 6a.m. - 11p.m. Friday and Saturday
Arrivals: April to October 6.15a.m. - 8p.m.
Departures: November to March 6a.m. - 8p.m.
Arrivals: November to March 6.15a.m. - 10p.m.

Shopping Hours: Generally speaking shops are open Monday to Saturday from 9a.m. - 5.30 or 6p.m. Closed all day Sundays and Bank holidays. Suburban shopping centres remain open until 9p.m. on Thursday and Friday with some opening for a limited periods on Sunday.

83 EMBASSIES

Apostolic Nunciature
183 Navan Road
Dublin
Tel: 838 0577

20 D4

Argentine Embassy
15 Ailesbury Drive
Dublin 4
Tel: 269 1546 / 269 4603

44 D1

Australian Embassy
2nd Floor,
Fitzwilton House
Wilton Terrace, Dublin 2
Tel: 676 1517

36 E4

Austrian Embassy
15 Ailesbury Court Apts.
93 Ailesbury Road
Dublin 4
Tel: 269 4577 / 269 1451

44 D1

Belgian Embassy
2 Shrewsbury Road
Dublin 4
Tel: 269 2082 / 269 1588

44 D1

Embassy of the Federative Republic of Brazil
Europa House
Harcourt Court
Harcourt Street, Dublin 2.
Tel: 475 6000

36 D4

British Embassy
31/33 Merrion Road
Dublin 4
Tel: 205 3700

44 D1

Bulgarian Embassy
22 Burlington Road
Dublin 4
Tel: 660 3293

36 E4

Canadian Embassy
4th Floor
65/68 St. Stephen's
Green South
Dublin 2
Tel: 478 1988

36 E3

Embassy of the People's Republic of China
40 Ailesbury Road
Dublin 4
Tel: 269 1707 / 269 6756

44 D1

Czech Embassy
57
Northumberland Road
Dublin 4
Tel: 688 1135 / 668 1343

36 F3

Royal Danish Embassy
121/122
St. Stephen's
Green West,
Dublin 2
Tel: 475 6404 / 475 6405

36 D3

Embassy of the Arab Republic of Egypt
12 Clyde Road
Ballsbridge, Dublin 4
Tel: 660 6566 / 660 6718

36 F4

Finnish Embassy
Russell House
Stokes Place
St. Stephen's Green South
Dublin 2
Tel: 478 1344

36 D3

French Embassy
36 Ailesbury Road
Dublin 4
Tel: 260 1666

44 D1

Embassy of the Federal Republic of Germany
31 Trimleston Avenue
Booterstown, Co. Dublin
Tel: 269 3011 / 269 3123

44 E2

Greek Embassy
1 Upper
Pembroke Street
Dublin 2
Tel: 676 7254 / 676 7255

36 E3

Embassy of the Republic of Hungary
2 Fitzwilliam Place
Dublin 2
Tel: 661 2902 / 661 2905

36 E3

Indian Embassy
6 Leeson Park
Dublin 6
Tel: 497 0843 / 496 6792

36 E4

Embassy of the Islamic Republic of Iran
72 Mount Merrion Avenue
Blackrock, Co. Dublin
Tel: 288 0252 / 288 2967

44 F3

Israel Embassy
122 Pembroke Road
Dublin 8
Tel: 668 0303

36 F4

Italian Embassy
63/65
Northumberland Road
Ballsbridge, Dublin 4
Tel: 660 1744

36 F4

Japanese Embassy
Nutley Building
Merrion Centre
Nutley Lane, Dublin 4
Tel: 269 4244 / 269 4033

44 E1

Embassy of the Republic of Korea
20 Clyde Road
Ballsbridge, Dublin 4
Tel: 660 8800

36 F4

Mexican Embassy
43 Ailesbury Road
Dublin 4
Tel: 260 0699

44 D1

Embassy of the Kingdom of Morocco
53 Raglan Road
Dublin 4
Tel: 660 9449

36 F4

Netherlands Embassy
160 Merrion Road
Dublin 4
Tel: 269 3444

44 D1

Embassy of the Federal Republic of Nigeria
56 Leeson Park
Dublin 6
Tel: 660 4366 / 660 4051

36 E4

Royal Norwegian Embassy
Hainault House
34 Molesworth Street,
Dublin 2
Tel: 662 1800

36 E3

Embassy of the Republic of Poland
5 Ailesbury Road
Dublin 4
Tel: 283 0855

44 D1

Portuguese Embassy
Knocksinna House
Knocksinna Road
Foxrock, Dublin 18
Tel: 289 4416

53 A

Embassy of the Russian Federation
184/186 Orwell Road
Rathgar, Dublin 14
Tel: 492 3525(Embassy)
Tel: 492 2048
492 3492 (Consular Section)

43 B

Embassy of South Africa
Alexandra House,
Earlsfort Centre,
Earlsfort Terrace, Dublin 2
Tel: 661 5553

36 E

Spanish Embassy
17A Merlyn Park
Dublin 4
Tel: 269 1640 / 269 2597

44 E

Swedish Embassy
Sun Alliance House
13-17 Dawson Street
Dublin 2
Tel: 671 5822

36 E

Swiss Embassy
6 Ailesbury Road
Ballsbridge
Dublin 4
Tel: 269 2515

44 D

Embassy of the Republic of Turkey
11 Clyde Road
Ballsbridge, Dublin 4
Tel: 668 5240

36 F

Embassy of the United States of America
42 Elgin Road
Ballsbridge, Dublin 4
Tel: 668 8777

36 F

This list contains only those Embassies in the Republic of Ireland A full list of Diplomatic and Consular Missions are contained in all Irish Telephone Directories.

DUBLIN BUS
CHANGING WITH THE CITY
GENERAL INFORMATION

Route Network

Dublin Bus operates the bus network in the greater Dublin area. This network extends from Balbriggan in North County Dublin to Kilcoole in County Wicklow and westwards as far as Kilcock, County Kildare.

Other Services:

In addition to the network described above, Dublin Bus operates other services including:

Nitelink – a network of 14 routes radiating from the City Centre which operate every Thursday, Friday and Saturday at 12 midnight, 1, 2 and 3 a.m.. An additional service to Maynooth and Celbridge operates at 2 a.m. and 3a.m. only.

Airlink – a special coach service between Heuston Rail Station and Dublin Airport serving Bus Áras on route.

Special services to the Ferryports.

Private Hire – Double Deckers, Single Deckers or Minibuses can be hired for group Outings, Parties, Weddings etc.

Sightseeing Tours – Dublin Bus operate a range of tours including open top tours of the City – see Tours Information section for more details.

Hours of operation

Scheduled services operate from 6a.m. throughout the day with last buses leaving the city centre at 11.30p.m. In addition to these services a special Nitelink network operates every Thursday, Friday and Saturday night with departures from the City Centre at 12 midnight, 1, 2 and 3 a.m.

Dublin Bus offices are located at 59 Upper O'Connell Street and are open from 9a.m. until 5.30p.m. Monday to Friday and up to 1p.m. on Saturdays. A telephone information service is available on 01-8734222 between 9a.m. and 7p.m. Monday to Saturday.

Timetables are provided on most of the important bus stops in the City. In addition, guides and timetables for local areas are available from Dublin Bus offices in O'Connell Street.

Fares

Fares are charged on the basis of distance travelled and range from 55p to £1.25 for Single journeys. On some longer distance routes, fares of up to £3.50 are applicable.

Prepaid Tickets:

Dublin Bus have a range of Weekly, Monthly and Annual tickets which offer significant discounts on cash fares. These are available for both adults and students. Day tickets are also available for adults and children as well as for families.

Travel Ten tickets are also available for adult second level students and students aged 16, 17 or 18 and Schoolchildren under 16. These allow the user to make ten bus journeys at a significant discount on the cash fare. Other tickets available from Dublin Bus include a Four Day Explorer ticket allowing the user to travel on all Dublin Bus, Suburban Rail and DART services on four consecutive days after 9.45a.m. on weekdays and all day Saturday and Sunday.

The Transfer Ninety is valid for travel on two bus journeys within ninety minutes of each other inside the Citizone area.

Nitelink tickets are available for Single journeys on Dublin Bus Nitelink services.

Dublin Bus tickets are available from the offices in O'Connell Street as well as from a network of over 200 Ticket Agents throughout the greater Dublin area.

Tours

Dublin City Tour – Open Deck

The Dublin City Tour is the most popular way for visitors to experience the true delights of Dublin City. The open top bus makes it a dream for the camera enthusiast.

Heritage Tour

The one hour tour which lasts all day. This continuous tour allows you the freedom of the city, with hourly departures and 10 specially located bus stops along the route. Hop on and off the bus as often as you wish during the day.

North – South Coastal Tours

North Coast: - View the fishing villages, quaint farms, and sweeping views of Dublin Bay. The North Dublin coastline is a wonder of magical sights for you to enjoy.

South Coast: - Enjoy the elegance of Dun Laoghaire, the charm of Dalkey, panoramic views of Killiney Bay and even more! Return through scenic mountains and villages – breathtakingly beautiful.

All tours depart from Dublin Bus 59 O'Connell St. Prices range from £5 to £10 for adults. Special family rates are available ranging from £12.00 to £25.00.

PLACE NAME	SERVED BY BUS NO.
Abbey Pk. (Baldoyle)	32B
Abbey Pk. (Blackrock)	114
Abbotstown Ave.	40, 40A, 220
Adelaide Rd.	14, 15A, 15B, 44, 47, 48A, 62
Ailesbury Rd.	3, 5, 7, 7A, 8, 52
Albert Rd.	8, 59
Alexandra Rd.	53A
All Saints' Rd.	29A
Allenton Estate	203
Amiens St.	20A, 30, 90
Angelsea Rd.	46, 63, 84
Annamoe Rd.	10
Anne Devlin Pk.	15B
Appian Way	11, 11A, 11B, 13, 18
Ardee St.	50, 56A, 150
Ardlea Rd.	20B, 27B
Artane S.Centre	20B, 103
Artane	27, 42, 42B
Arthur Griffith Pk.(Lucan)	25A
Ashtown	37, 38, 39, 70, 22B
Aughrim St.	10, 37, 38, 39
Baggot St.	10, 18
Balbriggan	33
Balbutcher	13, 220
Baldonnel	68
Baldoyle	32, 32A, 32B, 102
Balgaddy	78A
Balgriffin	42
Ballinclea Rd.	7, 86, 45A
Ballinteer	48A, 75
Ballsbridge	5, 7, 7A, 8, 18, 45
Ballybrack	7, 45A, 46, 111
Ballyboden	47, 47A, 47B
Ballybough	51A, 123
Ballydowd	25, 66, 66A, 67, 67A
Ballyfermot	18, 76, 76A, 76B, 78A, 79
Ballygall Rd. East	19, 134
Ballygall Rd. West	17A, 19A, 134, 103
Ballyknockan	65
Ballymore Eustace	65
Ballymount Rd.	56A
Ballymun	13, 17A, 36, 36A, 103, 220
Ballymun Rd.	11, 11A, 11B, 13, 19A
Ballyroan	15B
Ballyshannon	27B
Ballywaltrim	45
Balrothery (Tallaght)	65
Baltiboys (Ballyknockan)	65
Bangor Rd.	17, 18, 22A, 83
Barnaculla	44B
Barry's Bridge	84, 184
Bawnogue	51B, 210
Bawnville Rd.	76B, 77A
Beaumont Ave.(Churchtown)	14, 14A, 16A
Beaumont Rd.(Whitehall)	16, 16A, 20B, 51A, 103
Beaumont Hospital	27B, 51A, 101, 103
Beechwood Ave.	11, 11A, 11B, 13, 48A
Belcamp Rd.	42
Belfield (U.C.D.)	3, 10, 11, 11B, 17, 46, 46A, 46B, 52
Belgard Rd.	50, 76, 76A, 76B
Belgrave Square	13, 18
Berkeley Rd.	10, 22B, 38, 120
Binn's Bridge	11, 11A, 13, 16,16A, 16B, 40, 40A, 40B
Bird Ave.	11, 11A, 48A, 62
Biscayne(Malahide)	32A, 42, 102, 230
Blackhall Place	37, 39, 70
Blackhorse Ave.	10, 37
Blackrock	7, 7A, 8, 17, 45, 114
Blakestown	39, 76A, 220, 250
Blanchardstown	22B, 38, 39, 70, 76A, 250
Blessington	65
Blessington St.	10, 22B, 38, 120
Bluebell	51, 51B, 68, 69
Blunden Drive	42A, 42B, 101
Bohernabreena	203
Bolbrook	76B, 77A
Booterstown	5, 7, 7A, 8, 45
Botanic Gardens	13, 19, 134
Botanic Rd.	13, 19, 19A, 134
Braemor Rd.	14
Brandon Rd.	22, 22A, 123
Bray	45, 45A, 84, 145, 184, 185
Brewery Rd.	46A, 86
Brittas	65
Broadford	48A, 75
Broadstone	19, 19A, 134
Brookfield	56A, 77, 202
Brookwood Ave.	28, 42B, 101
Broombridge Rd.	120
Bulfin Rd.	19,
Bull Wall	30

PLACE NAME	SERVED BY BUS NO.
Burgage	65
Bushy Park	15B
Bushy Pk. Rd.	16, 16A, 47
Butterfield Ave.	15B, 16, 16A, 17, 75
Cabinteely	45, 46, 84, 86
Cabra	22, 22A, 22B, 120
Camden St.	16, 16A, 19, 19A, 22, 22A, 155, 83
Cappagh Hospital	40A, 220
Cappagh Rd.	40, 40A, 220
Cappaghmore	51
Captain's Rd.	54A, 83, 155
Cardiff Bridge Rd.	40A, 220
Carnlough Rd.	22, 22A, 120
Carpenterstown	37
Carrickmines	63, 86
Carysfort Ave.	7A, 8, 17, 114
Casement Park	40
Cashel Rd.	17, 18, 83, 155,
Castle Ave.	29A, 31, 103, 130
Castleknock	37, 250
Castle Lawns	65, 65B, 77A
Castletimon Rd.	27B
Cedarwood Rd.	19, 19A
Celbridge	67, 67A, 67X
Chapelizod	25, 26, 66, 66A, 66B, 67, 67A
Charlemont St.	44, 48A, 62
Chelmsford Rd.	11, 11A, 13, 18, 48A, 62
Cherry Orchard	18, 76, 76A, 76B, 78A
Christchurch Place	50, 51B, 54A, 56A, 68A, 78A, 123
Churchtown	14, 14A
Church St.	134
Clanbrassil St.	49, 54A
Clogher Rd.	22A
Cloghran	33, 41, 41B, 41C, 230
Clondalkin	51, 51B, 68, 69, 76, 76A, 76B, 210
Clonburris	51, 76, 76A, 76B
Clonee	70
Clonkeen Rd.	45
Clonsilla	39, 39X, 220, 250
Clonskea	11, 11A, 17, 62
Clontarf Castle	130, 103
Clontarf Rd.	130
Cloverhill Rd.	79
Colberts Rd.	50
Coldcut	18, 76, 76A, 76B, 78A
Collinstown	33, 41, 41A, 41B, 41C
Collins Ave.	3, 16, 20A, 20B, 103
Connolly Station	20A, 20B, 30, 44A, 90
Conyngham Rd.	25, 26, 51, 66, 67
Cooldrinagh Rd.	66, 67
Cooley Rd.	18, 22, 50, 56A, 123, 150
Coombe, The	50, 56A, 77, 77A, 150, 210
Coolmine Cross Rd.	39, 76A, 220
Coolock	17A, 27
Coolock Lane	17A, 41, 41A
Corduff	38, 220, 238
Cornelscourt Centre	46, 84, 86, 45
Cowper Rd.	13
Croke Park	3, 11, 11A, 16, 16A, 51A
Cromcastle Drive	27A
Cromwellsfort Rd.	155
Crooksling	65
Cross Chapel	65
Crumlin Village	17, 18, 150
Crumlin Rd.(Shopping Centre)	50, 56A, 77, 77A, 150, 210
Cushlawn	65B, 201
Dalkey	8
Dalymount Park	10, 19, 19A, 22, 38,120, 134
Danieli Rd.	27, 42, 42B
Darndale	27, 42,, 101
Dartry Rd.	14A
Deansgrange	45, 46A, 75
Deanstown Ave.	40A, 220
Delgany	184
Distillery Rd.	51A
Dodsboro'	25, 66, 67
Dollymount	130
Dolphin's Barn	17, 19, 22, 50, 56A, 150, 210
Donabate	33B
Donaghies	29A
Donaghmede S.C	29A
Donomore	65
Donnybrook	10, 46, 46A, 46B
Donnycarney	20A, 20B, 27, 42, 42B, 103
Donore Ave.	19, 22, 22A
Dorset St.	3, 11, 11A, 13, 16, 22, 36, 36A
Drimnagh	22, 123
Drimnagh Rd.	18, 50, 56A, 77, 150
Drumcondra	3, 11, 11A, 16, 36, 36A
Drumfin Rd.	18, 76, 76A, 76B, 78A

PLACE NAME	SERVED BY BUS NO.
Dubber Cross	40B
Dublin Airport	41, 41A, 41B, 41C, 230
Dunboyne	70
Dundrum	17, 44, 48A, 75
Dungriffin Rd.	31B
Dun Laoghaire(S.C.)	7, 7A, 8, 45A, 75, 111, 46A, 59
Dunsink Drive	40A
Earlsfort Terrace	14, 14A, 15A, 15B, 44, 48A
East Wall Rd.	53
Edenmore	28, 101
Edmonstown	47A
Embankment(Tallaght)	65
Enniskerry	44, 185
Errigal Rd.	50, 56A, 123
Exchequer St.	16, 19, 22, 83, 155
Fairview	20A, 130
Faussagh Ave.	22, 22A, 120
Feltrim Lane	43
Fettercairn	56A, 65, 65B, 76, 77, 202
Finglas	17A, 40, 40A, 40B, 103, 134 220
Finglas South	40, 40A, 40B, 220
Firhouse	49, 75
Fitzwilliam Sq.	11, 11A, 13, 46A
Fortfield Rd.	54A
Foster Ave.	11A, 17, 46B, 52
Four Courts	25, 26
Fox & Geese	51, 51B, 68, 69, 210
Foxrock	63, 86
Galtymore Rd.	123
George's St. Sth.	16, 19, 22, 83, 155
Gilford Rd.	3
Glasanaon Rd.	19, 134
Glassmore	41, 41X
Glasnevin	13, 19, 134
Glasnevin Ave.	13, 17A, 19, 19A, 103
Glasnevin Cemetery	40, 40A, 40B
Glasthule	8, 59
Glenageary Rd. Lr.	7, 7A, 45A, 111
Glenamuck	63
Glencullen	44B
Glen O'The Downs(Willow Gr.)	184
Glenview	54A, 65, 65B, 76B
Goatstown	62
Gracefield Rd.	42B
Gracepark Rd.	51A
Grand Canal St.	7, 7A, 8, 45
Grange Rd.(Rathfarnham)	16, 75
Grange X Rd.(Raheny)	29A
Granville Park	46A, 114
Greencastle Rd.	27
Greenhills Rd.	50, 77
Greenpark(Walkinstown)	15A, 77, 77A
Greystones	84, 184
Griffith Ave.	11, 11A, 19A, 36, 36A
Griffith Ave.(Extension)	40A, 40B, 220
Griffith Ave.(Whitehall)	3, 16, 36, 41, 41A
Griffith Ave.(Marino)	20A, 123
Grove Rd.(Finglas)	17A, 19, 19A, 103
Guild St.	53A
Haddington Rd.	7, 7A, 8, 45
Haddon Rd.	30, 44A
Halfway House(Walkinstown)	18, 50, 77, 77A, 210
Hanlon's Corner	10, 39, 70
Harcourt St.	14, 14A, 15A, 15B, 48A
Harrington St.	16, 16A, 19, 19A, 22, 22A,155
Hatch St.	14, 14A, 15A, 15B, 48A
Harmonstown Rd.	28, 42B, 101
Harold's Cross	16, 16A, 49, 65, 65B
Hartstown	39, 220
Hollybank Rd.	3, 11, 11A, 16, 41, 41C
Homefarm Rd.	3, 11, 11A, 16, 41, 41C
Howth	31, 31B
Howth Rd.	29A, 31, 31A, 42A
Howth Summit	31B
Hume St.(off St. Stephen's Gr.)	14, 14A, 15A, 15B, 44, 48A
Huntstown	39, 76A, 220, 250
Iona Rd.	13, 19, 19A, 36, 36A
Inchicore	51, 51B, 68, 68A, 69
Irishtown	1, 3
Islandbridge	25, 26, 51
James' St.	51B, 78A, 123
Jamestown Rd.(Finglas)	40, 40B, 220,134
Jamestown Rd.(Inchicore)	51, 51B, 68, 69
Jobstown	50, 65, 65B, 77, 201
Jones Rd.	51A

COLOUR CODES : ■ = Peripheral Service - does not operate via City Centre

PLACE NAME	SERVED BY BUS NO.
...enilworth Park	16, 16A, 18, 49, 83
...ennelsfort Rd.	26
...barrack	17A, 29A, 31, 31A, 32
...barron	27B
...cock	66
...coole	84, 84X
...cross	44, 114
...croney	44, 185
...dare Rd.	22A
...donan Rd.	17A, 40
...ll Avenue	46A
...llester	29A, 31, 42A
...llester Ave.	20A, 20B
...llinarden	50, 65, 65B, 77, 201
...llincarrick	84, 184
...lliney	59
...lliney Camp Site	45A
...lliney S.C.	7, 45A, 86
...ll O'The Grange	46A
...lmacud	5, 62, 75, 86
...lmainham	51B, 78A,
...lmainham Jail	68, 69, 79
...lmore	27B
...lnamanagh	50
...lternan	44, 63
...immage Rd. Lr.	54A, 155
...immage Rd. West	15A, 17, 155
...ingswood Heights	56A, 76, 76A, 76B
...insealy	42, 43
...invara Park	22, 22A, 22B, 37, 38, 39, 70
...nockmore	65, 77, 201
...ylemore Rd.	18, 51, 51B, 68, 69, 79
...ady's Well	38, 220
...akelands Park	15, 15B, 49, 65, 65B
...amb, The	65
...ambert Estate	14A
...amb's Cross	44, 44B, 44C
...andscape Rd.	14
...ansdowne Rd.	5, 7, 7A, 8
...archill	47
...arkhill	3, 16, 41, 41A, 41B, 103
...arkfield Gardens	18, 54A, 83, 155
...aurel Lodge	37
...eas Cross	60
...eeson St.	11, 11A, 13, 46A, 46B
...einster Rd.	47, 47A, 47B
...eixlip	66, 66A, 66B, 66X
...eonard's Corner	16, 16A, 19, 22, 22A, 155
...eopardstown Rd	46, 46A, 63, 86
...iam Mollowoe Rd.	17A, 40, 40A
...imekiln Rd.	15A, 54A, 150
...issenhall Bridge	33, 33B
...ondonbridge Rd	3
...ong Mile Rd.	18, 56A, 210
...ord Edward St.	50, 54A, 56A, 150
...oughlinstown	45, 84
...oughshinney	33
...ucan	25, 66, 66A, 66B, 67, 67A
...usk	33
...uttrellstown	250
...lacken St.	1, 3
...lacroom Rd.	27
...lalahide	32A, 42, 102, 230
...lalahide Rd.	20A, 27, 27B, 42, 42B
...lanor St.	37, 39, 70
...larian Park(Baldoyle)	32B
...larian Park(Templeogue)	15B
...larino	123
...larley Grange	47B
...lather Rd. Nth.	11A
...laynooth	66, 67A
...leadow Grove(Churchtown)	14, 14A
...lellowes Rd.	17A, 40
...lerchant's Quay	25, 26, 51, 79, 90
...lerrion Rd.	5, 7, 7A, 8, 45
...lerrion Row	10, 11, 13
...lerrion Sq.	5, 7, 7A, 8, 45
...lilltown	44, 44B, 48A, 86
...lilltown Cross	68
...lobhi Rd.	11, 11A, 19A
...lonkstown	7A, 8
...lorehampton Rd.	10, 46A, 46B
...lt. Jerome Cemetery	16, 16A, 54A, 155
...lount Merrion	5, 46, 46A, 46B, 63
...lount Merrion Ave.	5, 17
...lt Prospect Ave.	130, 103
...lountown	46A
...lount St.	5, 7, 7A, 8, 45
...lount Anville	62
...lourne Rd.	22

PLACE NAME	SERVED BY BUS NO.
Mulhuddart	38, 70, 220
Murphystown	44
McKee Ave.	134
McKee Rd.	19A
McKelvey Ave.	134
Naas Rd.	18, 51, 51B, 68, 69, 210
National Stadium	19, 22, 22A
Navan Rd.	22, 22A, 22B, 37, 38, 39, 70
Neilstown	51, 76, 76A, 76B, 210
Newcastle(Co. Dublin)	68
Newcastle(Co. Wicklow)	84
Newgrove Cross	29A
Newlands Cross	51, 76, 76A, 76B
Newtown Park Ave	45, 114
Nth. Circular Rd.	10, 22, 22A, 22B, 38, 120
North Rd. (Finglas)	40, 134
Northside S.C.	17A, 27, 27A, 27B
North Strand Rd.	20A, 20B, 30, 44A
North Wall	53A
Nutgrove S.C.	16A, 17, 75
Nutley Lane	3, 5, 7, 7A, 8, 46, 46A, 46B, 52, 63
Old Bawn Rd.	49, 75
Old Cabra Rd.	39, 70
Oldcourt (Bray)	45, 145
Omni Park S.C.	16A
Orwell Park Estate	54A, 150
Orwell Rd.	14, 14A, 47
Oscar Traynor Rd.	17A, 27A, 27B
Oxmanstown Rd.	10
Palmerston Park	13, 14, 14A
Palmerston Rd.	13
Palmerston	18, 25, 26, 66, 67, 76A
Parkgate St.	25, 26, 51
Patrick St.	50, 54A, 56A, 150
Peamount	68
Pearse St.	1, 3
Peck's Lane	37, 250
Pelican House(Mespil Rd.)	10, 11
Pembroke Park	10, 46A
Pembroke Rd.	5, 7, 7A, 8, 10, 18
Pembroke St.	10, 11, 11A, 13, 46A, 46B
Phibsboro	10, 19, 19A, 22, 22A, 22B, 134, 38, 120
Philipsburgh Ave.	123
Phoenix Park(N.C.R. Gate)	10
Phoenix Park(Parkgate St.)	25, 26, 51, 66, 67
Plunkett Rd.	40
Poppintree(Ballymun)	13, 220
Porterstown	250
Portmarnock	32, 32A, 32X, 102, 230
Portrane	33B, 33C
Powerscourt(Enniskerry)	44, 185
Priorswood	42C
Quarry Rd.	22, 22A, 120
Raheen(Tallaght)	56A, 65, 76, 77
Raheny	29A, 31, 31A, 32
Ranelagh	11, 11A, 13, 18, 48A, 62, 86
Rathbeale	41B
Rathcoole	69
Rathfarnham	16, 16A, 17, 47
Rathfarnham S.C.	15B, 16, 75
Rathgar	15A, 15B, 47
Rathmines	14, 14A, 15A, 15B, 18, 83
Ratoath Rd.	22, 40A, 120
R.D.S. (Ballsbridge)	7, 7A, 8, 18, 45
Rialto	17, 19
Richmond Rd.	3, 11, 11A, 16
Ringsend	1, 3
Riverside (Coolock)	27
Rivervalley (Swords)	41C, 230
Robinhood	51, 68, 69, 210
Rochestown Ave.	7, 45A, 86, 111
Rockbrook	47A
Roebuck Rd.	11A, 17, 62
Rolestown	41B
Rowlagh	76, 76A, 76B, 78A
Rush	33
St. Anne's Estate	29A
St. Assam's Ave.	31, 31A, 32
St. Brendan's Cres.	155
St. Maelruan's Park	49, 75, 203
St. Margaret's Rd.	134, 40B
St. Pappin's Rd.	11
St. Patrick's Coll(Drumcondra)	3, 11, 11A, 16, 41
St. Peter's Rd.(Walkinstown)	155
St. Stephen's Green	10, 11, 13, 15A, 15B
Saggart	69

PLACE NAME	SERVED BY BUS NO.
Sallynoggin	7, 7A, 45A, 111
Sandford Rd.	11, 11A, 48A, 62
Sandycove	8
Sandyford	44
Sandyford Ind. Est.	5, 62, 75, 114
Sandymount Ave.	5, 7, 7A, 8, 18
Sandymount Green	3, 18
Sandymount Tower	3, 18 (Sun)
Santry	16, 33, 41, 41A, 41B
Santry Ave.	17A, 41, 41A
Sarsfield Rd.	78A, 79
Scalp, The	44
Scholarstown	15
Seamount	42
Seskin View Rd.	76B, 77A
Shankill	45, 45A, 46, 84
Shanard Rd.	16
Shanboley Rd.	16
Shangan	36A
Shanganagh Cliffs Estate	45A
Shanowen Rd.	16
Sheepmoor	39, 76A, 220, 250
Shop River(Enniskerry)	185
Sillogue	36
Skerries	33
Spiddal Park	79
Springfield Estate(Tallaght)	50, 65, 76, 77, 201
Stannaway Rd.	18, 83
Stepaside	44
Stillorgan S.C.	46, 46A, 62, 63, 75, 84, 86
Stradbrook	45
Strand Rd. (Sutton)	31A, 31B
Strand Rd.(Sandymount)	3
Sth. Circular Rd.	16, 16A, 19, 22, 22A
Sth. Richmond St.	14, 14A, 15A, 15B, 83
Suir Rd.	123
Sundrive Rd.	17, 18, 50, 54A, 56A, 83, 150
Sutton Cross	31, 31A, 31B
Swords	33, 41, 41B, 230
Sycamore Rd.	19A
Sylvan Drive	56A
Tallaght	49, 50, 65, 76, 77, 77A
Templeogue	15B, 49, 65
Templeville Rd.	54A
Terenure	15A, 15B, 16, 16A, 17, 49
The Rise(Mt. Merrion)	46A, 46B
Thomas St.	51B, 78A, 123
Tibradden	47
Tinode	65
Toberburr	40B
Tolka Estate	19
Tonlegee Rd.	17A, 29A, 101
Tritonville Rd.	3
Tymon North	77A
Valleymount(Ballyknockan)	65
Vernon Ave.	30, 44A, 103
Villa Park	22, 22A, 22B, 37, 38, 39, 70
Wadelai Estate	11
Walkinstown Ave.	18, 56A
Walkinstown Cross	50, 56A, 77, 77A, 155
Waterloo Rd.	10, 18
Willington	54A, 150
Werburg St.	50, 56A, 150
Westland Row Stn.(Pearse Stn)	1, 3, 47, 48A
Wellmount Rd.	40
Weston Ave.	14A
West Rd.	53
Wexford St.	16, 16A, 19, 19A, 22, 22A, 155, 83
Whitechurch	47, 47B
Whitehall(Drumcondra)	3, 16, 33, 41, 41A, 41B, 41C
Whitehall Rd.(Terenure)	15A
Whitestown	39, 250
Whitworth Rd.	13, 40, 40A, 40B,
Willbrook	47, 47A, 47B
Willow Grove	184
Windgates	104
Woodford	51B, 210
Woodlawn(Firhouse)	49, 75
Wyattville Rd.	7, 111
Yellow Walls Rd.	42, 102, 230
Zion Rd.	47

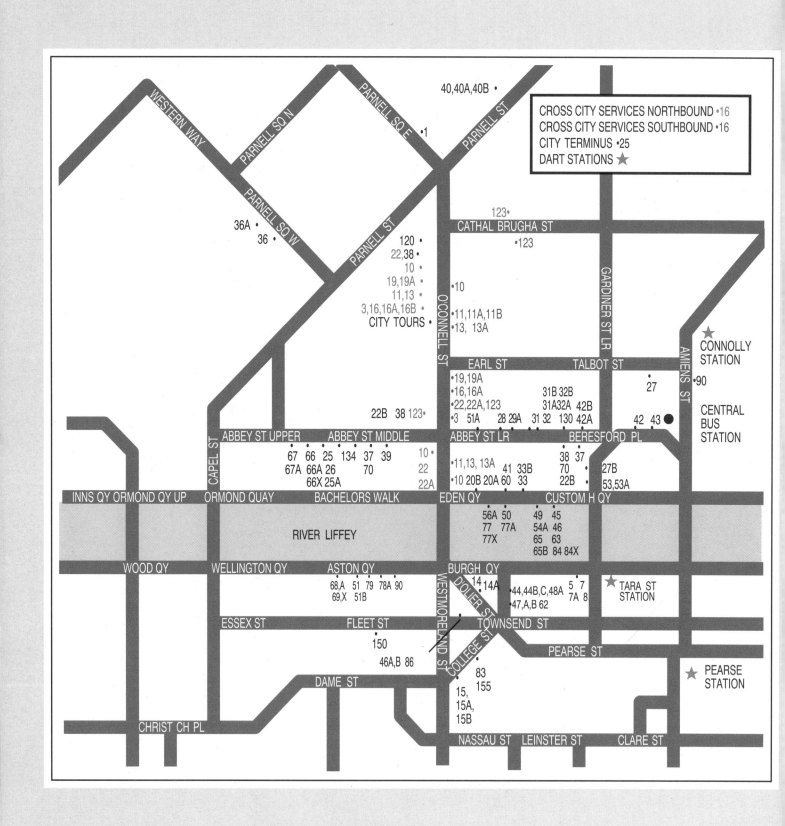

WESTERN WAY

PARNELL SQ N

PARNELL SQ E

PARNELL ST

40,40A,40B •

•1

PARNELL SQ W

36A •

36 •

PARNELL ST

PARNELL ST

120 •
22,38 •
10 •
19,19A •
11,13 •
3,16,16A,16B •
CITY TOURS

O'CONNELL ST

123•

CATHAL BRUGHA ST

•123

•10

•11,11A,11B
•13, 13A

GARDINER ST LR

AMIENS ST

★ CONNOLLY STATION

CROSS CITY SERVICES NORTHBOUND •16
CROSS CITY SERVICES SOUTHBOUND •16
CITY TERMINUS •25
DART STATIONS ★

EARL ST

TALBOT ST

•19,19A
•16,16A
•22,22A,123
•3 51A

31B 32B
31A 32A 42B
28 29A   31 32 130 42A

27 •

•90

42 43 ●

CENTRAL BUS STATION

22B 38 123•

ABBEY ST UPPER   ABBEY ST MIDDLE

CAPEL ST

67 66 25 134 37 39
67A 66A 26   70
66X 25A

10 •
22
22A

ABBEY ST LR

•11,13, 13A

•10 20B 20A 60

41 33B
33

BERESFORD PL

38 37

70

22B

27B •

53,53A •

INNS QY ORMOND QY UP   ORMOND QUAY   BACHELORS WALK   EDEN QY   CUSTOM H QY

RIVER LIFFEY

56A 50
77 77A
77X

49 45
54A 46
65 63
65B 84 84X

WOOD QY   WELLINGTON QY   ASTON QY   BURGH QY

68,A 51 79 78A 90
69,X 51B

WESTMORELAND ST

D'OLIER ST

14 •
14A

44,44B,C,48A •
47,A,B 62 •

COLLEGE ST

TARA ST STATION ★

5 7
7A 8

ESSEX ST   FLEET ST

150 •

46A,B 86 •

TOWNSEND ST

PEARSE ST

83 •
155 •

15,
15A,
15B

DAME ST

CHRIST CH PL

NASSAU ST LEINSTER ST   CLARE ST

PEARSE STATION ★

Name	Page	Grid Ref
Airport Industrial Estate	10	E4/F4
Airton Close	41	A4
Airton Road	41	A4
Airton Terrace	41	A4
Airways Industrial Estate	10	F4
Allied Industrial Estate	34	E4
Ardee Court	57	B2
Ashgrove Industrial Estate	53	C1
Avonbeg Industrial Estate	41	B1
Baldoyle Industrial Estate	23	C1
Balheary Industrial Park	2	D1
Ballyboggan Industrial Estate	20	D3
Ballycoolin Business Park	8	D4
Ballymount Business Park	41	B2
Ballymount Cross Ind Estate	41	A2
Ballymount Industrial Estate	41	B2
Ballymount Industrial Park	41	B2
Ballymount Trading Centre	41	B2
Ballymun Industrial Estate	9	C4
	10	D4
Beechlawn Industrial Complex	41	B2
Beechwood Close Industrial Estate	57	C4
Belgard Industrial Estate	40	F4
Bellevue Industrial Estate	20	E3
Benson Street Enterprise Centre	36	F2
Blackhorse Industrial Estate	35	B1
Blanchardstown Industrial Park	7	C4
Bluebell Business Centre	34	E4
Bluebell Industrial Estate	34	D4
Bracetown Business Park	5	C1
Bray Industrial Estate	57	B3
Bridgewater Business Centre	35	A2
Bridges Industrial Estate	41	A1
Broombridge Close	20	E3
Broombridge Industrial Estate	20	E3
Broomhill Close	41	A4
Broomhill Drive	41	A4
Broomhill Road	41	A4
Broomhill Terrace	41	A4
Burton Hall Road	52	E2
Carriglea Industrial Estate	41	B1
Castleforbes Industrial Estate	36	F2
Cherry Orchard Industrial Estate	33	C2/C3
Cian Park Industrial Estate	21	B4
Citywest Business Campus	39	B4
Clondalkin Commercial Park	33	B4
Clondalkin Industrial Estate	33	B4
Clonshaugh Industrial Estate	11	A4
Cloverhill Industrial Estate	33	B4
Collinstown Cross	10	F2
Collinstown Park	10	F3
Cookstown Enterprise Park	40	E4
Cookstown Industrial Estate	40	F4
Coolmine Industrial Estate	18	D2
Coolock Industrial Estate	22	F1
Croke Park Industrial Estate	36	E1
Crossbeg Industrial Estate	41	A2

No.	Name	Page	Grid Ref
57	Crosslands Industrial Park	41	A2
58	Damastown Business Park	6	E3
59	Deans Grange Industrial Estate	53	B1/B2
60	Doyles Industrial Estate	41	B1
61	Dublin Industrial Estate (Glasnevin)	20	E3
62	Dunboyne Industrial Estate	5	B2
63	Dun Laoghaire Industrial Estate	53	B2/C2
64	East Road Industrial Estate	36	F1
65	Elmfield	40	D1
66	Fairdale Industrial Estate	22	D2/E2
67	Feltrim Industrial Estate	2	E3
68	Finches Industrial Park	41	B1
69	Fingal Enterprise Centre	20	E2
70	Gaywood Industrial Estate	7	B3
71	Glen Abbey Complex	40	F4
72	Glen Industrial Centre	20	E3
73	Glen Industrial Estate	20	E3
74	Glenview Industrial Estate	35	B4
75	Glenville Industrial Estate	44	E3
76	Goldenbridge Industrial Estate	34	F3/F4
77	Greenhills Industrial Estate	41	C2
78	Greenmount Industrial Estate	35	C4
79	Grove Industrial Estate	20	E1
80	Grove Industrial Estate (2)	20	E1
81	Harbour Industrial Estate	57	C1
82	Hibernian Industrial Estate	41	A4
83	Hills Industrial Centre	28	D1
84	I.D.A. Centre	36	E1
85	I.D.A. Enterprise Centre	36	F3
86	I.D.A. Industrial Centre	35	C1
87	I.D.A. Small Industries Centre	36	F1
		37	A1
88	I.D.A. Small Industries Centre	11	A4
89	I.D.A. Tallaght Business Park	48	F2
90	Industrial Garden Estate	34	E2
91	Industrial Yarns Complex	57	B1
92	INTEL Collinstown Industrial Park	15	B3
93	Irish Farm Centre	34	E4
94	Jamestown Industrial Estate	34	E4/F4
95	Jamestown Little Industrial Estate	34	E4/F4
96	J.F.K. Avenue	41	A1
97	J.F.K. Drive	34	D4
		41	B1
98	J.F.K. Park	34	D4
99	J.F.K. Road	34	D4
100	KCR Industrial Estate	42	E2
101	Kilbarrack Industrial Estate	23	C1
102	Kylemore Industrial Estate	34	D4
103	Kylemore Park N	34	D3
104	Kylemore Park S	34	D4/E4
105	Kylemore Park W	34	D4
106	Landy's Industrial Estate	50	D1
107	Lansdowne Valley	41	C1
108	Leopardstown Retail Park	52	E2
109	Liberties Craft & Small Industries Centre	35	C3
110	Lilmar Industrial Estate	10	F4

No.	Name	Page	Grid Ref
111	Loughlinstown Industrial Estate	56	D1
112	McGarveys Industrial Park	41	B2
113	Metropolitan Industrial Estate	35	A3
114	Monarch Industrial Estate	40	F4
115	Mulcahy Keane Estate	41	C2
116	Newlands Business Park	40	E2
117	Newtown Industrial Estate	11	C4
118	North Richmond Industrial	36	E1
119	Oakfield Industrial Estate	33	A4
120	Old Court Industrial Estate	57	B4
121	Old Sawmills Industrial Estate	41	C2
122	Ossory Business Park & Ind. Est.	36	F1
123	Parkmore Industrial Estate	41	B1
124	Phoenix Industrial Estate	19	B3
125	Pineview Industrial Estate	49	C1
126	Pinewood Close Industrial Estate	57	C4
127	Poppintree Industrial Centre	9	B4
128	Pye Ireland Complex	51	C1
129	Richmond Road Industrial Estate	21	B4
130	Riversdale Industrial Estate	34	E4
131	Robinhood Industrial Estate	41	B1
132	Rohan Industrial Estate	34	F4
133	Rosemount Industrial Park	8	D4
134	St. Joans Industrial Estate	41	A2
134A	Sallynoggin Industrial Estate	54	D2
135	Sandyford Industrial Estate	52	E2
136	Sandyford Office Park	52	E2
137	Sandyford Business Park	52	E2
138	Santry Avenue Industrial Estate	10	E4
139	Santry Hall Industrial Estate	21	B1
140	Seaview Industrial Complex	57	C2
141	Shankill Business Centre	56	E2
142	Shanowen Road	21	B2
143	South County Business	52	F2
34	Stag Industrial Estate	20	E3
144	Stillorgan Industrial Park	52	D2
145	Sunbury Industrial Estate	41	B2
146	Sunshine Industrial Estate	35	A4/B4
147	Swiftbrook Industrial Estate	47	A2
148	Swords Business Park	2	D1
149	Tallaght Enterprise Centre	49	A1
150	The Liffey Enterprise Centre	36	F2
34	Tolka Industrial Park	20	E3
151	Turnpike Industrial Estate	37	A2
152	Unidare Industrial Estate	20	E1
153	Weatherwell Industrial Estate	33	A4
154	West Link Industrial Estate	34	E3
155	Western Industrial Estate	34	D4
156	Western Industrial Estate (2)	40	F1
157	Western Parkway Business Centre	41	B2
158	White Heather Industrial Estate	35	B4
159	White Swan Business Centre & Industrial Estate	35	C4
160	Whitestown Industrial Estate	48	F1
161	W.I.L. Industrial Complex	20	E1
162	Woodlawn Industrial Estate	10	F3

A

STREET NAME	PAGE/GRID REFERENCE
ABBERLEY	56 E1
Abbey Cottages	36 D2[43]
Abbey Court	22 E3
Abbey Court (Monkstown)	53 B1 [7]
Abbey Park (Baldoyle)	23 C1
Abbey Park (Kill o' the Grange)	53 B1
Abbey Park (Killester)	22 E3
Abbey Road	53 B1
Abbey Road	53 B1 [8]
Abbey Street (Howth)	26 D1
Abbey Street Lower	36 D2
Abbey Street Middle	36 D2
Abbey Street Old	36 E2[19]
Abbey Street Upper	36 D2
Abbey View	53 B1
Abbeydale Close	32 F3
Abbeydale Crescent	32 F3
Abbeydale Gardens	32 F3
Abbeydale Park	32 F3
Abbeydale Rise	32 F3
Abbeydale Walk	32 F3
Abbeyfarm	29 C4
Abbeyfield	43 B2
Abbeyfield	22 E3
Abbeylea Avenue	1 C1
Abbeylea Close	1 C1
Abbeylea Drive	1 C1
Abbeylea Green	1 C1
Abbeyvale Avenue	1 B1
Abbeyvale Close	1 B1
Abbeyvale Court	1 B1
Abbeyvale Crescent	1 B1
Abbeyvale Drive	1 B2
Abbeyvale Green	1 B2
Abbeyvale Grove	1 B1
Abbeyvale Lawn	1 B1
Abbeyvale Place	1 B1
Abbeyvale Rise	1 B1
Abbeyvale View	1 B2
Abbeyvale Way	1 B2
Abbeywood Avenue	32 E3
Abbeywood Close	32 F3
Abbeywood Court	32 E3
Abbeywood Crescent	32 F3
Abbeywood Park	32 F3
Abbeywood Way	32 F3
Abbotstown Avenue	19 C2
Abbotstown Drive	20 D2
Abbotstown Road	20 D1
Abercorn Road	36 F2
Abercorn Square	34 F3[19]
Abercorn Terrace	34 F3[10]
Aberdeen Street	35 B2
Accommodation Road	15 C4
Achill Road	21 B3
Achill Road	56 E1
Acorn Drive	51 B1
Acorn Road	51 B1
Acres Road	34 F2
Adair	37 A4[14]
*Adair Lane (Dorset Street)	36 D1
*Adair Terrace	36 D1
(on St.Joseph's Parade)	
*Adam Court (off Grafton Street)	36 D3
Adamstown Road	32 D2
Adare Avenue	22 E1
Adare Drive	22 E1
Adare Green	22 E1
Adare Park	22 E1
Adare Road	22 E1
Addison Place	21 A3 [9]
Addison Road	21 C4
Addison Terrace	21 A3[10]
Adelaide Mews	44 E1
Adelaide Road	57 C2
Adelaide Road (Dun Laoghaire)	54 E1
Adelaide Road (Leeson Street)	36 D4
Adelaide Street	46 D4
Adelaide Terrace (Dun Laoghaire)	54 E1[28]
*Adelaide Terrace	35 B3
(off Brookfield Road)	
Adelaide Villas	54 E1[27]
Adelaide Villas	57 B2
Admiral Park	13 A4
Adrian Avenue	42 F1
Aideen Avenue	42 E2
Aideen Drive	42 E2
Aideen Place	42 E2
Aikenhead Terrace	37 A3
Ailesbury	21 B1[1]
Ailesbury Drive	44 D1
Ailesbury Gardens	44 E1
Ailesbury Grove (Donnybrook)	44 D1
Ailesbury Grove (Dundrum)	51 B1
*Ailesbury Lane	44 D1
(off Ailesbury Road)	
Ailesbury Lawn	51 B1
Ailesbury Mews	44 E1
Ailesbury Park	44 E1
Ailesbury Road	44 D1
Airfield Court	44 D2
Airfield Drive	43 B4[13]
Airfield Park	44 D2
Airfield Road	42 F2
Airlie Heights	31 B2
Airton Close	41 A4
Airton Road	41 A4
Airton Terrace	40 A1
(off Greenhills Rd.)	
Aisling Close	35 B4
Albany Avenue	45 B4
Albany Court	56 E1
Albany Road	43 B1
Albert Avenue	57 C2
Albert College Avenue	21 A2
Albert College Crescent	21 A2
Albert College Drive	21 A2
Albert College Grove	21 A2 [1]
Albert College Lawn	21 A2
Albert College Park	21 A2
Albert College Terrace	21 A2
Albert Court	34 D4
Albert Court East	36 F3[30]
*Albert Court	36 F4
(off Grand Canal St.)	
Albert Park	54 E1 [3]
Albert Place East	36 F3[14]
Albert Place West	36 D4[15]
Albert Road Lower	54 E1
Albert Road Upper	54 E2
Albert Terrace	36 D4[18]
*Albert Terrace	46 D4
(Crofton Rd. Dun Laoghaire)	
Albert Walk	57 C2
Aldborough Parade	36 E1[17]
Aldborough Place	36 E1
*Aldborough Square	36 E1
(off Aldborough Place)	
Aldemere	17 B2
Alden Drive	23 C1
Alden Park	23 C1
Alden Road	23 C1
Alder Court	4 D4 [1]
Alderpark Court	48 F1
Alderwood Avenue	48 E1
Alderwood Close	48 E1
Alderwood Court	48 E1
Alderwood Drive	48 F1
Alderwood Green	48 E1
Alderwood Grove	48 F1
Alderwood Lawn	48 E1
Alderwood Park	48 F1
Alderwood Rise	48 E1
Alderwood Way	48 F1
Aldrin Walk	22 E1
Alexander Terrace	57 C2[43]
Alexander Terrace (North Wall)	36 F2[11]
Alexandra Quay	37 A2
Alexandra Road	37 A2
Alexandra Road Extension	37 C2
Alexandra Terrace (Dundrum)	43 C4
Alexandra Terrace (Portobello)	36 D4[45]
Alexandra Terrace (Terenure)	42 F2
Alexandra Terrace	43 C4 [3]
Alfie Byrne Road	36 F1
All Saints Drive	23 A3
All Saints Park	23 A3
All Saints Road	22 F3
Allen Park Drive	52 E1
Allen Park Road	52 E1
*Allen Terrace	35 C1
(off Avondale Avenue)	
Allenton Avenue	49 A2
Allenton Crescent	49 A2 [3]
Allenton Drive	49 A3
Allenton Gardens	49 B3
Allenton Green	49 A3
Allenton Lawns	49 A3
Allenton Park	49 A3
Allenton Road	49 B2 [1]
Allenton Way	49 A3
Allingham Street	35 C3[15]
Alma Place	45 C4[14]
Alma Road	45 B4
Alma Terrace	43 A1[13]
Almeida Avenue	35 B3[26]
Almeida Terrace	35 B3[27]
Alone Walk	22 E2
Alpine Heights	40 D1
Alpine Rise	40 E4
Altadore	54 D2
Alton Terrace	54 F2
Alverno	37 B1 [1]
Amber Vale	40 E4
Amiens Street	36 E2
Anastasia Lane	54 F2[3]
Anglesea Avenue	45 A3
Anglesea Lane	46 D4[20]
Anglesea Park	54 E2
Anglesea Road	43 C1
Anglesea Row	36 D2 [7]
Anglesea Street	36 D2
Ann Devlin Avenue	42 E4
Ann Devlin Drive	42 E4
Ann Devlin Park	50 E1
Ann Devlin Road	42 E4
Anna Villa	43 B1
Annabeg	54 D4 [1]
Annadale	43 B4[16]
Annadale Avenue	21 C4 [1]
Annadale Crescent	21 C3
Annadale Drive	21 C3
Annaly Road	20 F4
Annamoe Drive	35 C1
Annamoe Parade	35 C1 [2]
Annamoe Park	35 C1
Annamoe Road	35 B1
Annamoe Terrace	35 C1
Annaville Avenue	53 A1
Annaville Grove	43 C3 [1]
Annaville Park	43 C3
Annaville Terrace	43 C3
Anne Street North	36 D2 [5]
Anne Street South	36 D3
Anne's Lane	36 D3[33]
Anner Road	35 A3
Annesley Avenue	36 F1 [9]
Annesley Bridge Road	36 F1
Annesley Park	43 B1
Annesley Place	36 F1
Annsbrook	43 C2
Annville Drive	52 E1
Apollo Way	22 D1
*Appian Close (on Leeson Park)	36 E4
Apples	52 D2
Aran Avenue	56 E1
Aran Close	56 E1
Aran Drive	56 E1
Aranleigh Court	50 F1
Aranleigh Dell	51 A1
Aranleigh Gardens	50 F1
Aranleigh Mount	50 F1
Aranleigh Park	51 A1
Aranleigh Vale	50 F1
Aravon Court	57 C2 [2]
Arbour Hill	35 B2
Arbour Place	35 C2
Arbour Terrace	35 B2 [6]
Arbutus Avenue	35 C4 [8]
Arbutus Grove	57 B2 [2]
Arbutus Place	36 D4[51]
Ard Lorcain	52 F1
Ard Lorcain Villas	52 F1 [2]
Ard Mhacha	48 F2
Ard Mhuire Park	54 E2
Ard Righ Place	35 C2[27]
Ard Righ Road	35 C2
Ard na Mara	3 A3
Ard na Mara Crescent	3 A3
Ard na Meala	10 D4[1]
Ardagh Avenue	53 A1
Ardagh Close	53 A1[6]
Ardagh Court	52 F1
Ardagh Crescent	53 A1
Ardagh Drive	53 A1
Ardagh Grove	53 A1
Ardagh Park	53 A1
Ardagh Park Road	53 A1
Ardagh Road	35 B4
Ardara Avenue	12 D4
Ardbeg Crescent	22 E2
Ardbeg Drive	22 E2
Ardbeg Park	22 E2
Ardbeg Road	22 E2
Ardbrugh Close	54 F2[31]
Ardbrugh Road	54 F2
Ardbrugh Villas	54 F2[21]
Ardcian Park	1 C1
Ardcollum Avenue	22 E2
Ardee Grove	35 D4
Ardee Road	36 D4
Ardee Row	35 C3[34]
Ardee Street	35 C3
Ardeen	31 C2
Ardeevin Avenue	31 C2
Ardeevin Court	31 C2
Ardeevin Drive	31 C2
Ardeevin Road	54 F2
*Ardeevin Terrace	54 F2
(off Ardeevin Road)	
Ardenza Park	45 B3 [3]
Ardenza Terrace	45 B3 [1]
Ardglas Estate	51 C1
Ardilaun	12 F1
Ardilaun Road	36 E1 [3]
*Ardilaun Square	36 E1
(off Sackville Avenue)	
Ardilea Downs	44 D4
Ardlea Road	22 E2
Ardlui Park	53 A1
Ardmeen Park	53 A1
Ardmore Avenue	35 B1 [4]
Ardmore Close	22 D2
Ardmore Crescent	22 D2
Ardmore Crescent	57 B3
Ardmore Drive	22 D1
Ardmore Grove	22 D1
Ardmore Lawn	57 B3
Ardmore Park	57 B3
Ardmore Park (Artane)	22 D2
Ardmore Park	53 C1
(Kill o' the Grange)	
Ardmore Wood	57 A3
Ardpatrick Road	20 D4
Ardtona Avenue	43 B4 [6]
Arena Road	52 E2
Argyle Road	36 F4
Arkendale Court	54 E1[26]
Arkendale Road	54 E1
Arkendale Woods	54 E1[25]
Arkle Road	52 E2
*Arkle Square	52 F2
(Charles Sheil's Houses)	
Arklow Street	35 B1[13]
Armagh Road	42 D1
*Armstrong Street	35 C4
(off Harold's Cross Road)	
Armstrong Walk	22 E1
Army Road	35 A2
Arnold Grove	54 D2
Arnold Park	54 D2
Arnott Street	36 D3
Arran Green	57 C2
Arran Quay	35 C2
Arran Quay Terrace	35 C2[10]
Arran Road	21 B3
Arran Street East	36 D2
Arran Street West	35 C2[17]
Arranmore Avenue	36 D1[36]
Arranmore Road	43 C1
Artane	22 E2
Artane Cottages Lower	22 E2 [2]
Artane Cottages Upper	22 E2 [3]
Arthur Griffith Park	32 D3
*Asdill's Row (off Temple Bar)	36 D2
Asgard Park	26 D2
Asgard Road	26 D2
*Ash Grove (off Meath Street)	35 C3
Ash Street	35 C3
Ashhurst	54 E4
Ashurst	44 E4 [3]
Ashbrook	19 C3
Ashbrook	22 D4
*Ashbrook Terrace	43 B1
(on Sallymount Avenue)	
Ashbury Park	57 C2
Ashcroft	23 A2
Ashdale Avenue	42 F2
Ashdale Close	2 E3
Ashdale Gardens	42 F2
Ashdale Park	42 F2 [1]
Ashdale Road (Terenure)	42 F2
Ashdale Road (Swords)	2 E3
Ashfield	42 D4
Ashfield Avenue (Clondalkin)	40 F3
Ashfield Avenue (Ranelagh)	43 B3
Ashfield Close (Clondalkin)	40 F3
Ashfield Close (Templeogue)	42 D4
Ashfield Court	7 A4
Ashfield Drive	40 F3
Ashfield Gardens	7 A4
Ashfield Green	6 F4
Ashfield Grove	7 A4
Ashfield Lawn	6 F4
Ashfield Park (Booterstown)	44 E2
Ashfield Park (Clondalkin)	40 F3
Ashfield Park (Mulhuddart)	7 A4

STREET NAME	PAGE/GRID REFERENCE
Ashfield Park (Templeogue)	42 D4
Ashfield Park (Terenure)	42 F2
Ashfield Road (Ranelagh)	43 B1
Ashfield Way	6 F4
*Ashford Cottages (off Ross Street)	35 B1
*Ashford Place (off Ross Street)	35 B1
Ashford Street	35 B1[10]
Ashgrove	29 C2
Ashgrove (Kill o' the Grange)	53 C1
Ashgrove (Tallaght)	48 E1
Ashgrove Terrace	51 C1[2]
Ashington Avenue	20 D3
Ashington Close	20 D3
Ashington Court	20 D3
Ashington Crescent	19 C3
Ashington Dale	20 D3
Ashington Gardens	20 D3
Ashington Green	20 D3
Ashington Grove	20 D3
Ashington Heath	20 D3
Ashington Mews	20 D3
Ashington Park	20 D3
Ashington Rise	19 C3
Ashlawn	51 C1
Ashlawn Court	57 B2
Ashlawn Park	54 D4
Ashleigh Green	18 F3
Ashleigh Grove	18 F3
Ashleigh Lawn	3 B3
Ashley Avenue	2 D2
Ashley Drive	2 D2
Ashley Grove	2 D2
Ashley Heights	57 B2[4]
Ashley Rise	4 D4
Ashling Close	35 B4
Ashling Heights	18 E1
Ashmount	7 A4[1]
Ashmount Court	35 A3[23]
Ashton Avenue	50 D1
Ashton Close	50 D1
Ashton Grove	50 D1
Ashton Lawn	50 D1
Ashton Park	45 B4
Ashton Wood	57 A4
Ashtown	19 C3
Ashtown Gate Road	19 B4
Ashtown Grove	19 C4
Ashtown Villas	19 C4[4]
Ashurst	54 E4
Ashurst	44 E4[3]
Ashwood Avenue	39 C1
Ashwood Close	39 C1
Ashwood Drive	40 D1
Ashwood Lawns	40 D1
Ashwood Park	40 D1
Ashwood Road	40 D1
Ashwood Way	40 D1
*Ashworth Place (off Mount Drumond Avenue)	35 C4
Aspen Drive	2 E3
Aspen Park	2 E3
Aspen Park	53 C1[11]
Aspen Road	2 E3
Assumpta Park	56 D3
Aston Place	36 D2[39]
Aston Quay	36 D2
Athgoe Drive	56 E2[4]
Athgoe Road	56 E2
Atlumney Villas	36 D4[12]
Aubrey Grove	56 E3
Aubrey Park	56 E3
Auburn Avenue (Cabinteely)	54 D3
Auburn Avenue (Castleknock)	19 A3
Auburn Avenue (Donnybrook)	43 C1
Auburn Close	54 D3
Auburn Close	19 A3
Auburn Drive (Cabinteely)	54 D3
Auburn Drive (Castleknock)	19 A3
Auburn Green	19 A3
Auburn Grove	3 A3
Auburn Road (Cabinteely)	54 D3[1]
Auburn Road (Donnybrook)	43 C1[11]
Auburn Street	36 D1
*Auburn Terrace (on Old Kilmainham)	35 B3
Auburn Villas	43 A2
Auburn Villas	57 B2[27]
Auburn Walk	35 B1
Aughavannagh Road	35 C4
Aughrim Court	35 C1[21]
Aughrim Lane	35 C1[1]
Aughrim Place	35 B1[8]
Aughrim Street	35 B1
Aughrim Villas	35 B1[12]
Augustine Villas	57 C2[30]

STREET NAME	PAGE/GRID REFERENCE
Aulden Grange	10 F4
Aungier Lane	36 D3[23]
Aungier Place	36 D3[10]
Aungier Street	36 D3
Austin's Cottages	36 F1[23]
Avalo (Apts)	25 B1[2]
Ave Maria Road	35 B3[18]
Avenue Road	36 D4[26]
Avila Park	19 C1
Avoca Avenue	44 F4
Avoca Park	44 F4
Avoca Place	45 A3
Avoca Road	44 F4
Avonbeg Drive	49 A1
Avonbeg Gardens	49 B1
Avonbeg Park	49 B1
Avonbeg Road	49 B1
Avondale	16 D4
Avondale Avenue	35 C1
Avondale Crescent	54 E2
Avondale House	36 E1
Avondale Lawn	45 A4
Avondale Lawn Extension	45 A4
Avondale Park	57 B3
Avondale Park (Dalkey)	54 E2
Avondale Park (Dun Laoghaire)	45 A4[1]
Avondale Park (Raheny)	23 A2
Avondale Road (Dalkey)	54 D2
Avondale Road (Phibsborough)	35 C1
Avondale Terrace	41 C2
Avonmore	53 A2
Avonmore Avenue	49 B1[5]
Avonmore Close	49 B1
Avonmore Drive	49 B1
Avonmore Grove	49 B1
Avonmore Park	49 B1
Avonmore Road	49 B1
Aylesbury Estate	49 A2
Ayrefield Avenue	22 F1
Ayrefield Court	22 F1
Ayrefield Drive	22 F1
Ayrefield Grove	22 F1
Ayrefield Park	22 F1[2]
Ayrefield Place	22 F1
Ayrefield Road	22 F1

B

STREET NAME	PAGE/GRID REFERENCE
BACHELOR'S WALK	36 D2
Bachelor's Way	36 D2[30]
Back Lane (Baldoyle)	13 A4[3]
Back Lane (High Street)	36 D3
*Back Lane (off Sandwith St. Upr.)	36 E3
Back Road	3 B4
Baggot Court	36 E3[9]
Baggot Lane	36 F4
Baggot Road	19 C4
Baggot Street Lower	36 E3
Baggot Street Upper	36 E4
Baggot Terrace	19 C4[1]
Baggotrath Place	36 E3[28]
Bailey Green Road	26 E3
Bailey View	54 F1[15]
Bailey's Row	36 E1[11]
Balally Avenue	52 D1
Balally Close	52 D1
Balally Drive	52 D1
Balally Grove	52 D2
Balally Hill	52 D2
Balally Park	52 D1
Balally Road	51 C1
Balally Terrace	52 D2[1]
Balbutcher Drive	9 C4
Balbutcher Lane	9 C4
Balbutcher Way	9 C4
Balcurris Gardens	10 D4
Balcurris Road	10 D4
Baldoyle	13 A4
Baldoyle Road	24 D1
Balfe Avenue	41 C1
Balfe Gardens	30 D4[1]
Balfe Road	41 C1
Balfe Road East	42 D1
Balfe Street	36 D3[29]
Balglass Estate	26 D2
Balglass Road	26 D2
Balgriffin	12 D3
Balgriffin Cottages	12 D3
Balgriffin Road	12 D3
Balheary Road	2 D1
Balkill Park	26 D2
Balkill Road	26 D2
Ball's Lane	36 D2[23]
Ballawley Court	51 C2

STREET NAME	PAGE/GRID REFERENCE
Ballinclea Heights	54 E2
Ballinclea Road	54 D3
Ballinteer	51 B2
Ballinteer Avenue	51 B2
Ballinteer Close	51 B2
Ballinteer Court	51 B2[2]
Ballinteer Crescent	51 B2
Ballinteer Drive	51 B2
Ballinteer Gardens	51 C2
Ballinteer Grove	51 B2
Ballinteer Park	51 B2
Ballinteer Park	51 C2[2]
Ballinteer Road	51 C1
Ballintrane Wood	1 C2
Ballsbridge	36 F4
Ballsbridge Avenue	37 A4
Ballsbridge Park	37 A4[23]
Ballsbridge Terrace	36 F4[14]
Ballsbridge Wood	36 F4
Ballyboden	50 E1
Ballyboden Crescent	50 E1
Ballyboden Road	50 E1
Ballyboggan Road	20 E3
Ballybough Avenue	36 E1[42]
Ballybough Court	36 E1[43]
Ballybough Lane	36 E1[4]
Ballybough Road	36 E1
Ballybrack	54 E4
Ballybride Road	56 D3
Ballycoolin Road	8 D4
Ballycorus	55 A3
Ballycorus Road	55 A2
Ballycullen Avenue	49 B2
Ballycullen Drive	49 B2
Ballycullen Road	49 C2
Ballycullen View	49 C2
Ballydowd Grove	32 E1
Ballyfermot	34 D3
Ballyfermot Avenue	34 D3
Ballyfermot Crescent	34 D3
Ballyfermot Drive	34 D3
Ballyfermot Parade	34 D3
Ballyfermot Road	34 D3
Ballygall Avenue	20 E1
Ballygall Crescent	20 E2
Ballygall Parade	20 E2[4]
Ballygall Place	20 E2[1]
Ballygall Road	20 E2
Ballygall Road East	20 F2
Ballygall Road West	20 E1
Ballygihen Avenue	54 E1
Ballygihen Villas	54 F1[20]
Ballygorten	29 C2
Ballyhoy Avenue	23 A3
Ballymace Green	42 E4
Ballymadrough Road	2 F1
Ballymakealy	29 C4
Ballymakealy Grove	29 C4
Ballyman Lane	55 C4
Ballyman Road	57 A1
Ballymanagin Lane	33 A4[1]
Ballymorris	57 B4
*Ballymoss Parade (Charles Sheil's Houses)	52 F2
Ballymoss Road	52 E2
Ballymount Cottages	41 A2
Ballymount Drive	41 B2
Ballymount Road	40 F3
Ballymount Road Lower	41 B2
Ballymount Road Upper	41 A2
Ballymun	21 A1
Ballymun Road	21 A1
Ballyneety Road	34 F3
Ballynoe Court	57 B3[1]
Ballyogan Avenue	52 F4
Ballyogan Close	52 F4
Ballyogan Court	52 F4
Ballyogan Crescent	52 F4
Ballyogan Estate	52 F4
Ballyogan Green	52 F4
Ballyogan Lawn	52 F4
Ballyogan Road	52 F4
Ballyolaf Manor	51 C1[6]
Ballyoulster Park	30 E3
Ballyowen Avenue	32 F1
Ballyowen Court	32 F2
Ballyowen Crescent	32 F1
Ballyowen Drive	32 F2
Ballyowen Green	32 F1
Ballyowen Grove	32 F2
Ballyowen Lane	32 F2
Ballyowen Lawn	32 F1
Ballyowen Park	32 F1
Ballyowen View	32 F1
Ballyowen Way	32 F1

STREET NAME	PAGE/GRID REFERENCE
Ballyroan Court	50 D1[3]
Ballyroan Crescent	50 E1
Ballyroan Heights	50 E1
Ballyroan Park	50 D1
Ballyroan Road	50 E1
Ballyshannon Avenue	21 C1
Ballyshannon Road	22 D1
Ballytore Road	42 F3
Ballywaltrim Cottages	57 A4[1]
Ballywaltrim Heights	57 B4
Ballywaltrim Road	57 A4
Balnagowan	43 B2[4]
Balrothery Estate	41 B4
Balscadden Road	26 E1
Bancroft Avenue	49 A1
Bancroft Close	49 B1
Bancroft Crescent	41 B4
Bancroft Grove	41 B4
Bancroft Park	49 A1
Bancroft Road	49 B1
Bangor Drive	35 B4
Bangor Road	42 E1
Bankside Cottages	43 B2
Bann Road	20 E3
Bannaville	36 D4[41]
Bannow Road	20 E4
Bantry Road	21 A3
Barclay Court	45 A3
Bargy Road	36 F1
Barnacoille Park	54 F1
Barnacullia Road	52 D4
Barnamore Crescent	20 D3
Barnamore Grove	20 D3
Barnamore Park	20 D3
Barnaslingan Lane	55 A3
Barnhill Avenue	54 E2
Barnhill Cross Road	32 D1
Barnhill Grove	54 F2[7]
Barnhill Lawn	54 E2[1]
Barnhill Park	54 E2[3]
Barnhill Road	54 E2
*Barnhill Villas (on Barnhill Road)	54 F2
*Barrack Lane (off Irishtown Road)	37 A3
Barrett Street	45 C4[2]
Barron Place	21 A3[4]
Barrow Road	20 E3
Barrow Street	36 F3
Barry Avenue	20 D1
*Barry Close (off Barry Drive)	20 D1
Barry Drive	20 D1
Barry Green	20 D1
Barry Park	20 D1
Barry Road	20 D1
Barry's Court Road	22 E1
Barton Avenue	50 F1
Barton Drive	50 F1
Barton Road East	51 B1
Barton Road Extension	51 A1
Barton Road West	50 F1
Basin Street Lower	35 B3
Basin Street Upper	35 B3
*Basin View (off Basin Street Upper)	35 B3
Baskin Cottages	11 C1
Baskin Lane	11 B1
Bass Place	36 E3[3]
Bath Avenue (Malahide)	3 C2
Bath Avenue (Sandymount)	36 F3
Bath Avenue Gardens	36 F3
Bath Avenue Place	36 F3[10]
Bath Lane	36 D1[42]
Bath Place	45 A3[8]
Bath Street	37 A3
Bawnlea Avenue	48 D2
Bawnlea Close	48 D2
Bawnlea Crescent	48 D2
Bawnlea Drive	48 D2
Bawnlea Green	48 D2
Bawnogue Cottages	39 C1[1]
Bawnville Avenue	49 A2
Bawnville Close	49 A2
Bawnville Drive	49 B2
Bawnville Park	49 B2
Bawnville Road	49 A2
Baymount Park	23 A4
Bayshore Lane	56 E1
Bayside Boulevard North	23 C1
Bayside Boulevard South	23 C1
Bayside Crescent	23 C1
Bayside Park	23 C1
Bayside Square East	23 C1
Bayside Square North	23 C1

STREET NAME	PAGE/GRID REFERENCE
Bayside Square South	23 C1
Bayside Square West	23 C1
Bayside Walk	23 C1
Bayswater Terrace	54 F1 [7]
Bayview	56 E1
*Bayview (On Seapoint Road)	57 C2
Bayview Avenue	36 E1
Bayview Close	56 E1
Bayview Court	56 E1
Bayview Crescent	56 E1
Bayview Drive	56 E1
Bayview Glade	56 E1 [12]
Bayview Grove	56 E1
Bayview Lawn	56 E1
Beach Avenue	37 A3
Beach Drive	37 A3
Beach Park	13 A1
Beach Road	37 A3
Beach View	23 C2
*Beacon Hill(off Nerano Road)	54 F2
Beaconsfield Court	35 A3 [18]
Bearna Park	52 D3
Beatty Grove	30 D2
Beatty Park	30 D3
Beatty's Avenue	36 F4 [8]
Beaucourt	21 B3 [4]
Beaufield Manor	44 E4
Beaufield Mews	44 E4 [2]
Beaufield Park	44 E4
Beaufort	54 E1 [19]
Beaufort Court	42 F4 [10]
Beaufort Downs	42 F4
Beaufort Villas	42 F4 [3]
Beaumont	22 D1
Beaumont Avenue	43 B4
Beaumont Close	43 B4 [3]
Beaumont Cottages	32 D2
Beaumont Crescent	22 D2
Beaumont Drive	43 B4
Beaumont Gardens	44 F4
Beaumont Grove	21 C2
Beaumont Road	21 C2
Beauvale Park	22 D2
Beaver Close	36 E1 [51]
Beaver Row	43 C1
Beaver Street	36 E1
Bedford Court	42 E1 [5]
*Bedford Lane (off Aston Quay)	36 D2
*Bedford Row (off Aston Quay)	36 D2
Beech Drive	51 B1
Beech Grove (Blackrock)	44 F2
Beech Grove (Lucan)	32 E2
Beech Hill	43 C2
Beech Hill Avenue	43 C2
Beech Hill Crescent	43 C2 [3]
Beech Hill Drive	43 C2
Beech Hill Road	43 C2
Beech Hill Terrace	43 C2 [4]
Beech Hill Villas	43 C2 [2]
Beech Lawn	51 B1
Beech Park (Cabinteely)	53 C4
Beech Park (Castleknock)	18 F3
Beech Park (Lucan)	32 E1
Beech Park Avenue	19 A3
(Blanchardstown)	
Beech Park Avenue	53 B2
(Deans Grange)	
Beech Park Crescent	19 A3 [1]
Beech Park Drive	53 B2
Beech Park Grove	53 B2
Beech Park Lawn	19 A3
Beech Park Road	53 B2
Beech Road	41 A1
Beech Road	57 B2
Beech Row	33 A4
Beech Row	40 D1 [3]
Beech Walk	50 E2 [4]
Beechbrook Grove	12 D4 [4]
Beechdale	5 B3
Beechdale Mews	43 B1 [19]
Beeches	52 D1
Beeches Park	54 E1
Beechfield Avenue	41 C2
Beechfield Close	42 D2
Beechfield Haven	56 E2 [3]
Beechfield Manor	56 E2
Beechfield Mews	42 D2 [4]
Beechfield Road	41 C2
Beechlawn	44 F3
Beechlawn Avenue	51 B1
Beechlawn Avenue	22 E1
Beechlawn Close	22 E1
Beechlawn Green	22 E1
Beechlawn Grove	22 E1
Beechmount Drive	43 C3

STREET NAME	PAGE/GRID REFERENCE
(Windy Arbour)	
Beechpark Avenue	22 E1
Beechpark Court	22 E1
Beechurst	57 B2
Beechview Court	50 E2 [1]
Beechwood Avenue Lower	43 B1
Beechwood Avenue Upper	43 B1
Beechwood Close	17 C1
Beechwood Close	57 C4
Beechwood Court	54 D3
Beechwood Downs	17 C1
Beechwood Grove	54 D1 [11]
Beechwood Lawn	54 D2
Beechwood Park	54 D1
(Dun Laoghaire)	
Beechwood Park (Rathmines)	43 B1 [7]
Beechwood Road	43 B1
Beggar's Bush Buildings	36 F3
Belcamp Avenue	11 B4
Belcamp Crescent	11 B4
Belcamp Gardens	11 B4
Belcamp Green	11 B4
Belcamp Grove	11 B4
Belcamp Lane	11 C4
Belclare Avenue	9 C4
Belclare Crescent	9 C4
Belclare Drive	9 C4
Belclare Green	9 C4
Belclare Grove	9 C4
Belclare Lawns	9 C4
Belclare Park	9 C4
Belclare Terrace	9 C4
Belclare Way	9 C4
Belfield Close	43 C3 [8]
Belfield Court	44 D2
Belfield Downs	43 C4
Belgard Close	40 F3 [2]
Belgard Green	40 E4
Belgard Heights	40 F4
Belgard Road	40 E3
Belgard Square East	48 F1
Belgard Square North	48 F1
Belgard Square South	48 F1
Belgard Square West	48 F1
Belgrave Avenue	43 B1
Belgrave Place (Monkstown)	45 B4 [10]
Belgrave Place (Rathmines)	43 A1 [15]
Belgrave Road (Monkstown)	45 B4
Belgrave Road (Rathmines)	43 A1
Belgrave Square (Monkstown)	45 B4
Belgrave Square (Rathmines)	43 A1
Belgrave Square East	45 B4
Belgrave Square North	45 B4
Belgrave Square South	45 B4
Belgrave Square West	45 B4
(Monkstown)	
Belgrave Terrace (Monkstown)	45 B4 [11]
*Belgrave Terrace	57 C2
(On Meath Road)	
*Belgrave Villas	57 C2
(On Meath Road)	
Belgrave Villas (Rathmines)	43 B1 [16]
Belgrove Lawn	34 D2
Belgrove Park	34 D2
Belgrove Road	22 F4
Bell's Lane	36 E3 [30]
*Bella Avenue (off Bella St.)	36 E1
*Bella Place (off Bella St.)	36 E1
Bella Street	36 E1 [27]
Belleville Avenue	43 A2
Bellevue	35 C3
Bellevue Ave. (Merrion)	44 E2
Bellevue Avenue (Dalkey)	54 E2
Bellevue Copse	44 E2
Bellevue Cottages	20 F3 [4]
Bellevue Court	44 E2 [2]
Bellevue Park	44 E2
Bellevue Park Avenue	44 E2
Bellevue Road	54 D2
Bellman's Walk	36 F2 [13]
Belmont	52 F1
Belmont	57 C4
Belmont Avenue	43 C1
*Belmont Court	43 C1
(off Belmont Ave)	
Belmont Gardens	43 C1
Belmont Green	52 F1
Belmont Grove	52 F1
Belmont Lawn	52 F1
Belmont Park	23 A2
Belmont Park	43 C1 [3]
*Belmont Place	36 E1
(off Gardiner St. Middle)	
*Belmont Terrace	52 F1
(off Stillorgan Road)	

STREET NAME	PAGE/GRID REFERENCE
Belmont Villas	43 C1
Belton Park Avenue	22 D3
Belton Park Gardens	22 D3
Belton Park Road	22 D3
Belton Park Villas	22 D3
Belton Terrace	57 C2 [44]
Belvidere Avenue	36 E1 [19]
Belvidere Court	36 D1 [11]
Belvidere Place	36 D1
Belvidere Road	36 D1
Ben Edar Road	35 B1
Ben Inagh Park	45 A3 [3]
Benbulbin Avenue	35 A4
Benbulbin Road	35 A4
Benburb Street	35 C2
Beneavin Court	20 F2
Beneavin Drive	20 F2
Beneavin Park	20 F1
Beneavin Road	20 F1
Bengal Terrace	20 F4 [4]
Benmadigan Road	35 A4
Benson Street	36 F2
Bentley Avenue	57 C4 [3]
Bentley Park	57 C4
Bentley Road	57 C4
Bentley Villas	45 C4 [17]
Beresford	21 B3
Beresford Avenue	21 B3
Beresford Lane	21 B3
Beresford Lane	36 E2 [9]
Beresford Place	36 E2
Beresford Street	36 D2
Berkeley Avenue	36 D1 [55]
Berkeley Place	36 D1 [57]
Berkeley Road	36 D1
Berkeley Street	36 D1
Berkeley Terrace	36 F3 [36]
Bernard Curtis House	34 F4 [2]
Berryfield Crescent	20 D2
Berryfield Drive	20 D2
Berryfield Road	20 D2
Berwick Avenue	1 B2
Berwick Court	1 B1
Berwick Crescent	1 B1
Berwick Drive	1 B1
Berwick Grove	1 B1
Berwick Hall	43 A4
Berwick Lawn	1 B1
Berwick Place	1 B1
Berwick Rise	1 B2
Berwick View	1 B2
Berwick Walk	1 B2
Berwick Way	1 B1
Berystede	36 E4 [25]
Bessborough Avenue	36 F1
Bessborough Parade	36 D4 [9]
Besser Drive	33 B4
Bethany House	37 B4 [4]
Bethesda Place	36 D1 [58]
Bettyglen	23 B2
Bettysford	40 E1 [3]
Bettystown Avenue	22 F3
Beverly Avenue	50 D1
Beverly Court	22 F4
Beverly Crescent	49 C2
Beverly Downs	49 C2
Beverly Drive	50 D2
Beverly Green	49 C2
Beverly Grove	50 D1
Beverly Heights	50 D2
Beverly Lawns	50 D2
Beverly Park	49 C1
Beverly Rise	49 C2
Big Lane	30 D3
Bigger Road	41 C2
Binn Eadair View	25 A1
Birch Dale	53 A2 [9]
Birch Dale	53 C1 [12]
Birch's Lane	43 C4
Birchdale Close	2 E3
Birchdale Drive	2 E3
Birchdale Park	2 F3
Birchdale Road	2 E3
Birches	52 D1
Birchfield	43 C4
Birchgrove	53 C1
Birchview Avenue	41 A4
Birchview Close	41 A4
Birchview Court	41 A4
Birchview Drive	41 A4
Birchview Heights	41 A4
Birchview Lawn	41 A4
Birchview Rise	41 A4
Birchwood Close	40 E4
Birchwood Drive	48 E1

STREET NAME	PAGE/GRID REFERENCE
Birchwood Heights	48 E1
Bird Avenue	43 C3
Biscayne	3 C3
Bishop Street	36 D3
Bisset's Strand	3 B2
Black Street	35 B2 [9]
Blackberry Lane	13 A1
Blackberry Lane	36 D4 [8]
Blackberry Rise	13 A1
Blackcourt Road	18 E1
Blackditch Drive	33 C3
Blackditch Road	33 C3
Blackglen Court	52 D3
Blackglen Road	51 C3
Blackhall Parade	35 C2 [4]
Blackhall Place	35 C2
Blackhall Street	35 C2 [13]
Blackheath Avenue	22 E4
Blackheath Court	22 F4
Blackheath Drive	22 E4
Blackheath Gardens	22 E4
Blackheath Grove	22 E4
Blackheath Park	22 E4
Blackhorse Avenue	35 B1
Blackhorse Grove	35 B1
Blackpitts	35 C3
Blackrock	45 A3
Blackthorn Avenue	52 E2
Blackthorn Close	4 D4
Blackthorn Court	52 D2 [4]
Blackthorn Drive	52 D2
Blackthorn Green	52 D2 [6]
Blackthorn Grove	52 D2 [3]
Blackthorn Road	52 D2
Blackwater Road	20 E3
Blackwood Lane	3 C4
*Blakes Villas	35 C1
(on Grangegorman Lower)	
Blakesfield	17 C1
Blakestown Cottages	18 D1
Blakestown Drive	18 D1
Blakestown Road	18 D1
Blakestown Way	18 D1
Blanchardstown	18 F2
Blanchardstown Bypass	18 E1
Blanchardstown Road North	7 B4
Blanchardstown Road South	18 D2
Blarney Park	42 E1
Blessington Court	36 D1 [56]
Blessington Lane	36 D1 [53]
*Blessington Place	36 D1
(off St. Joseph's Parade)	
Blessington Road	47 C2
Blessington Road (Tallaght)	48 F1
Blessington Street	36 D1
Bloomfield Avenue (Donnybrook)	36 E4
Bloomfield Avenue (Portobello)	36 D4
Bloomfield Cottages	36 D4 [49]
Bloomfield Park	36 D4 [46]
Bluebell	34 E4
Bluebell Avenue	34 E4
Bluebell Road	34 E4
Blunden Drive	11 C4
Blythe Avenue	36 F2 [4]
*Boardman's Lane	35 C3
(off Cork Street)	
Boden Avenue	50 E2
Boden Close	50 E2
Boden Crescent	50 E2
Boden Dale	50 F1
Boden Drive	50 F1
Boden Green	50 E2
Boden Lawn	50 E1
Boden Park	50 E1
Boden Rise	50 E2
Boden Wood	42 F4
Boeing Road	10 F4
Boghall Road	57 B4
Bohernabreena Road	49 A3
Bolbrook Avenue	49 B1 [3]
Bolbrook Close	49 B1 [4]
Bolbrook Drive	49 B1 [1]
Bolbrook Grove	49 B1
Bolbrook Park	49 B1
Bolbrook Villas	49 B1
Bolton Street	36 D2
Bond Drive	37 A1
Bond Road	37 A1
Bond Street	35 C3
Bonham Street	35 C2
Boolavogue Road	36 F1 [13]
Boot Road	40 D2
Boot Road Inner	40 D2
Booterstown	44 E2
Booterstown Avenue	44 F3

STREET NAME	PAGE/GRID REFERENCE
*Booterstown Grove (off Booterstown Avenue)	44 F2
Booterstown Park	44 F3
Botanic Avenue	21 A4
Botanic Park	21 A4[14]
Botanic Road	21 A4
Botanic Villas	21 A4[10]
Boundary Road	37 A1
Bow Bridge	35 B3
Bow Lane East	36 D3[37]
Bow Lane West	35 B3
Bow Street	35 C2
Boyne Court	35 C4[31]
Boyne Lane	36 E3 [2]
Boyne Road	20 E3
Boyne Street	36 E3
Brabazon Cottages	57 C2[16]
Brabazon Place	35 C3[35]
Brabazon Row	35 C3[18]
Brabazon Square	35 C3[40]
Brabazon Street	35 C3[17]
Bracken Drive	4 D4
Bracken Road	52 D2
Bracken's Lane	36 E2[28]
Brackenbush Park	54 D4
Brackenbush Road	54 D4
Brackenstown Avenue	1 C2
Brackenstown Road	1 C2
Braemor Avenue	43 A3
Braemor Drive	43 A3
Braemor Grove	43 A3
Braemor Park	43 A3
Braemor Road	43 A3
Braithwaite Street	35 C3
Bramley Avenue	18 E3
Bramley Court	18 E3
Bramley Crescent	18 E3
Bramley Garth	18 E3
Bramley Green	18 E3
Bramley Grove	18 E3
Bramley Heath	18 E3
Bramley Park	18 E3
Bramley Road	18 E3
Bramley View	18 E3
Bramley Walk	18 E3
Bramley Way	18 E3
1 Branch Road North	37 A2
1 Branch Road South	37 A2
2 Branch Road North	37 B2
2 Branch Road South	37 A2
3 Branch Road South	37 A2
2 Branch Road North Extension	37 B1
4 Branch Road South	37 B2
Brandon Road	41 C1
Brandon Terrace	35 B3[32]
Bray	58 D2
Bray Commons	57 B2
Bray Head Terrace	57 C3[20]
Bray Road	53 B2
Bray Road	53 C4
Bray Southern Cross Route	57 B4
Breakwater Road North	37 B2
Breakwater Road South	37 B2
Breffni Gardens	13 A4 [5]
Breffni Road	54 E1
Bregia Road	20 F4
Bremen Avenue	37 A3
Bremen Grove	37 A3
Bremen Road	37 A3
Brendan Behan Court	36 E1[33]
Brendan Road	43 C1
Brennan's Cottages (Synge Street)	36 D4
Brennans Parade	57 C2 [8]
Brennans Terrace	58 D2 [4]
Brennanstown Road	53 B4
Brennanstown Vale	53 B4
Brewery Road	52 F2
Brian Avenue	21 C4
Brian Boru Avenue	37 C1
Brian Boru Street	37 C1
Brian Road	21 C4
Brian Terrace	21 C4
Briansboro Terrace	35 C4[23]
Briar Walk	4 D4
Briarfield Grove	23 B1
Briarfield Road	23 B2
Briarfield Villas	23 B1
Briarly Court	43 B4 [4]
Briarwood Avenue	18 D1
Briarwood Close	18 D1
Briarwood Gardens	18 D1
Briarwood Green	18 D1
Briarwood Lawn	18 D1
Briarwood Park	18 D1 [2]

STREET NAME	PAGE/GRID REFERENCE
Briarwood Road	18 D1 [4]
Brickfield	57 B3
Brickfield Drive	35 B4
Brickfield Lane	35 C3[48]
*Bride Close (off Bride Street)	36 D3
Bride Road	36 D3
Bride Street	36 D3
Bride Street New	36 D3
Brides Glen	55 C2
Bridge Street	2 D2
Bridge Street	35 C2
Bridge Street	37 A3
Bridge Street Lower	35 C2
Bridge Street Upper	35 C3
Bridgefoot Street	35 C2
Bridgewater Quay	35 A2
Brighton Avenue	53 A4
Brighton Avenue (Clontarf)	22 D4 [1]
Brighton Avenue (Monkstown)	45 B4
Brighton Avenue (Rathgar)	42 F2
Brighton Cottages	53 A3 [1]
Brighton Court	53 A4
Brighton Gardens	42 F2
Brighton Road (Foxrock)	53 A3
Brighton Road (Terenure)	42 F2
Brighton Square	42 F2
Brighton Terrace	45 B4 [9]
Brighton Terrace (Dun Laoghaire)	54 E1[13]
Brighton Vale	45 B3
Britain Place	36 D1[47]
Britain Quay	36 F2
Broadford Avenue	51 B2
Broadford Close	51 B2
Broadford Crescent	51 B2
Broadford Drive	51 B2
Broadford Hill	51 B2
Broadford Lawn	51 B2
Broadford Park	51 B2
Broadford Rise	51 B2
Broadford Road	51 B2
Broadford Walk	51 B1
Broadmeadow	1 C1
*Broadstone Avenue (off Royal Canal Bank)	36 D1
*Broadstone Place (off Royal Canal Bank)	36 D1
Broadway Drive	18 E2
Broadway Grove	18 E2
Broadway Park	18 E2
Broadway Road	18 E2
Brodin Row	35 B2[13]
Brompton Court	18 E3
Brompton Green	18 E2
Brompton Grove	18 E2
Brompton Lawn	18 E2
Brook Court	45 B4
Brookdale	49 A2
Brookdale Avenue	1 B3
Brookdale Close	1 B3
Brookdale Court	1 B3
Brookdale Drive	1 B2
Brookdale Green	1 B2
Brookdale Grove	1 B2
Brookdale Lawns	1 B2
Brookdale Park	1 B2
Brookdale Road	1 B2
Brookdale Walk	1 B2
Brookdale Way	1 B2
Brookdene	56 E2
Brookfield	43 C1[19]
Brookfield (Blackrock)	44 F3
Brookfield (Coolock)	22 F2
Brookfield (Milltown)	43 B2
Brookfield Avenue	45 A4
Brookfield Avenue	58 D3 [4]
Brookfield Court	42 E2 [6]
Brookfield Estate	42 E2
Brookfield Green	42 E2 [5]
Brookfield Place	45 A4
Brookfield Road (Kilmainham)	35 B3
Brookfield Road (Tallaght)	48 D1
Brookfield Street	35 B3
Brookfield Terrace	45 A4
Brookhaven Drive	18 E1
Brookhaven Grove	18 E1
Brookhaven Lawn	18 E1
Brookhaven Park	18 E1
Brookhaven Rise	18 E1
Brooklands	44 E1
Brooklawn (Blackrock)	44 F3
Brooklawn (Clontarf)	22 D4 [5]
Brooklawn Avenue	45 B4[12]
Brooklawn Wood	45 B4[13]

STREET NAME	PAGE/GRID REFERENCE
Brookmount Avenue	41 C4
Brookmount Lawn	49 C1 [1]
Brookstone Lane	13 A4 [6]
Brookstone Road	13 A4
Brookvale	32 D1 [8]
Brookvale Downs	42 F3
Brookvale Road (Donnybrook)	43 C1 [8]
Brookvale Road (Rathfarnham)	42 F3
Brookview Avenue	48 D1
Brookview Close	48 D1
Brookview Crescent	48 D1
Brookview Drive	48 D1
Brookview Gardens	48 D1
Brookview Green	48 D1
Brookview Grove	48 D1
Brookview Lawns	48 D1
Brookview Park	48 D1
Brookview Terrace	48 D1
Brookview Way	48 D1
Brookville	20 D1
Brookville Crescent	22 E1 [2]
Brookville Park (Artane)	22 E2
Brookville Park (Coolock)	22 E1
Brookville Park (Dean's Grange)	53 B1
Brookwood	50 E2
Brookwood Avenue	22 E2
Brookwood Crescent	22 F2
Brookwood Drive	22 E2
Brookwood Glen	22 F3
Brookwood Grove	22 E2
Brookwood Heights	22 F2
Brookwood Lawn	22 F2
Brookwood Meadow	22 E2
Brookwood Park	22 E3
Brookwood Rise	22 F3
Brookwood Road	22 E2
Broombridge Road	20 E4
Broomfield	3 B4
Broomhill Road	41 A4
*Broomhill Terrace	41 A4
Brown Street North	35 C2 [5]
Brown Street South	35 C3
Brunswick Place	36 F3[22]
Brunswick Street North	35 C2
Brunswick Villas (Pearse Street)	36 E2[30]
Brusna Cottages	45 A3[12]
Buckingham Place	36 E1[12]
Buckingham St. Lower	36 E1
Buckingham St. Upper	36 E1
Buckingham Terrace	36 E1[56]
Buckleys Lane	31 A1
Bulfin Gardens	35 A3
Bulfin Road	35 A3
Bull Alley Street	36 D3
*Bull Lane (Off Main Street)	57 C2
Bull Wall Cottages	38 D1
Bullock Steps	54 F1 [8]
Bunratty Avenue	22 E1
Bunratty Drive	22 E1
Bunratty Road	22 E1
Bunting Road	41 C1
Burdett Avenue	54 E1
Burgess Lane	35 C2[18]
Burgh Quay	36 E2
*Burke Place (off Mount Brown)	35 B3
Burleigh Court	36 E4[34]
Burlington Gardens	36 E4[33]
Burlington Road	36 E4
Burmah Close	54 F2[22]
Burnell Park Avenue	18 E4
Burnell Park Green	18 E4
Burren Court	9 C4
*Burris Court (off High Street)	36 D3
Burrow Court	13 A1
Burrow Road (Stepaside)	52 D4
Burrow Road (Sutton)	25 B1
Burrowfield Road	24 D1
Burton Hall Avenue	52 E2
Burton Hall Road	52 E2
Burton Road	54 F2
Bushfield Avenue	43 B1 [8]
Bushfield Park	40 D3
Bushfield Place	43 B1[17]
Bushfield Square	21 C4[15]
Bushfield Terrace	43 B1
Bushy Park Gardens	42 F3
Bushy Park Road	42 F3
Buttercup Close	11 C4
Buttercup Drive	11 C4
Buttercup Park	11 C4
Buttercup Square	11 C4
Butterfield Avenue	42 E4
Butterfield Close	42 E4
Butterfield Court	42 F4
Butterfield Crescent	42 F4

STREET NAME	PAGE/GRID REFERENCE
Butterfield Drive	42 F4
Butterfield Grove	42 E4
Butterfield Orchard	42 E4
Butterfield Park	42 E4
*Byrne's Cottages (Francis Street)	35 C3
Byrne's Lane (Jervis St.)	36 D2[31]
*Byrne's Lane (Pearse Sq. West)	36 F2

C

STREET NAME	PAGE/GRID REFERENCE
CABINTEELY	53 C4
Cabinteely Avenue	53 C3
Cabinteely Bypass	53 C3
Cabinteely Close	53 C3
Cabinteely Court	53 C3 [4]
Cabinteely Crescent	53 C3
Cabinteely Drive	53 C3
Cabinteely Green	53 C3
Cabinteely Grove	53 C3
Cabinteely Park	53 C3 [2]
Cabinteely Way	53 C3
Cabra	20 E3
Cabra Drive	35 B1
Cabra Grove	35 E2
Cabra Park	20 F4
Cabra Road	35 B1
Cadogan Road	21 C4
Cairn Court	10 D4
Cairn Hill	53 B2
Cairnwood Avenue	40 E4
Cairnwood Court	40 E4
Cairnwood Green	40 E4
Calderwood Avenue	21 C3
Calderwood Grove	21 C3 [3]
Calderwood Road	21 C3
Caledon Road	36 F1
Callary Road	44 D3
Camac Close	35 A3 [6]
Camac Court	35 A3[10]
Camac Park	34 E4
Camac Terrace	35 B3
Camac View (Bow Bridge)	35 B3
Camaderry Road	58 D3
Camberley	43 B4
Camberley Oaks	43 B4
Cambridge Avenue	37 A3 [7]
Cambridge Court	37 A3[24]
Cambridge Road (Rathmines)	43 A1
Cambridge Road (Ringsend)	37 A3
Cambridge Street	37 A3 [1]
Cambridge Terrace (Dun Laoghaire)	45 C4[24]
Cambridge Terrace (Ranelagh)	36 E4 [7]
Cambridge Villas	43 A1[16]
Camden Buildings	36 D4[30]
Camden Court	36 D4[31]
Camden Lock	36 F3[39]
Camden Market	36 D4[28]
Camden Place	36 D3
Camden Row	36 D3
Camden Street Lower	36 D3
Camden Street Upper	36 D4
Camden Villas	36 D3[22]
Cameron Square	35 B3 [5]
Cameron Street	35 C3
Camogie Road	35 A2
Campbell's Court	36 D2[34]
*Campbell's Lane (off Belvidere Ave.)	36 E1
*Campbell's Row (off Portland Street N.)	36 E1
Campfield Terrace	51 C1
Canal Road	36 D4
Canal Terrace	34 E4
Canal Turn	33 B4
Cannon Rock View	26 E2 [1]
Cannonbrook Park	32 D2
Canon Lillis Avenue	36 F1
Canon Mooney Gardens	37 A3[15]
Canonbrook Avenue	32 D2
Canonbrook Court	32 D2
Capel Street	36 D2
Cappagh Avenue	20 D1
Cappagh Drive	20 D1
Cappagh Green	20 D1
Cappagh Road	20 D1
Cappaghmore Estate	33 A4
Cappoge Cottages	8 E4
Captain's Avenue	42 D1
Captain's Drive	42 D2
Captain's Hill	16 D4
Captain's Road	42 D1
Car Ferry Terminal	37 C2
Cara Park	11 B3

STREET NAME	PAGE/GRID REFERENCE	STREET NAME	PAGE/GRID REFERENCE	STREET NAME	PAGE/GRID REFERENCE	STREET NAME	PAGE/GRID REFERENCE
Caragh Court	21 C4[12]	Casana View	26 E2	Castlegrange Road	2 D1	Celbridge Abbey	29 C4
Caragh Road	35 B1	*Casement Close	20 D1	Castlegrange Way	2 D1	Celbridge Road (Leixlip)	30 F1
Carberry Road	21 C3	(off Barry Road)		Castlekevin Road	22 D1	Celbridge Road (Lucan)	31 A2
Carbury Place	45 A3[20]	Casement Drive	20 D1	Castleknock	18 F3	Celtic Park Avenue	21 C2
Carbury Terrace	36 F2 [9]	Casement Green	20 D1	Castleknock Avenue	18 F3	Celtic Park Road	21 C3
Card's Lane (Pearse St.)	36 E2[13]	Casement Grove	20 D1	Castleknock Brook	18 F3	Chalet Gardens	32 E1
Cardiff Castle Road	20 D2	Casement Park	20 D1	Castleknock Close	18 E3	Chalfont Avenue	3 B2
Cardiff Lane	36 F2	Casement Road	20 D1	Castleknock Court	18 F3 [2]	Chalfont Park	3 B2
Cardiffs Bridge	20 D3	Casement Road	20 D2	Castleknock Crescent	18 F3	Chalfont Place	3 B2
Cardiffsbridge Avenue	20 D2	Casement Villas	53 B1	Castleknock Dale	18 F3	Chalfont Road	3 A2
Cardiffsbridge Grove	20 D1 [1]	Cashel Avenue	42 E2	Castleknock Downs	18 E3	*Chamber Court (Chamber St)	35 C3
Cardiffsbridge Road	20 D2	Cashel Road	42 D1	Castleknock Drive	18 F3	Chamber Street	35 C3
Careys Lane	2 F4	Casimir Avenue	42 F1	Castleknock Elms	18 F3	Champions Avenue	36 E2[32]
Carleton Road	21 C4	*Casimir Court	42 F1	Castleknock Gate	19 B4 [1]	Chancery Lane	36 D3
Carlingford Parade	36 F3 [4]	(off Casimir Avenue)		Castleknock Glade	18 F3	Chancery Place	36 D2
Carlingford Road	21 A4	Casimir Road	42 F1	Castleknock Grange	18 E3	Chancery Street	36 D2
Carlisle Avenue	43 B1	Casino Park	22 D3	Castleknock Green	19 A3	Chanel Avenue	22 E2
Carlisle Street	36 D4	Casino Road	21 C4	Castleknock Grove	18 F3	Chanel Grove	22 E1
Carlisle Terrace (Malahide)	3 B3	Castilla Park	22 F4	Castleknock Laurels	18 F3	Chanel Road	22 E2
*Carlisle Terrace (Off N.C. Rd.)	35 C1	Castle Avenue (Clondalkin)	40 E1	Castleknock Lodge	19 A4	*Chapel Avenue (off Bath St.)	37 A3
*Carlisle Terrace	57 C2	Castle Avenue (Clontarf)	22 E4	Castleknock Meadows	18 F3	Chapel Lane	57 B1
(On Seymour Road)		Castle Avenue (Swords)	2 D2	Castleknock Oaks	18 F3	Chapel Lane (Parnell Street)	36 D2[1]
*Carlisle Terrace	54 D1	Castle Close (Clondalkin)	40 E1	Castleknock Park	19 A3	Chapel Lane (Swords)	2 D2
(on Tivoli Road)		Castle Close (Dalkey)	54 F1	Castleknock Parklands	18 F3	Chapel Road	12 D1
Carlton Court	2 D2	Castle Court	43 A4 [1]	Castleknock Pines Lower	19 A3 [3]	Chapelizod	34 E2
Carlton Court	22 D4	Castle Court	56 E1	Castleknock Pines Upper	19 A3	Chapelizod Bypass	34 E2
Carlton Terrace	57 C2[41]	Castle Court (Booterstown)	44 F2	Castleknock Rise	18 E3	Chapelizod Court	34 E2
Carlton Villas	36 F4 [6]	Castle Court (Clontarf)	22 D4	Castleknock Road	19 A3	Chapelizod Hill Road	34 D2
Carlton Villas	57 C2[42]	Castle Court (Dundrum)	51 C1	Castleknock Vale	18 E3	Chapelizod Road	34 F2
Carman's Hall	35 C3	*Castle Court	42 D4	Castleknock View	18 F3	Charlemont	21 C3
Carmanhall Road	52 E2	(off Cypress Lawn)		Castleknock Walk	18 E3	Charlemont Avenue	46 D4 [5]
Carna Road	33 C3	Castle Cove	3 A2	Castleknock Way	18 F3	Charlemont Gardens	36 D4[20]
Carndonagh Drive	23 B1	Castle Cove	54 F2[32]	Castleknock Wood	18 F3	Charlemont Mall	36 D4
Carndonagh Lawn	23 B1	Castle Crescent	40 E1 [4]	Castlelands	54 F1[16]	Charlemont Parade	36 E1 [5]
Carndonagh Park	23 B1	Castle Down Croft	2 F2	Castlelands Grove	54 F1[12]	Charlemont Place	36 E4
Carndonagh Road	23 B1	Castle Down Grove	2 F2	Castlepark	31 A1	Charlemont Road	22 D4
Carne Court	6 F4	Castle Down Road	2 F2	Castlepark Road	54 E1	Charlemont Street	36 D4
Carnew Street	35 B1 [9]	Castle Drive	40 E1	Castleside Drive	42 F3	Charlemont Terrace	46 D4[18]
Carnlough Road	20 E4	Castle Drive (Swords)	2 D2	Castlethorn	44 F4	Charles Lane	36 E1
Caroline Row	37 A3[16]	Castle Grove (Clondalkin)	40 E1	Castletimon Avenue	21 C1	Charles Sheils Houses	52 F2
Carpenterstown	18 D4	Castle Grove (Clontarf)	22 E4	Castletimon Drive	21 C1	Charles Street Great	36 E1
Carpenterstown Avenue	18 E3	Castle Grove (Swords)	2 D2	Castletimon Gardens	21 C1	*Charles Street West	36 D2
Carpenterstown Park East	18 E3	Castle Lawns	2 F2	Castletimon Green	21 C1	(off Ormond Quay Upper)	
Carpenterstown Road	18 E4	Castle Lawns	41 B4	Castletimon Park	21 C1	Charleston Avenue	43 B1
Carraig Glen	53 C4	*Castle Market (off Drury Street)	36 D3	Castletimon Road	21 C1	Charleston Court Flats	43 B1 [9]
Carraroe Avenue	23 A1	Castle Park (Clondalkin)	40 E1	Castletown	30 F1	Charleston Road	43 B1
Carrick Court	12 F1	Castle Park (Monkstown)	45 C4	Castletown Court	30 D3 [2]	Charleville	43 B4
Carrick Lawn	52 D1 [2]	Castle Park (Swords)	2 D2	Castletown Grove	30 D3	Charleville Avenue	36 E1
Carrick Terrace	35 B3[29]	Castle Park Estate (Tallaght)	41 B4	Castletown Lawn	30 D3	Charleville Mall	36 E1
Carrickbrack Heath	25 B2	*Castle Place (on Breffni Road)	54 F1	Castleview	22 E2	*Charleville Road	35 C1
Carrickbrack Hill	25 B2	Castle Road	22 E4	Castleview	5 B3	(Phibsborough)	
Carrickbrack Lawn	25 B2	Castle Rosse	12 F4	Castleview Park	3 A3	Charleville Road (Rathmines)	43 A1
Carrickbrack Park	25 B2	*Castle Steps (off Castle St.)	36 D3	Castlewood	17 C1	*Charleville Terrace	35 C1
Carrickbrack Road	25 B2	Castle Street	57 C2	Castlewood Avenue	43 A1	(on Charleville Rd)	
Carrickbrennan Lawn	45 C4	Castle Street (Cork Hill)	36 D3 [3]	*Castlewood Close	43 A1	Charlotte Quay	36 F3
Carrickbrennan Road	45 C4	Castle Street (Dalkey)	54 F2	(on Castlewood Ave.)		Charlotte Terrace	54 F2[18]
Carrickfoyle Terrace	35 A3[15]	Castle Terrace	3 B2	Castlewood Park	43 A1	Charlotte Way	36 D4[32]
Carrickhill Close	4 D4	Castle Terrace	35 C1[17]	Castlewood Place	43 A1 [6]	Charlton Lawn	44 D4
Carrickhill Drive	13 A1	(Phibsborough Ave.)		Castlewood Terrace	43 A1 [5]	Charnwood	57 C3
Carrickhill Heights	13 A1	Castle Terrace	54 F1	Cathal Brugha Street	36 D2	*Chatham Court	36 D3
Carrickhill Rise	4 D4	(off Ulverton Road)		Cathedral Lane	36 D3 [5]	(on Chatham Street)	
Carrickhill Road	13 A4	*Castle Terrace(off Castle Street)	57 C2	Cathedral Street	36 D2[18]	*Chatham Lane	36 D3
Carrickhill Road Middle	13 A1	Castle View	40 E1	Cathedral View Court	36 D3[43]	(off Chatham Street)	
Carrickhill Road Upper	3 C4	Castle Village	29 C2	Cathedral View Walk	36 D3[44]	Chatham Row	36 D3[35]
Carrickhill Walk	4 D4	Castle Village Avenue	29 C2	*Catherine Court	36 E1	Chatham Street	36 D3
Carrickmines	53 B4	Castle Village Close	29 C2	(off William Street N.)		*Chaworth Terrace	35 C3
Carrickmines Little	53 A4	Castle Village Court	29 C2	Catherine Lane	35 C3[22]	(Hanbury Lane)	
Carrickmount Avenue	51 B1	Castle Village Crescent	29 C2	Catherine Street (Swift's Alley)	35 C3[45]	Cheeverstown Road	48 D1
Carrickmount Drive	51 A1	Castle Village Drive	29 C2	Cats Ladder	54 F2 [5]	Chelmsford Avenue	36 E4 [8]
Carrig Road	9 C4	Castle Village Lawns	29 C2	Causeway Road	23 B3	Chelmsford Lane	43 B1[15]
Carrigallen Drive	20 E3	Castle Village Park	29 C2	Cave's Strand	3 A2	Chelmsford Road	43 B1
Carrigallen Park	20 E3	Castle Village Rise	29 C2	Cavendish Row	36 D1[21]	Chelsea Gardens	22 F4
Carrigallen Road	20 E3	Castle Village Walk	29 C2	Ceanchor Road	26 D4	Cheltenham Place	36 D4[13]
Carriglea Avenue	49 B2	Castle Village Way	29 C2	*Ceannt Fort (off Mount Brown)	35 B3	Cherbury Court	44 F3
Carriglea Avenue	53 C2	Castle Village Woods	29 C2	Cecil Avenue	22 D4	Cherbury Gardens	44 F3
Carriglea Court	49 B2	Castlebrook	51 C1	*Cecilia Street (off Temple Bar)	36 D2	Cherbury Mews	44 F3 [4]
Carriglea Downs	53 C2	Castlebyrne Park	45 A4	Cedar Avenue	41 A3	Cherbury Park Avenue	32 D2
Carriglea Drive	49 B2	Castledawson Avenue	44 F3	Cedar Court	42 F2	Cherbury Park Road	32 D2
Carriglea Gardens	53 C1	Castlefarm	1 C1	Cedar Court	56 D1	Cherries	52 D2
Carriglea Grove	49 B2	Castlefarm	56 E3	Cedar Drive	33 B2	Cherrington Close	56 E3
Carriglea Rise	49 B2	Castlefield Avenue	49 C1	Cedar Hall	43 C1[16]	Cherrington Drive	56 E3
Carriglea View	49 B2	Castlefield Court	49 C1	Cedar Park	15 C4	Cherrington Road	56 E3
Carriglea Walk	49 B2	Castlefield Drive	49 C2	Cedar Park	23 A1	Cherry Avenue	18 E3
Carrigmore Drive	48 F2	Castlefield Green	49 C2	Cedar Square	44 F4 [4]	Cherry Avenue (Swords)	1 C3
Carrigmore Park	48 F3	Castlefield Grove	49 C2	Cedar Walk	23 B2	Cherry Court	42 F2
Carrigmore Road	48 F2	Castlefield Lawn	49 C2	Cedarmount Road	44 E4	Cherry Court	56 D1 [2]
Carrigwood	49 C2	Castlefield Manor	3 B3	Cedarwood	30 D3	Cherry Drive	18 E3
Carrow Road	34 F4	Castlefield Manor (Firhouse)	49 C1	Cedarwood Avenue	20 F1	Cherry Garth	44 E4
Carysfort Park	45 A4	Castlefield Way	49 C2	Cedarwood Close	20 F1	Cherry Garth (Swords)	1 B2
Carysfort Avenue	45 A4	Castlefield Park	49 C2	Cedarwood Green	20 F1	Cherry Grove	41 C2
Carysfort Downs	52 F1	Castleforbes Road	36 F2	Cedarwood Grove	20 F1	Cherry Grove (Swords)	1 B3
Carysfort Drive	54 F1 [1]	Castlegrange Avenue	2 D1	Cedarwood Park	20 F1	Cherry Lawn	18 E3
Carysfort Hall	45 A4	Castlegrange Close	2 D1	Cedarwood Rise	20 F1	Cherry Lawns	31 C2
Carysfort Road	54 F1	Castlegrange Heights	2 D1	Cedarwood Road	20 F1	Cherry Orchard Avenue	33 C3
		Castlegrange Hill	2 D1	Celbridge	30 D3	Cherry Orchard Crescent	33 C4

STREET NAME	PAGE/GRID REFERENCE
Cherry Orchard Drive	34 D3
Cherry Orchard Green	33 C3
Cherry Orchard Grove	33 C4
Cherry Park	18 E3
Cherry Park (Swords)	1B3
Cherry Tree Drive	57 C4 [1]
Cherry Wood	56 D1
Cherryfield Avenue	41 C2
Cherryfield Avenue Lr.	43 B1
Cherryfield Avenue Upr.	43 B1
Cherryfield Close	17 B1
Cherryfield Court	17 B1
Cherryfield Drive	41 C2
Cherryfield Lawn	17 C1
Cherryfield Park	17 C1
Cherryfield Road	41 C2
Cherryfield View	17 B1
Cherryfield Walk	17 B1
Cherrymount Crescent	22 D3 [1]
Cherrymount Grove	22 D3 [2]
Cherrymount Park	35 C1 [3]
Cherrywood	30 D3 [3]
Cherrywood Avenue	40 D1
Cherrywood Crescent	39 C1
Cherrywood Drive	39 C1
Cherrywood Grove	40 D1
Cherrywood Lawn	39 C2
Cherrywood Park	39 C2
Cherrywood Park	56 D1
Cherrywood Road	56 D2
Cherrywood Villas	40 D1
Chester Road	43 B1
Chester Square	54 E1 [23]
Chesterfield Avenue	19 B4
Chesterfield Avenue	34 F1
(Phoenix Park)	
Chesterfield Close	19 B4
Chesterfield Copse	19 B3
Chesterfield Grove	19 B4
Chesterfield Park	19 B3
Chesterfield View	19 B3
Chestnut Grove (Ballinteer)	51 B2
Chestnut Grove (Celbridge)	30 D3
Chestnut Grove (Clondalkin)	40 F3
Chestnut Grove (Dunboyne)	5 B3
Chestnut Park	53 A2 [5]
Chestnut Road (Clondalkin)	41 A1
Chestnut Road (Mount Merrion)	44 E3
Christchurch Place	36 D3
Christchurch Square	36 D3 [51]
Church Avenue	42 F1
Church Avenue (Blanchardstown)	18 F2
Church Avenue (Glasnevin)	21 A3 [2]
Church Avenue (Irishtown)	37 A3
Church Avenue (Killiney)	54 E4
Church Avenue (Rathmines)	43 A1
Church Avenue North	21 B3
(Drumcondra)	
Church Avenue South	35 B3 [22]
(Dolphin's Barn)	
Church Avenue West	35 C2 [25]
(Church Street)	
*Church Avenue	36 F2
(off Irvine Street)	
Church Court	18 F3
Church Drive	42 F1
Church Gardens	43 A1
Church Green	42 F1
Church Grove	48 F2
Church Lands	57 C3
Church Lane (College Green)	36 D2 [41]
Church Lane (Rathfarnham)	42 F3
*Church Lane South	36 D3
(off Kevin Street)	
Church Lawn	42 F1
Church Park Court	42 F1
Church Park Court	42 F1
*Church Place	36 F2
(off Irvine Terrace)	
Church Road	2 D2
Church Road (Bray)	57 B3
Church Road (Celbridge)	30 D4
Church Road (Dalkey)	54 F1
Church Road (East Wall)	36 F1
Church Road (Finglas)	20 D2
Church Road (Killiney)	54 D3
Church Road (Malahide)	3 B3
Church Road (Mulhuddart)	7 A4
Church Road (Sutton)	25 B1
Church Street	35 C2
Church Street (Finglas)	20 E2
Church Street (Howth)	26 D1
Church Street East	36 F2
Church Street New	35 C2 [11]

STREET NAME	PAGE/GRID REFERENCE
Church Street Upper	35 C2
Church Terrace	57 C2 [45]
*Church Terrace	35 C2
(off Church Street)	
Church View (Clondalkin)	40 D2 [1]
Church View (Finglas)	20 D2 [7]
Church View (Harold's Cross)	42 F1
Church Way	42 F1
Churchfields	43 C2
Churchgate Avenue	37 C1 [1]
Churchill Terrace	37 A4 [6]
Churchtown	43 B4
Churchtown Avenue	43 B3
Churchtown Close	43 B3
Churchtown Drive	43 B3
Churchtown Road	43 A4
Churchtown Road Lower	43 B3
Churchtown Road Upper	43 B4
Churchview Avenue	54 D3
Churchview Drive	54 D3
Churchview Park	54 D3
Churchview Road	54 D3
Cian Park	21 B4 [4]
Cianlea	1 B1
Cill Cais	48 F2
Cill Eanna	22 F2
Cill Manntan Park	57 C2 [9]
Cill Sarain	57 A3
City Quay	36 E2
Claddagh Green	33 C3
Claddagh Road	33 C3
*Claddagh Terrace	57 C2
(On Albert Avenue)	
Clanawley Road	22 E3
Clanboy Road	22 E3
Clanbrassil Close	35 C4 [17]
Clanbrassil Street Lower	35 C4
Clanbrassil Street Upper	35 C4
Clancarthy Road	22 D3
Clancy Avenue	20 E1
Clancy Road	20 E1
Clandonagh Road	22 D3
Clane Road	29 B4
Clanhugh Road	22 E3
Clanmahon Road	22 E3
Clanmaurice Road	22 D3
Clanmawr	56 E2
Clanmoyle Road	22 D3
Clanranald Road	22 D3
Clanree Road	22 D3
Clanwilliam Place	36 F3
Clanwilliam Square	36 F3 [41]
Clanwilliam Terrace	36 F3 [40]
Clare Hall	12 D4
Clare Lane	36 E3 [14]
Clare Park Villas	21 B3 [3]
Clare Road	21 B3
Clare Street	36 E3
Claremont Avenue	21 A3 [1]
Claremont Close	20 F4
Claremont Court	20 F3
Claremont Court	37 A4 [21]
Claremont Crescent	20 F4
Claremont Drive	20 F2
Claremont Grove	54 E3
Claremont Lawn	20 F4
Claremont Park	37 A4
Claremont Road (Killiney)	54 E3
Claremont Road (Sandymount)	37 A4
Claremont Road (Sutton)	25 B1
Claremont Terrace	43 C4 [7]
Claremont Villas	54 E1 [4]
Claremount Pines	53 B4
Claremount Terrace	57 C2 [32]
Clarence Mangan Road	35 C3
*Clarence Mangan Square	36 D3
(off John Dillon St.)	
Clarence Place Great	36 F3 [1]
Clarence St. Great Nth.	36 E1
Clarence Street	45 C4 [12]
*Clarendon Market	36 E1
(off William St.)	
*Clarendon Row	36 D3
(off King St. South)	
Clarendon Street	36 D3
Clareville Court	20 F4 [7]
Clareville Grove	20 F4
Clareville Road	42 F1
Clarinda Park East	54 D1
Clarinda Park North	46 D4
Clarinda Park West	46 D4
Clarke Terrace	35 B3 [16]
Clarkeville Terrace	33 C1 [3]
Claude Road	21 A4
Clayton Terrace	34 E2 [8]

STREET NAME	PAGE/GRID REFERENCE
Cleggan Avenue	33 C3
Cleggan Park	33 C3
Cleggan Road	33 C3
Clifden Drive	33 C3
Clifden Road	34 D3
Cliff Terrace	54 E1 [18]
Clifton Avenue	45 C4 [11]
Clifton Lane	45 C4 [10]
Clifton Park	56 E2
Clifton Terrace	45 C4 [13]
Cliftonville Road	21 A4
Clinch's Court	36 E1 [7]
Clogher Road	42 E1
Cloghran	1 C4
Cloister Avenue	45 A4
Cloister Gate	45 A4
Cloister Green	45 A4
Cloister Grove	45 A4
Cloister Park	45 A4
Cloister Square	45 A4
Cloister Way	45 A4
Clonard Avenue	51 C2
Clonard Close	51 C2
Clonard Drive	51 C2
Clonard Grove	51 C2
Clonard Lawn	51 C2
Clonard Park	51 C2
Clonard Road (Crumlin)	42 D1
Clonard Road (Sandyford)	51 C2
Clonasleigh	56 E2 [2]
Clondalkin	40 D1
Clonee	6 D3
Clonfert Road	42 E1
Clonkeen Crescent	53 B2
Clonkeen Drive	53 B2
Clonkeen Grove	53 B2
Clonkeen Lawn	53 B3 [5]
Clonkeen Road	53 B2
Clonlara Road	37 A3 [12]
Clonlea	51 C2
Clonlea Wood	51 C2 [1]
Clonliffe Avenue	36 E1
Clonliffe Gardens	21 B4
Clonliffe Road	21 B4
Clonmacnoise Grove	42 E1 [4]
Clonmacnoise Road	42 E1
Clonmel Road	21 A2
Clonmel Street	36 D3 [18]
Clonmellon Grove	12 D4 [3]
Clonmore Court	21 A3 [11]
Clonmore Road (Ballybough)	36 E1
Clonmore Road (Goatstown)	44 E4
Clonmore Terrace	36 E1 [6]
Clonmore Villas	36 E1 [39]
Clonrosse Court	22 F1
Clonrosse Drive	22 F1
Clonrosse Park	22 F1
Clonshaugh Avenue	11 A4
Clonshaugh Close	11 B4
Clonshaugh Crescent	11 A4
Clonshaugh Drive	11 B4
Clonshaugh Green	11 B4
Clonshaugh Grove	11 B4 [1]
Clonshaugh Heights	11 A4
Clonshaugh Lawns	11 B4
Clonshaugh Meadow	11 A4
Clonshaugh Park	11 B4
Clonshaugh Rise	11 B4 [2]
Clonshaugh Road	11 A4
Clonshaugh Walk	11 B4
Clonsilla	17 C2
Clonsilla Close	18 E2
Clonsilla Park	18 E2
Clonsilla Road	18 E2
Clonskeagh	43 C2
Clonskeagh Drive	43 C2 [6]
Clonskeagh Road	43 C2
Clonskeagh Square	43 C2 [7]
Clontarf	37 C1
Clontarf Park	37 C1
Clontarf Road	22 D4
Clonturk Avenue	21 B3 [1]
Clonturk Gardens	21 B4 [3]
Clonturk Park	21 B4
Cloonlara Crescent	20 E4
Cloonlara Drive	20 E2
Cloonlara Road	20 E2
Cloonmore Avenue	48 D2
Cloonmore Close	48 D2
Cloonmore Crescent	48 D2
Cloonmore Drive	48 D2
Cloonmore Gardens	48 D2
Cloonmore Green	48 D2
Cloonmore Grove	48 D2
Cloonmore Lawns	48 D2

STREET NAME	PAGE/GRID REFERENCE
Cloonmore Park	48 D2
Cloonmore Road	48 D2
Cloragh Road	50 E4
Clover Hill	57 A3
Clover Hill Drive	34 D3
Clover Hill Road	34 D4
Cloverhill Road	33 A4
Cloyne Road	42 E1 [2]
Cluain Mhuire	45 B4
(Newtown Park Avenue)	
Club Road	41 A1
Clune Road	20 E1
Cluny Grove	54 D3
Cluny Park	54 E2
Clyde Lane	36 F4
Clyde Road	36 F4
Coast Road (Malahide)	3 C2
Coburg Place	36 E1
*Coghill's Court	36 D2
(off Dame Street)	
Cois Coillte	56 D1 [3]
Cois Na Habhann	48 F2
*Coke Lane (off Arran Quay)	35 C2
Colbert's Fort Cottages	40 F4
*Colbert's Fort	35 B3
(off St. Jame's Walk)	
Coldcut Road	33 B2
Coldhurst Close	32 F2
Coldhurst Crescent	32 F2
Coldhurst Gardens	32 F2
Coldhurst Green	32 F2
Coldhurst Mews	32 F2
Coldhurst Park	32 F2
Coldhurst Road	32 F2
Coldhurst Rise	32 F2
Coldhurst Way	32 F2
Coldwell Street	54 D1
Colepark Avenue	34 D3
Colepark Drive	34 D3
Colepark Green	34 D3
Colepark Road	34 D3
Coleraine Street	36 D2
Coliemore Road	54 F2
Coliemore Villas	54 F2 [14]
College Crescent	42 D3
College Drive	42 E3
College Gate	18 F3
College Green	36 D2
College Grove	18 F4
College Lane	36 E3 [19]
College Manor	21 B4 [8]
College Mews	21 B4 [11]
College Park (Castleknock)	19 A4
College Park (Kimmage)	42 E3
College Park Avenue	51 C2
College Park Close	51 C2
College Park Court	51 C2
College Park Drive	51 C2
College Park Grove	51 C2
College Park Way	51 C2
College Road (Castleknock)	18 F4
College Road	51 A3
(Whitechurch Road)	
College Street	36 E2
College Street (Baldoyle)	13 A4
Collier's Avenue	43 B1 [3]
Collins Avenue	21 C2
Collins Avenue East	22 D3
Collins Avenue Extension	21 A2
Collins Avenue West	21 B2
Collins Court	21 C3 [6]
Collins Court	45 A3 [13]
Collins Drive	20 E1
Collins Green	20 E1
Collins Park	22 D3
Collins Place	20 E1
Collins Row	20 E2 [6]
Collinstown Crescent	33 A3 [1]
Collinstown Grove	33 B3
Collinstown Road	33 B3
Collinswood	21 C2
Comeragh Road	34 F4
Commons Road	40 D2
Commons Road	56 D2
Commons Street	36 E2
Comyn Place	21 A3 [5]
Con Colbert Road	35 A3
Confey	16 D4
Congress Gardens	54 E1 [2]
Congress Hall	5 B3
Congress Park	5 B3 [1]
Connaught Parade	20 F4 [6]
*Connaught Place	46 D4
(Crofton Road)	
Connaught Street	20 F4

STREET NAME	PAGE/GRID REFERENCE
Connawood Copse	57 B1
Connawood Crescent	57 B1
Connawood Drive	57 B1
Connawood Green	57 B1
Connawood Walk	57 B1
Connawood Way	57 B1
Connolly Avenue	3 A4
Connolly Avenue	35 A3
Connolly Gardens	35 A3 [3]
Conor Clune Road	19 C4
Conquer Hill Avenue	37 C1
Conquer Hill Road	37 C1
Constellation Road	10 F4
Constitution Hill	36 D1
Convent Avenue	21 B4
Convent Avenue	57 C3
Convent Close	36 E3 [40]
Convent Court	52 E1 [4]
Convent Lane	42 F4
Convent Place	36 E4 [12]
Convent Road (Blackrock)	45 A4
Convent Road (Clondalkin)	40 E2
Convent Road (Dalkey)	54 F2
Convent Road (Dun Laoghaire)	46 D4
Convent View Cottages	40 D2
Convent View Crescent	20 D4 [3]
Conway Court	36 F3 [23]
Conyngham Road	35 A2
Cook Street	35 C2
Cooks Road	1 A4
Cookstown Road	40 E4
Coolamber Court	50 D1 [1]
Coolamber Park	50 D1
Coolatree Close	21 C2
Coolatree Park	21 C2
Coolatree Road	21 C2
Cooldrinagh Lane	31 B1
Cooldrinagh Terrace	31 B1
Cooleen Avenue	21 C1
Coolevin (Ballybrack)	54 D4
Coolevin Lane	36 D3 [49]
Cooley Road	34 F4
Coolgariff Road	21 C1
Coolgreena Close	21 C2
Coolgreena Road	21 C1
Coolkill	52 D3
Coolmine Boulevard	18 E2
Coolmine Close	18 D2
Coolmine Cottages	7 A4
Coolmine Court	18 E2 [1]
Coolmine Green	18 D3
Coolmine Lawn	18 D2
Coolmine Mews	18 D2 [1]
Coolmine Park	18 E2
Coolmine Road	18 D3
Coolmine Woods	18 E2
Coolnevaun	52 E1
Coolock	22 E1
Coolock Drive	22 E1
Coolock Lane (Santry)	10 F4
Coolock Village	22 E1
Coolrua Drive	21 C1
Coombe Court	35 C3 [62]
Cope Street	36 D2 [22]
Copeland Avenue	22 D4
Copeland Grove	22 D4
*Copper Alley (off Lord Edward St.)	36 D3
Copper Beech Grove	57 B2 [6]
Coppinger Close	44 F4
Coppinger Glade	44 F4
Coppinger Row	36 D3 [34]
Coppinger Walk	45 A4
Coppinger Wood	44 F4
Corbally Avenue	47 C2
Corbally Close	47 C2
Corbally Court	48 D2
Corbally Drive	47 C2
Corbally Vale	47 C2
Corbally Way	47 C2
Corbawn Avenue	56 E2
Corbawn Close	56 E3
Corbawn Court	56 E2
Corbawn Dale	56 E2
Corbawn Drive	56 F2
Corbawn Glade	56 E3
Corbawn Grove	56 E2
Corbawn Lane	56 E2
Corbawn Lawn	56 E3
Corbawn Wood	56 E3
Corduff	18 F1
Corduff Avenue	18 F1
Corduff Close	18 F1
Corduff Cottages	18 E1
Corduff Crescent	18 F1
Corduff Gardens	18 F1
Corduff Green	18 F1
Corduff Grove	7 B4
Corduff Park	18 E1
Corduff Place	18 F1
Corduff Way	18 F1
*Cork Hill (off Dame St.)	36 D2
Cork Street	35 C3
Corkagh View	40 D2
Corke Abbey	57 C1
Corke Abbey Avenue	57 B1
Cormac Terrace	42 F2
Corn Exchange Place	36 E2 [24]
Cornelscourt	53 B3
Cornelscourt Hill Road	53 B3
Cornmarket	35 C3
Corporation Street	36 E2
*Corrbridge Terrace (off Claremont Road)	25 B1
Corrib Road	42 E2
Corrig Avenue	46 D4
Corrig Close	41 B3
Corrig Park	46 D4
Corrig Road (Dalkey)	54 F1
Corrig Road (Dun Laoghaire)	54 D1
Corrig Road (Stillorgan)	52 E2
Corrybeg	42 D4
Coulson Avenue	42 F2
Coultry Avenue	21 B1
Coultry Crescent	10 D4
Coultry Drive	10 D4
Coultry Gardens	10 D4
Coultry Grove	10 E4
Coultry Lawn	10 E4
Coultry Park	10 E4
Coultry Road	10 D4
Coultry Way	21 B1
Coundon Court	54 E4
Courthill Drive	5 B2
Courtlands	53 C3
Courtney Place	36 F1 [8]
Cow Parlour	35 C3 [24]
Cowbooter Lane	26 E2
Cowley Place Lower	36 D1 [37]
Cowley Place Upper	36 D1 [18]
Cowper Downs	43 A1
Cowper Drive	43 B2
Cowper Gardens	43 A2
Cowper Mews	43 A2 [4]
Cowper Road	43 B2
Cowper Street	35 B1
Cowper Village	43 A2
Crag Avenue	33 B4
Crag Crescent	33 B4
Crag Terrace	33 B4
Craigford Avenue	22 E3
Craigford Drive	22 E3
Craiglands	54 F2 [26]
Craigmore Gardens	45 A3 [5]
*Crampton Court (off Dame St.)	36 D2
Crampton Quay	36 D2 [40]
*Crane Lane (off Dame Street)	36 D2
Crane Street	35 C3
Cranfield Place	37 A3
Crannagh Castle	42 F3
Cranford Court	44 D2
Cranmer Lane	36 F3 [19]
Crannagh	43 C2 [9]
Crannagh Court	42 F3
Crannagh Grove	43 A3
Crannagh Park	42 F3
Crannagh Road	42 F3
Crannagh Way	43 A3 [8]
Crannogue Close	9 C4
Crannogue Road	9 C4
Crawford Avenue	21 A4
*Crawford Terrace (off Kings Avenue)	36 E1
Creighton Street	36 E2
Cremona Road	34 E3
Cremore Avenue	20 F3
Cremore Crescent	20 F3
Cremore Drive	20 F3
Cremore Heights	20 F2
Cremore Lawn	20 F3
Cremore Park	20 F3
Cremore Road	20 F3
Cremore Villas	20 F3 [5]
Cremorne	50 D1
Crescent Gardens	36 F1 [11]
Crescent House	22 D4 [6]
Crescent Place	22 D4
Crescent Villas	21 A4
Crestfield Avenue	21 B2
Crestfield Close	21 B2
Crestfield Drive	21 B2
Crestfield Park	21 B2
Crestfield Road	21 B2
Crinken Glen	56 D3
Crinken Lane	56 D4
Croaghpatrick Road	20 D4
Crodaun Forest Park	30 D2
Crofton Avenue	46 D4
*Crofton Mansions (Crofton Rd. Dun Laoghaire)	46 D4
Crofton Road	46 D4
Crofton Terrace	45 C4 [6]
Croftwood Crescent	33 C3
Croftwood Drive	33 C3
Croftwood Gardens	33 C3
Croftwood Green	34 D3
Croftwood Grove	33 C3
Croftwood Park	34 D3
Cromcastle Avenue	22 D1
Cromcastle Drive	22 D1
Cromcastle Green	22 D1
Cromcastle Park	22 D1
Cromcastle Road	22 D1
Cromlech Court	9 C4
Cromlech Fields	56 E1
Cromwell's Quarters	35 B3 [3]
Cromwellsfort Road	41 C2
Cross Avenue (Booterstown)	44 F3
Cross Avenue (Dun Laoghaire)	46 D4
Crosthwaite Park East	54 D1
Crosthwaite Park South	54 D1
Crosthwaite Park West	54 D1
Crosthwaite Terrace	46 D4 [15]
*Crostick Alley (off Meath St.)	35 C3
Crotty Avenue	41 C1
*Crow Street (off Dame St.)	36 D2
*Crown Alley (off Temple Bar)	36 D2
Croydon Gardens	21 C4
Croydon Green	21 C4
Croydon Park Avenue	21 C4
Croydon Terrace	21 C3 [4]
Crumlin	42 D1
Crumlin Park	42 D1
Crumlin Road	35 B4
Cuala Grove	58 D3
Cuala Road	20 F4
Cuckoo Lane	36 D2
Cuffe Lane	36 D3
Cuffe Street	36 D3
Cul na Greine	48 F2
Cullen's Cottages	45 A4 [7]
*Cullenswood Court (off Cullenswood Park)	43 B1
Cullenswood Gardens	43 B1
Cullenswood Park	43 B1
Cullenswood Road	43 B1 [11]
Culmore Park	33 C2 [1]
Culmore Road	33 C2
*Cumberland PlaceNorth (on North Circular Road)	35 C1
Cumberland Road	36 E4
Cumberland Street	45 C4
Cumberland Street North	36 E1
Cumberland Street South	36 E3 [1]
Cunningham Drive	54 F2
Cunningham Road	54 F2
Curlew Road	34 F4
Curraghcloe Drive	12 D4 [5]
Curzon Street	36 D4
Cushlawn Park	48 F2
Custom House Quay	36 E2
Cymric Road	37 A3
Cypress Avenue	50 E2 [2]
Cypress Court	56 E1
Cypress Drive	42 D3
Cypress Garth	42 D4
Cypress Grove Road	42 D3
Cypress Grove North	42 D3
Cypress Grove South	42 D4
Cypress Lawn	42 D4
Cypress Park	42 D4
Cypress Road	44 E3

D

STREET NAME	PAGE/GRID REFERENCE
*DAISY MARKET (on Parnell Street)	36 D2
Dakota Avenue	10 F4
Dal Riada	3 C4
Dalcassian Downs	20 F4
Dale Close	52 E1 [1]
Dale Drive	52 E1
Dale Road	52 E1
Dale View	54 E4
Dale View Park	54 E4 [2]
Dalepark Road	49 A2
Daletree Road	49 C2
Dale View Road	1 C1
Dalkey	54 F1
Dalkey Avenue	54 F2
Dalkey Court	54 F2 [23]
Dalkey Grove	54 F2 [6]
Dalkey Park	54 E2
Dalymount	35 C1
Dame Court	36 D3 [16]
Dame Lane	36 D2 [42]
Dame Lane	36 D3 [7]
Dame Street	36 D2
Dane Road	9 C4
Danes Court	23 A4
Danesfort	37 B1
Daneswell Road	21 A4
Dangan Avenue	42 D2
Dangan Drive	42 D2
Dangan Park	42 D2
Daniel Street	36 D3
Danieli Drive	22 E2
Danieli Road	22 E2
Dara Court	30 D3
Dara Crescent	30 D3
Dargan Street	57 B2 [10]
Dargle Crescent	57 B2 [5]
Dargle Drive	51 A1
Dargle Heights	57 B2
Dargle Road (Dean's Grange)	53 A1
Dargle Road (Drumcondra)	21 A4
*Dargle Terrace (On Lower Dargle Road)	57 B2
Dargle Valley	51 A1
Dargle View	51 A1
Dargle Wood	50 D1
Darley Cottages	57 C2 [15]
Darley Street	36 D4
Darley's Terrace	35 C3 [9]
Darling Estate	19 C4
Dartmouth Lane	36 E4 [6]
Dartmouth Place	36 E4 [4]
Dartmouth Road	36 E4
Dartmouth Square East	36 E4 [16]
Dartmouth Square North	36 E4 [14]
Dartmouth Square South	36 E4 [15]
Dartmouth Square West	36 E4 [17]
Dartmouth Terrace	36 E4 [5]
Dartry Cottages	43 B1 [1]
Dartry Park	43 B2
Dartry Road	43 A2
David Park	21 A4
David Road	21 A4
*Davis Place (off Thomas Davis St Sth)	35 C3
Davitt Road	34 F4
Davitt Road	57 B2
Dawson Court	44 F3
*Dawson Court (off Stephen St. Lower)	36 D3
Dawson Lane	36 E3 [18]
Dawson Street	36 E3
De Burgh Road	35 B2 [14]
De Courcy Square	21 A4 [2]
De Selby Close	47 C2
De Selby Grove	48 D2
De Selby Lawns	48 D2
De Selby Park	47 C2
De Velara Place	36 D1 [19]
*De Vesci Court (Flats) (off Sloperton)	45 C4
De Vesci Terrace	45 C4
Dean Street	36 D3
Dean Swift Green	21 A2
Dean Swift Road	21 A2
Dean Swift Square	35 C3
Dean's Grange Road	53 B1
Deans Court	53 B1 [10]
Deans Grange	53 B2
Deansrath Avenue	32 F4
Déansrath Crescent	39 C1
Deansrath Green	39 C1
Deansrath Grove	32 F4
Deansrath Lawn	32 F4
Deansrath Park	39 C1
Deansrath Road	39 B1
Deanstown Avenue	20 D2
Deanstown Drive	20 D2
Deanstown Green	20 D2
Deanstown Park	20 D2
Deanstown Road	20 D2
Decies Road	34 E3
Deerpark	57 B4
Deerpark Avenue	19 A4
Deerpark Close	19 A3

STREET NAME	PAGE/GRID REFERENCE
Deerpark Drive	19 A3
Deerpark Lawn	19 B3
Deerpark Road	44 D4
Deerpark Road (Castleknock Road)	19 A3
Del Val Avenue	23 C2
Del Val Court	23 C2 [2]
Delaford Avenue	49 C1
Delaford Drive	49 C1
Delaford Grove	49 C1
Delaford Lawn	49 C1
Delaford Park	49 C1
Delbrook Manor	51 C2
Delbrook Park	51 C2
Delville Road	21 A2
Delvin Road	20 F4 [3]
Delwood Close	18 E3
Delwood Drive	18 E3
Delwood Grove	18 E3
Delwood Lawn	18 E3
Delwood Park	18 E3
Delwood Road	18 E3
Delwood Walk	18 E3
Demesne	22 E3
Denmark Street Great	36 D1
Denzille Lane	36 E3
*Derby Square (off Werburgh St.)	36 D3
Dermot O'Hurley Avenue	37 A3
Derravaragh Road	42 E2
Derry Drive	42 D1
Derry Park	42 D1
Derry Road	42 D1
Derrynane Gardens	37 A3
Derrynane Parade	36 D1[33]
Deselby	48 D2
Desmond Avenue	46 D4 [3]
Desmond Cottages	54 F2[20]
Desmond Street	36 D4 [2]
Devenish Road	42 E1
Deverell Place	36 E2 [5]
Devery's Lane	21 A4[18]
Devitt Villas	54 E1 [8]
Devlin's Place	36 E3[22]
Devon Close	53 B1[11]
Devoy Road	35 A3
Dewberry Park	4 D4
Dexter Terrace	36 E4[29]
Diamond Terrace	57 B2[15]
Digges Lane	36 D3[38]
Digges Street Upper	36 D3
*Dillon Place South (off John Dillon St.)	36 D3
Dingle Road	20 E4
Dispensary Lane (Lucan)	32 D1 [6]
Dispensary Lane (Willbrook)	42 F4
Distillery Lane	16 D4
Distillery Road	21 B4
Diswellstown Cottages	18 E4
Dixon Villas	54 E1 [9]
D'Olier Street	36 E2
Dodder Avenue	49 B2
Dodder Court	49 B2
Dodder Crescent	49 B2
Dodder Dale	42 F4
Dodder Green	49 B2
Dodder Lawn	49 B2
Dodder Park Drive	42 F3 [3]
Dodder Park Grove	42 F3
Dodder Park Road	42 F3
Dodder Road Lower	43 A3
Dodder Terrace	37 A3[18]
Dodder View Cottages	36 F4 [9]
Doddervale	43 A3
Dodsboro Cottages	31 C2
Dodsboro Road	31 C2
Dollymount	23 A4
Dollymount Avenue	23 A4
Dollymount Grove	22 F4
Dollymount Park	23 A4
Dollymount Rise	23 A4
Dolmen Court	10 D4
Donmore Green	42 E2
Donnelly Estate	18 F2
Dolphin Avenue	35 C4
Dolphin House	35 B4 [1]
*Dolphin Market (off Dolphin's Barn St.)	35 B4
Dolphin Park	35 B4 [5]
Dolphin Road	35 B4
Dolphin's Barn	35 B4
Dolphin's Barn Street	35 B4
Domhnach's Well	24 D1
*Dominick Court (off Dominick St Upper)	36 D1

STREET NAME	PAGE/GRID REFERENCE
Dominick Lane	36 D2[35]
Dominick Place	36 D1
Dominick Street	46 D4
Dominick Street Lower	36 D2
Dominick Street Upper	36 D1
Domville Drive	42 D4
Domville Green	42 D4
Domville Grove	56 E1[9]
Domville Road	42 D4
Donaghmede	12 E4
Donaghmede Avenue	23 B1
Donaghmede Drive	23 B1
Donaghmede Park	23 B1
Donaghmede Road	23 B1
Donard Road	34 F4
Donmore Green	42 E2
Donnellan Avenue	35 B3 [7]
Donnelly Estate	18 F2
Donnybrook	43 C1
Donnybrook Close	44 D2 [2]
Donnybrook Court	43 C1
Donnybrook Green	44 D2
Donnybrook Manor	43 C1
Donnybrook Road	43 C1
Donnycarney	22 D3
Donnycarney Road	22 D3
Donomore Avenue	48 E2
Donomore Crescent	48 E2
Donomore Green	48 E2
Donomore Park	48 E2
Donore Avenue	35 C3
Donore Road	35 C3
Donore Terrace	35 C3[55]
Donovan Lane	35 C4[21]
Doon Avenue	35 B1 [6]
Doon Court	9 C4
Doonamana Road	54 D3
Doonanore Park	54 D3
Doonsalla Drive	54 D3
Doonsalla Park	54 D3
Doris Street	36 F3
Dornden Park	44 E2
Dorney Court	56 E3
Dorset Lane	36 D1
*Dorset Place (off Dorset Street Lower)	36 D1
Dorset Street Lower	36 D1
Dorset Street Upper	36 D1
Dowland Road	42 D1
Dowling's Court	36 E2[15]
Downpatrick Road	35 B4
Dowth Avenue	20 F4
Drapier Green	20 F2 [1]
Drapier Road	20 F2
Drimnagh	34 F4
Drimnagh Road	41 C1
Drimnigh Road	12 E3
Drinagh Avenue	52 F4
Drinagh Close	52 F4
Drinagh Court	52 F4
Drinagh Park	52 F4
Drinaghmore	52 F4
Dromard Road	34 F4
Dromard Terrace	37 A4[17]
Dromawling Road	21 C2
Drombawn Avenue	21 C2
Dromcarra Avenue	48 E2
Dromcarra Drive	48 E2
Dromcarra Green	48 D2
Dromcarra Grove	48 E2
Dromeen Avenue	21 C2
Dromheath Avenue	7 B4
Dromheath Drive	7 B4
Dromheath Gardens	7 B4
Dromheath Grove	7 B4
Dromheath Park	7 B4
Dromlee Crescent	21 C2
Dromnanane Park	21 C2 [2]
Dromnanane Road	21 C2 [1]
Dromore Road	35 A4
Druid Court	9 C4
Drumahill	52 D1
Drumalee Avenue	35 B1
Drumalee Court	35 B1[14]
Drumalee Drive	35 B1
Drumalee Grove	35 B1
Drumalee Park	35 B1
Drumalee Road	35 B1
Drumcairn Avenue	48 D1
Drumcairn Drive	48 D1
Drumcairn Gardens	48 D1
Drumcairn Green	48 D1
Drumcairn Park	48 E1
Drumcliffe Drive	20 E4
Drumcliffe Road	20 E4

STREET NAME	PAGE/GRID REFERENCE
Drumcondra	21 B4
Drumcondra Park	36 E1[18]
Drumcondra Road Lower	21 B4
Drumcondra Road Upper	21 B4
Drumfinn Avenue	33 C2
Drumfinn Park	34 D3
Drumfinn Road	34 D2
Drumkeen Manor	54 D3
Drummartin Close	44 D4
Drummartin Crescent	52 D1 [1]
Drummartin Park	52 D1
Drummartin Road	44 D4
Drummartin Terrace	44 D4
*Drummond Place (off Mount Drummond Ave)	35 C4
Drury Street	36 D3
Drynam Court	2 D2
Drynam Lane	2 E2
Drynam Road	2 D2
Drysdale Close	49 A2
Dublin Road	25 A1
Dublin Road	44 E4
Dublin Road (Bray)	57 B1
Dublin Road (Celbridge)	30 D3
Dublin Road (Kilbarrack)	23 C2
Dublin Road (Malahide)	3 A3
Dublin Road (Shankill)	56 E3
Dublin Road (Swords)	1 C3
Dublin Street (Portmarnock)	13 A4
Dublin Street (Swords)	2 D2
Dufferin Avenue	35 C4
Duke Lane Lower	36 E3[17]
Duke Lane Upper	36 D3[32]
Duke Row	36 E1[57]
Duke Street	36 D3
Dun Aonghasa	48 F2
Dun Emer Drive	51 C1
Dun Emer Park	51 C1
Dun Emer Road	51 C1
Dun Laoghaire	46 D4
Dun an Oir	48 F2
Dunamase	44 F3
Dunard Avenue	35 A1
Dunard Court	35 B1
Dunard Drive	35 B1
Dunard Park	35 B1
Dunard Road	35 B1[11.]
Dunard Walk	35 B1
Dunawley Avenue	40 D1
Dunawley Drive	40 D1
Dunawley Grove	40 D1
Dunawley Way	40 D1
Dunbo Cottages	26 D1 [3]
Dunbo Hill	26 D1 [4]
Dunbo Terrace	26 D1 [1]
Dunboyne	5 B2
Dunbro Lane	9 C1
Dunbur Terrace	57 C2[21]
Duncairn Avenue	57 C2
Duncairn Terrace	57 C2
Duncarraig	25 B2
Dundaniel Road	22 D1
Dundela Avenue	54 E1
Dundela Crescent	54 E1
Dundela Haven	54 E1[24]
Dundela Park	54 E1
Dundrum	51 C1
Dundrum Castle	51 C1 [7]
Dundrum Court	51 C1 [4]
Dundrum Road	43 C3
Dundrum Wood	51 B1
Dunedin Drive	53 C1 [8]
Dunedin Terrace	53 C1
Dungar Terrace	46 D4[12]
Dungriffan Road	26 D2
Dungriffan Villas	26 D2 [8]
Dunleary Hill	45 C4
Dunleary Road	45 C4
Dunluce Road	22 E3
Dunmanus Road	20 E4
Dunmore Grove	40 F2
Dunmore Lawn	40 F2
Dunmore Park	40 F2
Dunne Street	36 E1
Dunree Park	22 F1
Dunsandle Court	19 A3
Dunsandle Grove	19 A3
Dunseverick Road	22 E4
Dunsink Avenue	20 D2
Dunsink Drive	20 D2
Dunsink Gardens	20 D2
Dunsink Green	20 D2
Dunsink Lane	19 A2
Dunsink Park	20 D2
Dunsink Road	20 D2

STREET NAME	PAGE/GRID REFERENCE
Dunville Avenue	43 B1
Dunville Terrace (on Canal Road)	32 D4
Durham Road	37 B4
Durrow Road	42 E1
Dwyer Park	57 C2

E

STREET NAME	PAGE/GRID REFERENCE
EAGLE HILL	45 A3[15]
Eagle Hill Avenue	42 F2 [4]
Eagle Park	22 D1
Eagle Terrace	51 C1 [3]
*Eagle Terrace (Dalkey) (Sorento Rd)	54 F2
Earl Place	36 D2[19]
Earl Street North	36 D2
Earl Street South	35 C3
Earls Court	35 B1
Earlscroft	57 C4
Earlsfort	32 F3
Earlsfort Terrace	36 E4
East Pier (Dun Laoghaire)	46 E3
East Pier (Howth)	26 D1
East Road	36 F2
East Wall	36 F1
East Wall Road	36 F1
Eastmoreland Lane	36 F4 [2]
Eastmoreland Place	36 F4 [1]
Easton Park	15 C4
Easton Road	30 F1
Eaton Brae	43 A3
Eaton Brae	56 E2
Eaton Place	45 B4
Eaton Road	42 F2
Eaton Square (Monkstown)	45 B4
Eaton Square (Terenure)	42 F2
Eaton Wood Avenue	56 E3
Eaton Wood Court	56 E3
Eaton Wood Grove	56 E3
Ebenezer Terrace	35 C3[53]
Eblana Avenue	46 D4
Eblana Villas (Lr. Grand Canal St.)	36 F3 [2]
*Eblana Villas (off Arbour Hill)	35 B2
Eccles Court	36 D1[20]
Eccles Place	36 D1
Eccles Street	36 D1
Echlin Street	35 C3
Eden Park	54 D1
Eden Park Avenue	52 D1
Eden Park Drive	44 D4
Eden Park Road	52 D1
Eden Quay	36 E2
Eden Road Lower	54 D1
Eden Road Upper	54 D1
*Eden Terrace (Botanic Ave)	21 A4
Eden Terrace (Dun Laoghaire)	54 D1
Eden Villas	54 D1 [5]
Edenbrook Court	50 F1 [5]
Edenbrook Drive	42 E4
Edenbrook Park	42 E4
Edenmore Avenue	22 F1
Edenmore Crescent	23 A2
Edenmore Drive	22 F2
Edenmore Gardens	22 F2
Edenmore Green	22 F2
Edenmore Grove	22 F2
Edenmore Park	22 F1
Edenvale Road	43 B1
Edgewood	21 B4[10]
Edgewood Lawns	18 E1
Edmondstown	50 E3
Edmondstown Court	50 E2
Edmondstown Green	50 E2
Edmondstown Road	50 E2
Edward Road	58 D3
*Edward Terrace (Off Nerano Rd)	54 F2
Edwin Court	54 E2 [5]
Effra Road	43 A1
Eglinton Road	57 C2 [3]
Eglinton Court	43 C1
Eglinton Park (Donnybrook)	43 C1
Eglinton Park (Dun Laoghaire)	45 C4
Eglinton Road	43 C1
Eglinton Square	43 C1[13]
Eglinton Terrace (Donnybrook)	43 C1
Eglinton Terrace (Dundrum)	43 C4
*Eglinton Terrace (Royal Canal Bank)	36 D1
Eglinton Wood	43 C1
Elderwood Road	33 B2
(off Donore Avenue)	
*Elford Terrace	35 C3

STREET NAME	PAGE/GRID REFERENCE
Elgin Heights	57 A4
Elgin Road	36 F4
Elgin Wood	57 A4
Elizabeth Street	21 B4
Elkwood	50 E1
Ellenfield Road	21 C2
Ellesmere	52 F2 [4]
Ellesmere Avenue	35 B1
Ellis Court	35 C2[38]
Ellis Quay	35 C2
*Ellis Street (off Benburb Street)	35 C2
Elm Grove Cottages	19 C4 [3]
Elm Mount Avenue	21 C2
Elm Mount Close	22 D2
Elm Mount Court	22 D3
Elm Mount Crescent	22 D2
Elm Mount Drive	22 D2
Elm Mount Grove	22 D2
Elm Mount Heights	22 D2
Elm Mount Lawn	22 D2
Elm Mount Park	22 D2
Elm Mount Rise	22 D2
Elm Mount Road	22 D2
Elm Mount View	22 D2
Elm Park	44 D1
Elm Park (Celbridge)	30 D3
Elm Park Terrace	42 F2
Elm Road (Donnycarney)	22 D3
Elm Road (Fox & Geese)	41 A1
Elmbrook	32 E2
Elmbrook Crescent	32 E2
Elmbrook Lawn	32 E2
Elmbrook Walk	32 E2
Elmcastle Close	41 A3
Elmcastle Court	41 A3
Elmcastle Drive	41 A3
Elmcastle Green	41 A3
Elmcastle Park	41 A3
Elmcastle Walk	41 A3
Elmdale Crescent	33 C3
Elmdale Drive	33 C3
Elmdale Park	33 C3
Elmfield	52 E4
Elmfield Avenue	12 D4
Elmfield Court	12 D4
Elmfield Crescent	12 E4
Elmfield Drive	12 E4
Elmfield Green	12 D4
Elmfield Grove	12 D4
Elmfield Lawn	12 E4
Elmfield Park	12 E4
Elmfield Rise	12 D4
Elmfield Vale	12 E4
Elmfield Walk	12 D4
Elmfield Way	12 D4
Elmgrove	45 A4
Elmgrove	54 D4
Elmgrove Terrace	57 C2[22]
Elmpark Avenue	43 B1
Elms	44 F3
Elmwood	17 B1
Elmwood Avenue Lower	43 B1
Elmwood Avenue Upper	43 B1
Elmwood Close	17 B1
Elmwood Drive	1 C1
Elmwood Park	1 C1
Elmwood Road	1 C1
Elner Court	4 D4
Elton Court	22 F1 [1]
Elton Court	30 F1
Elton Drive	23 A1
Elton Park (Coolock)	23 A1
Elton Park (Dalkey)	54 E1
Elton Walk	23 A1 [1]
Ely Close	49 B3
Ely Manor	49 B3
Ely Place	36 E3
Ely Place Upper	36 E3[31]
Embassy Lawn	43 C2
Emerald Cottages	36 F3[34]
Emerald Place	36 E2[23]
Emerald Square	35 B3[20]
Emerald Street	36 F2 [1]
Emerald Terrace	35 C3[63]
Emmet Court	35 A3
Emmet Road	35 A3
Emmet Square	44 F3
Emmet Street (Harold's Cross)	35 C4[10]
Emmet Street (Nth. Circular Rd.)	36 E1
Emmet Street (Sallynoggin)	54 D1[4]
Emor Street	36 D4
Emorville Avenue	36 D4
Empress Place	36 E1
*Enaville Avenue	36 F1
(off Annesley Place)	

STREET NAME	PAGE/GRID REFERENCE
Enaville Road	36 F1[10]
*Engine Alley (off Meath St.)	35 C3
English Row	30 D4
Ennafort Avenue	22 F2
Ennafort Court	22 F3
Ennafort Drive	22 F3
Ennafort Grove	22 F2
Ennafort Park	22 F3
Ennafort Road	22 F2
Ennel Avenue	22 F2
Ennel Court	56 E1 [6]
Ennel Drive	22 F2
Ennel Park	22 F2
Ennis Grove	37 A3[19]
Enniskerry Road (Phibsborough)	21 A4 [3]
Enniskerry Road (Sandyford)	52 D4
Erne Place	36 F3·[21]
Erne Place Little	36 E3 [4]
Erne Place Lower	36 E2 [2]
Erne Street Lower	36 E2
Erne Street Upper	36 E3
Erne Terrace Front	36 E3[20]
Erne Terrace Rere	36 E3[21]
Errigal Gardens	41 C1
Errigal Road	34 F4
Erris Road	20 E4
Esker Drive	32 D2
Esker Glebe	32 D2
Esker Lane	32 E1
Esker Lawns	32 D1
Esker Lodge	32 E2
Esker Lodge Avenue	32 E2
Esker Lodge Close	32 E2
Esker Lodge View	32 E2
Esker Park	32 E2
Esker Road	32 D3
Esker South	32 D3
Esker Villas	43 A1[11]
Esker Wood Close	32 E2
Esker Wood Court	32 E2
Esker Wood Drive	32 E2
Esker Wood Grove	32 E2
Esker Wood Rise	32 E2
Esker Wood View	32 E2
Esker Wood Walk	32 E2
Esker Woods	32 E2
Esmond Avenue	21 C4
Esmonde Terrace	57 B2[18]
Esplanade Terrace	58 D2 [3]
Esposito Road	41 C1 [5]
*Essex Gate (off Essex Quay)	36 D2
Essex Quay	36 D2
Essex Street East	36 D2
*Essex Street West	36 D2
(off Fishamble St.)	
Estate Avenue	44 E1
Estate Cottages	36 F3[16]
(Northumberland Rd.)	
Estate Cottages (Shelbourne Rd.)	36 F4[13]
Estuary Court	2 D1
Estuary Road	2 F2
Eugene Street	35 C3
Eustace Street	36 D2
Everton Avenue	35 B1 [3]
Evora Park	26 D1
Evora Terrace	26 D1 [2]
Ewington Lane	35 B3[12]
*Exchange Street Lower	36 D2
(off Wood Quay)	
*Exchange Street Upper	36 D2
(off Lord Edward St.)	
Exchequer Street	36 D3

F

STREET NAME	PAGE/GRID REFERENCE
FABER GROVE	53 B1 [9]
Fade Street	36 D3[39]
Fairbrook Lawn	42 F4
Fairfield Avenue	36 F1
Fairfield Park	43 A2
Fairfield Road	21 A4
Fairgreen Road	57 B2[11]
Fairgreen Terrace	57 B2[14]
Fairhaven	3 B2
Fairlawn Park	20 E2
Fairlawn Road	20 E2
Fairlawns	54 E2 [6]
Fairview	21 C4
Fairview Avenue Lower	21 C4
Fairview Avenue Upper	21 C4
Fairview Court	21 C4[14]
Fairview Green	21 C4 [7]
Fairway's Grove	20 F2
Fairview Passage	21 C4[10]

STREET NAME	PAGE/GRID REFERENCE
Fairview Strand	21 C4
Fairview Terrace	21 C4[11]
Fairway's Avenue	20 F2
Fairway's Green	20 F2
Fairway's Park	20 F2
Fairways	42 E4
Fairyhill	53 A1
Fairyhill	57 B3
Faith Avenue	36 F1
Falcarragh Road	21 B2
Falls Road	56 D2
Farmhill Drive	43 C4
Farmhill Park	43 C4
Farmhill Road	43 C4
Farmleigh Avenue	52 F1
Farmleigh Close	52 F1
Farmleigh Park	52 F1
Farney Park	37 A4
Farnham Crescent	20 E2
Farnham Drive	20 E2
Farrenboley Cottages	43 B3
Farrenboley Park	43 B3
Fassaroe	57 A2
Fassaroe Lane	57 A3
Father Colohan Terrace	57 C2[11]
Father Mathew Square	35 C2[26]
Fatima Mansions	35 B3[23]
(off James's Walk)	
Fatima Terrace	57 C2
Faughart Road	42 E1 [3]
Faussagh Avenue	20 E4
Faussagh Road	20 F4
Feltrim	3 A4
Feltrim Road	2 F4
Fenian Street	36 E3
Fergus Road	42 F2
Ferguson Road	21 A3
Ferndale	49 A2
Ferndale Avenue	20 F 2
Ferndale Road	20 F 2
Ferndale Road (Bray)	57 A1
Ferndale Road (Shankill)	56 D3
Fernhill Avenue	41 C3
Fernhill Park	41 C3
Fernhill Road	41 C3
Fernleigh (Est)	52 D3
Ferns Road	42 E1
Fernvale Drive	42 D1
Fernwood Avenue	48 E1
Fernwood Close	48 E1
Fernwood Court	48 E1
Fernwood Lawn	48 E1
Fernwood Park	48 E1
Fernwood Way	48 E1
Ferrard Road	42 F2
Ferrycarrig Avenue	11 B4
Ferrycarrig Drive	11 B4
Ferrycarrig Park	11 B4
Ferrycarrig Road	11 B4
Ferryman's Crossing	36 F2[14]
Fertullagh Road	20 F4.5
Fettercairn Road	40 D4
Field Avenue	41 C1 [1]
Field's Terrace	43 B1 [5]
Fieldview Cottages	45 A4 [6]
Findlater Place	36 D2[25]
Findlater Street (Dun Laoghaire)	54 E1 [7]
Findlater Street	35 B2[10]
(Nth. Circular Rd.)	
Fingal Place	35 C1 [5]
Fingal Street	35 C3[11]
Finglas	20 D1
Finglas East	20 E1
Finglas Park	20 E1
Finglas Place	20 E2
Finglas Road	20 E2
Finglas Road Old	20 F3
Finglas South	20 E2
Finglas West	20 D1
Finglaswood Road	20 D1
Finn Street	35 B2[12]
Finnstown Abbey	32 D3
Finsbury Park	43 B4
Firgrove	54 E4 [8]
Firhouse	49 C1
Firhouse Road	49 B2
Firhouse Road West	49 A2
First Avenue (Sarsfield Road)	34 F3
First Avenue (Seville Place)	36 F2 [3]
Fishamble Street	36 D2
Fishermans Wharf	37 A2 [1]
Fitzgerald Park	53 C1 [6]
Fitzgerald Street	36 D4 [1]
Fitzgibbon Lane	36 E1[21]
Fitzgibbon Street	36 E1

STREET NAME	PAGE/GRID REFERENCE
Fitzmaurice Road	20 F2
Fitzpatrick's Cottages	42 F1 [6]
Fitzroy Avenue	21 B4
Fitzwilliam Court	36 E3[38]
Fitzwilliam Lane	36 E3
Fitzwilliam Place	36 E3
Fitzwilliam Place North	35 C2[23]
(Grangegorman)	
Fitzwilliam Quay	37 A3
Fitzwilliam Square East	36 E3
Fitzwilliam Square North	36 E3
Fitzwilliam Square South	36 E3
Fitzwilliam Square West	36 E3
Fitzwilliam Street (Ringsend)	37 A3 [2]
Fitzwilliam Street Lower	36 E3
Fitzwilliam Street Upper	36 E3
Fitzwilliam Terrace	57 C2[36]
Fleet Street	36 D2
Fleming Road	21 A3
Fleming's Place	36 E4
Flemingstown Park	43 B4
Fleurville	45 A4
Floraville Avenue	40 E1
Floraville Drive	40 E2
Floraville Estate	40 E1
Floraville Lawn	40 E1
Florence Road	57 C2
Florence Street	36 D4[17]
Florence Terrace	57 C2[39]
*Florence Terrace	36 E4
(Leeson Park Avenue)	
Florence Villas	57 C2[40]
*Florence Villas	37 A4
(Sandymount)	
Flower Grove	54 D2
Foley Street	36 E2
Fontenoy Street	36 D1
Fontenoy Terrace	58 D3
Fonthill Abbey	50 F1 [3]
Fonthill Park	50 F1
Fonthill Road (Clondalkin)	33 A2
Fonthill Road (Rathfarnham)	50 F1
Forbes Lane	35 C3
Forbes Street	36 F2
Forest Avenue	1 B3
Forest Avenue	41 A3
Forest Boulevard	1 B3
Forest Close	41 A3
Forest Court	1 B2
Forest Crescent	1 B3
Forest Dale	1 B2
Forest Drive	1 B3
Forest Drive	41 A3
Forest Fields	1 C3
Forest Fields Road	1 C3
Forest Green	1 B3
Forest Green	41 A3
Forest Grove	1 B3
Forest Lawn	41 A2
Forest Park	1 B2
Forest Park	30 F1
Forest Park	41 A3
Forest Road	1 B4
Forest View	1 B3
Forest Walk	1 B3
Forest Way	1 B3
Fortfield Avenue	42 E3
Fortfield Court	42 E3[2]
Fortfield Drive	42 E3
Fortfield Gardens	43 A2
Fortfield Grove	42 E3
Fortfield Park	42 E3
Fortfield Road	42 E3
Fortfield Terrace	43 A2
Forth Road	36 F1
Fortlawn Avenue	18 D1
Fortlawn Drive	18 D1
Fortlawn Park	18 D1
Fortlawns	54 E2
Fortrose Park	42 E4
Fortunestown Close	47 C1
Fortunestown Crescent	47 C1
Fortunestown Lane	47 B1
Fortunestown Road	48 D2
Fortunestown Way	48 D1
Fortview Avenue	37 C1
Foster Place North	36 E1[41]
Foster Place South	36 D2[38]
(College Green)	
Foster Terrace	36 E1
Fosterbrook	44 E3
Fosters Avenue	44 E3
Fountain Place	35 C2
Fountain Road	35 B2
Fourth Avenue (Seville Place)	36 F2 [8]

STREET NAME	PAGE/GRID REFERENCE
*Fownes Street Lower (off Temple Bar)	36 D2
*Fownes Street Upper (off Dame St.)	36 D2
Fox and Geese	41 A1
Fox's Lane	23 B2
Foxborough	32 E3
Foxborough Avenue	32 E3
Foxborough Drive	32 E3
Foxborough Park	32 E3
Foxborough Road	32 F3
Foxdene Avenue	32 F3
Foxdene Drive	32 F3
Foxdene Gardens	32 F3
Foxdene Green	32 F3
Foxdene Grove	32 F3
Foxdene Park	32 F3
Foxes Grove	56 E3
Foxfield	32 D3
Foxfield Avenue	23 B2
Foxfield Crescent	23 B2
Foxfield Drive	23 B2
Foxfield Green	23 B2
Foxfield Grove	23 B2
Foxfield Heights	23 B2
Foxfield Lawn	23 B2
Foxfield Park	23 B2
Foxfield Road	23 B2
Foxfield St. John	23 B2
Foxford	32 F2
Foxhill Avenue	23 A1
Foxhill Close	23 A1
Foxhill Court	23 A1
Foxhill Crescent	23 A1
Foxhill Drive	23 A1
Foxhill Green	12 D4
Foxhill Grove	23 A1
Foxhill Lawn	23 A1
Foxhill Park	23 A1
Foxhill Way	23 A1
Foxpark	32 D3
Foxrock	53 A3
Foxrock Avenue	53 A2
Foxrock Close	53 B2
Foxrock Court	53 A2
Foxrock Crescent	53 B2
Foxrock Green	53 A2
Foxrock Grove	53 B2
Foxrock Manor	52 F2
Foxrock Mount	53 A2 [4]
Foxrock Park	53 A2
Foxrock Wood	53 B2
Foxwood	2 D2
Foxwood	32 D3
Foyle Road	21 C4
Francis Street	35 C3
Frankfort	43 B4 [10]
Frankfort Avenue	43 A2
Frankfort Cottages	36 E1
Frankfort Court	42 F2 [8]
Frankfort Flats	42 F2 [9]
Frankfort Park	43 B4
Frascati Park	45 A3
Frascati Road	45 A2
Frederick Court	36 D1 [46]
Frederick Lane North	36 D1 [14]
Frederick Lane South	36 E3 [10]
Frederick Street North	36 D1
Frederick Street South	36 E3
Frenchman's Lane	36 E2 [20]
Friar's Walk	40 E1 [5]
Friarsland Avenue	43 C3 [3]
Friarsland Road	43 C3
Friary Avenue	35 C2 [6]
*Friary Grove (off Friary Avenue)	35 C2
Fumbally Lane	36 D3
Furry Park	22 E3
Furry Park Court	22 E3
Furry Park Road	22 F3
Furze Road	34 E1
Furze Road	52 E2

G

STREET NAME	PAGE/GRID REFERENCE
GABLES	23 A1 [6]
Gaelic Street	36 F1 [6]
Gallanstown Drive	33 C4
Gallanstown Green	33 C4
Gallanstown Way	33 C4 [1]
Gallaun Road	9 C4
Galloping Green	52 F1
Galmoy Road	20 F4
Galtrim Park	57 C2
Galtrim Road	57 C2

STREET NAME	PAGE/GRID REFERENCE
Galtymore Close	34 F4
Galtymore Drive	35 A4
Galtymore Park	34 F4
Galtymore Road	35 A4
Gandon Close	42 F1 [9]
Garden Lane	35 C3 [21]
*Garden Terrace (off Clanbrassil St Upper)	35 C4
Garden View	36 D4 [42]
Gardiner Lane	36 E1
Gardiner Lane	36 E1
Gardiner Place	36 D1
Gardiner Row	36 D1 [40]
Gardiner St. Middle	36 E1
Gardiner Street Lower	36 E1
Gardiner Street Upper	36 D1
Garrynisk Close	40 F3
Garrynisk Road	40 F3
Garryowen Road	34 E3
Gartan	2 E1
Gartan Avenue	21 A4
Gartan Court	2 E1
Gartan Drive	2 E1
Garter Lane	47 B1
Garville Avenue	43 A2
Garville Avenue Upper	42 F2
*Garville Drive (off Garville Ave)	43 A2
Garville Lane	43 A2
Garville Road	43 A2
Gas Yard Lane	3 B2
Gaybrook Lawns	3 A3
Geoffrey Keating Road	35 C3 [30]
*George Reynolds Flats (off Oliver Plunkett Ave.)	37 A3
George's Avenue (Blackrock)	45 A3
George's Hill	36 D2 [6]
George's Lane	35 C2 [3]
George's Place	36 D1 [43]
George's Place (Blackrock)	45 A3 [6]
George's Place (Dun Laoghaire)	46 D4
George's Quay	36 E2
George's Road	20 E1 [1]
George's Street Great North	36 D1
George's Street Great South	36 D3
George's Street Lower (Dun Laoghaire)	46 D4
George's Street Upper (Dun Laoghaire)	46 D4
Georges Road	20 E1 [1]
Georgian Hamlet	13 A4
Georgian Village	19 A4
Gerald Street	36 F3 [9]
Geraldine Street	36 D1
Gertrude Terrace	57 B2 [25]
Gilbert Road	35 C4 [12]
Gilford Avenue	37 B4
Gilford Court	37 A4 [10]
Gilford Drive	37 A4
Gilford Park	37 A4
Gilford Place	36 E1 [30]
Gilford Road	37 A4
Gilford Terrace	37 B4 [1]
Glandore Park	53 C1
Glandore Road	21 C3
Glasanaon Court	20 E2
Glasanaon Park	20 E2
Glasanaon Road	20 E2
Glasaree Road	20 E2
Glasilawn Avenue	20 F2
Glasilawn Road	20 F2
Glasmeen Road	20 F2
Glasmore Park	1 C1
Glasnamana Place	20 F2 [2]
Glasnamana Road	20 F2
Glasnevin	20 F3
Glasnevin Avenue	20 F1
Glasnevin Court	20 E3
Glasnevin Downs	20 F3
Glasnevin Drive	21 A2
Glasnevin Hill	21 A3
Glasnevin North	20 F1
Glasnevin Oaks	20 F3 [3]
Glasnevin Park	20 F1
Glasnevin Woods	20 E3
Glasson Court	43 B3
Glasthule Buildings	54 E1 [11]
Glasthule Road	54 E1
Gleann na Smol	45 B4
Gleann na Smol	48 F2
Glebe View	20 E2 [7]
Gledswood Avenue	43 C3
Gledswood Close	43 C3
Gledswood Drive	43 C3 [5]
Gledswood Park	43 C3

STREET NAME	PAGE/GRID REFERENCE
Glen Avenue	53 B3
Glen Close	53 B3
Glen Dale	53 B3
Glen Drive	53 B3
Glen Druid	56 E1 [11]
Glen Garth	53 B3
Glen Grove	53 B3
Glen Lawn Drive	53 B3
Glen Terrace	54 E1 [10]
Glen Walk	53 B3
Glen na Smol	57 B4
Glenaan Road	21 B2
Glenabbey Road	44 E4
Glenageary Avenue	54 D2
Glenageary Court	54 D2
Glenageary Hall	54 E2
Glenageary Lodge	54 D2
Glenageary Park	54 D2
Glenageary Road Lower	54 D1
Glenageary Road Upper	54 D1
Glenageary Woods	54 D1
Glenagle Grove	56 E1
Glenalbyn Road	52 F1
Glenalua Heights	54 E3
Glenalua Road	54 E3
Glenalua Terrace	54 E3
Glenamuck Cottages	55 A1
Glenamuck Road	55 A1
Glenann	42 F4 [4]
Glenanne	42 E2
Glenard Avenue	35 B1 [5]
Glenard Avenue	57 C2
Glenard Hall	43 C3 [7]
Glenarm Avenue	21 B4
Glenarriff Road	19 C3
Glenart Avenue	44 F4
Glenaulin	34 D2
Glenaulin Drive	34 D2
Glenaulin Green	34 C2 [2]
Glenaulin Park	34 D2
Glenaulin Road	33 C2
Glenavon Park	56 D1
Glenavy Park	42 E2
Glenayle Road	22 F1
Glenayr Road	42 F2
Glenbeigh Park	35 B1
Glenbeigh Road	35 B1
Glenbourne Avenue	52 F4
Glenbourne Close	52 F4
Glenbourne Crescent	52 F4
Glenbourne Drive	52 F4
Glenbourne Green	52 F4
Glenbourne Grove	52 F4
Glenbourne Park	52 F4
Glenbourne Road	52 F4
Glenbourne View	52 F4
Glenbourne Walk	52 F4
Glenbourne Way	52 F4
Glenbower Park	43 B4 [1]
Glenbrook Park	42 F4
Glenbrook Road	19 C3
Glenburgh Terrace	57 B2 [28]
Glencairn	52 E3
Glencairn Avenue	52 E3
Glencairn Close	52 E3
Glencairn Court	52 E4
Glencairn Crescent	52 E3
Glencairn Dale	52 E3
Glencairn Drive	52 E3
Glencairn Garth	52 E3 [1]
Glencairn Green	52 E3
Glencairn Heath	52 E3 [2]
Glencairn Lawn	52 E3
Glencairn Park	52 E3
Glencairn Road	52 E3
Glencairn View	52 E3
Glencairn Walk	52 E3
Glencairn Way	52 E3
Glencar Road	35 B1 [2]
Glencarr Court	56 E1 [8]
Glencarr Lawn	56 E1
Glencarraig	25 B1
Glencarrig Court	49 B2
Glencarrig Drive	49 B2
Glencarrig Green	49 B2
Glencloy Road	21 B2
Glencorp Road	21 C2
Glencourt Estate	57 B3
Glendale	16 D4
Glendale Drive	57 C4
Glendale Meadows	16 E4
Glendale Park	42 D3
Glendalough Road	21 A4 [6]
*Glendenning Lane	36 D3

STREET NAME	PAGE/GRID REFERENCE
(off Wicklow Street)	
Glendhu Park	19 C3
Glendhu Road	19 C3
Glendhu Villas	21 A4 [4]
Glendoher Avenue	50 F1
Glendoher Close	50 E1
Glendoher Drive	50 F1
Glendoher Park	50 E1
Glendoher Road	50 E1
Glendoo Close	41 B3
Glendown Avenue	42 D3
Glendown Close	42 D3
Glendown Court	42 D3
Glendown Crescent	42 D3
Glendown Green	42 D3
Glendown Grove	42 D3
Glendown Lawn	42 D3
Glendown Park	42 D3
Glendown Road	42 D3
Glendun Road	21 B2
Glenealy Downs	6 F4
Glenealy Road	35 B4
Glenfarne Road	22 F1
Glenfield Avenue	33 A2
Glenfield Close	33 A2
Glenfield Drive	33 A2
Glenfield Grove	33 A2
Glenfield Park	33 A2
Glengara Close	54 D1 [15]
Glengara Park	54 D1
Glengarriff Parade	36 D1
Glenhill Avenue	20 E2
Glenhill Court	20 E2
Glenhill Drive	20 E2
Glenhill Grove	20 E2
Glenhill Road	20 E2
Glenhill Villas	20 E2 [2]
Glenlucan	57 B3
Glenlyon	49 C2
Glenlyon Crescent	49 C2
Glenlyon Grove	49 C2
Glenlyon Park	49 C2
Glenmalure Park	35 B3 [13]
Glenmalure Square	43 B2
*Glenmalure Villas (Rialto)	35 B3
Glenmaroon Park	33 C2
Glenmaroon Road	33 C2
Glenmore Court	50 F2
Glenmore Park	50 F2
Glenmore Road	35 B1 [1]
Glenmurry Park	41 C3 [2]
Glenomena Grove	44 E2
Glenomena Park	44 E2
Glenpark Close	33 B1
Glenpark Drive	33 B1
Glenpark Road	33 B1
Glenshane Close	48 D1
Glenshane Crescent	48 D1
Glenshane Drive	48 D1
Glenshane Gardens	48 D1
Glenshane Green	48 D1
Glenshane Grove	48 D1
Glenshane Lawns	48 D1
Glenshane Park	48 D1
Glenshesk Road	21 C2
Glenside Villas	33 C1 [2]
Glenties Drive	20 D2
Glenties Park	20 D2
Glentow Road	21 B2
Glentworth Park	23 A1 [2]
Glenvar Park	44 F3
Glenvara Park	49 C2
Glenview	54 D3
Glenview Drive	49 B1 [2]
Glenview Lawn	49 B1
Glenview Park	49 B1
Glenville Avenue	18 E2
Glenville Court	18 E3
Glenville Drive	18 E2
Glenville Garth	18 E3
Glenville Green	18 E2
Glenville Grove	18 E2
Glenville Lawn	18 E2
Glenville Road	18 E3
Glenville Terrace	43 C4 [8]
Glenville Way	18 E2
Glenwood	57 B2
Glenwood Road	22 F1
Glin Avenue	11 B4
Glin Crescent	11 B4
Glin Drive	11 B4
Glin Grove	11 B4
Glin Park	11 B4
Glin Road	11 B4
Gloucester Diamond	36 E1 [52]

STREET NAME	PAGE/GRID REFERENCE
*Gloucester Lane (off Sean McDermott Street Lower)	36 E1
Gloucester Place	36 E1[25]
Gloucester Place Lower	36 E1[53]
Gloucester Place Lower	36 E1[54]
Gloucester Place Upper	36 E1[24]
Gloucester Street South	36 E2
Glovers Alley	36 D3[28]
*Glovers Court (off York Street)	36 D3
Goatstown	44 D4
Goatstown Avenue	43 C4
Goatstown Road	43 C4
*Godfrey Place (off Oxmanstown Road)	35 B1
Gofton Hall	20 E1[2]
Golden Lane	36 D3
Goldenbridge Avenue	35 A3
Goldenbridge Gardens	35 A3[4]
Goldenbridge Terrace	35 A3[5]
Goldenbridge Walk	34 F4
Goldenbridge Walk	35 A3[16]
Goldsmith Street	36 D1
Goldsmith Terrace	57 C2[25]
Gordon Avenue	53 A3
Gordon Place	36 D4[23]
Gordon Street	36 F3
Gorsefield Court	22 F2[1]
Gort na Mona Drive	53 B3
Gortbeg Avenue	20 E3
Gortbeg Drive	20 E3
Gortbeg Park	20 E3
Gortbeg Road	20 E3
Gortmore Avenue	20 E2
Gortmore Drive	20 E2
Gortmore Park	20 E3
Gortmore Road	20 E2
Gosworth Park	54 E1
Gowrie Park	54 D1
Grace O'Malley Drive	26 D2
Grace O'Malley Road	26 D2
Grace Park Avenue	21 B4
Grace Park Court	21 C2
Grace Park Gardens	21 B4
Grace Park Heights	21 C3
Grace Park Meadows	21 C3
Grace Park Road	21 C3
Grace Park Terrace	21 C3
Gracefield Avenue	22 F2
Gracefield Road	22 E2
Grafton Street	36 D3
Graham Court	36 D1[13]
Graham's Row	36 D1[54]
Graigue Court	9 C4
Granby Lane	36 D1
Granby Place	36 D2
Granby Row	36 D1
Grand Canal Docks	36 F3
Grand Canal Place	35 C3[2]
Grand Canal Quay	36 F3
Grand Canal Street Lower	36 F3
Grand Canal Street Upper	36 F3
Grand Canal View	35 A3
Grand Parade	36 E4
Grange Abbey Crescent	12 E4
Grange Abbey Drive	12 E4
Grange Abbey Grove	12 E4
Grange Avenue	12 F4
Grange Brook	50 F2
Grange Close	23 C1
Grange Cottages	53 B1[6]
Grange Court	51 A1
Grange Crescent	53 B2
Grange Downs	51 A1
Grange Drive	23 C1
Grange Grove	53 B1[2]
Grange Manor Avenue	51 A1
Grange Manor Close	51 A1
Grange Manor Drive	51 A1
Grange Manor Grove	51 A1
Grange Manor Road	51 A1
Grange Parade	23 C1
Grange Park (Baldoyle)	12 F4
Grange Park (Cornelscourt)	53 B2
Grange Park (Willbrook)	50 F1
Grange Park Avenue	23 A2
Grange Park Close	23 B2
Grange Park Crescent	23 B2
Grange Park Drive	23 A2
Grange Park Green	23 B2
Grange Park Grove	23 A2
Grange Park Rise	23 B1
Grange Park Road	23 A2
Grange Park View	23 B1
Grange Park Walk	23 A2
Grange Rise	12 F4
Grange Road (Baldoyle)	12 F4
Grange Road (Marley Park)	51 A2
Grange Road (Rathfarnham)	42 F4
Grange Road (The Priory)	50 F1
Grange Way	23 C1
Grange Wood (Ballinteer)	51 A2
*Grangegorman Villas (Grangegorman Upper)	35 C1
Grangegorman Lower	35 C2
Grangegorman Upper	35 C1
Grangemore	12 E4
Grangemore Avenue	12 E4
Grangemore Court	12 D4[6]
Grangemore Crescent	12 D4
Grangemore Drive	12 E4
Grangemore Grove	12 E4
Grangemore Lawn	12 E4
Grangemore Park	12 E4
Grangemore Rise	12 D4
Grangemore Road	12 D4
Grangewood (Kill O' The Grange)	53 C1
Granite Hall	54 D1[7]
Granite Place	36 F4[10]
Granite Terrace	34 F3[11]
Granitefield	53 C3
Grant's Row	36 E3[5]
Grantham Place	36 D4
Grantham Street	36 D4
Granville Close	54 D3
Granville Crescent	54 D3[2]
Granville Park	53 A1
Granville Road (Cabinteely)	53 C3
Granville Road (Deans Grange)	53 A2
Grattan Court	29 C4
Grattan Court East	36 F3[28]
Grattan Crescent	34 F3
Grattan Parade	21 A4
Grattan Place	36 F3[29]
Grattan Street	36 E3
Gray Square	35 C3[41]
*Gray Street (off Meath St.)	35 C3
Graysbrook	26 D2
Great Western Avenue	35 C1[18]
Great Western Square	35 C1[8]
Great Western Villas	35 C1[9]
Greek Street	36 D2
Green Acre Court	50 D1
Green Isle Court	40 D2[2]
Green Lane	29 A2
Green Lane (Leixlip)	15 C4
Green Park (Rathgar)	43 B3
Green Park Road	57 B2
Green Road (Blackrock)	44 F3
Green Street	36 D2
Green Street East	36 F2
Green Street Little	36 D2[8]
Greencastle Avenue	22 E1
Greencastle Crescent	22 E1
Greencastle Drive	11 B4
Greencastle Parade	22 F1
Greencastle Park	11 B4
Greencastle Road	22 E1
Greendale Avenue	23 C2
Greendale Court	23 B2[2]
Greendale Road	23 B2
Greenfield Crescent	44 D2
Greenfield Park	44 D2
Greenfield Park	49 C2
*Greenfield Place (off Mount Drummond Ave)	35 C4
Greenfield Road (Mount Merrion)	44 E3
Greenfield Road (Sutton)	25 B1
Greenfort Avenue	33 A2
Greenfort Close	33 A2
Greenfort Crescent	33 A2
Greenfort Drive	33 A2
Greenfort Gardens	33 A2
Greenfort Lawns	33 A2
Greenfort Park	33 A2
Greenhills	41 B3
Greenhills Road	41 A4
Greenlands	48 D2
Greenlea Avenue	42 E2
Greenlea Drive	42 E2
Greenlea Grove	42 E2
Greenlea Park	42 E3
Greenlea Road	42 E3
Greenmount Avenue	35 C4[9]
Greenmount Court	35 C4[19]
Greenmount Lane	35 C4
Greenmount Lawns	42 F2
Greenmount Road	42 F2
Greenmount Square	35 C4[14]
Greenore Terrace	36 F3[26]
Greenpark Road	31 C2
Greenridge Court	18 E1
Greentrees Drive	41 C2
Greentrees Park	41 C2
Greentrees Road	41 C2
Greenville Avenue	35 C4[11]
*Greenville Parade (Blackpitts)	35 C3
Greenville Road	45 B4
Greenville Terrace	35 C4
Grenville Lane	36 D1[15]
Grenville Street	36 D1
Grey's Lane	26 D2
Greygates	44 E3
Greygates	44 E4[1]
Greythorn Park	54 D1
Griffith Avenue	21 B3
Griffith Close	20 F2
Griffith Court	21 C4
Griffith Downs	21 B3
Griffith Drive	20 F2
Griffith Lawns	21 A3
Griffith Parade	20 F2
Griffith Road	20 F2
Griffith Square	35 C4[22]
Grosvenor Avenue	58 D3[3]
Grosvenor Court	22 E4
Grosvenor Court	42 D3
Grosvenor Lane	43 A1[8]
Grosvenor Lodge	43 A1
Grosvenor Park	43 A1[7]
Grosvenor Place	43 A1
Grosvenor Road	43 A1
Grosvenor Square	43 A1
Grosvenor Terrace (Dalkey)	54 F2[17]
Grosvenor Terrace (Dun Laoghaire)	45 C4[9]
*Grosvenor Villas (Dalkey) (Off Sorento Rd.)	54 F2
Grosvenor Villas (Rathmines)	43 A1
Grotto Avenue	44 F2
Grotto Place	44 F2
Grove Avenue	3 C3
Grove Avenue (Finglas)	20 E1
Grove Avenue (Harold's Cross)	36 D4[47]
Grove Avenue (Mount Merrion)	44 F4
Grove Lane	11 C4
Grove Lawn	44 F4
Grove Lawns (Malahide)	3 C3
Grove Park (Rathmines)	36 D4
Grove Park Avenue	20 F1
Grove Park Crescent	20 F1
Grove Park Drive	20 F1
Grove Park Road	20 F1
Grove Road	3 B3
Grove Road (Finglas)	20 E1
Grove Road (Malahide)	3 C3
Grove Road (Rathmines)	36 D4
Grove Wood	20 E1
Guild Street	36 F2
Guilford Terrace	56 E3[1]
Gulistan Cottages	43 A1
Gulistan Place	43 A1
Gulistan Terrace	43 A1
Gurteen Avenue	34 D3
Gurteen Park	34 D3
Gurteen Road	34 D2

H

STREET NAME	PAGE/GRID REFERENCE
HACKETSLAND	56 E1
Haddington Lawns	54 E2
Haddington Park	54 E2
Haddington Place	36 F3[18]
Haddington Road	36 F3
Haddington Terrace	46 D4[7]
Haddon Court	37 B1[2]
Haddon Park	22 D4
Haddon Road	22 E4
Hadleigh Court	19 A3
Hadleigh Green	19 A3[2]
Hadleigh Park	19 A3
Hagan's Court	36 E3[39]
Haigh Terrace	46 D4
Hainault Drive	53 B3
Hainault Grove	53 B3[2]
Hainault Lawn	53 B3[3]
Hainault Park	53 A3
Hainault Road	53 A3
Halliday Road	35 C2
Halliday Square	35 B2[2]
Halston Street	36 D2
*Hamilton Court (off Strand St. Little)	36 D2
Hamilton Street	35 C4[1]
Hammond Lane	35 C2
Hammond Street	35 C3[56]
Hampstead Avenue	21 A2
Hampstead Court	21 A2
Hampstead Park	21 A3
Hampton Court	34 F3[16]
Hampton Court (Clontarf)	22 F4
Hampton Crescent	44 E3
Hampton Green	35 B1
Hampton Park	44 E3
Hanbury Lane (Lucan)	32 D1[3]
Hanbury Lane (The Coombe)	35 C3
Hanlon's Lane	3 B2
Hannaville Park	42 F2
Hanover Lane	36 D3[1]
Hanover Quay	36 F2
Hanover Square	36 D3[4]
Hanover Street East	36 E2
Hanover Street West	35 C3[47]
Harbour Court	36 E2[18]
Harbour Crescent	54 F1
Harbour Road (Dalkey)	54 F1
Harbour Road (Dun Laoghaire)	46 D4
Harbour Road (Howth)	26 D1
Harbour Terrace	45 C4[8]
Harbour View	26 D1[1]
Harcourt Lane	36 D4[14]
Harcourt Lodge	35 A3[22]
Harcourt Road	36 D4
Harcourt Street	36 D3
Harcourt Terrace	36 E4
*Harcourt Villas (off Dundrum Rd/Mulvey Pk.)	43 C3
Hardebeck Avenue	41 C1
Hardiman Road	21 A3
*Hardwicke Arch (off Hardwicke St.)	36 D1
Hardwicke Lane	36 D1[45]
Hardwicke Place	36 D1[12]
Hardwicke Street	36 D1
Harelawn Avenue	33 A3
Harelawn Crescent	33 A3
Harelawn Drive	33 A2
Harelawn Green	33 A3
Harelawn Grove	33 B2
Harelawn Park	33 A2
Harlech Crescent	44 D3
Harlech Downs	43 C3
Harlech Grove	44 D3
Harlech Villas	43 C3[4]
Harman Street	35 C3[54]
Harmonstown Road	22 F2
Harmony Avenue	43 C1[5]
Harmony Court	43 C1[20]
Harmony Row	36 E3[23]
*Harold Crescent (off Eden Rd. Lower)	54 E1
Harold Road	35 C2
Harold Ville Avenue	35 B3
Harold's Cross	42 F1
Harold's Cross Cottages	35 C4[18]
Harold's Cross Road	42 F1
Harold's Grange Road	51 B3
Harrington Street	36 D4
Harrison Row	42 F2
Harry Street	36 D3[17]
Hartstown	17 B1
Hartstown Road	17 C2
Harty Avenue	41 C1
Harty Court	41 C1
*Harty Court (off Daniel Street)	36 D3
Harty Place	36 D3
Harvard	44 D3
Hastings Street	36 F3[5]
Hastings Terrace	54 E1[12]
Hatch Lane	36 E4[2]
Hatch Place	36 E4[13]
Hatch Street Lower	36 E4
Hatch Street Upper	36 D4
Hatter's Lane	35 C4[15]
Havelock Square	36 F3
Havelock Terrace	37 A3[17]
Haven View	3 B2[1]
Haverty Road	21 C4
Hawkins Street	36 E2
Hawthorn Avenue	36 F1
Hawthorn Drive	51 B1[2]
Hawthorn Lawn	18 F3
Hawthorn Lodge	18 F3
Hawthorn Manor	53 A1[4]
Hawthorn Road	40 F1
Hawthorn Road	52 D2

STREET NAME	PAGE/GRID REFERENCE	STREET NAME	PAGE/GRID REFERENCE	STREET NAME	PAGE/GRID REFERENCE	STREET NAME	PAGE/GRID REFERENCE
Hawthorn Terrace	36 F1	Hermitage Green (Lucan)	32 F1	Holles Place	36 E3[34]	Idrone Drive	50 D1
Hawthorn View	30 D2	Hermitage Grove (Grange Road)	51 A1	Holles Row	36 E3 [7]	Idrone Mews	45 A3[11]
Hawthorns	52 D2	Hermitage Lawn (Grange Road)	51 A1	Holles Street	36 E3	Idrone Park	50 D1
Hayden's Lane	32 D3	Hermitage Manor (Lucan)	32 F1	Holly Court	56 D1 [4]	Idrone Terrace	45 A3
Haymarket	35 C2	Hermitage Park (Grange Road)	51 A1	Holly Park	56 E2	Imaal Road	35 C1
Hazel Avenue	52 D1	Hermitage Park (Lucan)	32 F1	Holly Park Avenue	53 A1	Inagh Court	56 E1
Hazel Grove	12 F2	Hermitage Place (Lucan)	32 F1	Holly Road (Donnycarney)	22 D3	Inagh Road	34 D3
Hazel Lawn	18 E2	Hermitage Road (Lucan)	32 F1	Holly Road (Fox and Geese)	40 F1	Inbhir Ide	3 A2
Hazel Lawn	53 C2 [4]	Hermitage Valley (Lucan)	32 F1	Hollybank Avenue Lower	43 B1	Inbhir Ide Close	3 A2
Hazel Park	42 E2 [2]	Hermitage View (Grange Road)	50 F1	Hollybank Avenue Upper	43 B1	Inbhir Ide Drive	3 A2
Hazel Road	22 D3	Hermitage Way (Lucan)	32 F1	Hollybank Road	21 A4	Inchicore	34 F3
Hazel Villas	52 D1	Heuston Square	35 A3[11]	Hollybrook Court	22 D4 [3]	Inchicore Road	35 A3
Hazelbrook Court	42 E2	*Hewardine Terrace	36 E1	Hollybrook Court Drive	22 D4 [2]	Inchicore Square	34 F3[13]
Hazelbrook Drive	42 E2	(off Killarney Street)		Hollybrook Grove	22 D4	Inchicore Terrace North	34 F3 [3]
Hazelbrook Road	42 E2	Heytesbury Lane	36 F4	Hollybrook Park	22 D4	Inchicore Terrace South	34 F3
Hazelcroft Gardens	20 E2	Heytesbury Street	36 D3	Hollybrook Road	22 D4	Infirmary Road	35 B2
Hazelcroft Park	20 E2	Hibernian Avenue	36 F1 [5]	Hollystown	7 B1	Inglewood Close	17 C2
Hazelcroft Road	20 E2	Hibernian Terrace	34 E2 [3]	Hollyville Lawn	33 C1	Inglewood Crescent	17 C2
Hazeldene	43 C1	High Park	21 C2	Hollywood Drive	44 D4	Inglewood Drive	17 C2
Hazelwood (Bray)	57 B2	High Street	36 D3	Hollywood Park	44 D4	Inglewood Road	17 C2
Hazelwood (Shankill)	56 E2	Highbridge Green	52 E1	*Holme's Cottages	43 A1	Ingram Road	35 C4 [2]
Hazelwood Avenue	17 C1	Highfield Avenue (Dundrum)	51 A2	(Church Avenue Rathmines)		Inis Fail	48 F2
Hazelwood Bank	40 D2	Highfield Close	1 C2	Holmston Avenue	54 D1	Inis Thiar	48 F2
Hazelwood Close	40 D2	Highfield Court	43 A2 [3]	Holmwood	53 B4	*Inkerman Cottages	36 E2
Hazelwood Court	17 C1	Highfield Crescent	1 C2	Holycross Avenue	21 B4 [5]	(off Amiens Street)	
Hazelwood Court	22 D1	Highfield Downs	1 C2	*Holycross Cottages	21 B4	Innisfallen Parade	36 D1
Hazelwood Crescent	17 C1	Highfield Drive	51 A2	(off Holycross Avenue)		Innishmaan Road	21 B2
Hazelwood Crescent	40 D2	Highfield Green	1 C2	Holyrood Park	37 A4	*Innishmore Terrace	42 D1
Hazelwood Drive	22 D2	Highfield Grove	43 A2	Holywell	52 D1	(St Mary's Road)	
Hazelwood Green	17 C1	Highfield Lawn	1 C2	Holywell Crescent	23 B1	Innismore	42 D1
Hazelwood Grove	22 E1	Highfield Park	31 A1	Holywell Road	23 B1	*Inns Court	36 D2
Hazelwood Lane	40 D2	Highfield Park	43 B3	Home Farm Park	21 B3	(on Winetavern Street)	
Hazelwood Park	22 E1	Highfield Road	43 A2	Home Farm Road	21 A3	Inns Quay	35 C2
Hazelwood View	40 D2	Highland Avenue	53 B3	Home Villas	43 C1	Inver Road	20 E4
Headford Grove	43 B4	Highland Grove	53 B3	Homelawn Avenue	49 B1	Invermore Grove	23 A1 [3]
Healthfield Road	42 F2	Highland Lawn	53 B3	Homelawn Drive	49 B1	Inverness Road	21 C4
*Healy Street	36 E1	Highland View	53 B3	Homelawn Gardens	49 B1	Iona Crescent	21 A4
(off Rutland Place North)		Highridge Green	52 E1	Homelawn Road	49 B1	Iona Drive	21 A4
Heany Avenue	54 F2[19]	Highthorn Park	53 C1	*Homelawn Villas	49 A1	Iona Park	21 A4
Heatfield Road	42 F2	Highthorn Woods	53 C1[10]	(Homelawn Road)		Iona Road	21 A4
Heather Close	51 A2	Hill Cottages	54 E3 [1]	Homelee	37 A4[11]	Iona Villas	21 A4
Heather Drive	51 A2	Hill Court	12 F1	Homeleigh	18 D4	Iris Grove	44 E3
Heather Gardens	4 D4	Hill Drive	3 B3	Homeville	43 A1	Irishtown	37 A3
Heather Grove (Ballinteer)	51 B2	Hill Street	36 D1	Honey Park	54 D2 [1]	Irishtown (Bray)	57 B4
Heather Grove (Palmerston)	33 B2	Hill View	51 B1	Hope Avenue	36 F1	Irishtown Road	37 A3
Heather Lawn	51 A2	Hill View Court	51 B1	*Hope Street (off Gordon Street)	36 F3	Irvine Cottages	36 F2[10]
Heather Park	51 B2	Hillcourt Park	54 D2	Horton Court	42 F2	Irvine Terrace	36 F2
Heather Road	51 A2	Hillcourt Road	54 D2	Hospital Lane	35 A2 [2]	Irwin Court	35 B3[24]
Heather Road	52 E2	Hillcrest	3 A2 [1]	Hotel Yard	36 D2[29]	Irwin Street	35 B3 [1]
Heather View Avenue	48 F2	Hillcrest	42 D4	Houghton Terrace	35 C2[28]	Island Street	35 C2
Heather View Close	48 F2	Hillcrest (Templeogue)	42 D4	*Howard Street	36 F3	Island View	3 C3
Heather View Drive	48 F2	Hillcrest Avenue	31 C2	(off Gordon Street)		Island Villa	36 F3 [3]
Heather View Lawn	48 F2	Hillcrest Close	31 C2	Howth	26 D2	Islandbridge	35 A2
Heather View Park	48 F2	Hillcrest Court	32 D2	Howth Junction Cottages	23 B1 [1]	Islandbridge Court	35 A2 [1]
Heather View Road	48 F2	Hillcrest Downs	52 D3	Howth Road (Howth)	25 C1	Islington Avenue	46 E4
Heather Walk	4 D4	Hillcrest Drive	31 C2	Howth Road (Killester)	22 E3	Isolda Road	37 A3
Heatherwood	57 B4	Hillcrest Green	31 C2	Howth Road (Marino)	22 D4	Isolde Gardens	34 E2 [6]
*Heatley Villas (on Pearse Road)	53 C2	Hillcrest Grove	32 D2	Howth Road (Raheny)	22 F3	Ivar Street	35 C2
Heidelberg	44 D3	Hillcrest Heights	31 C2	Howth Road (Sutton)	25 B1	Iveagh Buildings	36 D3 [4]
Hempenstal Terrace	37 B4 [5]	Hillcrest Lawns	31 C2	Howth Terrace	26 D1 [5]	Iveagh Gardens	35 A4
Hendrick Place	35 C2 [9]	Hillcrest Park	20 F2	Howth View Park	23 B1	Iveleary Road	21 B2
Hendrick Street	35 C2	Hillcrest Park	31 C2	Huband Road	34 F4	Iveragh Road	21 B2
Henley Court	43 B4 [8]	Hillcrest Road (Lucan)	32 D2	Hudson Road	54 E1	Ivy Terrace	35 C3[61]
Henley Park	43 B4	Hillcrest Road (Sandyford)	52 D3	Hughes Road East	41 C1		
Henley Villas	43 B4	Hillcrest View	31 C2	Hughes Road North	41 C1	**J**	
Henrietta Lane	36 D1	Hillcrest Walk	31 C2	Hughes Road South	41 C1		
Henrietta Place	36 D2	Hillcrest Way	31 C2	Hume Street	36 E3	JAMES CONNOLLY PARK	33 A4
Henrietta Street	36 D2	Hillsbrook Avenue	42 D2	Huntstown Avenue	17 C1	James Connolly Square	57 C2 [5]
Henry Place	36 D2[16]	Hillsbrook Crescent	42 D2	Huntstown Close	17 C1	James Everett Park	57 B2
Henry Street	36 D2	Hillsbrook Drive	42 D2	Huntstown Court	6 F4	James Larkin Road	23 B2
Herbert Avenue	44 E1	Hillsbrook Grove	42 D2	Huntstown Drive	6 F4	James McCormack Gardens	24 E1 [1]
Herbert Cottages	36 F4 [4]	Hillside	54 E2	Huntstown Glen	6 F4	James's Place East	36 E3
Herbert Crescent	18 F2 [1]	Hillside Drive	43 A3	Huntstown Green	6 F4	James's Street	35 B3
Herbert Lane	36 E3[41]	Hillside Park	50 E1	Huntstown Grove	6 F4	James's Street East	36 E3
Herbert Park	36 F4	Hillside Terrace	26 D2 [7]	Huntstown Lawn	18 D1 [1]	James's Street North	36 F1[20]
Herbert Park	57 B3	Hillside View	23 C2 [1]	Huntstown Park (Mulhuddart)	6 F4	James's Terrace	3 B2
Herbert Park Lane	36 F4	Hilltop Lawn	56 D3	Huntstown Rise	7 A4	Jamestown Avenue	34 F4
*Herbert Place	36 E3	Hilltown	1 B3	Huntstown Road	17 C1	Jamestown Court	34 F4
(Baggot Street Lower)		Hilltown Close	1 C2	Huntstown Way	7 A4	Jamestown Road (Finglas)	20 E1
*Herbert Place (off Bath St.)	37 A3	Hilltown Court	1 C2	Huntstown Wood	6 F4	Jamestown Road (Inchicore)	34 F4
Herbert Road	57 B3	Hilltown Green	1 C2	Hutchinson's Strand	2 E1	*Jane-Ville (Off Tivoli Road)	46 D4
Herbert Road (Blanchardstown)	18 F2	Hilltown Grove	1 C2	Huxley Crescent	35 C3 [8]	Jervis Lane Lower	36 D2[11]
Herbert Road (Sandymount)	37 A4	Hilltown Lawn	1 C2	Hyacinth Street	36 F1 [7]	Jervis Lane Upper	36 D2[10]
Herbert Street	36 E3	Hilltown Park	1 C2	Hybreasal	35 A3 [1]	Jervis Street	36 D2
Herbert View	57 B2[26]	Hilltown Road	1 C2	Hyde Park (Dalkey)	54 E1	Jobstown	48 D2
Herberton Drive	35 B4	Hilltown Way	1 C2	Hyde Park (Templeogue)	42 E3	Jobstown Road	48 D2
Herberton Park	35 B3[15]	Hillview	51 B1	Hyde Park Avenue	44 F3	John Dillon Street	36 D3
Herberton Road	35 B3	Hillview Cottages	53 C2 [1]	Hyde Park Gardens	44 F3	John F. Kennedy Avenue	41 A1
Hermitage Avenue (Grange Road)	50 F1	Hillview Drive	53 C2	Hyde Road	54 F1	John F. Kennedy Drive	41 A1
Hermitage Close (Grange Road)	51 A1	Hillview Lawn	53 C2			John F. Kennedy Park	34 D4
Hermitage Court (Grange Road)	51 A1	Hilton Gardens	51 C2	**I**		John F. Kennedy Road	34 D4
Hermitage Crescent (Lucan)	32 F1	*Hoeys Court	36 D3			John Field Road	36 D3[40]
Hermitage Downs	51 A1	(off Werburgh Street)		IDRONE AVENUE	50 D1	John MacCormack Avenue	41 C1
Hermitage Drive (Grange Road)	50 F1	Hogan Avenue	36 F3[27]	Idrone Close	50 D1	*John Street North	35 C2
Hermitage Garden (Lucan)	32 F1	Hogan Place	36 E3			(off Ellis Quay)	

STREET NAME	PAGE/GRID REFERENCE
John Street South	35 C3
John Street West	35 C3
John's Lane East	36 D3[52]
John's Lane West	35 C3[50]
Johnson Place	36 D3[36]
Johnson's Court	36 D3[30]
Johnstown Avenue	53 C3
Johnstown Court	53 C2
Johnstown Gardens	20 E2[5]
Johnstown Grove	53 E3
Johnstown House	20 F2[3]
Johnstown Lane	53 C3
Johnstown Park (Cornelscourt)	53 C3
Johnstown Park (Glasnevin)	20 F2
Johnstown Road	53 C3
Jones's Road	36 E1
Josephine Avenue	36 D1[25]
*Joy Street (off Gordon Street)	36 F3
Joyce Avenue	53 A3
Joyce Road	21 A3
Jugback Lane	1 C1

K

STREET NAME	PAGE/GRID REFERENCE
KEADEEN AVENUE	41 B3
Kearn's Place	35 A3[7]
*Keegan's Cottages (off Merrion Rd.)	44 E1
Keeper Road	35 B4
Kells Road	42 E1
Kelly's Avenue	46 D4
Kelly's Lane	36 D1[22]
Kelly's Row	36 D1
Kellystown Road	51 B3
Kelvin Close	4 D4
Kempton	19 C3
Kempton Avenue	19 C3
Kempton Court	19 C3
Kempton Green	19 C3
Kempton Grove	19 C3
Kempton Heath	19 C3
Kempton Lawn	19 C3
Kempton Park	19 C3
Kempton Rise	19 C3
Kempton View	19 C3
Kempton Way	19 C3
Kenilworth Lane	42 F1
Kenilworth Park	42 F1
Kenilworth Road	43 A1
Kenilworth Square	42 F1
Kenilworth Square East	43 A1
Kenilworth Square North	42 F1
Kenilworth Square South	42 F1
Kenilworth Square West	42 F1
Kenmare Parade	36 D1[31]
Kennedy Park	57 C4[5]
Kennedy's Villas	35 B3[2]
Kennelsfort Green	33 B2
Kennelsfort Road Lower	33 C1
Kennelsfort Road Upper	33 C2
Kennington Close	41 C4
Kennington Crescent	41 C4
Kennington Lawn	41 C4
Kennington Road	41 C3
*Kent Terrace (on Barnhill Road Dalkey)	54 F2
Kerlogue Road	37 A3
Kerrymount Avenue	53 A4
Kerrymount Close	53 B3[1]
Kerrymount Green	53 B3
Kerrymount Mall	53 B3
Kerrymount Rise	53 B3
Kettles Lane	2 E4
*Kevin Barry (off Church Street Upper)	35 C2
*Kevin Street Cross (on Bride St. New)	36 D3
Kevin Street Lower	36 D3
Kevin Street Upper	36 D3
Kew Park	31 C1
Kew Park Avenue	31 B2
Kew Park Crescent	31 B1
Kickham Road	35 A3
Kilakee Close	41 B3
Kilakee Drive	41 B3
Kilakee Road	50 D4
Kilbarrack	23 C1
Kilbarrack Avenue	23 C2
Kilbarrack Gardens	23 C2
Kilbarrack Grove	23 C2
Kilbarrack Parade	23 C1
Kilbarrack Road	23 B1
Kilbarrack Way	23 B1
Kilbarron Avenue	22 D1
Kilbarron Court	22 D1[1]

STREET NAME	PAGE/GRID REFERENCE
Kilbarron Drive	22 D1
Kilbarron Park	22 D1
Kilbarron Road	22 D1
Kilbegnet Close	54 F2[24]
Kilbogget Grove	53 C4
Kilbogget Villas	53 C4[1]
*Kilbride Cottages (Killarney Road)	57 B3
*Kilbride Court (Killarney Road)	57 B3
*Kilbride Grove	57 B3
Kilbride Lane	57 B3
Kilbride Road	22 E3
Kilbrina	5 B2
Kilcarrig Avenue	40 E4
Kilcarrig Close	48 D1
Kilcarrig Crescent	40 E4
Kilcarrig Green	40 E4
Kilclare Avenue	48 E2
Kilclare Crescent	48 E2
Kilclare Drive	48 E2
Kilclare Gardens	48 E2
Kilcolman Court	54 E2[4]
Kilcroney Lane	57 A4
Kilcross Avenue	52 D3
Kilcross Close	52 D3
Kilcross Court	51 C3
Kilcross Crescent	51 C3
Kilcross Drive	51 C3
Kilcross Grove	51 C3
Kilcross Lawn	52 D3
Kilcross Park	51 C3
Kilcross Road	52 D3
Kilcross Way	51 C3
Kildare Park	42 D1
Kildare Place	36 E3[25]
Kildare Road	42 D1
Kildare Street	36 E3
Kildonan Avenue	20 D1
Kildonan Drive	20 D1
Kildonan Road	20 D1
Kilfenora Drive	23 A1
Kilfenora Road	42 E1
Kilgobbin Heights	52 E4
Kilgobbin Road	52 E3
Kilkieran Court	20 E4[1]
Kilkieran Road	20 E4
Kill Abbey	53 B1
Kill Avenue	53 C1
Kill Lane	53 B2
Kill O' the Grange	53 C1
Killadoon Park	29 C4
Killakee Avenue	49 B2
Killakee Court	49 B2
Killakee Gardens	49 B2
Killakee Green	49 B2
Killakee Lawns	49 B2
Killakee Park	49 B2
Killakee View	49 B2
Killakee Way	49 B2
Killala Road	20 E4
Killan Road	36 F2
Killarney Avenue	36 E1[13]
Killarney Heights	57 B3
Killarney Lane	57 B3
Killarney Parade	36 D1[30]
Killarney Park	57 B3
Killarney Road	57 B3
Killarney Street	36 E1
Killarney Villas	57 C2[48]
Killary Grove	23 B1
Killeck Lane	1 A3
Killeen	2 F3
Killeen Avenue	2 F2
Killeen Court	2 F3
Killeen Crescent	2 F3
Killeen Mews	3 B3
Killeen Park	2 F3
Killeen Road (Fox and Geese)	41 A1
Killeen Road (Rathmines)	43 B1
Killeen Terrace	3 B2
*Killery Terrace (Upper Dargle Road)	57 B2
Killester	22 E3
Killester Avenue	22 E3
Killester Park	22 E3
Killinarden Estate	48 E2
Killinarden Heights	48 E2
Killinarden Road	48 E3
Killiney	54 E3
Killiney Avenue	54 E4
Killiney Avenue	54 E4[7]
Killiney Court	56 E1[1]
Killiney Gate	54 E4
Killiney Grove	54 E2
Killiney Heath	54 E4

STREET NAME	PAGE/GRID REFERENCE
Killiney Hill Road	54 E3
Killiney Hill Road	56 E1
Killiney Oaks	56 E1[2]
Killiney Road	54 E2
Killiney Terrace	54 E1[15]
Killiney Towers	54 E2[2]
*Killiney View (off Albert Road)	54 E1
Kilmacud Avenue	52 E1
Kilmacud Park	52 E1
Kilmacud Road Upper	52 E1
Kilmahuddrick Avenue	39 B1
Kilmahuddrick Close	39 B1
Kilmahuddrick Court	39 B1
Kilmahuddrick Crescent	39 B1
Kilmahuddrick Drive	39 B1
Kilmahuddrick Green	39 B1
Kilmahuddrick Grove	39 B1
Kilmahuddrick Lawn	39 B1
Kilmahuddrick Place	39 B1
Kilmahuddrick Road	39 B1
Kilmahuddrick Walk	39 B1
Kilmahuddrick Way	39 B1
Kilmainham	35 A3
Kilmainham Lane	35 B3
Kilmantain Place	57 C2[10]
Kilmartin Avenue	48 D1
Kilmartin Crescent	40 D4
Kilmartin Drive	48 D1
Kilmartin Gardens	48 D1
Kilmartin Green	48 D1
Kilmartin Park	48 D1
Kilmashogue Close	41 B3
Kilmashogue Drive	41 B3
Kilmashogue Grove	41 B3
Kilmashogue Lane	50 F3
Kilmore	22 D1
Kilmore Avenue (Coolock)	22 E1
Kilmore Avenue (Killiney)	54 E4
Kilmore Close	22 E1
Kilmore Crescent	22 E1
Kilmore Drive	22 E1
Kilmore Road	22 D1
Kilmorony Close	23 A1[4]
Kilnamanagh	41 A3
Kilnamanagh Road	41 C1
Kilohan Grove	41 B3
Kilrock Road	26 E2
Kilronan Court	22 D4[7]
Kilshane Road	19 C2
Kiltalown Avenue	48 D2
Kiltalown Close	48 D2
Kiltalown Court	48 D2
Kiltalown Crescent	48 D2
Kiltalown Drive	48 D2
Kiltalown Green	48 D2
Kiltalown Grove	48 D2
Kiltalown Heights	48 D2
Kiltalown Hill	48 D2
Kiltalown Park	48 D2
Kiltalown Road	48 D2
Kiltalown View	48 D2
Kiltalown Walk	48 D2
Kiltalown Way	48 D2
Kilteragh Drive	53 A3
Kilteragh Pines	53 A3[2]
Kilteragh Road	53 A3
Kiltiernan	55 A2
Kiltipper Avenue	49 A2
Kiltipper Close	49 A2
Kiltipper Drive	49 A2
Kiltipper Road	49 A3
Kiltuck Park	56 E4[1]
Kilvere	42 E4
Kilworth Road	34 F4
Kimmage	42 D2
Kimmage Court	42 E2[3]
Kimmage Grove	42 E2
Kimmage Road Lower	42 F1
Kimmage Road West	42 D2
Kinahan Street	35 B2[4]
Kincora Avenue	22 E4
Kincora Court	37 C1
Kincora Drive	22 E4
Kincora Grove	22 E4
Kincora Park	22 E4
Kincora Road	22 E4
King Edward Lawn	57 B2
King Edward Park	57 B2
King Edward Road	57 B2
King Street North	35 C2
King Street South	36 D3
King's Avenue	36 E1
King's Court	35 C1[19]
King's Inns Street	36 D2
Kingram Place	36 E4

STREET NAME	PAGE/GRID REFERENCE
Kings Hall	34 E2
Kings Inns	36 D2
Kingscourt	57 B4[1]
Kingsland Parade	36 D4[5]
Kingsland Park Avenue	36 D4[4]
Kingsmill Road	57 C2
Kingston	51 B3
Kingston Avenue	51 B3
Kingston Close	51 B3
Kingston Court	50 F2[1]
Kingston Crescent	51 B3
Kingston Drive	51 C3
Kingston Green	51 B3
Kingston Grove	51 B3
Kingston Heights	51 C3
Kingston Lawn	51 B3
Kingston Lodge	21 B4[12]
Kingston Park	51 B3
Kingston Rise	51 B3
Kingston View	51 B3
Kingston Walk	51 B3
Kingswood Avenue	40 F3
Kingswood Castle	41 A2
Kingswood Drive	40 F3
Kingswood Heights	40 F3
Kingswood View	40 F3
Kinsaley	12 D1
Kinsaley Lane	3 A4
Kinsealy Court	2 E3
Kinsealy Downs	2 E3
Kinvara Avenue	20 D4
Kinvara Drive	19 C4
Kinvara Grove	19 C4
Kinvara Park	19 C4
Kinvara Road	19 C4
Kippure Avenue	41 B3
Kippure Park	20 D3
Kirkfield	18 D2[2]
Kirkpatrick Avenue	18 D3
Kirkpatrick Drive	18 D3
Kirkwood	37 A4
Kirwan Street	35 C2
Kirwan Street Cottages	35 C1[10]
Kitestown Road	26 E3
Knapton Court	45 C4[21]
Knapton Lawn	45 C4[22]
Knapton Road	45 C4
Knapton Terrace	45 C4[27]
*Knapton Villas (Knapton Road)	45 C4
Knights Bridge	22 E4[3]
Knights Wood	10 F4
Knock-na-Cree Grove	54 F2
Knock-na-Cree Park	54 F2
Knock-na-Cree Road	54 F2
Knockaire	50 D1
Knockaulin	16 D4
Knockcullen Drive	50 D1
Knockcullen Lawn	50 D1
Knockcullen Park	50 D1
Knockcullen Rise	50 D1
Knockfield Green	49 C1
Knockfield Manor	49 C1
Knocklyon Avenue	49 C1
Knocklyon Close	50 D1
Knocklyon Court	50 D1
Knocklyon Drive	50 D1
Knocklyon Green	50 D1
Knocklyon Grove	50 D1
Knocklyon Heights	49 C1
Knocklyon Mews	49 C1[2]
Knocklyon Park	50 D1
Knocklyon Road	50 D1
Knockmaroon Hill	34 D1
Knockmaroon Road	34 D1
Knockmeenagh Lane	40 E2
Knockmeenagh Road	40 E2
Knockmitten Close	40 F1[1]
Knockmitten Lane	41 A1
Knockmitten Lane North	40 F1[2]
Knockmore Avenue	48 E2
Knockmore Crescent	48 E2
Knockmore Drive	48 E2
Knockmore Gardens	48 E2
Knockmore Green	48 E2
Knockmore Grove	48 E2
Knockmore Park	48 E2
Knocknacree Park	54 F2
Knocknarea Avenue	35 A4
Knocknarea Road	35 A4
Knocknarrow Terrace	35 B3[34]
Knocknashee	43 C4
Knocknashee	44 D4
Knocksinna	53 A2
Knocksinna Court	53 A2[2]
Knocksinna Crescent	53 A2

STREET NAME	PAGE/GRID REFERENCE
Knocksinna Grove	53 A2 [1]
Knocksinna Park	53 A2
Knowth Court	9 C4
Kyber Road	34 F2
Kyle-Clare Road	37 A3[13]
Kylemore Avenue	34 D3
Kylemore Drive	34 D3
Kylemore Park North	34 D4
Kylemore Park South	34 D4
Kylemore Park West	34 D4
Kylemore Road	34 D2

L

STREET NAME	PAGE/GRID REFERENCE
LA TOUCHE COURT	34 F4 [3]
La Touche Court	51 B2
La Touche Drive	34 E4
La Touche Road	34 F4
La Vista Avenue (Howth)	25 B2
Labre Park	34 E4
Laburnum Road	43 C2
Laburnum Walk	33 B2
Lad Lane	36 E3
Lad Lane Upper	36 E4
Lady's Lane	35 A3[13]
Lady's Well Road	7 A4
Lagan Road	20 E3
Lakelands Avenue	52 D1
Lakelands Close	52 D1
Lakelands Crescent	52 E1
Lakelands Drive	52 E1
Lakelands Grove	52 D1
Lakelands Lawn	52 D1
Lakelands Park	42 E3
Lakelands Place	52 D1
Lakelands Road	52 E1
Lally Road	34 E3
Lamb Alley	35 C3
Lamb's Brook	52 D3 [1]
*Lamb's Court (off James Street)	35 B3
Lambay Close	56 E1
Lambay Court	3 C3
Lambay Drive	56 E1
Lambay Road	21 A3
Lambourne Avenue	17 C2
Lambourne Court	17 C2
Lambourne Drive	17 C2
Lambourne Park	17 C2
Lambourne Road	17 C2
Lambourne Village	22 E4 [3]
Lambourne Wood	53 C4
Landen Road	34 F3
Landscape Avenue	43 A3
Landscape Crescent	43 A4
Landscape Gardens	43 B4
Landscape Park	43 A3
Landscape Road	43 A3
Lanesville	53 B1
Langrishe Place	36 E1[23]
Lanndale Lawn	48 E1
Lansdowne Crescent	36 F3[43]
Lansdowne Gardens	36 F4 [7]
Lansdowne Hall	37 A3[25]
Lansdowne Lane	36 F3[20]
Lansdowne Park (Ballsbridge)	36 F3
Lansdowne Park (Templeogue)	50 D1
Lansdowne Road	36 F4
Lansdowne Square	37 A4[24]
Lansdowne Terrace	36 F3[37]
Lansdowne Valley Park	34 F4
Lansdowne Village	37 A3
Lansdowne Villas	36 F3[44]
Laracor Gardens	23 A1 [5]
Laragh (Flats)	21 C2 [4]
Laragh Close	23 A1
Laragh Grove	23 A1
Larch Drive	50 E2 [3]
Larch Grove (Clonsilla)	17 C2
Larch Grove (Donnybrook)	43 B1
Larchfield	43 C4
Larchfield Park	43 C4
Larchfield Road	43 C4
Larkfield Avenue	42 F1
Larkfield Gardens	42 F1
Larkfield Grove	42 F1
Larkfield Mews	30 D3 [1]
Larkfield Park	42 F1
Larkhill Road	21 B2
Lauder's Lane	25 A1
Lauderdale Estate	57 C3 [1]
Lauderdale Terrace	57 C3[16]
*Lauderdale Terrace (on New Row South)	36 D3

STREET NAME	PAGE/GRID REFERENCE
Laundry Lane	42 F1
Laurel Avenue	51 B1
Laurel Court	18 E3
Laurel Drive	51 B1
Laurel Hill	54 D1 [6]
Laurel Lodge Road	18 F3
Laurel Park	40 E1
Laurel Road	51 B1
Laurelton	42 F3
Laurence Place East	36 F2 [5]
Laurleen	52 F1
Lavarna Grove	42 E2
Lavarna Road	42 E2
Laverna Avenue	18 E3
Laverna Dale	18 E3
Laverna Grove	18 E3
Laverna Way	18 E3
Lavista Avenue (Killester)	22 E3
Lawnswood Park	52 F1
Lawrence Grove	22 D4
Lawson Spinney	3 A3
Lawson Terrace	54 E1[14]
Le Bas Terrace	42 F1 [7]
Le Fanu Drive	34 D3 [1]
Le Fanu Road	34 D3
*Le Vere Terrace (off Harold's Cross Road)	42 F1
Lea Crescent	37 B4
Lea Road	37 B4
Leahy's Terrace	37 A3
Lealand Avenue	39 C1
Lealand Close	39 C1
Lealand Crescent	39 C1
Lealand Drive	39 C1
Lealand Gardens	39 C1
Lealand Grove	39 C1
Lealand Road	39 C1
Lealand Walk	39 C1
Ledwidge Crescent	57 B1
Lee Road	20 E3
Leeson Close	36 E4 [1]
Leeson Lane	36 E3[16]
Leeson Park	36 E4
Leeson Park Avenue	36 E4
Leeson Place	36 E4 [3]
Leeson Street Lower	36 E3
Leeson Street Upper	36 E4
Leeson Village	36 E4[30]
Leeson Walk	36 E4[19]
Leicester Avenue	43 A1
Leighlin Road	42 E1
Lein Gardens	22 F2
Lein Park	22 F2
Lein Road	22 F2
Leinster Avenue	36 F1
Leinster Lane	36 E3[13]
Leinster Lawn	43 C3
*Leinster Market (off d'Olier Street)	36 E2
Leinster Place	42 F1
Leinster Road	43 A1
Leinster Road West	42 F1
Leinster Square	43 A1 [2]
Leinster Street East	36 F1[21]
Leinster Street North	20 F4
Leinster Street South	36 E3
Leinster Terrace	40 D1 [2]
Leitrim Place	36 F3[33]
Leix Road	35 C1
Leixlip	31 B1
Leixlip Park	30 F1
Leixlip Road	31 B1
Leland Place	36 E2[31]
Lemon Street	36 D3[31]
Lennox Place	36 D4
Lennox Street	36 D4
*Lennox Terrace (off Lennox Street)	36 D4
Lentisk Lawn	23 A1
Leo Avenue	36 D1[24]
Leo Street	36 D1
Leopardstown	52 F3
Leopardstown Avenue	52 F2
Leopardstown Court	52 F2 [1]
Leopardstown Drive	52 F2
Leopardstown Gardens	52 F2
Leopardstown Grove	52 F2
Leopardstown Heights	52 E3
Leopardstown Lawn	52 F2 [2]
Leopardstown Oaks	52 F2
Leopardstown Park	52 F2
Leopardstown Road	52 F2
Leopardstown Valley	52 F4
Leslie Avenue	54 F1
Leslie's Buildings	35 C1 [7]

STREET NAME	PAGE/GRID REFERENCE
Leukos Road	37 A3[11]
Liberty House	36 E1
Liberty Lane	36 D3[20]
Library Road	46 D4
Library View Terrace	36 D1[61]
Liffey Junction	20 E3
Liffey Street Lower	36 D2
Liffey Street South	34 F3
Liffey Street Upper	36 D2
Liffey Street West	35 C2[19]
Liffey Terrace	34 E2 [7]
Lime Street	36 E2
Limekiln Avenue	41 C3
Limekiln Close	41 C3
Limekiln Drive	41 C3
Limekiln Green	41 B3
Limekiln Grove	41 C2
Limekiln Lane (Harold's Cross)	35 C4[16]
Limekiln Lane (Kimmage)	41 C2
Limekiln Park	41 C3
Limekiln Road	41 C3
Limetree Avenue	3 C4
Limewood Avenue	22 F1
Limewood Park	22 F1
Limewood Road	23 A1
*Lincoln Lane (off Arran Quay)	35 C2
Lincoln Place	36 E3
Linden Grove	44 F4
Linden Lea Park	52 F1
Lindenvale	45 A4 [4]
Lindisfarne Avenue	39 C1
Lindisfarne Drive	39 C1
Lindisfarne Green	39 C1
Lindisfarne Grove	39 C1
Lindisfarne Lawns	39 C1
Lindisfarne Park	39 C1
Lindisfarne Vale	39 C1
Lindisfarne Walk	39 C1
Lindsay Road	21 A4
Linenhall Parade	36 D2 [4]
*Linenhall Street (off King Street North)	36 D2
Linenhall Terrace	36 D2 [1]
Link Road	54 E1
Lios na Sidhe	48 F2
Lisburn Street	36 D2 [2]
Liscannor Road	20 E4
Liscanor	54 F1 [9]
Liscarne Court	33 A3
Liscarne Gardens	33 A3
Lisle Road	42 D1
Lismeen Grove	22 E1 [1]
Lismore Road	42 E1
Lissadel Avenue	35 A4
Lissadel Court	35 A4
Lissadel Crescent	2 F2
Lissadel Drive	35 A4
Lissadel Grove	2 F2
Lissadel Park	2 F2
Lissadel Road	35 A4
Lissen Hall	2 D1
Lissenfield	36 D4[53]
Lissenhall Avenue	2 D1
Lissenhall Court	2 D1
Lissenhall Drive	2 D1
Lissenhall Park	2 D1
Little Britain Street	36 D2
Little Fitzwilliam Place	36 E3[29]
Little Meadow	53 C3 [1]
Littlepage Paddocks	6 E4
*Litton Lane (off Bachelors Walk)	36 D2
Llewellyn Close	51 A1
Llewellyn Court	51 A1
Llewellyn Grove	51 A1
Llewellyn Lawn	51 A1
Llewellyn Park	51 A1
Llewellyn Way	51 A1
Lock Road	32 D3
Loftus Lane	36 D2
Lohunda Crescent	17 C2
Lohunda Dale	18 D2
Lohunda Downs	18 D2
Lohunda Drive	17 C2
Lohunda Grove	18 D2
Lohunda Park	17 C2
Lohunda Road	18 D2
Lombard Court	36 E2[33]
Lombard Street East	36 E2
Lombard Street West	36 D4
Lomond Avenue	21 C4
Londonbridge Drive	37 A3[20]
Londonbridge Road	37 A3
Long Lane	36 D3

STREET NAME	PAGE/GRID REFERENCE
Long Lane (New Street)	36 D1[49]
*Long Lane Close (off Long Lane)	36 D3
Long Mile Road	41 B1
Long's Place	35 C3 [5]
Longford Lane	36 D3[45]
Longford Place	45 C4
Longford Street Great	36 D3 [8]
Longford Street Little	36 D3 [9]
Longford Terrace	45 C4
Longlands	2 D2
Longmeadow	53 C3
Longwood Avenue	36 D4
Longwood Park	42 F4
Lorcan Avenue	21 C1
Lorcan Crescent	21 C1
Lorcan Drive	21 B1
Lorcan Green	21 C1
Lorcan Grove	21 C1
Lorcan O'Toole Court	42 D2 [2]
Lorcan O'Toole Park	42 D2
Lorcan Park	21 C1
Lorcan Road	21 B1
Lorcan Villas	21 C1
Lord Edward Street	36 D3
Lordello Road	56 D3
Lords Walk	35 A1
Loreto Abbey	42 F4
Loreto Avenue	43 A4
Loreto Avenue (Dalkey)	54 F1
Loreto Court	43 A4
Loreto Crescent	43 A4
Loreto Gardens	57 C3
Loreto Grange	57 C3
Loreto Park	43 A4
Loreto Road	35 C3
Loreto Row	43 A4
Loreto Terrace	42 F4
Loretto Avenue	57 C3 [3]
Loretto Terrace	57 C3 [4]
Loretto Villas	57 C3[12]
*Lorne Terrace (off Almeida Avenue)	48 D1
Lotts	36 D2
Lough Conn Avenue	34 D2
Lough Conn Drive	34 D2
Lough Conn Road	34 D2
Lough Conn Terrace	34 D2
Lough Derg Road	23 A2
Loughlinstown	56 D1
Loughlinstown Drive	56 D1
Loughlinstown Park	56 D1
Loughlinstown Wood	56 D1
*Louis Lane (off Leinster Road)	43 A1
Lourdes House	36 E1
Lourdes Road	35 B3
Louvain	44 D3
Louvain Glade	44 D3
Love Lane East	36 F3[15]
Lower Dargle Road	57 B2
Lower Glen Road	34 D1
Lower Kilmacud Road (Goatstown)	52 D1
Lower Kilmacud Road (Stillorgan)	52 E1
Lower Lucan Road	17 C4
Lower Road (Shankill)	56 E3
Lower Road (Strawberry Beds)	33 B1
Luby Road	35 A3
Lucan	32 D2
Lucan Bypass	32 D2
Lucan Heights	32 D1
Lucan Road (Lucan)	32 D1
Lucan Road (Palmerston)	33 C1
Lucan-Newlands Road	33 A4
Ludford Drive	51 B1
Ludford Park	51 B1
Ludford Road	51 B2
Lugmore Lane	47 C3
Lugnaquilla Avenue	41 B3
Luke Street	36 E2[25]
Lurgan Street	36 D2 [3]
Luttrell Park	18 D3
Luttrell Park Close	18 D3
Luttrell Park Court	18 D3
Luttrell Park Crescent	18 E3
Luttrell Park Drive	18 D3
Luttrell Park Green	18 D3
Luttrell Park Grove	18 D3
Luttrell Park Lawn	18 D3
Luttrell Park View	18 D3
Luttrellstown Park	18 D4
Luttrellstown View	18 E4
Luttrellstown Walk	18 D4

STREET NAME	PAGE/GRID REFERENCE
Luttrellstown Wood	18 E4
Lullymore Terrace	35 C4 [6]
Lynch's Lane	32 D2
Lynch's Lane	34 E3 [2]
Lynch's Place	36 D1 [2]
Lyndon Gate	20 D4 [4]
Lynton Court	37 A4 [12]
Lynwood	51 C1

M

STREET NAME	PAGE/GRID REFERENCE
MABBOT LANE	36 E2 [17]
Mabel Street	21 B4
Macken Street	36 F3
Macken Villa	36 F3 [31]
Mackies Place	36 E3 [33]
Mackintosh Park	53 C2
Macroom Avenue	11 B4
Macroom Road	11 B4
Madden Road	35 C3 [31]
*Madden's Court	35 C3
(off Thomas Street)	
Madden's Lane	54 E4
Madison Road	35 B3 [10]
*Magdalen Terrace	37 A3
(off Oliver Plunket Ave.)	
Magennis Place	36 E2 [3]
Magennis Square	36 E2 [29]
Magenta Crescent	21 B1
Magenta Hall	21 B1
Magenta Place	54 D1 [8]
*Maher's Terrace	43 C4
(Main Street Dundrum)	
Maidens Row	34 E2 [2]
Main Street	57 C2
Main Street (Baldoyle)	13 A4
Main Street (Blackrock)	45 A3
Main Street (Blanchardstown)	18 F2
Main Street (Celbridge)	30 D3
Main Street (Clondalkin)	40 E1
Main Street (Dundrum)	43 C4
Main Street (Finglas)	20 E2
Main Street (Howth)	26 D2
Main Street (Leixlip)	31 A1
Main Street (Lucan)	32 D1
Main Street (Raheny)	23 A2
Main Street (Rathfarnham)	42 F4
Main Street (Swords)	2 D2
Maitland Street	57 B2
Malachi Place	36 F1 [18]
*Malachi Road	35 C2
(off Halliday Road)	
Malahide	3 C2
Malahide Road	2 E2
Malahide Road (Artane)	22 E2
Malahide Road (Balgriffin)	12 D3
Malahide Road (Coolock)	22 F1
Malahide Road (Marino)	22 D4
Mallin Avenue	35 B3 [17]
Malone Gardens	36 F3 [12]
Malpas Court	36 D3 [50]
Malpas Place (off Malpas Street)	36 D3
Malpas Street	36 D3
Malpas Terrace	36 D3 [46]
Mander's Terrace	36 E4 [10]
Mangerton Road	34 F4
Mannix Road	21 A4
Manor Avenue	42 E3
Manor Close	51 A2
Manor Drive	12 D4
Manor Green	51 A2
Manor Heath	51 A1
Manor Park (Ballinteer)	51 A2
Manor Park (Palmerston)	33 C2
Manor Place	35 C2
Manor Rise	51 A2
Manor Road	33 C2
Manor Street	35 C1
Manor Villas	42 F1 [4]
Maolbuille Road	21 A2
Mapas Avenue	54 E2
Mapas Road	54 E2
Maple Avenue	18 E3
Maple Close	18 E3
Maple Drive	18 E3
Maple Drive	42 F2 [6]
Maple Glen	18 E3
Maple Green	18 E3
Maple Grove	18 E3
Maple Grove	57 B2
Maple Lawn	18 E3
Maple Manor	53 C3
Maple Road	43 C2
Maples Road	52 D2
Maplewood Avenue	48 E1

STREET NAME	PAGE/GRID REFERENCE
Maplewood Close	48 E1
Maplewood Court	48 E1
Maplewood Drive	48 E1
Maplewood Green	48 E1
Maplewood Lawn	48 E1
Maplewood Park	48 E1
Maplewood Road	48 E1
Maplewood Way	48 E1
Maretimo Gardens East	45 A3
Maretimo Gardens West	45 A3 [4]
Maretimo Place	45 A3 [17]
Maretimo Road	45 A3 [2]
Maretimo Terrace	45 A3 [16]
Maretimo Villas	45 A3 [18]
Margaret Place	36 F3 [11]
Marguerite Road	21 A4
Marian Crescent	42 E4
Marian Drive	42 E4
Marian Grove	42 E4
Marian Park (Baldoyle)	23 C1
Marian Park (Blackrock)	53 A1
Marian Park (Templeogue)	42 E4
Marian Road	42 E4
Marie Villas	57 C3 [13]
Marigold Court	11 C4
Marigold Crescent	11 C4
Marigold Grove	11 C4
Marigold Park	11 C4
Marina Village	3 B2
Marine Avenue	54 E1
Marine Court	54 E1
Marine Drive	37 A4
Marine Parade	46 E4
Marine Terrace	46 D4 [9]
Marine Terrace	57 C2 [19]
Mariners Cove	26 E2
Marino	21 C4
Marino Avenue	22 D4
Marino Avenue West	54 E4
Marino Court	21 C4 [13]
Marino Crescent	22 D4
Marino Green	21 C4
Marino Mart	21 C4 [9]
Marino Park	21 C4
Marino Park Avenue	21 C4
Marion Villas	35 C3 [59]
Mark Street	36 E2 [26]
Mark's Alley West	35 C3 [22]
Mark's Lane	36 E2 [4]
Market Square	57 C2 [49]
Market Street South	35 C3 [4]
Marlborough Mews	35 B1
Marlborough Park	54 D1 [9]
Marlborough Place	36 E2 [7]
Marlborough Road (Donnybrook)	43 C1
Marlborough Road (Glenageary)	54 E1
Marlborough Road (Nth. Circular Rd.)	35 B1
Marlborough Street	36 D2
Marlborough Terrace	57 C2 [37]
Marley Avenue	51 A1
Marley Close	51 A1
Marley Court (North)	51 A1
Marley Court (South)	51 A1
Marley Drive	51 A1
Marley Grove	51 A1
Marley Lawn	51 A1
Marley Rise	51 A1
Marley Villas	51 A1 [1]
Marley Walk	51 A1
Marlfield	53 C3
Marlfield Gardens	53 C3
*Marmion Court	35 C2
(on Blackhall Street)	
Marne Villas	35 C1 [13]
Marrowbone Lane	35 C3
*Marrowbone Lane Close	35 C3
(off Marrowbone Lane)	
Marshal Lane	35 C3 [1]
Marshalsea Lane	35 C2 [12]
Marsham Court	52 E1
Mart Lane	53 B3
Martello Avenue	46 D4 [14]
Martello Court	4 D4
Martello Mews	44 E1
Martello Terrace	57 C2 [38]
Martello Terrace	25 B3 [2]
Martello Terrace (Booterstown)	44 F3 [1]
Martello Terrace (Dun Laoghaire)	46 E4 [2]
Martello View	37 B4 [3]
Martello Wood	37 B4 [6]
Martin Grove	20 D4
Martin Savage Park	19 C3
Martin Savage Road	19 C4 [1]
Martin Street	36 D4 [34]

STREET NAME	PAGE/GRID REFERENCE
Martin's Row	34 E2
*Martin's Terrace	36 E2
(off Hanover Street East)	
Mary Street	36 D2
Mary Street Little	36 D2 [32]
Mary's Abbey	36 D2
Mary's Lane	36 D2
Maryfield Avenue	22 E2 [1]
Maryfield Crescent	22 E2
Maryfield Drive	22 D2
Maryville Road	22 F3
Mask Avenue	22 E2
Mask Crescent	22 E2
Mask Drive	22 E2
Mask Green	22 E2
Mask Road	22 E2
Mather Road North	44 D3
Mather Road South	44 D4
Matt Talbot Court	36 E1 [28]
Maunsell Place	36 D1 [52]
Maxwell Court	43 A1 [18]
Maxwell Road	43 A1
Maxwell Street	35 C3 [10]
May Lane	35 C2
May Park	22 D3
*May Street	21 B4
(off Fitzroy Ave)	
Mayberry Park	41 A4
Mayberry Road	41 A4
Mayfair	3 C2
Mayfield	43 A2
Mayfield Park	33 B4
Mayfield Road (Kilmainham)	35 B3 [11]
Mayfield Road (Terenure)	42 F2
Mayfield Terrace	57 C3 [17]
Mayne Road	12 E3
Mayola Court	43 B4
Mayor Street Lower	36 E2
Mayor Street Upper	36 F2
Mayville Terrace	54 F1 [11]
Maywood Avenue	23 B2
Maywood Close	23 B2
Maywood Crescent	23 B3
Maywood Drive	23 B2
Maywood Grove	23 B2
Maywood Lawn	23 B3
Maywood Park	23 B2
Maywood Road	23 B2
McAuley Avenue	22 F2
McAuley Drive	22 F2
McAuley Park	22 F2
McAuley Road	22 F2
McCabe Villas	44 E3
McCarthy Terrace	35 B3 [25]
McDowell Avenue	35 B3 [8]
McGrane Court	51 C1 [5]
McKee Avenue	20 E1
McKee Drive	35 B1
McKee Park	35 B1
McKee Road	20 E1
McKelvey Avenue	9 A4
McKelvey Road	9 A4
McMahon Street	36 D4 [27]
McMorrough Road	42 F2
Meade's Terrace	36 E3 [6]
Meadow Avenue	51 B1 [1]
Meadow Bank	42 F3
Meadow Close (Dundrum)	51 A1
Meadow Close (Newtown Park Ave.)	53 A1
Meadow Copse	17 C1
Meadow Court	54 D4 [2]
Meadow Dale	17 C1 [1]
Meadow Downs	17 C1
Meadow Drive	17 C1
Meadow Green	17 C1
Meadow Grove	51 A1
Meadow Mount	51 A1
Meadow Park	51 A1
Meadow Park Avenue	43 A4
Meadow Vale	53 B2
Meadow View(Dunboyne)	5 B2
Meadow View	51 A1
Meadow Villas	51 A1 [2]
Meadow Way	17 C1
Meadowbrook Avenue	24 D1
Meadowbrook Estate	24 D1
Meadowbrook Lawn	24 D1
Meadowbrook Park	24 D1
Meadowvale	53 B2
Meadowview Grove	31 C2
Meakstown Cottages	9 B3
Meath Market	35 C3 [16]
Meath Place	35 C3

STREET NAME	PAGE/GRID REFERENCE
Meath Place	57 C2
Meath Road	57 C2
Meath Square	35 C3 [42]
Meath Street	35 C3
*Meath Terrace (on Meath Place)	35 C3
*Meathville Terrace	36 D3
(on Long Lane)	
Meetinghouse Lane	36 D2 [33]
Mellifont Avenue	46 D4
Mellowes Avenue	20 D1
Mellowes Court	20 D2 [3]
Mellowes Crescent	20 D2 [4]
Mellowes Park	20 D1
Mellowes Road	20 D1
Melrose Avenue (Clondalkin)	32 F4
Melrose Avenue (Fairview)	21 C4
Melrose Crescent	39 C1
Melrose Green	39 C1
Melrose Grove	39 C1
Melrose Lawn	32 F4
Melrose Park	2 E3
Melrose Park	39 C1
Melrose Road	32 F4
Melrose Square	21 C4
Melvin Road	42 F2
Memorial Road	35 A3 [9]
Memorial Road	36 E2
Mercer Street Lower	36 D3
Mercer Street Upper	36 D3
Merchamp	22 F4
Merchant's Quay	35 C2
Merchant's Road	37 A1
*Merchants Arch	36 D2
(off Temple Bar)	
Meretimo Villas	58 D3 [2]
Merlyn Drive	44 D1
Merlyn Park	44 D1
Merlyn Road	44 D1
Merrion	44 E1
Merrion Close	36 E3 [26]
Merrion Court	44 E1 [1]
Merrion Gates	44 E1 [2]
Merrion Grove	44 E3
Merrion Park	44 E3
Merrion Place	36 E3 [8]
Merrion Road	37 A4
Merrion Row	36 E3
Merrion Square East	36 E3
Merrion Square North	36 E3
Merrion Square South	36 E3
Merrion Square West	36 E3
Merrion Strand	44 E1
Merrion Street Lower	36 E3 [27]
Merrion Street Upper	36 E3
Merrion View Avenue	44 D1 [1]
Merrion Village	44 E1
Merton Avenue	35 C4 [25]
Merton Drive	43 B1
Merton Park	35 C4 [27]
Merton Road	43 B2
Merville Avenue (Fairview)	21 C4
Merville Avenue (Stillorgan)	52 F1
Merville Road	52 F1
Mespil Road	36 E4
Michael Collins Park	40 D1
Middle Third	22 E3
Milesian Avenue	2 E2
Milesian Court	2 E2
Milesian Grove	2 E2
Milesian Lawn	2 E2
Milestown	15 C1
Milford	3 A2
Military Road	35 B3
Military Road (Killiney)	54 E4
Military Road (Phoenix Park)	34 F2
Military Road (Rathmines)	36 D4
Mill Lane	31 A1
Mill Lane (Ashtown)	19 B3 [1]
Mill Lane (Loughlinstown)	56 E2
Mill Lane (Newmarket)	35 C3 [2]
Mill Lane (Palmerston)	33 C1
*Mill Lane	57 C2
(off Castle Street Bray)	
Mill Road (Blanchardstown)	18 F2
Mill Road (Saggart)	47 A2
Mill Street	35 C3
Mill Street (Dun Laoghaire)	46 D4 [19]
Millbourne Avenue	21 A4
Millbrook Avenue	23 A1
Millbrook Court	35 B3 [35]
Millbrook Drive	23 A1
Millbrook Grove	23 A1
Millbrook Lawns	49 A1
Millbrook Road	23 A1
Millbrook Terrace	35 A3

STREET NAME	PAGE/GRID REFERENCE
(off Lady's Lane)	
Millbrook Village	43 C1[17]
Millfarm	5 C2
Millgate Drive	41 C3
Millmount Avenue	21 A4
Millmount Grove	43 B3
Millmount Place	21 B4
Millmount Terrace (Drumcondra)	21 B4
Millmount Terrace (Dundrum)	43 A3 [4]
Millmount Villas	21 A4 [1]
Millrose Estate	34 E4 [2]
Millstead	18 F2
Millstream Road	31 C2
Milltown	43 C2
Milltown Bridge Road	43 C2
*Milltown Collonade (on Milltown Road)	43 B2
Milltown Drive	43 A3
Milltown Grove	43 A3
Milltown Grove	43 B2 [6]
Milltown Hill	43 B2 [7]
Milltown Park	43 B2
Milltown Path	43 B2
Milltown Road	43 B2
Milltown Terrace (Dundrum)	43 B3 [4]
Millview Close	3 A3
Millview Court	3 A2
Millview Lawns	3 A3
Millview Road	3 A3
Millwood Park	23 A1
Millwood Villas	23 A1
Milton Terrace	57 C2[13]
Milward Terrace	57 C2[35]
Mine Hill Lane	55 B3
*Minstrel Court (Charles Sheil's Houses)	52 F2
Misery Hill	36 F2
Moatfield Avenue	22 F1
Moatfield Park	22 F1
Moatfield Road	22 F1
Moatview Avenue	11 B4
Moatview Court	11 B4
Moatview Drive	11 B4
Moatview Gardens	11 B4
Moeran Road	41 C1
*Moira Road (off Oxmanstown Road)	35 B1
Moland Place	36 E2[21]
Molesworth Place	36 E3[24]
Molesworth Street	36 E3
Molyneux Yard	35 C3[19]
Monalea Grove	49 C1
Monalea Park	49 C1
Monalea Wood	49 C1
Monaloe Avenue	53 C3
Monaloe Court	53 B3 [6]
Monaloe Crescent	53 B3 [4]
Monaloe Drive	53 C3
Monaloe Park	53 C3
Monaloe Park Road	53 C3
Monaloe Way	53 C3
Monasterboice Road	42 E1
Monastery Crescent	40 E1
Monastery Drive	40 E1
Monastery Heights	40 E1 [2]
Monastery Park	40 E1
Monastery Rise	40 E1
Monastery Road	40 E1
Monastery Walk	40 E1
Monck Place	35 C1
Monks Meadow	4 D4
Monksfield	40 F1
Monksfield Court	40 F1
Monksfield Downs	40 F1
Monksfield Grove	40 F1
Monksfield Heights	40 F1
Monksfield Lawn	40 F1
Monksfield Meadows	40 F1
Monksfield Walk	40 F1
Monkstown	45 B4
Monkstown Avenue	53 B1
Monkstown Crescent	45 C4
Monkstown Farm	53 C1
Monkstown Grove	53 C1
Monkstown Road	45 B4
Monkstown Valley	45 B4
Montague Court	36 D3[25]
Montague Lane	36 D3[13]
Montague Place	36 D3[26]
Montague Street	36 D3
Monte Vella	54 F2 [9]
Montebello Terrace	58 D2 [2]
Montpelier Drive	35 B2

STREET NAME	PAGE/GRID REFERENCE
Montpelier Gardens	35 B2 [5]
Montpelier Hill	35 B2
Montpelier Manor	45 B4 [2]
Montpelier Parade	45 B4
Montpelier Park	35 B2
Montpelier Place	45 B4 [1]
Montrose Avenue	22 D2
Montrose Close	22 D2
Montrose Court	22 D2
Montrose Crescent	22 D1
Montrose Drive	22 D1
Montrose Grove	22 D2
Montrose Park	22 D2
Moore Lane	36 D2[15]
Moore Street	36 D2
Moore's Cottages	53 A1 [3]
Mooretown	1 B1
Mooretown Avenue	1 C1
Mooretown Grove	1 C1
Mooretown Park	1 C1
Mooretown Road	1 C1
Moorfield Avenue	33 A4
Moorfield Close	33 A4. [2]
Moorfield Drive	33 A4
Moorfield Green	33 A4
Moorfield Lawns	33 A4
Moracrete Cottages	35 B4 [4]
Moran's Cottages	43 B1[12]
Moreen Avenue	52 D2
Moreen Close	52 D2
Moreen Lawn	52 D2 [2]
Moreen Road	52 D2
Moreen Walk	52 D2
Morehampton Lane	36 F4
Morehampton Mews	36 F4[12]
Morehampton Road	36 F4
Morehampton Square	36 F4[11]
Morehampton Terrace	43 C1
Morgan Place	35 C2[14]
Morning Star Avenue	35 C2[24]
Morning Star Road	35 B3[19]
Mornington Avenue	46 E4 [1]
Mornington Grove	22 E2
Mornington Park	22 E2
Mornington Road	43 B1
Morrogh Terrace	21 C3 [2]
Moss Street	36 E2
Mount Albany	53 A1
Mount Albion Road	51 B1
Mount Albion Road	51 B1 [3]
Mount Alton	50 D1
Mount Alton Court	50 D1
Mount Annville Lawn	44 D4
Mount Annville Park	44 D4
Mount Annville Road	44 D4
Mount Annville Wood	44 D4
Mount Anthony's Flats	43 A1[22]
Mount Argus Close	42 F1
Mount Argus Court	42 F1
Mount Argus Crescent	42 F1
Mount Argus Green	42 F1
Mount Argus Grove	42 F1
Mount Argus Park	42 F1
Mount Argus Road	42 F1
Mount Argus Terrace	42 F1
Mount Argus View	42 F1
Mount Argus Way	42 F1
Mount Auburn	54 E3 [2]
Mount Brown	35 B3
Mount Carmel Avenue	43 C4
Mount Carmel Park	49 C1
Mount Carmel Road	43 C4
Mount Dillon Court	22 E2
Mount Drinan Avenue	2 E3
Mount Drinan Crescent	2 E3
Mount Drinan Grove	2 E3
Mount Drinan Lawn	2 E3
Mount Drinan Park	2 E3
Mount Drinan Walk	2 E3
Mount Drummond Avenue	35 C4
Mount Drummond Court	35 C4[30]
Mount Drummond Square	36 D4
Mount Eagle Court	52 E3
Mount Eagle Drive	52 E3
Mount Eagle Green	52 E3
Mount Eagle Grove	52 E3
Mount Eagle Lawn	52 E3
Mount Eagle Park	52 E3
Mount Eagle Rise	52 D3
Mount Eagle View	52 E3
Mount Eden Road	43 C1
Mount Gandon	32 D1 [9]
Mount Harold Terrace	42 F1 [1]
Mount Merrion	44 E4

STREET NAME	PAGE/GRID REFERENCE
Mount Merrion Avenue	44 F3
Mount Norris Villas	58 D3 [6]
Mount Olive Grove	23 B1
Mount Olive Park	23 B1
Mount Olive Road	23 B1
Mount Prospect Avenue	22 F4
Mount Prospect Drive	22 F4
Mount Prospect Grove	22 F4
Mount Prospect Lawn	22 F4
Mount Prospect Manor	50 E2
Mount Prospect Park	22 F4
Mount Salus Road	54 F2
Mount Sandford	43 C1[14]
Mount Street Crescent	36 F3[32]
Mount Street Lower	36 E3
Mount Street Upper	36 E3
Mount Tallant Avenue	42 F2
Mount Temple Road	35 C2
Mount Venus Road	50 D4
Mount View Road	18 D2
Mount Wood	53 C1
Mountain Park	49 A1
Mountain View	48 D2
Mountain View Apartments	57 C3[11]
Mountain View Avenue	42 F1 [3]
Mountain View Cottages (Castleknock)	18 D4
Mountain View Cottages (Ranelagh)	43 B1[13]
*Mountain View Court (off Summerhill Place)	36 E1
Mountain View Drive	51 A1
Mountain View Park	43 A4
Mountain View Road	43 B1
Mountain View Road	54 E4 [5]
Mountain Villa	54 E4 [3]
Mountainview Drive	57 B4
Mountdown Avenue	41 C3
Mountdown Drive	41 C3
Mountdown Park	41 C3
Mountdown Road	41 C3
Mountjoy Parade	36 E1[36]
Mountjoy Place	36 E1[22]
Mountjoy Square	36 E1
Mountjoy Square East	36 E1
Mountjoy Square North	36 D1
Mountjoy Square South	36 E1
Mountjoy Square West	36 D1
Mountjoy Street	36 D1
Mountjoy Street Middle	36 D1 [9]
Mountpleasant Avenue Lower	36 D4
Mountpleasant Avenue Upper	36 D4
Mountpleasant Parade	36 D4[39]
Mountpleasant Place	36 E4[22]
Mountpleasant Square	36 D4
Mountpleasant Terrace	36 D4[40]
*Mountpleasant Terrace Upper (off Mountpleasant Place)	36 E4
Mountpleasant Villas	57 B2[13]
*Mountpleasant Villas (off Mountpleasant Place)	36 E4
Mountsandel	53 B4
Mountshannon Road	35 B3
Mounttown Cottages	45 C4[26]
Mounttown Lower	53 C1
Mounttown Park	53 C1 [3]
Mounttown Upper	45 C4
Mourne Road	35 A4
Moy Elta Road	36 F1
Moyclare Avenue	24 D1
Moyclare Close	24 D1
Moyclare Drive	24 D1
Moyclare Park	24 D1
Moyclare Road	24 D1
Moycullen Road	33 C3
Moyle Crescent	40 E1
Moyle Road	20 E3
Moyne Road	43 B1
Moyville	50 E2
Moyville Lawns	50 E1
Muckross Avenue	42 D2
Muckross Crescent	42 D2
Muckross Drive	42 D2 [1]
Muckross Green	42 D2
Muckross Grove	42 D2
Muckross Parade	36 D1[32]
Muckross Park	42 D2
Muirfield Drive	34 F4 [1]
Muldowney Court	3 C3
Mulgrave Street	46 D4
Mulgrave Terrace	46 D4
Mulhuddart	7 A4
Mulhuddart Wood	7 A4
Mullinastill Road	56 D2
Mullingar Terrace	34 E2[10]

STREET NAME	PAGE/GRID REFERENCE
Mulroy Road	20 E4
Mulvey Park	43 C3
Munster Street	20 F4
Munster Terrace	54 E1[16]
Murphy's Lane	55 B4
Murphystown Road	52 E3
Murray's Cottages	34 F3 [4]
Murtagh Road	35 C1[30]
Muskerry Road	34 E3
Mutton Lane	50 E4
Myra Cottages	35 A3[21]
Myrtle Avenue	54 D1 [1]
Myrtle Grove	52 F1 [1]
Myrtle Park	54 D1
Myrtle Street	36 D1[23]

N	
NAAS ROAD	41 A1
Naas Road (Saggart)	47 B1
Naas Road Old	34 E4
Nangor Crescent	39 C1 [2]
Nangor Road (Clondalkin)	40 D1
Nangor Road (Fox & Geese)	40 F1
Nanikin Avenue	23 A3
Nash Street	34 F3
Nashville Park	26 E2
Nashville Road	26 D2
Nassau Place	36 E3[11]
Nassau Street	36 E3
Naul Road	1 C4
Navan Road (Blanchardstown)	18 E1
Navan Road (Cabra)	20 D4
Navan Road (Clonee)	6 E3
Neagh Road	42 E2
Neill's Court	45 A3
Neillstown Avenue	33 A3
Neillstown Crescent	33 A3
Neillstown Drive	33 A3
Neillstown Gardens	33 A3
Neillstown Park	33 A3
Neilstown Cottages	33 A4 [3]
Neilstown Road	33 A3
Nelson Street	36 D1
Nephin Road	20 D4
Neptune Terrace	54 E1[17]
Nerano Road	54 F2
Nerney's Court	36 D1[44]
Neville Road	43 A2
Nevinstown Lane	1 C3
New Bawn Drive	49 A2
New Bawn Park	49 A2
New Brighton Terrace	57 C2[47]
New Grange Park	57 C3 [7]
New Grange Road (Deans Grange)	53 A1
New Grove Estate	12 E4
New Ireland Road	35 B3
New Park Lodge	53 A2 [3]
New Park Road	53 A1
New Rathmore Terrace	57 B2[23]
New Ravenswell Row	57 B2[20]
New Road (Portmarnock)	12 E2
New Road (Clondalkin)	40 E2
New Road (Howth)	26 E3
New Road (Inchicore)	34 F3
New Road (Portmarnock)	12 E2
*New Row (off Maidens Row)	34 E2
New Row Square	35 C3[32]
New Row South	35 C3
New Street	3 B2
New Street	36 D3
*New Street Garden's (off New Street)	36 D3
*New Street North (off Church Street)	35 C2
New Vale Cottages	56 D3
New Vale Crescent	56 D3
New Wapping Street	36 F2
Newbridge Avenue	37 A3
Newbridge Drive	37 A3
Newbrook Avenue	23 B1
Newbrook Road	23 B1
Newbury Avenue	11 A4
Newbury Drive	11 A4
Newbury Grove	11 A4
Newbury Heights	11 A4
Newbury Lawns	11 B4
Newbury Park	11 A4
Newbury Terrace	11 A4 [1]
Newcastle Road	32 D2
Newcomen Avenue	36 E1
Newcomen Court	36 E1[29]
Newcourt	2 D1

STREET NAME	PAGE/GRID REFERENCE
Newcourt	58 D4
Newcourt Avenue	58 D3
Newcourt Road	58 D3
Newcourt Villas	57 C3 [8]
Newgrange Road (Cabra)	20 F4
Newgrove Avenue	37 B4
Newlands Avenue	40 E2
Newlands Drive	40 E2
Newlands Park	40 E2
Newlands Road	40 E2
Newmarket	35 C3
Newmarket Street	35 C3 [25]
Newport Street	35 C3
Newtown Avenue	45 A3
Newtown Cottages	22 F1
Newtown Cottages	9 A1
Newtown Court	43 A3 [5]
Newtown Drive	22 F1
Newtown Glendale	16 D4
Newtown Park	16 D4
Newtown Park (Blackrock)	53 A1
Newtown Park (Tallaght)	49 B1
Newtown Park Avenue	45 A4
Newtown Road	30 D4
Newtown Villas	45 A3 [1]
Newtownsmith	46 E4
Niall Street	35 B2 [11]
Nicholas Avenue	35 C2 [7]
Nicholas Street	36 D3
Ninth Lock Road	40 D1
Nore Road	20 E3
Norfolk Road	20 F4
Norseman Place	35 C2
North Avenue	44 E4
North Bull Island	23 B4
North Circular Road (Phibsborough)	35 C1
North Circular Road (Phoenix Park)	35 B1
North Great George's St.	36 D1
North Quay Extension	37 A2
North Road	9 A4
North Road (Phoenix Park)	35 A1
North Strand Road	36 F1
North Street	2 D1
North Wall	36 F2
North Wall Quay	36 F2
Northbrook Avenue (Ranelagh)	36 E4
Northbrook Avenue Lower	36 F1
Northbrook Avenue Upper	36 F1
Northbrook Lane	36 E4 [20]
Northbrook Road	36 E4
Northbrook Terrace	36 F1 [1]
*Northbrook Villas (on Northbrook Road Ranelagh)	36 E4
Northcote Avenue	45 C4
Northcote Place	45 C4 [23]
Northcote Terrace	45 C4 [20]
Northland Drive	20 F3 [2]
Northland Grove	20 F3 [1]
Northumberland Avenue	46 D4
Northumberland Park	46 D4 [11]
Northumberland Place	36 F3 [42]
Northumberland Place	46 D4 [10]
Northumberland Road	36 F3
Northumberland Square	36 E2 [8]
Northway Estate	9 A4
Norton's Avenue	35 C1 [11]
Norwood	56 E1
Norwood Park	43 C1 [7]
Nottingham Street	36 F1
Novara Avenue	57 C2
Novara Park	57 C2 [7]
Novara Terrace	57 C2 [27]
Nowlan Avenue	51 B1
Nugent Road	43 A4
Nunciature Road	19 C4
Nurney Lawn	12 D4
Nutgrove Avenue	43 A4
Nutgrove Avenue	43 B4 [14]
Nutgrove Court	43 A4 [2]
Nutgrove Park (Clonskeagh)	43 C2
Nutgrove Park (Sandymount)	37 A4
Nutgrove Way	51 A1
Nutley Avenue	44 D1
Nutley Lane	44 D2
Nutley Park	44 D2
Nutley Road	44 D1
Nutley Square	44 D2 [1]

O

STREET NAME	PAGE/GRID REFERENCE
OAK APPLE GREEN	43 A2
Oak Avenue	10 F4
Oak Court	10 F4

STREET NAME	PAGE/GRID REFERENCE
Oak Crescent	10 F4
Oak Dene	54 E3
Oak Downs	40 D2
Oak Drive	10 F4
Oak Glen	57 C4
Oak Green	10 F4
Oak Grove	10 F4
Oak Lawn	10 F4
Oak Lawn (Castleknock)	18 F3
Oak Rise	10 F4
Oak Rise	40 D2
Oak Road (Donnycarney)	22 D3
Oak Road (Fox & Geese)	40 F1
Oak Way	40 D2
Oakcourt Avenue	33 C2
Oakcourt Close	33 C2
Oakcourt Drive	33 C2
Oakcourt Grove	33 C2
Oakcourt Lawn	33 C2
Oakcourt Park	33 C2
Oakdale Drive	53 C2
Oakdown Road	43 A4
Oakfield Place	36 D [50]
Oaklands Avenue	2 D2
Oaklands Crescent	43 A2
Oaklands Drive (Rathgar)	43 A2
Oaklands Drive (Sandymount)	37 A4
Oaklands Park	2 D2
Oaklands Park	37 A4
Oaklands Terrace	42 F2
Oaklawn	15 C4
Oaklawn Close	15 C4
Oaklawn West	15 C4
Oakleigh	29 C4
Oakley Court (Flats)	43 B1 [10]
Oakley Grove	45 A4
Oakley Park (Blackrock)	45 A4
Oakley Park (Clontarf)	22 F4
Oakley Road	43 B1
Oakley Square	43 B1 [20]
Oaklodge	19 A4
Oakpark Avenue	21 C1
Oakpark Close	21 C1
Oakpark Drive	21 B1
Oakpark Grove	21 C1
Oakton Court	54 E4 [1]
Oakton Drive	54 D4
Oakton Green	54 D4 [3]
Oakton Park	54 D4
Oaktree Avenue	18 E3
Oaktree Drive	18 E3
Oaktree Green	18 E3
Oaktree Grove	18 E3
Oaktree Lawn	18 E3
Oaktree Road	52 F1
Oakview	10 E4
Oakview Avenue	17 C1
Oakview Close	17 C1
Oakview Court	17 C1
Oakview Drive	17 C1
Oakview Grove	17 C1 [2]
Oakview Lawn	17 C1
Oakview Park	17 C1
Oakview Rise	17 C1
Oakview Walk	17 C1
Oakview Way	17 C1
Oakwood	45 C4 [7]
Oakwood Avenue	1 C2
Oakwood Avenue	20 E1
Oakwood Close	20 E1
Oakwood Grove Estate	33 A4
Oakwood Park	20 E1
Oakwood Road	20 E1
Oatfield Avenue	33 B3
Oatfield Close	33 B3
Oatfield Crescent	33 B2
Oatfield Drive	33 B3
Oatfield Grove	33 B3
Oatfield Lawn	33 B3
Oatfield Park	33 B3
Oblate Drive	34 F3 [14]
O'Brien Road	41 C1
O'Brien's Place North	21 A3 [13]
O'Brien's Terrace	21 A4 [15]
Observatory Lane	43 A1 [14]
O'Byrne Road	57 C3
O'Byrne Villas	57 C3 [9]
O'Carolan Road	35 C3 [29]
O'Connell Avenue	36 D1 [6]
O'Connell Gardens	37 A3
O'Connell Street Lower	36 D2
O'Connell Street Upper	36 D2
*O'Curry Avenue (off O'Curry Road)	35 C3
O'Curry Road	35 C3

STREET NAME	PAGE/GRID REFERENCE
O'Daly Road	21 A3
Odd Lamp Road	34 F1
O'Devaney Gardens	35 B2
O'Donnell Gardens	54 D1 [1]
O'Donoghue Street	34 F3
O'Donovan Road	35 C4
O'Dwyer Road	41 C1 [4]
Offaly Road	20 F4
Offington Avenue	25 B2
Offington Court	25 B2
Offington Drive	25 B2
Offington Lawn	25 B2
Offington Manor	25 B1
Offington Park	25 B1
O'Hanlon's Lane	3 B2
*O'Hara Avenue (off Rathgar Road)	36 D4
O'Hogan Road	34 E3 [1]
Olaf Road	35 C2 [33]
Oldbawn	49 A2
Old Bawn Avenue	49 A2
Old Bawn Close	49 A2
Old Bawn Drive	49 A2
Old Bawn Park	49 A2
Old Bawn Road	49 A2
Old Bawn Terrace	49 A2
Old Bawn Way	49 A2
Old Bridge Road	42 D4
Old Brighton Terrace	57 C2 [46]
Old Cabra Road	35 B1
Old Conna Wood	57 B1
Old Connaught	57 A1
Old Connaught Avenue	57 B1
Old Connaught Grove	57 B2
Old Connaught View	57 B2
Old Corduff Road	18 E1
Old Cornmill Road	31 C2
Old County Glen	35 B4
Old County Road	35 A4
Old Dunleary	45 C4
Old Hill	16 D4
Old Kilmainham	35 B3
Old Kilmainham Village	35 B3 [2]
Old Mill Court	35 C3 [52]
Old Mountpleasant	36 E4 [9]
Old Naas Road	34 E4
Old Naas Road Cottages	34 E4 [1]
Old Quarry	54 F2
Old Rathmore Terrace	57 B2 [22]
Old Ravenswell Row	57 B2 [19]
Old Rectory	32 D1
Old Rectory Park	43 C4
Old Road (Portmarnock)	12 E2
Old Street	3 B2
Old Tower Crescent	33 A2
Old Yellow Walls Road	2 F2
Oldbawn	49 A2
Oldcastle Avenue	25 B2
Oldcastle Drive	39 B1
Oldchurch Avenue	39 C1
Oldchurch Close	39 C1
Oldchurch Court	39 C1
Oldchurch Crescent	39 C1
Oldchurch Drive	39 C1
Oldchurch Grove	49 C1
Oldchurch Lawn	39 C1
Oldchurch Park	39 C1
Oldchurch Way	39 C1
Oldcourt	57 B3
Oldcourt Avenue	49 B2
Oldcourt Avenue	57 B4
Oldcourt Close	49 B2
Oldcourt Cottages	49 B3
Oldcourt Drive	57 B4
Oldcourt Grove	57 B4
Oldcourt Lawn	49 B2 [2]
Oldcourt Manor	49 B3
Oldcourt Park	57 B3
Oldcourt Road	49 B3
Oldcourt Terrace	57 C3 [15]
Oldcourt View	49 B2
Oldtown Avenue	21 A1
Oldtown Cottages	29 C3
Oldtown Park	21 A1 [3]
Oldtown Road	21 A1
O'Leary Road	35 A3
Olivemount Grove	43 C3 [2]
Olivemount Road	43 C3
Olivemount Terrace	43 C3 [6]
Oliver Bond Street	35 C2
Oliver Plunkett Avenue (Dun Laoghaire)	53 C1
Oliver Plunkett Avenue (Ringsend)	37 A3
Oliver Plunkett Road	53 C1

STREET NAME	PAGE/GRID REFERENCE
Oliver Plunkett Square	53 C1 [1]
Oliver Plunkett Terrace	53 C1 [5]
Oliver Plunkett Villas	53 B1 [3]
Olney Crescent	42 F2
Omni Park	21 B1
O'Moore Road	34 E3
O'Neachtain Road	21 A3 [14]
O'Neill's Buildings	36 D3 [14]
Ontario Terrace	36 D4 [11]
Onward Close	3 C4
Onward Walk	3 C4
Ophaly Court	43 C4 [1]
*O'Quinn Avenue (off Mount Brown)	35 B3
O'Rahilly Parade	36 D2 [26]
Oranmore Road	33 C3
Orchard Avenue	17 C2
Orchard Close	18 D2
Orchard Cottages	53 A1 [1]
Orchard Court	18 E2
Orchard Green	18 D2
Orchard Grove	18 E2
Orchard Lane	36 E4 [24]
Orchard Lane (Blackrock)	53 A1
Orchard Lane (Clondalkin)	40 E1
Orchard Lawns	33 C3
Orchard Road (Ballybough)	21 B4
Orchard Road (Raheny)	23 B2
Orchard Road South	43 B2
Orchard Terrace	57 C3 [19]
*Orchard Terrace (Grangegorman Upper)	35 C1
*Orchard View (Grangegorman Upper)	35 C1
Orchardstown Avenue	42 E4
Orchardstown Drive	42 E4
Orchardstown Park	42 E4
Orchardstown Villas	42 E4
Orchardston	50 E1 [1]
Ordnance Survey Road	34 E1
O'Reilly Avenue	35 B3 [9]
Oriel Place	36 F1 [12]
Oriel Street Lower	36 F1
Oriel Street Upper	36 E2
Orlagh Avenue	50 D2
Orlagh Close	50 D2
Orlagh Court	50 D2
Orlagh Crescent	50 D2
Orlagh Dale	50 D2
Orlagh Downs	50 D2
Orlagh Grange	50 D2
Orlagh Green	50 D2
Orlagh Grove	50 D2
Orlagh Lawn	50 D2
Orlagh Lodge	50 D2
Orlagh Meadows	50 D2 [1]
Orlagh Park	50 D2
Orlagh Rise	50 D2
Orlagh View	50 D2
Orlagh Way	50 D2
Ormeau Drive	54 F1 [1]
Ormeau Street	36 F3 [7]
Ormond Avenue	1 B1
Ormond Close	1 B1
Ormond Drive	1 B1
Ormond Grove	1 B1
Ormond Lawn	1 B1
*Ormond Market (off Ormond Quay Upper)	36 D2
*Ormond Place (off Ormond Quay Upper)	36 D2
Ormond Quay Lower	36 D2
Ormond Quay Upper	36 D2
Ormond Road	21 B4
Ormond Road South (Rathmines)	43 B1
Ormond Square	36 D2 [37]
Ormond Street	35 C3
*Ormond Terrace (off Sorrento Road)	54 F2
Ormond View	1 B1
Ormond Way	1 B1
O'Rourke Park (Sallynoggin)	53 C2
Orpen	52 F1
Orpen Close	44 F4
Orpen Dale	44 F4 [2]
Orpen Green	52 F1
Orpen Hill	52 F1
Orpen Rise	52 F1
Orwell Bank	43 A3 [7]
Orwell Court	43 A3 [3]
Orwell Gardens	43 A3
Orwell Park	43 A3
Orwell Park Avenue	42 D3
Orwell Park Close	42 D3

STREET NAME	PAGE/GRID REFERENCE
Orwell Park Crescent	42 D3
Orwell Park Dale	41 C4
Orwell Park Drive	42 D3
Orwell Park Estate	41 C4
Orwell Park Glade	41 C3
Orwell Park Glen	42 D3
Orwell Park Green	42 D3
Orwell Park Grove	41 C3
Orwell Park Heights	41 C3
Orwell Park Lawns	41 C3
Orwell Park Rise	41 C4
Orwell Park View	41 C4
Orwell Park Way	42 D3
Orwell Road	43 A2
Orwell Woods	43 A2
*Osborne Terrace (Northbrook Road)	36 E4
Oscar Square	35 C3[23]
Oscar Traynor Road	22 E1
Oscar Wilde Court	23 C1
O'Shea's Cottages	53 C3 [3]
Osprey Avenue	41 C3
Osprey Drive	41 C3
Osprey Lawn	41 C3
Osprey Park	41 C3
Osprey Road	41 C3
Ossory Road	36 F1
Ostman Place	35 C2 [1]
O'Sullivan Avenue	36 E1[1]
Oswald Road	37 A3
Otranto Place	54 E1
Oulart	1 C3
Oulton Road	22 E4
*Our Lady's Close (off Our Lady's Road)	35 C3
Our Lady's Road	35 C3
Outlands	1 C1
Ovoca Road	36 D4
*Owen's Avenue (off Mount Brown)	35 B3
Owendore Avenue	42 F4
Owendore Crescent	42 F4
Owenstown Park	44 D3
Oxford Road	36 E4
*Oxford Terrace (on Hawthorn Terrace)	36 F1
*Oxford Terrace (off Church Road)	36 F1
Oxmantown Lane	35 C2[21]
Oxmantown Road	35 B1

P

STREET NAME	PAGE/GRID REFERENCE
PACELLI AVENUE	23 C1
Pairc Mhuire	47 A2
Pakenham	45 C4[28]
Pakenham Road	45 C4
*Palace Street (off Dame Street)	36 D2
Palatine Square	35 B2
Palmer Park	50 F2
Palmers Avenue	33 B2
Palmers Close	33 B2
Palmers Copse	33 B2
Palmers Court	33 B2
Palmers Crescent	33 B2
Palmers Drive	33 B2
Palmers Glade	33 B2
Palmers Grove	33 B2
Palmers Lawn	33 B2
Palmers Park	33 B2
Palmers Road	33 B2
Palmers Walk	33 B2
Palmerston	33 C1
*Palmerston Close (rere of Palmerston Road)	43 B1
Palmerston Gardens	43 B2
Palmerston Grove	43 C2[5]
Palmerston Lane	43 B2
Palmerston Park	33 B2
Palmerston Park	43 B2
Palmerston Place	36 D1[8]
Palmerston Road	43 B1
Palmerston Villas	43 A2
Palmerstown Avenue	33 C2
Palmerstown Close	33 B2
Palmerstown Court	33 C2
Palmerstown Drive	33 C2
Palmerstown Green	33 B2
Palmerstown Heights	33 B2
Palmerstown Lawn	33 B2
Palmerstown Manor	33 B2
Palmerstown Woods	33 B3
Paradise Place	36 D1
Park Avenue	1 B2
Park Avenue	18 F3
Park Avenue (Deans Grange)	53 A1
Park Avenue (Sandymount)	37 B4
Park Avenue (Willbrook)	50 F1
Park Avenue West	35 B2[13]
Park Close (Sallynoggin)	54 D2
Park Court (Sandymount)	37 A4[16]
Park Crescent	35 A1
Park Crescent (Kimmage)	42 D2
Park Drive (Cabinteely)	53 B3
Park Drive (Castleknock)	18 F3
Park Drive (Ranelagh)	43 B1
Park Drive Avenue	18 F3
Park Drive Close	18 F3
Park Drive Court	18 F3
Park Drive Crescent	18 F3
Park Drive Green	18 F3
Park Drive Grove	18 F3
Park Drive Lawn	18 F3
Park Lane (Chapelizod)	34 E2 [1]
Park Lane (Sandymount)	37 A4
Park Lane East	36 E2[11]
Park Lawn	23 A4
Park Lodge	18 F3
Park Place	35 A2 [4]
Park Road (Dun Laoghaire)	46 D4
Park Road (Sallynoggin)	54 D2
Park Road (off Navan Road)	19 C3
Park Street	34 F3 [1]
*Park Street (off Hanover St. West)	35 C3
Park Terrace (Coombe)	35 C3 [6]
*Park Terrace (on Lower Dargle Road)	57 B2
Park View (Cabra)	35 B1
Park View (Castleknock)	19 B4
Park View (Clonsilla)	18 D2
Park View (Portmarnock)	13 A1
Park View Lawns	40 D2
Park Villas	19 A3
Park Villas	44 F4 [3]
Parker Hill	43 A1[12]
Parkgate Street	35 B2
Parkhill Avenue	40 F3
Parkhill Close	41 A3
Parkhill Court	40 F3
Parkhill Drive	40 F3
Parkhill Green	40 F3
Parkhill Heights	41 A3 [1]
Parkhill Lawn	40 F3
Parkhill Rise	40 F3
Parkhill Road	40 F3
Parkhill Way	41 A3
Parkhill West	40 F4
Parkmore Drive	42 E2
Parknasilla Avenue	56 D2
Parknasilla Close	56 D2
Parknasilla Lane	56 D2
Parknasilla Rise	56 D2
Parkvale	24 D1
Parkvale	51 C1
Parkview	41 A3 [2]
Parkview Avenue (Harold's Cross)	42 F1
Parkview Court	42 F1 [8]
*Parkview Court (on Blackhorse Avenue)	35 A1
Parkview Place	37 A3[14]
Parkview Terrace	57 B2[16]
Parkwood Avenue	49 A2
Parkwood Grove	49 A2
Parkwood Lawn	49 A2
Parkwood Road	49 A2
Parliament Row (off Fleet Street)	36 D2
Parliament Street	36 D2
Parlickstown Court	7 A4
Parlickstown Gardens	7 A3
Parlickstown Green	7 A4
Parnell Avenue	35 C4
Parnell Cottages	3 B3
Parnell Court	35 C4[13]
Parnell Place	36 D1[16]
Parnell Road	35 C4
Parnell Road	57 B2
Parnell Square East	36 D1
Parnell Square North	36 D1
Parnell Square West	36 D1
Parnell Street	36 D2
Parnell Street (Sallynoggin)	54 D1
Parochial Avenue	13 A4 [2]
Parslickstown Avenue	7 A4
Parslickstown Close	7 A4
Parslickstown Drive	7 A4
Partridge Terrace	34 F3 [5]
Patrician Park	53 C1 [2]
Patrician Villas	44 F4
Patrick Doyle Road	43 B2
Patrick Street	36 D3
Patrick Street (Dun Laoghaire)	46 D4
Patrick's Row	45 A3[14]
Patrickswell Place	20 D2
Paul Street	35 C2[36]
Pea Field	44 F3
Pearse Avenue	54 D2
Pearse Brothers Park	50 F1
Pearse Close	54 D2 [3]
Pearse Drive	54 D2
Pearse Gardens	53 C2
Pearse Green	54 D2
Pearse Grove	36 F3[38]
Pearse House	36 E2 [1]
Pearse Park	54 D2
Pearse Road	57 B2[12]
Pearse Square (Bray)	57 B2
Pearse Street	36 E2
Pearse Street (Sallynoggin)	54 D2
Pearse Villas	54 D2
Peck's Lane	19 A3
Pembroke Cottages (Booterstown)	44 F3 [2]
Pembroke Cottages (Donnybrook)	43 C1[2]
Pembroke Cottages (Dundrum)	43 C4 [5]
Pembroke Cottages (Ringsend)	37 A2
Pembroke Gardens	36 F4
Pembroke Lane (Lr. Baggot Street)	36 E3
Pembroke Lane (Pembroke Road)	36 F4
Pembroke Park	36 F4
Pembroke Place (Ballsbridge)	36 F4[15]
Pembroke Place (Pembroke St. Upr.)	36 E4[32]
Pembroke Road	36 F4
Pembroke Row	36 E3
Pembroke Street	37 A3
Pembroke Street Lower	36 E3
Pembroke Street Upper	36 E3
Pembroke Terrace	43 C4 [6]
Penrose Street	36 F3 [6]
Percy French Road	41 C1 [3]
Percy Lane	36 F3
Percy Place	36 F3
Peter Place	36 D4[19]
Peter Row	36 D3
Peter Street	36 D3
Peter's Court	36 D1[38]
Peterson's Court	36 E2[16]
Petrie Road	35 C4
Phibsboro	35 C1[22]
Phibsboro	36 D1
Phibsborough Avenue	36 C1 [6]
Phibsborough Place	36 D1 [1]
Phibsborough Road	36 D1
Philipsburgh Avenue	21 C4
Philipsburgh Terrace	21 C4
*Philomena Terrace (off Oliver Plunket Ave.)	37 A3
Phoenix Avenue	19 A3
Phoenix Court	19 A3
Phoenix Court	35 B2[17]
Phoenix Court	35 B1[15]
Phoenix Drive	19 A3
Phoenix Gardens	19 A3
Phoenix Manor	35 B1
Phoenix Place	19 A3
Phoenix Street	34 F3 [2]
Phoenix Street West	35 C2[15]
Phoenix Terrace	44 F3
*Pig Lane (off Summer Place)	36 E1
Pigeon House Road	37 B3
*Pile's Terrace (Sandwith St. Upper)	36 E3
Pilot View	54 F1[14]
Pim Street	35 C3
Pimlico	35 C3
Pimlico Cottages	35 C3[12]
Pine Avenue	53 A2
Pine Copse Road	51 B1
Pine Court	53 A1
Pine Grove	50 D1 [2]
Pine Grove Park	1 C1
Pine Grove Road	1 C1
Pine Haven	44 F3
Pine Hurst	20 E4
Pine Lawn (Deans Grange)	53 A1
Pine Lawn (Tallaght)	49 A2
Pine Lodge	4 D4
Pine Road	37 A3
Pine Valley Avenue	51 B2
Pine Valley Drive	51 B3
Pine Valley Grove	51 B3
Pine Valley Park	51 B3
Pine Valley Way	51 B3
Pinebrook Avenue	22 D2
Pinebrook Close	17 C1 [4]
Pinebrook Crescent	22 D2
Pinebrook Downs	17 C1
Pinebrook Drive	22 E2
Pinebrook Glen	17 C1
Pinebrook Grove	22 E2
Pinebrook Heights	17 C1
Pinebrook Lawn	17 C1
Pinebrook Rise	22 D2
Pinebrook Road	22 D2
Pinebrook Vale	17 C1
Pinebrook View	17 C1
Pinebrook Way	17 C1 [3]
Pinetree Crescent	40 F4 [1]
Pinetree Grove	40 F3 [1]
Pineview Avenue	49 A2
Pineview Drive	49 A2
Pineview Grove	49 A2
Pineview Lawn	49 A2
Pineview Park	49 A2
Pineview Rise	49 A2
Pineview Road	49 A2
Pinewood	54 D4
Pinewood Avenue	20 F1
Pinewood Close	57 C4
Pinewood Court	6 F4
Pinewood Crescent	20 F1
Pinewood Drive	20 F1
Pinewood Green	20 F1
Pinewood Grove	21 A1 [1]
Pinewood Park	50 E1
Pinewood Villas	20 F1
Pinewoods	40 D2
Pleasants Lane	36 D3[15]
Pleasants Place	36 D3[21]
Pleasants Street	36 D3
Plums	52 D1
Plunkett Avenue (Finglas)	20 D1
Plunkett Avenue (Foxrock)	53 A3
Plunkett Crescent	9 A4
Plunkett Drive	20 D1
Plunkett Green	20 D1
Plunkett Grove	20 D1
Plunkett Road	20 D1
Poddle Park	42 E2
Polo Road	35 A1
Poolbeg Street	36 E2
Poole Street	35 C3[38]
Poplar Row	36 F1
Poppintree	9 C4
Porters Avenue	18 D2
Porters Gate	17 B2
Porters Gate Avenue	17 C2
Porters Gate Close	17 B2
Porters Gate Court	17 B2
Porters Gate Crescent	17 B2
Porters Gate Drive	17 B2
Porters Gate Green	17 B2
Porters Gate Grove	17 C2
Porters Gate Heights	17 C2
Porters Gate Rise	17 C2
Porters Gate View	17 B2
Porters Gate Way	17 B2
Porters Road	18 D2
Porterstown Road	18 D2
Portland Close	36 E1[50]
*Portland Court (off Portland Place)	36 D1
Portland Place	36 D1
Portland Row	36 E1
*Portland Square (off Portland St. North)	36 E1
Portland Street North	36 E1
Portland Street West	35 C3
Portmahon Drive	35 B3
Portmarnock	13 A1
Portmarnock Avenue	13 A1
Portmarnock Crescent	13 A1
Portmarnock Drive	4 D4
Portmarnock Grove	4 D4
Portmarnock Park	4 D4
Portmarnock Rise	13 A1
Portmarnock Walk	4 D4
Portobello Harbour	36 D4 [6]
Portobello Place	36 D4[36]
Portobello Road	36 D4
Pottery Road	53 C2
Pound Street	31 A1
Power's Court	36 F3
*Power's Square (off John Dillon Street)	36 D3
Prebend Street	35 C2

STREET NAME	PAGE/GRID REFERENCE
Preston Street	36 E1[14]
*Price's Lane (Aston Quay)	36 D2
Price's Lane (Ranelagh)	36 D4
Priestfield Cottages	35 C4[4]
Priestfield Drive	35 C4[28]
Primrose Avenue	36 D1
Primrose Grove	11 C4
Primrose Hill	45 C4[25]
Primrose Lane	32 D2
*Primrose Street (off Wellington Street Upper)	36 D1
Prince Arthur Terrace	43 A1[3]
Prince Edward Terrace Lower	45 A4[2]
Prince Edward Terrace Upper	45 A4[3]
Prince of Wales Terrace	37 A4[7]
Prince of Wales Terrace	57 C2[26]
Prince's Street North	36 D2[20]
Prince's Street South	36 E2[12]
Princeton	44 D3
Prior Hall	35 B3[36]
Priorswood Estate	11 B4
Priorswood Road	11 C4
Priory Avenue	44 F4
Priory Court	51 A2[1]
Priory Drive	44 F4
Priory East	20 D4
Priory Grove	44 F4
Priory Hall	44 E4
Priory North	20 D3
Priory Road	42 F1
Priory West	20 D4
Proby Garden	45 A4
Proby Hall	54 E2
Proby Square	45 A4
Proby's Lane	36 D2[28]
Promenade Road	37 A1
Prospect Avenue	21 A4
Prospect Downs	50 E2
Prospect Lane	43 C2[1]
Prospect Lawn	53 B3
Prospect Manor	50 E2
Prospect Road	21 A4
Prospect Square	21 A4[5]
Prospect Terrace (Kilmainham)	35 A3[14]
Prospect Terrace (Sandymount)	37 B3[1]
Prospect Way	21 A4
Protestant Row	36 D3[12]
Proud's Lane	36 D3[24]
Prussia Street	35 C1
Pucks Castle Lane	55 C3
*Purcell Lane (off Main Street Bray)	57 C2
Purley Park	3 C4
Purser Gardens	43 A1[10]
Putland Road	57 C3
Putland Villas	57 C3[14]
Pyro Villas	35 C3[60]

Q

STREET NAME	PAGE/GRID REFERENCE
QUARRY COTTAGES	22 E3[3]
Quarry Drive	41 C2
Quarry Road	20 E4
Queen's Park	45 B4
Queen's Road	46 D4
Queen's Street	35 C2
Quinn's Lane	36 E3
Quinn's Road	56 E3
Quinsborough Road	57 C2

R

STREET NAME	PAGE/GRID REFERENCE
RADLETT GROVE	4 D4
*Rafter's Avenue (off Rafter's Road)	35 A4
Rafter's Lane	35 A4
Rafter's Road	35 A4
Raglan Lane	36 F4
Raglan Road	36 F4
Raheen Avenue	48 E1
Raheen Close	48 E1
Raheen Court	48 E1
Raheen Crescent	48 E1
Raheen Drive (Ballyfermot)	34 D3
Raheen Drive (Tallaght)	48 E1
Raheen Green	48 E1
Raheen Lawn	58 D3[1]
Raheen Park (Ballyfermot)	34 D3
Raheen Park (Bray)	58 D3
Raheen Park (Tallaght)	48 E1
Raheen Road	48 E1
Raheny	23 A2
Raheny Park	23 A3
Raheny Road	23 A2
Railway Avenue	3 B2
Railway Avenue (Baldoyle)	24 D1
Railway Avenue (Inchicore)	34 F3
Railway Cottages	37 A4[8]
Railway Road	54 F2[2]
Railway Street	36 E1
*Railway Tce. (off Macken St.)	36 F3
Rainsford Avenue	35 C3[3]
Rainsford Lane	54 E4[6]
Rainsford Street	35 C3
Ralahine	54 D4
Raleigh Square	42 D1
Ralph Square	31 A1
Ramillies Road	34 E3
Ramleh Close	43 C2
Ramleh Park	43 C2
Ramor Park	18 E2
Ranelagh	36 E4
Ranelagh Avenue	36 E4
Ranelagh Road	36 E4
Raphoe Road	42 D1
Rath Row	36 E2[27]
Rathbeale Court	1 C1
Rathbeale Crescent	1 C1
Rathbeale Rise	1 C2
Rathbeale Road	1 C1
Rathclaren	57 B3[2]
Rathdown Avenue	42 F3
Rathdown Court	42 F2[10]
Rathdown Crescent	42 F3
Rathdown Drive	42 E3
Rathdown Park	42 F3
Rathdown Road	35 C1
Rathdown Square	35 C1[20]
Rathdown Terrace (Sandyford)	52 D2[5]
Rathdown Villas	42 F3
Rathdrum Road	35 B4
Rathfarnham	42 F3
Rathfarnham Park	42 F3
Rathfarnham Road	42 F3
Rathfarnham Wood	42 F4
Rathgar	43 A2
Rathgar Avenue	42 F2
Rathgar Place	43 A1
Rathgar Road	43 A1
Rathingle	1 B3
Rathingle Road	1 B3
Rathland Drive	42 E2[4]
Rathland Road	42 E2
Rathlin Road	21 A3
Rathlyon	49 C2
Rathlyon Grove	49 C2
Rathlyon Park	49 C2
Rathmichael	55 C3
Rathmichael Dales	56 D3
Rathmichael Hill	55 C3
Rathmichael Manor	56 D2
Rathmichael Road	55 C2
Rathmichael Woods	56 E2
Rathmines	43 A1
Rathmines Avenue	43 A1
Rathmines Close	43 A2
Rathmines Park	43 A1[1]
Rathmines Road Lower	43 A1
Rathmines Road Upper	43 A1
Rathmintan Close	48 D2
Rathmintan Court	48 D2
Rathmintan Crescent	48 D2
Rathmintan Drive	48 D2
Rathmore Avenue	52 D1
Rathmore Park	23 A2
Rathmore Villas	42 F2
Rathsallagh Avenue	56 E2
Rathsallagh Drive	56 E2
Rathsallagh Grove	56 E2
Rathsallagh Park	56 E2
Rathland Drive	42 E2[1]
Rathland Road	42 E2
Rathvale Avenue	22 F1
Rathvale Drive	22 F1
Rathvale Grove	22 F1
Rathvale Park	22 F1
Rathvilly Drive	20 D2
Rathvilly Park	20 D2
Ratoath Avenue	20 D2
Ratoath Drive	19 C2
Ratoath Estate	20 D3
Ratoath Road	20 E4
Ratoath Road (Hollystown)	7 B1
Ratra Park	19 C4
Ratra Road	19 C4
Ravens Court	20 D2[5]
Ravens Rock Road	52 E2
*Ravensdale Drive (off Ravensdale Par k)	42 E2
Ravensdale Park	42 E2
Ravensdale Road	36 F1
Ravenswell Road	57 C2
Raverty Villas	57 B1[1]
Raymond Street	35 C4
Rectory Slopes	57 A3
Red Brick Terrace	53 A1[2]
Red Cow Cottages	33 C1[4]
Red Cow Lane	35 C2
Redesdale Crescent	44 D4
Redesdale Road	44 D4
Redfern Avenue	3 C4
Redmond's Hill	36 D3[11]
Redwood Avenue	41 A4
Redwood Close	41 A4
Redwood Court (Churchtown)	43 A3
Redwood Court (Tallaght)	40 F4
Redwood Drive	40 F4
Redwood Heights	41 A4
Redwood Lawn	40 F4
Redwood Park	41 A4
Redwood Rise	41 A4
Redwood View	41 A4
Redwood Walk	40 F4
Reginald Square	35 C3[43]
Reginald Street	35 C3
Rehoboth Avenue	35 C4[3]
Rehoboth Place	35 B4
Reilly's Avenue	35 B4[6]
Reuben Avenue	35 B3
Reuben Street	35 B3
*Rhodaville (off Mountpleasant Ave)	36 D4
Rialto Buildings	35 B3[14]
*Rialto Cottages (off Rialto Street)	35 B3
Rialto Drive	35 B4[3]
*Rialto Park (off Echlin Street)	35 B3
Rialto Street	35 B3
Ribh Avenue	22 F2
Ribh Road	22 F2
Richelieu Park	44 E1
Richmond	53 A1
Richmond Avenue (Fairview)	21 B4
Richmond Avenue (Monkstown)	45 C4
Richmond Avenue South	43 B2
Richmond Cottages (Summerhill)	36 E1[9]
Richmond Cottages North	36 E1[37]
Richmond Court	43 B2
Richmond Crescent	36 E1[8]
Richmond Estate	21 C4
Richmond Grove	45 C4
Richmond Hill (Monkstown)	45 C4
Richmond Hill (Rathmines)	36 D4
Richmond Lane	36 E1[20]
Richmond Manor	36 D4
Richmond Mews	36 D4[43]
Richmond Parade	36 E1[10]
Richmond Park	45 B4
Richmond Park	57 A4
Richmond Place (Rathmines)	36 D4[10]
Richmond Place South (Sth. Richmond St.)	36 D4[44]
Richmond Road	21 B4
Richmond Row	36 D4[7]
Richmond Street North	36 E1
Richmond Street South	36 D4
Richmond Terrace	57 C2[34]
Richmond Villas	36 D4[22]
Richview	43 C2
Richview Park	43 B2
*Richview Villas (Clonskeagh Rd.)	43 C2
Riddlesford	57 C4
Ridge Hill	56 E1
Ridgeford	51 C1
Ring Street	34 F3[12]
Ring Terrace	34 F3
Ringsend	37 A3
Ringsend Park	37 A2
Ringsend Road	36 F3
Ripley Court	57 B3
Ripley Hills	57 B3
River Court	5 B3
River Forest	16 D3
River Forest View	15 C3
River Gardens	21 A3[15]
River Lane (Bray)	57 B2
River Lane (Loughlinstown)	56 E2[1]
River Lawn	29 C4
River Road	19 C3
River Road Cottages	19 A2
River Valley Avenue	1 C2
River Valley Close	1 B2
River Valley Court	1 B2
River Valley Drive	1 C2
River Valley Grove	1 C3
River Valley Heights	1 C2
River Valley Lawn	1 C2
River Valley Park	1 C2
River Valley Rise	1 C3
River Valley Road	1 B3
River Valley View	1 B2
River Valley Way	1 B2
Riverbank	43 A3[6]
Riverdale	16 D4
Riversdale	33 C1
Riversdale Avenue	42 F3
Riversdale Avenue (Clondalkin)	40 E1
Riversdale Avenue (Palmerston)	33 C1
Riversdale Court	33 C1
Riversdale Crescent	40 E1
Riversdale Drive	40 E1
Riversdale Green	33 B4
Riversdale Grove	33 B1
Riversdale Grove	42 E2[2]
Riversdale Park	33 C1
Riversdale Park	40 E1
Riversdale Road	40 E1
Riverside Avenue	11 A4
Riverside Cottages	42 E4
Riverside Crescent	11 A4
Riverside Drive (Coolock)	11 B4
Riverside Drive (Palmerston)	33 C1
Riverside Drive (Rathfarnham)	43 A3
Riverside Grove	11 A4
Riverside Park	11 A4
Riverside Road	11 A4
Riverside Walk	43 C1[21]
Riverston Abbey	20 D4
Riverview	33 C1
Riverview Court	34 E2
Robert Place	21 B4[7]
Robert Street (James's Street)	35 C3
Robert Street (Jones's Road)	21 B4[6]
Robin Villas	33 C1
Robinhood Park	41 B1
Robinhood Road	41 B1
Roby Place	46 D4[17]
Rochestown Avenue	53 C2
Rochestown Park	54 D2
Rochfort Downs	32 F2
Rochfort Park	32 F2
Rock Hill	45 A3
*Rock Lane (Baggot St. Lower)	36 E3
Rock Lodge	54 E3
Rock Road	45 A3
Rockbrook	50 E4
Rockfield	32 D3
Rockfield Avenue	42 D2
Rockfield Close	18 D3
Rockfield Drive (Clondalkin)	40 D2
Rockfield Drive (Coolmine)	18 D3
Rockfield Drive (Kimmage)	42 D2
Rockfield Park	18 D2
Rockford Park	53 B1
Rockford Terrace	45 B4[4]
Rockfort Avenue	54 F2
Rockingham	15 C4
Rockingham Terrace	2 D2
Rocklands	54 F1[6]
Rockville Crescent	45 B4
Rockville Drive	45 B4
Rockville Drive	55 A1
Rockville Estate	45 A4[9]
Rockville Park	45 B4
Rockville Road	45 A4
Rockwell Cove	45 A3[9]
Rockwood	32 D3
Rocwood	52 F2
Roebuck Avenue	44 E3
Roebuck Castle	44 D3
Roebuck Crescent	43 C3
Roebuck Downs	43 C3
Roebuck Drive	42 D2
Roebuck Hall	44 D3
Roebuck Road	44 D3
Roger Casement Park	57 B2
Roger's Lane	36 E3[15]
Roland Court	43 A1[20]
Rollins Court	54 D1[12]
Rollins Villas	54 D1
Ronanstown	33 A4
Roncalli Road	23 C1
Roosevelt Cottages	20 D4[1]
Rope Walk Place	37 A3
Rory O'Connor Park	53 B1
Rosapenna Drive	12 D4
Rosary Gardens East	46 D4[2]
Rosary Gardens West	45 C4[1]
Rosary Road	35 B3
Rosary Terrace (Ringsend)	37 A3

STREET NAME	PAGE/GRID REFERENCE
*Rosary Terrace (off Library Road)	46 D4
Rosbeg Court	23 C2
Rose Park	53 C1
Rosebank	49 A2
*Rosedale Terrace (Lower Clanbrassil St)	35 C4
Roseglen Avenue	23 B2
Roseglen Road	23 B2
Rosehill	53 A1 [5]
Roselawn	32 E1
Roselawn Avenue	18 E2
Roselawn Close	18 F2
Roselawn Court	18 F2
Roselawn Crescent	18 E2
Roselawn Drive	57 C4
Roselawn Drive (Castleknock)	18 E2
Roselawn Glade	18 E2
Roselawn Grove	18 E2
Roselawn Park	57 C4 [2]
Roselawn Road	18 F2
Roselawn View	18 E2
Roselawn Walk	18 E2
Roselawn Way	18 F2
Rosemount	22 D3
Rosemount (Churchtown)	43 C4
Rosemount Avenue	22 E2
Rosemount Court	43 C4
Rosemount Court	44 E3
Rosemount Court (Inchicore Rd)	35 A3 [19]
Rosemount Crescent (Roebuck Road)	43 C3
Rosemount Park	43 C4
Rosemount Road	35 C1 [4]
Rosemount Terrace (Arbour Hill)	35 C2 [29]
Rosemount Terrace (Booterstown)	44 E3
Rosemount Terrace (Dundrum)	43 B4 [11]
Rosevale Court	22 F3
Rosevale Mansions	22 F3
Roseville Terrace	43 C4 [4]
Rosewood Grove	32 F3
Rosmeen Gardens	46 D4
Rosmeen Park	54 D1
Ross Road	36 D3
Ross Street	35 B1
Ross View	33 C1
Rossfield Avenue	48 D1
Rossfield Crescent	48 D1
Rossfield Drive	48 D1
Rossfield Gardens	48 D1
Rossfield Grove	48 D1
Rossfield Park	48 D1
Rossfield Way	48 D1
Rosslyn	57 C3 [6]
Rosslyn Court	57 C3
Rosslyn Grove	57 C2 [4]
Rossmore Avenue (Ballyfermot)	34 D3
Rossmore Avenue (Templeogue)	42 D4
Rossmore Close	42 D4
Rossmore Crescent	42 D4
Rossmore Drive (Ballyfermot)	34 D2
Rossmore Drive (Templeogue)	41 C4
Rossmore Grove	42 D4
Rossmore Lawn	42 D4
Rossmore Park	42 D4
Rossmore Road (Ballyfermot)	34 D2
Rossmore Road (Templeogue)	42 D4
Rostrevor Road	43 A3
Rostrevor Terrace (Lr. Grand Canal St.)	36 F3 [25]
Rostrevor Terrace (Orwell Road)	43 A2
Rothe Abbey	35 A3
Rowan Close	30 D3
Rowan Grove	57 B2
Rowan Hall	43 C1 [15]
Rowan Park Avenue	45 B4
Rowanbyrn	45 B4
Rowans	52 D2
Rowlagh Avenue	33 A3
Rowlagh Crescent	33 A3
Rowlagh Gardens	33 A3
Rowlagh Green	33 A3
Rowlagh Park	33 A3
Rowserstown Lane	35 A3 [20]
Royal Canal Bank	21 A4 [16]
Royal Canal Bank	36 D1
Royal Canal Terrace	35 C1 [12]
Royal Canal Way	21 A4
Royal Canal Way	36 E2
Royal Hibernian Way	36 E3 [42]
Royal Marine Road	46 D4
Royal Marine Terrace	57 C2 [12]
Royal Oak	10 F4

STREET NAME	PAGE/GRID REFERENCE
Royal Terrace Lane	54 D1 [10]
Royal Terrace East	54 D1
Royal Terrace North	54 D1 [2]
Royal Terrace West	54 D1
Royse Road	21 A4
Royston	42 D2
Ruby Hall	53 C2
Rugby Road	43 B1
Rugby Villas	43 B1 [6]
*Rus in Urbe Terrace (on Glenageary Road Lr.)	54 D1
Rushbrook	18 E2
Rushbrook Avenue	41 C3
Rushbrook Court	41 C4
Rushbrook Crescent	41 C3
Rushbrook Drive	41 C3
Rushbrook Grove	41 C3
Rushbrook Park	41 C3
Rushbrook Road	41 C3
Rushbrook View	41 C3
Rushbrook Way	41 C3
Russell Avenue	36 E1
Russell Avenue East	36 F1 [14]
Russell Street	36 E1
Rutland Avenue	35 B4
Rutland Cottages	36 E1 [55]
Rutland Grove	42 F1
Rutland Place North	36 E1 [48]
Rutland Place West	36 D1
Rutland Street Lower	36 E1
Rutledge Terrace	35 C4 [26]
Ryan's Cottages (Harold's Cross)	42 F1 [7]
Ryder's Row	36 D2 [9]
Rye River Avenue	16 D4
Rye River Close	16 D4
Rye River Court	16 D4
Rye River Crescent	16 D4
Rye River Gardens	16 D4
Rye River Grove	16 D4
Rye River Mall	16 D4
Rye River Park	16 D4
Ryecroft	57 B3
Ryevale Lawns	16 D4
Rynville Manor	57 A4

S

STREET NAME	PAGE/GRID REFERENCE
*ST. AGATHA COURT (off William St. N.)	36 E1
St. Agnes Park	42 D1
St. Agnes Road	42 D1
*St. Agnes Terrace (on St. Agnes Road)	42 D1
St. Agnes Terrace (Rathfarnham)	42 F3 [2]
St. Aidan's Drive	44 D4
St. Aidan's Park	21 C4 [6]
St. Aidan's Park Avenue	21 C4
St. Aidan's Park Road	21 C4
St. Aidan's Terrace	57 C2 [23]
St. Alban's Park	44 E1
St. Alban's Road	35 C4
St. Alphonsus Avenue	21 A4 [11]
St. Alphonsus Rd.	21 A4
St. Andrew Street	36 D3
St. Andrew's Grove	3 B3
*St. Andrew's Lane (off Exchequer Street)	36 D3
St. Andrews Park	1 C1
St. Ann's	23 A3
St. Anne's Avenue	23 A3
St. Anne's Court	23 A3 [2]
St. Anne's Drive	23 A3
St. Anne's Park	56 E3
St. Anne's Road North	21 A4
St. Anne's Road South	35 C4 [5]
St. Anne's Square (Blackrock)	45 A3 [7]
St. Anne's Square (Portmarnock)	12 F2
St. Anne's Terrace (Cabra)	20 F4
St. Anne's Terrace (Raheny)	23 A3
St. Annes	42 E2
St. Anthony's Avenue	40 E2
St. Anthony's Crescent	41 C2
*St. Anthony's Place (off Temple Street North)	36 D1
St. Anthony's Road	35 B3
St. Aongus Court	41 B4
St. Aongus Crescent	41 B4
St. Aongus Green	41 B4
St. Aongus Grove	41 B4
St. Aongus Lawn	41 B4
St. Aongus Road	41 B4
St. Assam's Avenue	23 A2
St. Assam's Drive	23 B2
St. Assam's Park	23 A2

STREET NAME	PAGE/GRID REFERENCE
St. Assam's Road East	23 B2
St. Assam's Road West	23 A2
St. Attracta Road	20 F4
St. Aubyn's Court	56 E1 [5]
*St. Audoen's Terrace (off High Street)	36 D3
St. Augustine Street	35 C2
St. Augustine's Park	53 A1
St. Barnabas Gardens	36 F1 [12]
St. Begnet's Villas	54 E1
St. Benedicts Gardens	36 D1 [35]
St. Bernadette's Park	7 C4
St. Brendan's Avenue	22 E2
St. Brendan's Cottages	37 A3 [6]
St. Brendan's Crescent	41 B2
St. Brendan's Drive	22 E2
St. Brendan's Park	22 F2
St. Brendan's Road	21 A4 [12]
St. Brendan's Terrace (Coolock)	22 E1
St. Brendan's Terrace (Dun Laoghaire)	45 C4 [19]
St. Brendan's Terrace (Rockbrook)	50 E4
St. Bricin's Park	35 B2
St. Bridget's Avenue (North Strand)	36 F1
St. Bridget's Drive (Greenhills)	41 B2
St. Bridget's Flats	43 C2 [8]
St. Brigid's Church Road	52 F1
St. Brigid's Cottages (Blanchardstown)	18 F2
St. Brigid's Cottages (Clondalkin)	40 F2
St. Brigid's Cottages (North Strand)	36 F1 [24]
St. Brigid's Court	22 E3 [2]
St. Brigid's Crescent	22 E2
St. Brigid's Drive (Clondalkin)	40 E2
St. Brigid's Drive (Killester)	22 E3 [1]
St. Brigid's Gardens	36 F2 [12]
St. Brigid's Green	22 E2
St. Brigid's Grove	22 E2
St. Brigid's Lawn	22 E2
St. Brigid's Park (Clondalkin)	40 E2 [1]
St. Brigid's Park (Cornelscourt)	53 B3
St. Brigid's Pk (Blanchardstown)	18 F2
St. Brigid's Road (Artane)	22 E2
St. Brigid's Road (Clondalkin)	40 E2
St. Brigid's Road Lower	21 A4
St. Brigid's Road Upper	21 A4
St. Brigid's Terrace	57 B2 [24]
St. Broc's Cottages	43 C1 [1]
St. Canice's Park	20 F2
St. Canice's Road	21 A2
St. Catherine's Avenue	35 C4
St. Catherine's Lane West	35 C3 [14]
St. Catherine's Park	54 E1
St. Catherine's Road	54 E1
St. Catherine's Terrace	24 E1 [2]
St. Catherine's View	16 E4
St. Clair's Lawn	57 B3
St. Clair's Terrace	57 B3 [3]
St. Clare's Avenue	35 C4 [2]
*St. Clare's Terrace (on Mount Drummond Avenue)	36 D4
St. Clement's Road	21 A4 [13]
St. Columba's Road	41 B2
St. Columba's Road Lower	21 A4
St. Columba's Road Upper	21 A4
St. Columbanus Avenue	43 B3
St. Columbanus Place	43 B3 [1]
St. Columbanus Road	43 B3
St. Columbas Heights	1 C2
St. Columbas Rise	1 C2
St. Columcille's Crescent	2 D2 [1]
St. Columcille's Drive	2 D2
St. Columcille's Terrace	57 C2 [18]
St. Columcills Park	2 D2
St. Conleth's Road	41 C2
St. Cronan's Avenue	1 B1
St. Cronan's Close	1 B2
St. Cronan's Court	1 B1
St. Cronan's Grove	1 C1
St. Cronan's Lawn	1 B1
St. Cronan's Road	57 B2 [8]
St. Cronan's View	1 B2
St. Cronan's Way	1 C2
St. David's	22 D2
St. David's Court	22 E4 [5]
St. David's Terrace (Blackhorse Avenue)	35 B1 [7]
St. David's Terrace (Glasnevin)	21 A3 [3]
St. Declan's Road	21 C4
St. Declan's Terrace	21 C4 [5]
St. Dominic's Avenue	49 A1
St. Dominic's Road	49 A1

STREET NAME	PAGE/GRID REFERENCE
St. Dominic's Terrace	49 A1
St. Donagh's Crescent	23 B1
St. Donagh's Park	23 B1
St. Donagh's Road	23 B1
St. Eithne Road	20 F4
St. Elizabeth's Court	35 C1 [14]
St. Enda's Drive	50 F1
St. Enda's Park	50 F1
St. Enda's Road	42 F2
St. Finbarr's Close	41 B3
St. Finbarr's Court	20 E4 [2]
St. Finbarr's Road	20 E4
St. Finnians Avenue	32 D2
St. Finnians Close	32 D2
St. Finnians Crescent	32 D2
St. Fintan Road (Cabra)	20 F4
St. Fintan Terrace (Cabra)	20 F4
St. Fintan's Crescent	25 B3
St. Fintan's Grove	25 B3
St. Fintan's Park (Dean's Grange)	53 B1
St. Fintan's Park (Sutton)	25 B2
St. Fintan's Road (Sutton)	25 B3
St. Fintan's Terrace	33 C1 [5]
St. Fintan's Villas	53 B1
St. Francis Square	36 D3 [48]
St. Gabriel's Court	23 A4 [2]
St. Gabriel's Road	22 F4
St. Gall Gardens North	43 B3 [2]
St. Gall Gardens South	43 B3 [3]
St. Gatien Road	50 F1 [2]
St. George's Avenue (Clonliffe Road)	21 B4
St. George's Avenue (Killiney)	54 E3
St. George's Villas (Inchicore)	34 F3 [18]
St. Gerard's Road	41 C2
St. Helen's	54 E1 [22]
St. Helen's Road	44 E2
St. Helen's Villas	44 F2 [1]
St. Helen's Wood	44 E3
St. Helena's Court	20 E2 [3]
St. Helena's Drive	20 E2
St. Helena's Road	20 E2
St. Helier's Copse	44 F4 [1]
St. Ignatius Avenue	36 D1 [17]
St. Ignatius Road	21 A4
St. Ita's Road	21 A3 [6]
St. Ives	3 B2
St. James Avenue (Clonliffe Road)	36 E1
*St. James Place (Sandymount Road)	37 A3
St. James Terrace (Sandymount)	37 A3 [2]
St. James's Avenue (James's Street)	35 B3 [21]
St. James's Place (Inchicore)	34 F3 [17]
St. James's Road	41 B2
St. James's Terrace (Dolphin's Barn)	35 B4 [1]
St. James's Walk	35 B3
St. Jarlath Road	20 F4
St. John Street	35 C3 [58]
St. John's	44 E1
St. John's Avenue	35 C3 [39]
St. John's Avenue	40 D2
St. John's Close	40 D2
St. John's Cottages	35 B3 [28]
St. John's Court	22 D1
St. John's Court	40 D2
St. John's Crescent	40 D2
St. John's Drive	40 D2
St. John's Green	40 D2
*St. John's Lane (off Strand Road)	44 E1
St. John's Lawn	40 D2
St. John's Meadows	40 D2
St. John's Park (Clondalkin)	40 D2
St. John's Park (Dun Laoghaire)	45 C4
St. John's Park East	40 D2
St. John's Road	40 D2
St. John's Road East	44 E1
St. John's Road West	35 B2
St. John's Road West	40 D2
St. John's Terrace (Mount Brown)	35 B3 [33]
St. John's Wood	22 E4 [2]
St. John's Wood	40 D2
St. John's Wood West	40 D2
St. Joseph Street	36 D1 [27]
St. Joseph's Avenue (Ballybough)	21 B4 [2]
St. Joseph's Avenue (Drumcondra)	21 A4
St. Joseph's Cottages	19 C4 [3]
St. Joseph's Court	35 C1 [16]
St. Joseph's Grove	43 C4 [9]
St. Joseph's Mansions	36 E1
St. Joseph's Parade	36 D1

STREET NAME	PAGE/GRID REFERENCE
St. Joseph's Place	35 C1[15]
St. Joseph's Place	36 D1[59]
St. Joseph's Road (Aughrim Street)	35 C1
St. Joseph's Road (Walkinstown)	41 C2
St. Joseph's Square	37 C1[2]
*St. Joseph's Street (off Leo Street)	36 D1
St. Joseph's Terrace	36 E1[35]
St. Joseph's Terrace (Fairview)	21 C4[4]
*St. Joseph's Terrace (off Dolphin's Barn)	35 B4
*St. Joseph's Terrace (off Pembroke Street)	37 A3
*St. Joseph's Terrace (on Tivoli Road)	46 D4
St. Joseph's Villas (Summerhill)	36 E1[38]
*St. Kevin's Avenue (off Blackpitts)	35 C3
St. Kevin's Cottages	36 D4[29]
St. Kevin's Court	43 A2
St. Kevin's Gardens	43 A2
St. Kevin's Parade	36 D4[52]
St. Kevin's Park (Rathgar)	43 A2
St. Kevin's Park (Stillorgan)	52 D1
St. Kevin's Road	36 D4[3]
St. Kevin's Square	57 C2
St. Kevin's Terrace	57 C2[14]
*St. Kevin's Terrace (New Bride St.)	36 D3
St. Kevin's Villas	54 D1
St. Killian's Avenue	41 B2
St. Killian's Park	40 E1[1]
St. Laurence Grove	34 E2[4]
St. Laurence's Park	44 F4
*St. Laurence Place (Fontenoy Street)	36 D1
*St. Laurence Place (Lr. Sheriff Street)	36 F2
St. Laurence Road	34 E2
St. Laurence Terrace (Chapelizod)	34 E2[9]
St. Laurence's Mansions	36 E2[34]
St. Laurence's Terrace	57 C2[17]
St. Lawrence Road (Clontarf)	22 D4
St. Lawrence Road (Howth)	26 D1
St. Lawrence's Court	22 D4
St. Lawrence's Terrace (Howth)	26 D2[1]
St. Luke's Crescent	43 B2[3]
St. Maelruans Park	49 A1[1]
St. Maignenn's Terrace	35 B3[6]
St. Malachy's Drive	41 C2
St. Malachy's Road	21 A3[7]
St. Margaret's	9 B1
St. Margaret's Avenue	3 B3
*St. Margaret's Avenue (off Pimlico)	35 C3
St. Margaret's Avenue North	36 E1[34]
St. Margaret's Park	3 B3
St. Margaret's Road	3 B3
St. Margaret's Road (Ballymun)	10 D4
St. Margaret's Road (Finglas)	9 A4
St. Margaret's Terrace	35 C3[7]
St. Mark's Avenue	33 A2
St. Mark's Crescent	33 A3
St. Mark's Drive	33 A3
St. Mark's Gardens	33 A3
St. Mark's Green	33 A3
St. Mark's Grove	33 A3
St. Martin's Drive	42 E2
St. Martin's Park	42 E1
St. Mary's Ave. North (Mountjoy Street)	36 D1[7]
St. Mary's Avenue (Rathfarnham)	42 F4
St. Mary's Avenue West	34 F3
St. Mary's Crescent	41 C1
St. Mary's Drive	41 C1
St. Mary's Lane	36 F3[17]
St. Mary's Mansions	36 E1
St. Mary's Park	16 D4
St. Mary's Park	19 C2
St. Mary's Park	41 C1
St. Mary's Place (Howth)	26 D2[4]
St. Mary's Place North	36 D1[48]
St. Mary's Road (Crumlin)	42 D1
St. Mary's Road (Howth)	26 D2[3]
St. Mary's Road North (East Wall)	36 F1
St. Mary's Road South (Ballsbridge)	36 F4
St. Mary's Street	45 C4[5]
St. Mary's Terrace	57 C4[6]
St. Mary's Terrace	58 D3[7]
St. Mary's Terrace (Arbour Hill)	35 C2[34]
*St. Mary's Terrace (Bath Street)	37 A3
St. Mary's Terrace (Chapelizod)	34 E2[5]
St. Mary's Terrace (Mountjoy Street)	36 D1[10]
St. Mary's Terrace (Rathfarnham)	42 F4[5]
St. Mel's Avenue	41 B3
*St. Michael's Close (off High Street)	36 D3
St. Michael's Estate	35 A3[8]
*St. Michael's Hill (off High Street)	36 D3
St. Michael's Place	36 D1[51]
St. Michael's Road	21 A3[8]
St. Michael's Terrace (Blackpitts)	35 C3[57]
St. Michael's Terrace (Dun Laoghaire)	45 C4[18]
*St. Michan's Place (off Chancery Street)	36 D2
St. Michan's Street	36 D2[44]
St. Mobhi Boithirin	21 A3
*St. Mobhi Avenue (off St.Mobhi Road)	21 A3
St. Mobhi Court	21 A3[16]
St. Mobhi Drive	21 A3
St. Mobhi Grove	21 A3[10]
St. Mobhi Road	21 A3
St. Mura's Terrace	36 F1[17]
St. Nathy's House	43 B4[5]
St. Nessan's Close	26 D2[9]
St. Nessan's Court	26 D2[10]
St. Nessan's Terrace	26 D2[5]
St. Nicholas Place	36 D3[2]
St. Oliver's Park	33 B3
St. Pappin's Green	20 F2
St. Pappin's Road	21 A2
St. Patrick's Avenue (Clondalkin)	40 D1[1]
St. Patrick's Avenue (Dalkey)	54 F2[1]
St. Patrick's Avenue (Fairview)	36 F1[16]
St. Patrick's Close	36 D3
St. Patrick's Close	53 C1[9]
St. Patrick's Cottages	42 F4
St. Patrick's Crescent	53 C1
St. Patrick's Parade	21 A4
St. Patrick's Park	30 D3
St. Patrick's Park	5 B2
St. Patrick's Park (Blanchardstown)	18 E2
St. Patrick's Park (Clondalkin)	33 A4
*St. Patrick's Place (off Royal Canal Bank)	21 A4
St. Patrick's Road (Clondalkin)	33 A4
St. Patrick's Road (Dalkey)	54 F2[8]
St. Patrick's Road (Drumcondra)	21 A4
St. Patrick's Road (Walkinstown)	41 C2
St. Patrick's Square	54 F2[4]
St. Patrick's Square	57 B2[7]
St. Patrick's Terrace (Inchicore)	34 F3[9]
St. Patrick's Terrace (Kill O' the Grange)	53 C1[7]
*St. Patrick's Terrace (Nth. Brunswick St.)	35 C2
*St. Patrick's Terrace (off Fitzroy Avenue)	21B4
St. Patrick's Terrace (Russell Street)	36 E1
St. Patrick's Villas	37 A3[3]
*St. Paul's Street (Off Blackhall Place)	54 E1
St. Paul's Terrace	54 E1[5]
St. Peter's Avenue	35 C1
*St. Peter's Close (off Royal Canal Bank)	36D1
St. Peter's Crescent	41 C2
St. Peter's Drive	41 C2
St. Peter's Park	5 B2
St. Peter's Road (Bray)	57 B1
St. Peter's Road (Phibsborough)	35 C1
St. Peter's Road (Walkinstown)	41 C2
St. Peter's Terrace (Dun Laoghaire)	54 E1[6]
St. Peter's Terrace (Howth)	26 D2
*St. Peter's Terrace (Walkinstown)	41 C2[1]
St. Peter's Terrace	57B1[2]
St. Philomena's Road	20 F4[1]
St. Ronan's Avenue	33 A3
St. Ronan's Close	33 A3
St. Ronan's Crescent	33 A3
St. Ronan's Drive	33 A3
St. Ronan's Gardens	33 A3
St. Ronan's Green	33 A3
St. Ronan's Grove	33 A3
St. Ronan's Park	33 A3
St. Ronan's Way	33 A3
St. Stephen's Green East	36 E3
St. Stephen's Green North	36 E3
St. Stephen's Green South	36 D3
St. Stephen's Green West	36 D3
St. Sylvester Villas	3 B3
St. Teresa's Place	21 A4[9]
St. Teresa's Road (Glasnevin)	21 A4[8]
St. Teresa's Gardens	35 C3
St. Teresa's Road (Crumlin)	42 D2
St. Thomas Mead	44 E3
St. Thomas Road (Ardee Street)	35 C3
St. Thomas's Road (Mount Merrion)	44 E3
St. Ultan's Flats	36 D4[21]
St. Vincent Street North	36 D1[4]
St. Vincent Street South	36 D4
St. Vincent Street West	35 A3
St. Vincent's Cottages	19 C4[2]
St. Vincent's Court	21 C3[7]
St. Vincent's Park	45 A4
Sackville Avenue	36 E1
Sackville Gardens	36 E1[2]
Sackville Place	36 D2[24]
Sadleir Hall	5 A2
Saggart	47 B2
Saintbury Avenue	54 E4
Salamanca	44 D4
Salem Court	43 A1[17]
Sally Park	49 C1
Sally Park Close	49 C1
Sallymount Avenue	43 B1
Sallymount Gardens	43 B1[1]
Sallymount Terrace	43 B1[14]
Sallynoggin	54 D2
Sallynoggin Park	53 C2
Sallynoggin Road	53 C2
*Salthill Place (off Crofton Road)	46 D4
Saltzburg	44 D4
Sampson's Lane	36 D2[14]
Sandford Avenue (Donnybrook)	43 C1
Sandford Avenue (Donore Ave)	35 C4
Sandford Close	43 B1
Sandford Gardens (Donnybrook)	43 C1[10]
*Sandford Gardens (off Donore Avenue)	35 C4
*Sandford Park (off O'Donovan Road)	35 C4
Sandford Road	43 B1
Sandford Terrace	43 B1
Sandon Cove	22 E4
Sandwith Street Lower	36 E2
Sandwith Street Upper	36 E3
Sandycove Avenue East	54 E1
Sandycove Avenue North	46 E4
Sandycove Avenue West	54 E1
Sandycove Point	46 E4
Sandycove Road	54 E1
Sandyford	52 D2
Sandyford Downs	52 D3
Sandyford Hall	52 E3
Sandyford Hall Avenue	52 E3
Sandyford Hall Close	52 E4
Sandyford Hall Court	52 E3
Sandyford Hall Crescent	52 E3
Sandyford Hall Drive	52 E4
Sandyford Hall Green	52 E3
Sandyford Hall Grove	52 E3
Sandyford Hall Lawn	52 E3
Sandyford Hall Park	52 E3
Sandyford Hall Place	52 E3
Sandyford Hall Rise	52 E3
Sandyford Hall View	52 E3
Sandyford Hall Walk	52 E3
Sandyford Park	52 D2
Sandyford Road	51 C1
Sandyford Village	52 D3
Sandyhill Avenue	20 F1
Sandyhill Gardens	20 F1
Sandymount	37 A4
Sandymount Avenue	37 A4
Sandymount Castle	37 A4[5]
Sandymount Castle Drive	37 A4[3]
Sandymount Castle Park	37 B4[2]
Sandymount Castle Road	37 A4[2]
Sandymount Court	37 A3[26]
Sandymount Green	37 A4[1]
Sandymount Road	37 A3
Sans Souci Park	44 F3
Santa Sabina Manor	25 B2
Santry Avenue	10 E4
Santry Close	10 F4
Santry Court	10 F4
Santry Villas	10 E4
Sarah Curran Avenue	50 F1
Sarah Curran Road	50 F1[1]
Sarah Place	35 A2[3]
Sarsfield Court	32 D1[4]
Sarsfield Park	32 D1
Sarsfield Quay	35 C2[8]
Sarsfield Road	34 F3
Sarsfield Street (Phibsborough)	36 D1[5]
Sarsfield Street (Sallynoggin)	54 D1
Sarsfield Terrace	32 D1[1]
Sarto Lawn	23 C1
Sarto Park	23 C1
Sarto Rise	23 C1
Sarto Road	23 C2
Saul Road	42 E1
Saval Grove	54 E2
Saval Park Crescent	54 E2
Saval Park Gardens	54 E2
Saval Park Road	54 E2
Scholarstown Park	50 D2
Scholarstown Road	50 D2
School Avenue	22 E2
School Street	35 C3
Schoolhouse Lane	21 B1
Schoolhouse Lane	36 E3[12]
*Schoolhouse Lane West (off High Street)	36 D3
Scott Park	57 C4
Sea Road	3 A2
Seabank Court	54 E1[21]
Seabury	44 E1
Seabury Avenue	2 F2
Seabury Close	2 F2
Seabury Court	2 F2
Seabury Crescent	2 F2
Seabury Dale	2 F2
Seabury Downs	2 F2
Seabury Drive	3 A2
Seabury Gardens	2 F2
Seabury Glen	2 F2
Seabury Green	2 F2
Seabury Grove	2 F2
Seabury Heights	2 F2
Seabury Lane	2 F2
Seabury Lawns	2 F2
Seabury Meadows	2 F2
Seabury Orchard	2 F2
Seabury Parade	2 F2
Seabury Park	2 F2
Seabury Place	2 F2
Seabury Road	2 F2
Seabury Vale	2 F2
Seabury View	2 F2
Seabury Walk	2 F2
Seabury Wood	2 F2
Seacliff Avenue	23 C1
Seacliff Drive	23 C1
Seacliff Road	23 C1
Seacourt	22 F4
Seacrest	57 C3
Seafield (Shankill)	56 F2
Seafield (Sutton))	24 D1
Seafield Avenue (Clontarf)	22 F4
Seafield Avenue (Monkstown)	45 B4
Seafield Close	44 E2
Seafield Court	24 D1[2]
Seafield Court	56 E1
Seafield Court (Malahide)	3 B2
Seafield Crescent	44 E2
*Seafield Downs (off Kincora Road Clontarf)	22E4
Seafield Drive	44 E2
Seafield Grove	23 A4[1]
Seafield Park	44 E2[1]
Seafield Road (Ballybrack)	56 E1
Seafield Road (Booterstown)	44 E2
Seafield Road (Killiney)	54 E4
Seafield Road East	22 F4
Seafield Road West	22 E4
Seafield Terrace	54 F2[15]
Seafort Avenue	37 A4
Seafort Cottages	37 A4[18]
Seafort Gardens	37 A3[10]
Seafort Parade	44 F3
Seafort Terrace	37 A4[19]
Seafort Villas	37 A4[20]
Seagrange Avenue	12 F4
Seagrange Drive	23 C1
Seagrange Road	23 C1
Seamount Drive	3 C3
Seamount Heights	3 C3
Seamount Road	3 C3
Seamus Ennis Road	20 E1
Sean MacDermott Street Upper	36 D2
Sean MacDermott Street Lower	36 E1
Sean Moore Road	37 A3
Sean O'Casey Avenue	36 E1[47]

STREET NAME	PAGE/GRID REFERENCE
Seapark	3 C3
Seapark (Dollymount)	22 F4
Seapark Drive	22 F4
Seapark Hill	3 C3
Seapark Road	22 F4
Seapoint Avenue	45 B3
Seapoint Avenue (Baldoyle)	13 A4 [1]
Seapoint Court	57 C2
Seapoint Road	57 C2
Seapoint Terrace	37 A3 [4]
Seapoint Terrace (Blackrock)	45 B3 [4]
Seapoint Terrace	57 C2 [24]
Seapoint Villas	57 C2 [20]
Seatown West	2 E1
Seaview Avenue East	36 F1
Seaview Avenue North	22 D4
Seaview Lawn	56 E2
Seaview Park	56 E2
Seaview Terrace (Donnybrook)	44 D1
Seaview Terrace (Dun Laoghaire)	45 C4 [15]
Seaview Terrace (Howth)	26 D2 [2]
Second Avenue (Seville Place)	36 F2 [6]
Sefton	53 C2
Sefton Green	53 C2
Selskar Terrace	36 E4 [21]
Serpentine Avenue	37 A4
Serpentine Park	37 A4
Serpentine Road	37 A4
Serpentine Terrace	37 A4
Seskin View Avenue	49 A2
Seskin View Drive	49 A2
Seskin View Park	49 A2
Seskin View Road	49 A2
Seven Houses	54 D1 [13]
Seven Oaks	21 B3
Seville Place	36 E1
Seville Terrace	36 E1 [59]
Seymour Road	57 C2
Shamrock Cottages	36 E1 [31]
Shamrock Place	36 E1 [15]
*Shamrock Street (off Royal Canal Bank)	36 D1
Shamrock Terrace	36 E1 [16]
Shamrock Villas	42 F1
Shanard Avenue	21 A1
Shanard Road	21 A1
Shanboley Road	21 C1
Shancastle Avenue	33 A2
Shancastle Close	33 A2
Shancastle Crescent	33 A2
Shancastle Drive	33 A2
Shancastle Lawns	33 A2
Shancastle Park	33 A2
Shandon Crescent	20 F4
Shandon Drive	20 F4
Shandon Gardens	20 F4
Shandon Park (Monkstown)	45 B4
Shandon Park (Phibsborough)	20 F4
Shandon Road	20 F4
Shangan Avenue	21 B1
Shangan Gardens	21 B1
Shangan Green	21 B1
Shangan Park	21 B1
Shangan Road	21 A1
Shanganagh Cliffs	56 E2
Shanganagh Grove	56 E3
Shanganagh Road	21 A4
Shanganagh Road	56 E1
Shanganagh Terrace	54 E4
Shanganagh Vale	54 D4
Shanglas Road	21 C1
Shanid Road	42 F1
Shankill	56 E3
*Shankill View (on Seapoint Rd)	57 C2
Shanliss Avenue	21 B1
Shanliss Drive	21 B1
Shanliss Gardens	21 A1 [2]
Shanliss Grove	21 B1
Shanliss Park	21 B1
Shanliss Road	21 A1
Shanliss Walk	21 B1
Shanliss Way	21 B1
Shannon Terrace	35 B3 [4]
Shanowen Avenue	21 A1
Shanowen Crescent	21 B1
Shanowen Drive	21 B1
Shanowen Grove	21 A1
Shanowen Park	21 A1
Shanowen Road	21 B1
Shanrath Road	21 B1
Shantalla Avenue	21 C1
Shantalla Drive	21 C2
Shantalla Park	21 C2
Shantalla Road	21 C2
Shanvarna Road	21 B1
Sharavogue	54 E2
Shaw Street	36 E2 [10]
Shaw's Lane	36 F3 [13]
Sheelin Avenue	56 E1
Sheelin Drive	56 E1 [15]
Sheelin Grove	56 E1 [7]
Sheelin Hill	56 E1 [13]
Sheelin Walk	56 E1 [14]
Sheephill Avenue	7 C4
Sheephill Green	7 C4
Sheephill Park	7 C4
Sheepmoor Avenue	18 D1
Sheepmoor Close	18 D1
Sheepmoor Crescent	18 D1
Sheepmoor Gardens	18 D1
Sheepmoor Green	18 D1
Sheepmoor Grove	18 D1
Sheepmoor Lawn	18 D1
Sheepmoor Way	18 D1
Shelbourne Avenue	36 F4 [5]
Shelbourne Lane	36 F4 [3]
Shelbourne Road	36 F3
Shelerin Road	17 C2
Shelmalier Road	36 F1
Shelmartin Avenue	21 C4
Shelmartin Terrace	21 C4 [2]
Shelton Drive	42 D2
Shelton Gardens	42 D2
Shelton Grove	42 D2
Shelton Park	42 D2
Sheriff Street Lower	36 E2
Sheriff Street Upper	36 F2
Sherkin Gardens	21 B3
Sherrard Avenue	36 D1 [28]
*Sherrard Court (off Portland Place)	36 D1
Sherrard Street Lower	36 D1
Sherrard Street Upper	36 D1
Shielmartin Drive	25 B3
Shielmartin Park	25 B3 [1]
Shielmartin Road	25 B3
Ship Street Great	36 D3
Ship Street Little	36 D3
Shrewsbury	37 A4
Shrewsbury Hall	56 E3
Shrewsbury Lawn	53 C4
Shrewsbury Park	44 D1
Shrewsbury Road	44 D1
Shrewsbury Road	56 E3
Shrewsbury Woods	53 C4
Sibthorpe Lane	36 E4 [28]
Sidmonton Avenue	57 C2
Sidmonton Court	57 C3
Sidmonton Court	58 D3 [5]
Sidmonton Gardens	57 C3 [5]
Sidmonton Park	57 C3 [2]
Sidmonton Place	57 C2 [6]
Sidmonton Road	57 C2
Sidmonton Square	57 C2 [1]
Sigurd Road	35 C2 [31]
Silchester Court	54 D1
Silchester Crescent	54 D1
Silchester Park	54 D1
Silchester Road	54 D1
Silchester Wood	54 D1 [16]
Silleachain Lane	16 D4
Silloge Avenue	21 A1
Silloge Gardens	21 A1
Silloge Road	21 A1
Silver Birches	43 C4
Silver Pines	52 F2 [3]
Silverbridge	57 A3
Silverpine	57 B3
Silverwood Drive	42 E4
Silverwood Road	42 E4
Simmon's Court	44 D1 [3]
*Simmon's Place	36 E1
Simmonscourt Avenue (off Thompson's Cottages)	44 D1 [2]
Simmonscourt Castle	44 D1
Simmonscourt Road	37 A4
Simmonscourt Terrace	43 C1 [18]
Simmonstown Park	30 D4
*Simpson's Lane (off Irishtown Road)	37 A3
Sion Hill Avenue	42 F1
Sion Hill Court	21 C3 [5]
Sion Hill Road	21 C3
Sion Road	54 D2
*Sir Ivor Hall (Charles Sheil's Houses)	52 F2
Sir John Rogerson's Quay	36 F2
*Sitric Place (off Sitric Road)	35 C2
Sitric Road	35 C2
Skelly's Lane	22 D2
Skreen Road	35 A1
Slade Row	35 C2 [35]
Slademore Avenue	22 F1
Slademore Close	22 F1
Slademore Court	11 C4
Slademore Court	22 F1
Slademore Drive	22 F1
Slane Road	35 B4
Slaney Close	20 E3
Slaney Road	20 E3
Slate Cabin Lane	51 C3
Slemish Road	20 D4
Slieve Rua Drive	52 D1
Slievebloom Park	41 C1
Slievebloom Road	41 C1
Slievemore Road	35 A4
Slievenamon Road	35 A4
*Sloan Terrace (on Meath Road)	57 C2
Sloperton	45 C4
Smith's Cottages (Donnybrook)	43 B1 [18]
Smith's Villas	45 C4 [3]
Smithfield	35 C2
Smithfield Terrace	35 C2 [37]
Snowdrop Walk	11 C4
Snugborough Road	18 F1
Somerset Street	36 F3 [8]
Somerton	53 C2
Somerton Mews Est.	53 C2
Somerville Avenue	41 C1
Somerville Drive	42 D1
Somerville Park	41 C1 [7]
Sommerton Road	33 B1
Sommerville	43 C4
Sonesta	3 A2
Sorbonne	44 D4
Sorrento Close	54 F2 [25]
Sorrento Court	54 F2 [29]
Sorrento Drive	54 F2 [12]
Sorrento Heights	54 F2 [30]
Sorrento Lawn	54 F2 [13]
Sorrento Mews	54 F2 [28]
*Sorrento Park (on Sorrento Rd)	54 F2
Sorrento Road	54 F2
Sorrento Terrace	54 F2
South Avenue	44 E4
South Circular Road (Dolphin's Barn)	35 B3
South Circular Road (Islandbridge)	35 A2
South Circular Road (Kilmainham)	35 B3
South Circular Road (Portobello)	35 C3
*South City Market (on South Great Georges St)	36 D3
South Dock Place	36 F3 [35]
South Dock Road	36 F3 [24]
South Dock Street	36 F3
South Esplanade	58 D2
South Great George's St.	36 D3
South Hill	25 C3
South Hill	43 B2
South Hill Avenue	44 F3
South Hill Park	44 E3
South Lotts Road	36 F3
South Park	53 B2
South Park Drive	53 B2
South Winds	54 F1 [4]
South Wood Park	44 F3
Southern Cross Avenue	35 A3
Southview Terrace	35 B3 [38]
Spa Road	34 F3
Spa Road (Phoenix Park)	35 A1
Spafield Terrace	37 A4 [13]
Spencer Avenue	36 F2 [2]
Spencer Dock (Guild Street)	36 F2
*Spencer Place (off Spencer Street N.)	36 F1
Spencer Row	36 E2 [22]
Spencer Street North	36 F1
Spencer Street South	36 D4 [48]
*Spencer Terrace (off Cork Street)	35 B3
Spencer Villas	54 E1
Sperrin Road	35 A4
Spiddal Park	33 C3
Spiddal Road	33 C3
Spire View Lane	43 A1
Spitalfields	35 C3 [46]
Spittal Hill	2 D1
Spring Garden Lane	36 E2 [14]
Spring Garden Street	36 E1
Springbank Cottages	47 A2
Springdale Road	22 F2
Springfield (Cabra)	35 A1
Springfield (Tallaght)	48 F1
Springfield Avenue	42 E4
Springfield Crescent	42 E4
Springfield Drive	42 E4
Springfield Park (Deans Grange)	53 A2
Springfield Park (Templeogue)	42 E4
Springfield Road	42 E3
Springhill Avenue	53 A1
Springhill Cottages	53 B1 [5]
Springhill Park (Dalkey)	54 E2
Springhill Park (Deans Grange)	53 B1
Springlawn	18 E2
Springlawn Court	18 E2
Springlawn Drive	18 E2
Springlawn Park	18 E2
Springlawn Road	18 E2
Springvale	50 E2
Stable Lane (Harcourt Street)	36 D3 [19]
Stable Lane (Leeson St. Lr.)	36 E3 [37]
*Stable Lane (Londonbridge Road)	37 A3
Stable Lane (Smithfield)	35 C2 [16]
Stamer Street	36 D4
Stanford Green	41 C1
Stanhope Street	35 C2 [2]
*Stanley Street (off Brunswick Street North)	35 C2
Stannaway Avenue	42 D1
Stannaway Court	42 D2 [3]
Stannaway Drive	42 E1
Stannaway Road	42 E1
Stapolin Estate	12 F4
Stapolin Lawns	12 F4
Station Road	15 C4
Station Road (Glenageary)	54 E1
Station Road (Killiney)	54 E4
Station Road (Portmarnock)	12 E2
Station Road (Raheny)	23 A2
Station Road (Sutton)	25 A1
*Station Road (off Clover Hill Road)	34 D4
Steeven's Lane	35 B2
Stella Avenue	21 A3
Stella Gardens	37 A3
Stepaside	52 E4
Stephen Street Lower	36 D3
Stephen Street Upper	36 D3
Stephen's Lane	36 E3
Stephen's Place	36 E3 [36]
Stephen's Road	35 A3
Stillorgan	52 E1
Stillorgan Court	52 E1 [2]
Stillorgan Grove	44 F4
Stillorgan Heath	52 E1
Stillorgan Heath	52 E1 [3]
Stillorgan Park	44 F4
Stillorgan Park Avenue	52 F1
Stillorgan Road (Donnybrook)	44 D1
Stillorgan Road (Foxrock)	53 A2
Stillorgan Road (Mount Merrion)	44 E3
Stillorgan Road (Stillorgan)	44 E4
Stillorgan Wood	52 E1
Stirling Park	43 A3 [2]
*Stirrup Lane (off Church Street)	35 C2
Stockhole Lane	10 F1
Stocking Lane	50 D3
Stockton Court	19 A3
Stockton Drive	19 A3
Stockton Green	19 A3
Stockton Grove	19 A3
Stockton Lawn	19 A3
Stockton Park	19 A3
Stokes Place	36 D3 [27]
Stonebridge	17 B2
Stonebridge Avenue	17 B2
Stonebridge Close	56 E3 [2]
Stonebridge Drive	17 B2
Stonebridge Road	17 B2
Stonebridge Road	56 D2
Stonemasons Way	51 A2
Stonepark Abbey	42 F4
Stoneview Place	46 D4 [13]
Stoney Road (Dundrum)	43 C4
Stoney Road (East Wall)	36 F1 [7]
Stoneybatter	35 C2
Stoneylea Terrace	57 C3 [10]
Store Street	36 E2
Stormanstown Road	21 A2
Stradbrook Close	53 B1
Stradbrook Gardens	45 B4 [8]
Stradbrook Hill	53 B1 [4]
Stradbrook Lawn	45 B4
Stradbrook Park	45 B4
Stradbrook Road	45 B4
Strand Lane	44 E.4
Strand Road (Baldoyle)	13 A4

STREET NAME	REFERENCE	STREET NAME	REFERENCE	STREET NAME	REFERENCE	STREET NAME	REFERENCE
Strand Road (Ballybrack)	54 E4	*Swift's Row (off Ormond Quay)	36 D2	Taney Court	43 C4	Terenure Road West	42 E2
Strand Road (Bray)	57 C2	Swilly Road	20 E4	Taney Crescent	43 C4	Terminal Road North	37 C2
Strand Road (Malahide)	3 C2	Swords	2 D1	Taney Drive	43 C4	Terminal Road South	37 C2
Strand Road (Merrion)	44 E1	Swords Manor Avenue	1 B2	Taney Grove	43 C4	Termon Court	9 C4 [4]
Strand Road (Portmarnock)	12 F2	Swords Manor Court	1 B1	Taney Lawn	43 C4	*Terrace Place (off Bella St.)	36 E1
Strand Road (Portmarnock)	13 A1	Swords Manor Crescent	1 B1	Taney Manor	43 C4	Texas Lane	3 A2
Strand Road (Portmarnock)	4 D4	Swords Manor Drive	1 B1	Taney Park	43 C4	The Alders	45 B4 [6]
Strand Road (Sandymount)	37 B4	Swords Manor Grove	1 B2	Taney Rise	43 C4	The Appian Way	36 E4
Strand Road (Sutton)	25 B2	Swords Manor View	1 B1	Taney Road	43 C4	The Avenue (Ballinteer)	51 C2
Strand Street Great	36 D2	Swords Manor Way	1 B1	*Tangier Lane (off Grafton St.)	36 D3	The Avenue (Ballyboden)	50 E2
Strand Street Little	36 D2 [36]	Swords Road	21 B1	Tara Hill Crescent	42 F4	The Avenue (Celbridge)	30 D3
Strand Terrace	43 B2 [2]	Swords Road (Collinstown)	10 F2	Tara Hill Grove	42 F4 [2]	The Avenue (Kinsaley)	2 E3
Strandmill Avenue	12 F2	Swords Road (Malahide)	3 A3	Tara Hill Road	42 F4	The Avenue (Mulhuddart)	7 A4
Strandmill Park	13 A2	Swords Street	35 B2 [8]	Tara Lawn	23 A1	The Avenue (Swords)	2 D1
Strandmill Road	13 A2	Sybil Hill Avenue	22 F3	Tara Street	36 E2	The Avenue (Tallaght)	40 F3
Strandville Avenue (North Strand)	36 F1 [4]	Sybil Hill Road	22 F3	Taylor's Lane (Ballyboden)	50 E1	The Avenue (Templeogue)	42 D3
Strandville Avenue East (Clontarf)	22 D4	Sycamore Avenue (Cabinteely)	53 B3	Taylor's Lane (Pimlico)	35 C3 [13]	The Bawn	3 B3
Strandville House	22 D4 [4]	Sycamore Avenue (Castleknock)	18 E3	Temple Bar	36 D2	The Bawn Grove	3 B3
Strandville Place	36 F1 [19]	Sycamore Avenue (Tallaght)	41 A3	Temple Buildings	36 D1 [60]	The Beeches	23 A1
Strangford Gardens	36 F1	Sycamore Close	40 F3	Temple Cottages	36 D1	The Belfry	35 A3 [17]
Strangford Road	36 F1	Sycamore Close	53 B3	Temple Court	35 B2 [16]	The Birches	53 A3
Strasburg Terrace	37 A3 [21]	Sycamore Court	53 C2 [3]	Temple Crescent	45 B4	The Black Avenue	31 B1
Strathmore Road	54 E4	Sycamore Crescent (Cabinteely)	53 B3	Temple Gardens	43 B2	The Bramblings	22 E3
Strawberry Beds	33 B1	Sycamore Crescent (Mt. Merrion)	44 E4	Temple Hill	45 B4	The Briars	33 C1
Streamville Court	56 E1 [10]	Sycamore Drive (Cabinteely)	53 B3	*Temple Hill (on Terenure Road West)	42 E2	The Burgage	54 F2
Streamville Road	23 A1	Sycamore Drive (Castleknock)	18 E3	Temple Lane North	36 D1 [41]	The Castlelands	42 F4 [11]
*Strong's Court (off Findlater Place)	36 D2	Sycamore Drive (Dundrum)	51 B1 [4]	*Temple Lane South (off Temple Bar)	36 D2	The Cedars	45 B4 [5]
Suffolk Street	36 D2	Sycamore Drive (Tallaght)	41 A3	Temple Lawn	12 D4	*The Chase (Charles Sheil's Houses)	52 F2
Sugarloaf Crescent	57 C3	Sycamore Green (Cabinteely)	53 B3	Temple Manor	41 C3	The Cherries	51 A2 [2]
*Sugarloaf Terrace(off Vevay Rd.)	57 C3	Sycamore Grove	53 A2 [7]	Temple Manor	5 B2	The Cloisters	42 F2
Suir Road	35 A3	Sycamore Grove	53 B4	Temple Manor Avenue	41 C3	The Close (Ballinteer)	51 C2
Sullivan Street	35 B2 [3]	Sycamore Lawn (Cabinteely)	53 B3	Temple Manor Close	41 C3	The Close (Ballyboden)	50 E2
*Summer Arch (off Summer St. N.)	36 E1	Sycamore Lawn (Castleknock)	18 E3	Temple Manor Court	41 C3	The Close (Kinsaley)	2 E3
Summer Place	36 E1 [46]	Sycamore Park (Castleknock)	18 E3	Temple Manor Drive	41 C3	The Close (Mount Merrion)	44 E3
*Summer Row (off Summer St. N.)	36 E1	Sycamore Park (Finglas)	20 E1	Temple Manor Grove	41 C3	The Close (Tallaght)	40 F3
Summer Street North	36 E1	Sycamore Park (Tallaght)	41 A3	Temple Manor Way	41 C3	The Close (Tallaght)	49 A2 [2]
Summer Street South	35 C3	Sycamore Road (Dundrum)	51 B1	Temple Park	43 B2	The Close (Templeogue)	42 D3
Summerfield	49 A2 [1]	Sycamore Road (Finglas)	20 E1	Temple Park Avenue	45 B3	The Coombe	35 C3
Summerfield Close	54 F2 [10]	Sycamore Road (Fox & Geese)	41 A1	Temple Place	36 E4 [26]	The Coppice	33 C1
Summerhill	36 E1	Sycamore Road (Mount Merrion)	44 E4	Temple Road (Blackrock)	45 A3	The Coppins	30 D3
Summerhill Parade (Dun Laoghaire)	46 D4 [6]	Sycamore Street	36 D2 [21]	Temple Road (Rathgar)	43 B2	The Coppins (Foxrock)	53 A3
Summerhill Parade (Summerhill)	36 E1	Sycamore View	18 E3	Temple Square	43 B2 [5]	The Court	21 C2
Summerhill Place	36 E1 [26]	Sycamore Walk	53 B4	Temple Street North	36 D1	The Court	23 B3 [2]
Summerhill Road	46 D4	Sydenham Mews	57 C3	Temple Street West	35 B2 [7]	The Court (Ballinteer)	51 B2
Summerville	37 B1	*Sydenham Place (on Kilmacud Rd Upr.)	43 C4	Temple Terrace	54 F2 [16]	The Court (Celbridge)	29 C4
Summerville Park	43 A1	Sydenham Road (Ballsbridge)	37 A4 [4]	Temple Road (Blackrock)		The Court (Clontarf)	22 D4
*Summerville Terrace (on Dalkey Ave)	54 F2	Sydenham Road (Dundrum)	43 C4	*Temple Villas (Arbour Hill)	35 C2	The Court (Mulhuddart)	7 A4
Sunbury Gardens	43 A2	Sydenham Villas	57 C3 [1]	*Temple Villas (on Palmerston Road)	43 B1	The Court (Sutton)	25 A1
Suncroft Drive	48 D2	Sydenham Villas (Dundrum)	43 C4	Templemore Avenue	43 A2	The Court (Swords)	2 D1
Suncroft Park	48 D2	Sydney Avenue	45 A3	Templeogue	42 D4	The Court (Tallaght)	40 F3
Sundale Avenue	48 D2	Sydney Parade Avenue	44 E1	Templeogue Road	42 E3	The Court (Tallaght)	40 F4
Sundale Close	48 D2	Sydney Terrace	45 A3	Templeogue Wood	42 D4	The Court (Templeogue)	42 D3
Sundale Road	48 D2	Sykes Lane	42 F2	Templeroan Avenue	50 D1	The Courtyard	42 F4
Sundrive Park	42 E1	Sylvan Avenue	41 A3	Templeroan Close	50 E1	The Cove	3 A2
Sundrive Road	42 E1	Sylvan Close	40 F3	Templeroan Court	50 D1	The Covert	33 C1 [1]
Sunnyside Mews	22 F4	Sylvan Drive	40 F3	Templeroan Crescent	50 D1	The Crescent	31 C2
Sunville Green	42 D1 [1]	Sylvester Villas	3 B3	Templeroan Downs	50 E1	The Crescent (Abbeyfarm)	29 C4
Susan Terrace	35 C3	Synge Lane	36 D4 [25]	Templeroan Drive	50 D1	*The Crescent (Ballinteer)	51 B2 [1]
Susanville Road	21 B4	Synge Place	36 D4 [24]	Templeroan Green	50 D1	The Crescent (Ballyboden)	50 E2
Sussex Road	36 E4	Synge Street	36 D4	Templeroan Grove	50 D1	The Crescent (Castleknock)	18 F3 [1]
Sussex Street	46 D4 [16]	Synnott Place	36 D1	Templeroan Lodge	50 D2	The Crescent (Donnybrook)	43 C1 [4]
SussexTerrace	36 E4 [11]	Synnott Row	36 D1 [26]	Templeroan Meadows	50 E1	The Crescent (Kinsaley)	2 E3
Sutton	25 A1	Synnott Terrace	45 C4 [16]	Templeroan Park	50 E1	The Crescent (Sutton)	25 A1
Sutton Court	24 D1 [1]			Templeroan View	50 E1	The Crescent (Swords)	2 D1
Sutton Downs	24 D1	**T**		Templeroan Way	50 E1	The Crescent (Tallaght)	40 F3
Sutton Grove	24 D1			Templeview Avenue	12 D4	The Crescent (Whitehall)	21 B3
Sutton Lane	55 A3	TAAFFE'S PLACE	36 F1 [15]	Templeview Close	12 D4	The Crescent (Tallaght)	49 A1
Sutton Lawns	24 D1	Talbot	2 F3	Templeview Copse	12 D4	The Crescent (Tallaght)	40 E4
Sutton Park	24 D1	Talbot Court	18 F2	Templeview Court	12 D4	The Croft	30 D2
Sutton Road	57 B2 [9]	Talbot Court	3 A2	Templeview Crescent	12 D4 [2]	The Dale	40 F3
Sutton Villas	57 B2 [17]	Talbot Downs	18 F2	Templeview Downs	12 D4	The Dale	40 F4
Swan Alley	35 C3 [51]	Talbot Lane	36 E2 [6]	Templeview Drive	12 D4	The Deanery	29 C3 [1]
Swan Grove	36 E4 [23]	Talbot Lodge	44 F4	Templeview Green	12 D4	The Dell	51 A2
Swan Place	36 E4 [31]	Talbot Place	36 E2	Templeview Grove	12 D4	The Demesne (Killester)	22 E3
*Swan Yard (off Harry Street)	36 D3	Talbot Road	54 E3 [3]	Templeview Lawn	12 D4	The Dingle	33 B2
Swan's Nest Avenue	23 B1 [3]	Talbot Street	36 E2	Templeview Lawn	12 D4	The Donahies	23 B1
Swan's Nest Court	23 B1 [2]	Tallaght	49 A1	Templeview Park	12 D4	The Drive	57 B1
Swan's Nest Road	23 B1	Tallaght Bypass	48 F1	Templeview Place	12 D4	The Drive (Ballinteer)	51 B2
Swanville Place	43 A1 [4]	Tallaght Road	41 C4	Templeview Rise	12 D4	The Drive (Ballyboden)	50 E1
Sweeney's Terrace	35 C3 [36]	Tallaght Road	49 A1	Templeview Row	12 D4	The Drive (Celbridge)	29 C4
Sweetbriar Lane	52 D1	Tamarisk Avenue	41 A3	Templeview Square	12 D4	The Drive (Kinsaley)	2 E3
Sweetman's Avenue	45 A3	Tamarisk Close	41 A3	Templeview Vale	12 D4 [1]	The Drive (Mulhuddart)	7 A4
Sweetmount Avenue	43 B4	Tamarisk Court	41 A3	Templeview Walk	12 D4	The Drive (Swords)	2 D1
Sweetmount Avenue	43 B4 [15]	Tamarisk Dale	41 A3	Templeview Way	12 D4	The Drive (Tallaght)	49 A1
Sweetmount Drive	51 B1	Tamarisk Drive	41 A3	Templeville Avenue	42 D3	The Dunes	13 A2
Sweetmount Park	43 B4	Tamarisk Grove	41 A3	Templeville Drive	42 D3	The Elms	44 E2
Swift's Alley	35 C3	Tamarisk Heights	41 A3	Templeville Park	42 E3 [1]	The Elms	56 E1 [4]
Swift's Grove	11 A3	Tamarisk Lawn	41 A3	Templeville Road	42 D3	The Elms (Celbridge)	30 D2
		Tamarisk Park	41 A3	Terenure	42 F2	The Fairways	57 C1
		Tamarisk View	41 A3	Terenure Park	42 F2	The Fosters	44 E3
		Tamarisk Walk	41 A3	Terenure Place	42 F2 [3]	The Gallops	52 E3
		Tamarisk Way	41 A3	Terenure Road East	42 F2	The Garth	40 E4
		Tandys Lane	31 C3	Terenure Road North	42 F2	The Garth	40 F3
		Taney Avenue	43 C4	Terenure Road North	42 F2	The Glade (Ballinteer)	51 B2

STREET NAME	PAGE/GRID REFERENCE	STREET NAME	PAGE/GRID REFERENCE	STREET NAME	PAGE/GRID REFERENCE	STREET NAME	PAGE/GRID REFERENCE
The Glade (Palmerston)	33 B2	The Pines	19 A3	Three Rock Close	41 B3 [1]	Tymon Close	49 A2
The Glade (Tallaght)	40 F4	The Pines	22 E3	Three Rock Road	52 E2	Tymon Crescent	48 F2
The Glebe	32 E2	The Pines	52 D1 [3]	Thundercut Alley	35 C2[20]	Tymon Grove	49 A2
The Glen	54 D1[14]	The Pines	57 B3	Tibradden Close	41 B2 [1]	Tymon Heights	49 B2
The Glen (Ballinteer)	51 B2	The Poplars	45 B4 [7]	Tibradden Drive	41 B2	Tymon Lane	41 B4
The Glen (Ballyboden)	50 E1	The Priory	20 D4	Tibradden Grove	41 B3	Tymon Lawn	49 A2
The Golf Links	3 C3	The Priory	50 F1	Tibradden Lane	50 F4	Tymon North	41 B4
The Grange	53 B1	The Rise	3 B3	Ticknock Road	51 B4	Tymon North Avenue	41 B4
The Green (Ballinteer)	51 B2	The Rise (Ballinteer)	51 B2	Tinkler's Path	34 E1	Tymon North Court	41 B4 [1]
The Green (Ballyboden)	50 E2	The Rise (Ballyboden)	50 E2	Tivoli Avenue	42 F1	Tymon North Gardens	41 B4
The Green (Bray)	57 C1	The Rise (Dalkey)	54 E2	Tivoli Close	53 C1	Tymon North Green	41 B4
The Green (Celbridge)	29 C4	The Rise (Glasnevin)	21 A2	Tivoli Road	46 D4	Tymon North Grove	41 B4
The Green (Kinsaley)	2 E3	The Rise (Kinsaley)	2 E3	Tivoli Terrace East	46 D4	Tymon North Lawn	41 B4
The Green (Malahide)	3 B2	The Rise (Mount Merrion)	44 E4	Tivoli Terrace North	45 C4	Tymon North Park	41 B4
The Green (Mulhuddart)	7 A4	The Rise (Tallaght)	40 F3	Tivoli Terrace South	45 C4	Tymon North Place	41 B4 [2]
The Green (Swords)	2 D1	The Rise (Tallaght)	40 E4	Tobernea Terrace	45 B3 [2]	Tymon North Road	41 B4
The Green (Tallaght)	40 F3	The Rookery	50 D2	Tolka Cottages	20 F3	Tymonville Avenue	41 B3
The Green (Templeogue)	42 D3	The Sand Holes	18 F4 [1]	Tolka Estate Road	20 F3	Tymonville Court	41 A4
The Green Road	54 F2	The Scalp	55 A4	Tolka Quay	37 A2	Tymonville Crescent	41 A4
The Greenlands	42 F4	The Slopes	45 C4	Tolka Quay Road	37 A2	Tymonville Drive	41 A3
The Grove	23 B3 [1]	The Square (Irishtown)	37 A3 [5]	Tolka Road	21 B4	Tymonville Grove	41 B3
The Grove	30 D4	The Square (Lucan)	32 D1 [5]	Tolka Valley Road	20 D3	Tymonville Lawn	41 B4
The Grove (Abbeyfarm)	29 C4	The Stables	44 E3 [1]	Tom Clarke House	21 B4 [1]	Tymonville Park	41 B4
The Grove (Ballinteer)	51 B2	The Steeples	34 E3	Tom Kelly Road	36 D4[16]	Tymonville Road	41 A4
The Grove (Bray)	57 C1	The Stiles Road	22 E4	Tonduff Close	41 B3	Tyrconnell Park	34 F3
The Grove (Celbridge)	30 D4	The Summit (Howth)	26 E3	Tonguefield Road	42 E1 [1]	Tyrconnell Road	34 F3
The Grove (Kinsaley)	2 E3	The Sweepstakes	37 A4[22]	Tonlegee Avenue	22 F1	Tyrconnell Street	34 F3 [6]
The Grove (Tallaght)	40 F3	The Sycamores	56 E1 [3]	Tonlegee Drive	22 F1	Tyrconnell Villas	34 F3 [7]
The Grove (Tallaght)	40 E4	The Thatch Road	21 C2	Tonlegee Road	23 A1	Tyrone Place	35 A3[12]
The Grove (Tallaght)	49 A1	The Thicket	53 A3	Torca Road	54 F2	*Tyrrel's Lane	37 A3
The Grove (Whitehall)	21 B3	The Turrets	37 A4	Torca View	54 F2[33]	(off Fitzwilliam St Ringsend)	
The Haggard (Howth)	26 D2 [6]	The Vale	33 C1	Torlogh Gardens	21 C4 [8]	Tyrrell Place	36 E1[45]
The Haven	21 A3[17]	The Valley	41 C1 [6]	Torlogh Parade	21 C3 [1]		
The Haven	3 B2	The View (Ballinteer)	51 B2	Torquay Road	52 F2	**U**	
The Heath (Tallaght)	40 F4	The View (Tallaght)	40 F4	Torquay Wood	52 F2		
The Heath (Templeogue)	42 D3	The View (Tallaght)	49 B1	Tourmakeady Road	21 B2 [1]	ULLARDMOR	54 F2[27]
The Hedgerows	53 A3	The Villa (Kinsaley)	2 E3	Tower Avenue	42 F2	Ulster Street	20 F4
The Heights (Ballinteer)	51 B2	The Village	21 B3 [2]	Tower Road	40 D1	Ulster Terrace (North Strand)	36 E1[58]
The Heights (Kinsaley)	2 E3	The Village	23 B3	Tower Road (Castleknock)	18 F4	Ulster Terrace (Stillorgan Grove)	52 F1 [3]
The Hill	3 B3	The Village	54 F2	*Tower Terrace	35 B3	Ulverton Close	54 F1 [5]
The Hill (Ballinteer)	51 C2	The Village (Clonsilla)	17 C3	(off Kilmainham Lane)		Ulverton Court	54 F1[13]
The Hill (Monkstown)	45 C4	The Village Gate	54 F2	Tower View Cottages	20 F4 [2]	Ulverton Road	54 F1
The Hill (Mulhuddart)	7 A4	The Village Square	49 A1	Townsend Street	36 E2	Upper Cliff Road	26 E2 [2]
The Hill (Stillorgan)	52 F1	The Walk (Ballinteer)	51 B2	Townyard Lane	3 B2	Upper Dargle Road	57 A2
The Hole in the Wall Rd.	12 E4	The Walk (Kinsaley)	2 E3	Trafalgar Lane	45 B4	Upper Glen Road	34 E1
The Lakelands	42 F4 [8]	The Walk (Tallaght)	49 A1	Trafalgar Terrace	45 B3	Uppercross	32 F1
The Lane	29 C4	The Walk (Templeogue)	42 D3	Trafalgar Terrace	57 C2[31]	Uppercross Road	35 B3
The Laurels (Dundrum)	43 B4	The Walled Gardens	30 D2	Tramway Court	25 A1	Urney Grove	54 E2 [7]
The Laurels (Terenure)	42 F2	The Warren	2 F2	Tranquility Grove	22 E1	Usher Street	35 C2
The Lawn	57 C1	The Willows	30 D3	*Traynor Place	35 B3	Usher's Island	35 C2
The Lawn (Ballinteer)	51 B2	The Willows	43 A3 [1]	(off Mount Brown)		Usher's Quay	35 C2
The Lawn (Ballyboden)	50 E1	The Willows (Glasnevin)	20 F3	Treepark Avenue	41 A3	Ushers Lane	1 A2
The Lawn (Finglas)	20 E2	The Willows (Monkstown)	45 B4 [3]	Treepark Close	41 A3		
The Lawn (Kinsaley)	2 E3	The Wood	49 A2	Treepark Drive	41 A3	**V**	
The Lawn (Tallaght)	40 E4	The Woodlands	30 D3	Treepark Road	41 A3		
The Lawns (Abbeyfarm)	29 C4	The Woodlands	42 F4 [9]	Trees Avenue	44 E4	*VALE TERRACE	57 B2
The Mall	3 B2	Third Avenue (Seville Place)	36 F2 [7]	Trees Road Lower	44 E4	(on Lower Dargle Road)	
The Mall	31 A1	Thirlestane Terrace	35 C3[64]	Trees Road Upper	44 E4	Vale View Avenue	53 B3
The Mall (Baldoyle)	13 A4 [4]	Thomas Court	35 C3	Tresilian	53 A3	Vale View Close	53 B3
The Mall (Lucan)	32 D1	Thomas Davis Street South	35 C3[49]	Trim Road	22 D1	Vale View Grove	53 B3
The Maltings	57 C2	Thomas Davis Street West	34 F3	Trimleston Avenue	44 E2	Vale View Lawn	53 B3
The Maples	43 C3	Thomas Lane	36 D2[17]	Trimleston Drive	44 E2	Vale view	57 B2[21]
The Maples	45 B4 [4]	Thomas Moore Road	41 C1	Trimleston Gardens	44 E2	Valentia Parade	36 D1[34]
The Meadow	51 B2	Thomas Street	35 C3	Trimleston Park	44 E2	Valentia Road	21 A3
The Meadows	22 F3	Thomas Street West	35 C3[65]	Trimleston Road	44 E2	Valeview Crescent	20 D2 [6]
The Meadows East	40 F4	Thomastown Crescent	54 D2 [2]	Trinity Square	36 E2[35]	Valeview Drive	20 D2
The Meadows West	40 E4	Thomastown Road	54 D3	Trinity Street	36 D2	Valeview Gardens	20 D2 [2]
The Mews	22 E4	Thomond Road	34 E3	Trinity Terrace	36 E1[44]	Valley Park Avenue	20 D2 [1]
The Mews	43 A1[19]	Thompson's Cottages	36 E1[49]	Tritonville Avenue	37 A3 [8]	Valley Park Drive	19 C2
The Moorings	3 C3	Thor Place	35 B2 [1]	Tritonville Close	37 A3[22]	Valley Park Road	19 C2
The New Road	19 B1	Thormanby Lawns	26 D2	Tritonville Court	37 A4	Valley View	1 B2
The Nurseries (Swords)	1 C3	Thormanby Lodge	26 E2	Tritonville Crescent	37 A3 [9]	Vanessa Close	29 C3
The Nurseries	54 E4 [4]	Thormanby Road	26 E2	Tritonville Road	37 A3	Vanessa Lawns	29 C3
The Nurseries	57 B3	Thormanby Woods	26 E2	Trosyrafon Terrace	58 D2 [1]	Vauxhall Avenue	35 B3[30]
The Oaks	30 D3	Thorncastle Street	37 A2	Tubber Lane Road	31 B2	Vavasour Square	36 F3
The Oaks	32 F3	Thorncliff	43 B2 [8]	Tubbermore Avenue	54 F2	Venetian Hall	22 E3
The Oaks	43 B4	Thorncliffe Park	43 B3	Tubbermore Road	54 F2	Ventry Drive	20 D4
The Oaks	56 D1 [1]	Thorndale Avenue	22 D2	Tuckett's Lane	26 D2	Ventry Park	20 E4
The Oaks	40 E4	Thorndale Court	21 C2 [3]	Tudor Court	2 F2	Ventry Road	20 E4
The Oaks	40 F4	Thorndale Crescent	22 D2	Tudor Lawns	52 F2	Verbena Avenue	23 C1
The Old Hill	32 D1	Thorndale Drive	22 D3	Tudor Road	43 B1	Verbena Avenue	53 A3
The Orchard	53 A1	Thorndale Grove	22 D3	Tulip Court	11 C4	Verbena Grove	23 C1
The Orchard (Killester)	22 E3	Thorndale Lawn	22 D2	Turnapin Cottages	10 F3	Verbena Lawn	23 C1
The Orchard (Kimmage)	42 E2	Thorndale Park	22 D2	Turnapin Green	10 F3	Verbena Park	23 C1
The Orchard (Palmerston)	33 B1	Thornhill Gardens	29 C2	Turnapin Grove	10 F3	Vergemount	43 C1[12]
The Oval	33 C2	Thornhill Grove	57 B2 [3]	Turnapin Lane	10 F3	Vergemount Hall	43 C1 [9]
The Paddock	19 C4	Thornhill Heights	29 C2	Turnberry	24 D1	Vergemount Park	43 C1 [6]
The Paddocks	5 B2	Thornhill Meadows	29 C2	Turnpike Road	41 A2	Vernon Avenue	22 F4
The Paddocks	54 F1 [3]	Thornhill Road	44 E4	Turret Road	33 C2	Vernon Court	22 F4
The Palms	44 D3	Thornhill Road	57 A2	Turrets Flats	43 A1 [9]	Vernon Court	37 C1 [3]
The Park (Kinsaley)	2 E3	Thornville Avenue	23 B1	Turvey Avenue	35 A3 [2]	Vernon Drive	22 F3
The Park (Tallaght)	40 F3	Thornville Drive	23 B2	Tuscany Downs	23 A2	Vernon Gardens	22 F4
The Park (Tallaght)	49 A2	Thornville Park	23 C1	Tuscany Park	24 D1	Vernon Grove (Clontarf)	22 F4
The Park (Templeogue)	42 D3	Thornville Road	23 B1	Twin Cottages	45 A4 [5]	Vernon Grove (Rathgar)	43 A2
The Park Lands	42 F4 [7]	Thornville Terrace	23 B2 [1]			Vernon Heath	22 F4

STREET NAME	PAGE/GRID REFERENCE
Vernon Park	22 F4
Vernon Rise	22 F3
Vernon Street	36 D3
*Veronica Terrace	37 A3
(off Oliver Plunket Ave.)	
Verschoyle Court	36 F3
*Verschoyle Place	36 E3
(off Lr. Mount St)	
Vesey Mews	45 C4
Vesey Park (Lucan)	32 D2
Vesey Place	45 C4
Vesey Terrace (Lucan)	32 D1 [2]
*Vevay Arcade (on Vevay Road)	57 C3
Vevay Road	57 C3
Vevay Villas	57 C3[18]
Vicar Street	35 C3[20]
Vico Road	54 F3
*Vico Terrace (Vico Road)	54 F3
Victoria Avenue	43 C1
Victoria Avenue	58 D2
*Victoria Cottages	37 A3
(off Irishtown Rd.)	
Victoria Lane	21 B4 [9]
*Victoria Lane	43 A2
(South Zion Road)	
Victoria Quay	35 C2
Victoria Road (Clontarf)	22 E4
Victoria Road (Dalkey)	54 F2
Victoria Road (Killiney)	54 E3
Victoria Road (Terenure)	42 F2
Victoria Street	36 D4
Victoria Terrace (Dalkey)	54 F2[11]
Victoria Terrace (Dun Laoghaire)	46 D4 [8]
Victoria Terrace (Dundrum)	43 C4
Victoria Village	42 F2 [7]
Victoria Villas (Clontarf)	22 D4
Victoria Villas (Rathgar)	42 F2 [5]
*Viking Place (off Sitric Road)	35 C2
Viking Road	35 C2[32]
*Villa Bank (Royal Canal Bank)	36 D1
Villa Blanchard	18 F2
Villa Park Avenue	20 D4
Villa Park Drive	20 D4
Villa Park Gardens	20 D4
Villa Park Road	20 D4
Village Court	42 F4 [6]
*Village Gate Arcade	57 C2
(on Main Street Bray)	
Village Heights	7 A4
Village Weir	32 D1 [7]
Villarea Park	54 E1
Villiers Road	43 A2
Vincent Street	36 D4
Violet Hill Drive	20 F3
Violet Hill Park	20 F3
Violet Hill Road	20 F3
Virginia Drive	20 D2
Virginia Heights	48 F1
Virginia Park	20 D2
Viscount Avenue	10 F4

W

STREET NAME	PAGE/GRID REFERENCE
WADE'S AVENUE	23 A3
Wadelai Green	21 A2
Wadelai Road	21 A2
Wainsfort Avenue	42 D3
Wainsfort Crescent	42 D3
Wainsfort Drive	42 E2
Wainsfort Gardens	42 D3
Wainsfort Grove	42 E3
Wainsfort Park	42 E3
Wainsfort Road	42 D3
Waldemar Terrace	43 B4[12]
Walker's Cottages	36 D4[37]
Walker's Court	36 D4[38]
Walkinstown	41 B1
Walkinstown Avenue	41 B1
Walkinstown Crescent	41 B1
Walkinstown Drive	41 B1
Walkinstown Green	41 B1
Walkinstown Parade	41 B1
Walkinstown Park	41 B1
Walkinstown Road	41 C1
Wallace Road	41 C1 [2]
Walnut Avenue (Clondalkin)	40 F3
Walnut Avenue (Whitehall)	21 B3
Walnut Close	41 A3
Walnut Court	21 B2
Walnut Drive	40 F3
Walnut Lawn	21 B3
Walnut Park	21 B3
Walnut Rise	21 B3
Walnut View	50 E2 [5]
Walsh Road	21 A3
Waltersland Road	52 F1
Waltham Terrace	44 F3
Walworth Road	36 D4[33]
Warburton Terrace	57 C2[33]
Ward's Hill	35 C3
Warner's Lane	36 E4[18]
Warren Avenue	18 E3
Warren Close	18 E3
Warren Crescent	18 E4
Warren Green	18 E3
Warren Green	24 D1
Warren Park	18 D3
Warren Street	36 D4[35]
Warrenhouse Road	24 D1
Warrenmount	35 C3[27]
Warrenmount Place	35 C3[28]
Warrenpoint	22 E4 [1]
*Warrington Lane	36 F3
(off Warrington Place)	
Warrington Place	36 F3
Warwick Terrace	36 E4[27]
Wasdale Grove	42 F2
Wasdale Park	42 F2
Washington Lane	42 E4
Washington Park	42 E4
Washington Street	35 C4
Waterfall Avenue	21 B4
Waterfall Road	22 F3
Watergate Estate	49 A1
Waterloo Avenue	36 F1
Waterloo Lane	36 E4
Waterloo Road	36 E4
Watermeadow Drive	48 F2
Watermeadow Park	49 A2
Watermill Avenue	23 A3
Watermill Close	49 A2
Watermill Drive	23 A3
Watermill Grove	49 A2
Watermill Lawn	23 A3 [1]
Watermill Lawn	49 A2
Watermill Park	23 A3
Watermill Road	23 A3
Waterside Crescent	3 C4
Waterstown Avenue	33 C1
Watery Lane	1 C1
Watery Lane	40 E1
*Watkin's Buildings	35 C3
(off Ardee Street)	
Watling Street	35 C2
Watson Avenue	54 D4
Watson Drive	54 D4
Watson Park	54 D4
Watson Road	54 D3
Watson's Estate	54 D3
Waverley Avenue	21 C4
Waverley Terrace (Bray)	57 C2[28]
*Waverley Terrace	42 F1
(off Harolds Cross Road)	
Weaver Lane	36 D1[39]
Weaver's Close	35 C3[33]
Weaver's Row	17 C2
Weaver's Square	35 C3[37]
Weaver's Street	35 C3
Webster's Cottages	45 A4 [8]
Wedgewood Estate	52 D2
Weirview	32 D1
Weirview Drive	52 F1
Weldon's Lane	13 A4
Well Road	2 D2 [2]
Wellesley Place	36 E1[32]
Wellfield	12 D4
Wellington Court·	42 D2 [5]
*Wellington Gardens	43 B1
(off Oakley Road)	
Wellington Lane (Tallaght Road)	41 C3
Wellington Lane	36 F4
(Wellington Road)	
Wellington Lawn	41 C3 [1]
Wellington Place (Leeson Street)	36 E4
Wellington Place North	36 D1[50]
Wellington Quay	36 D2
Wellington Road	36 F4
Wellington Road (Phoenix Park)	35 A2
Wellington Road (Templeogue)	42 D3 [1]
Wellington Street	46 D4 [1]
(Dun Laoghaire)	
Wellington Street Lower	36 D1
Wellington Street Upper	36 D1
Wellmount Avenue	20 D2
Wellmount Court	20 D2
Wellmount Crescent	20 D2
Wellmount Drive	20 D2
Wellmount Green	20 D2
Wellmount Parade	20 D2
Wellmount Park	20 D2
Wellmount Road	20 D2
Wellpark Avenue	21 B3
Wellview Avenue	7 A3
Wellview Crescent	7 A3
Wellview Green	7 A3
Wellview Grove	7 A3
Wellview Park	7 A3
Wendell Avenue	4 D4
Werburgh Street	36 D3
Wesbury	52 E1
Wesley Heights	51 C2
Wesley Lawns	51 C2
Wesley Place	35 C4 [7]
Wesley Road	43 A2
West Park Drive	20 F2
West Pier (Dun Laoghaire)	45 C3
West Pier (Howth)	26 D1
West Road	36 F1
West Terrace	34 F3
Westbourne Avenue	39 C1
Westbourne Castle	39 C1
Westbourne Close	39 C1
Westbourne Court	39 C1
Westbourne Drive	39 C1
Westbourne Grove	39 C1
Westbourne Lodge	50 D1
Westbourne Manor	39 C1
Westbourne Road	42 F3
*Westbourne Terrace	57 C2
(on Quinnsborough Road)	
Westbrook	42 D2
Westbrook Glen	47 B2
Westbrook Lawns	47 C2
Westbrook Park	31 C2
Westbrook Road (Windy Arbour)	43 B3
Westbury Court	32 D2
Western Parkway Motorway	18 E4
Western Road	35 C4[29]
Western Way	36 D1
Westerton Rise	51 C1 [1]
Westfield Avenue	31 B1
Westfield Park	57 C3
Westfield Road	42 F1
Westfield Terrace	45 A3[10]
Westhampton Place	42 F2 [2]
Westland Row	36 E3
Westminister Lawns	52 F2
Westminister Road	53 A3
Westminster Park	53 A2
Westmoreland Park	43 B1 [4]
Westmoreland Street	36 D2
Weston Avenue	43 B4
Weston Close	31 B1
Weston Close	43 B4
Weston Court	31 B2
Weston Crescent	31 B1
Weston Drive	31 B1
Weston Green	31 B1
Weston Grove	43 B4
Weston Heights	31 B2
Weston Lawn	31 B1
Weston Meadow	31 B2
Weston Park	31 B1
Weston Park	43 B4
Weston Road	43 B4
Weston Terrace	43 B4 [9]
Weston Way	31 B2
Westpark (Coolock)	22 F2
Westpark (Tallaght)	49 A1
Westview Terrace	57 C2[29]
Westway Close	7 C4
Westway Grove	7 C4
Westway Lawns	18 F1
Westway Park	7 C4
Westway Rise	7 C4
Westway View	7 C4
Westwood Avenue	19 C2
Westwood Road	19 C2
Wexford Street	36 D3
Wheatfield	57 B3
Wheatfield Grove	4 D4
Wheatfield Road	33 C2
Wheatfield Road	4 D4
Wheatfields Avenue	33 B3
Wheatfields Close	33 B3
Wheatfields Court	33 B3
Wheatfields Crescent	33 B3
Wheatfields Drive	33 B3
Wheatfields Grove	33 B3
Wheatfields Park	33 B3
Whelan's Terrace	45 A3[19]
White Hall (Ballymount Road)	40 F3
White Oak	43 C3
White's Lane North	36 D1 [3]
White's Road	19 A4
White's Villas	54 F1[10]
Whitebarn Road	43 A4
Whitebeam Avenue	43 C2
Whitebeam Road	43 C2
Whitebeams	52 D2
Whitebrook Park	48 E1
Whitechapel Avenue	18 D2
Whitechapel Court	18 D2
Whitechapel Crescent	18 D2
Whitechapel Green	18 D2
Whitechapel Grove	18 D2
Whitechapel Lawn	18 D2
Whitechapel Park	18 D2
Whitechapel Road	18 D2
Whitechurch Abbey	50 F1 [4]
Whitechurch Avenue	50 F2
Whitechurch Close	50 F2
Whitechurch Court	50 F2
Whitechurch Crescent	50 F2
Whitechurch Drive	50 F2
Whitechurch Green	50 F2
Whitechurch Grove	50 F2
Whitechurch Hill	50 F2
Whitechurch Lawn	50 F2
Whitechurch Park	50 F2
Whitechurch Place	50 F2
Whitechurch Road	50 F2
Whitechurch View	50 F2
Whitechurch Walk	50 F2
Whitechurch Way	50 F2
Whitecliff	50 F1
*Whitefriar Gardens	36 D3
(off Whitefriar St.)	
Whitefriar Place	36 D3[42]
Whitefriar Street	36 D3[41]
Whitehall	21 B2
Whitehall Close	42 D3
Whitehall Gardens	42 D2
Whitehall Park	42 D3
Whitehall Road (Churchtown)	43 A4
Whitehall Road (Kimmage)	42 D2
Whitehall Road West	42 D2
Whites Lane	36 D1 [3]
Whitestown	18 D1
Whitestown Avenue	18 D1
Whitestown Crescent	18 D1
Whitestown Drive	18 D1
Whitestown Gardens	18 D1
Whitestown Green	18 D1
Whitestown Park	18 D1
Whitestown Road	48 E2
Whitethorn Avenue	22 D2
Whitethorn Close	22 D2
Whitethorn Crescent	33 B3
Whitethorn Drive	33 B3
Whitethorn Gardens	33 B3
Whitethorn Grove	22 D2
Whitethorn Park	22 D2
Whitethorn Park	33 B3
Whitethorn Rise	22 D2
Whitethorn Road (Artane)	22 D2
Whitethorn Road (Milltown)	43 C2
Whitethorn Walk	53 A2 [8]
Whitethorn Walk	53 C2 [2]
Whitethorn Way	33 B3
Whitton Road	42 F2
Whitworth Avenue	36 E1[40]
(off Whitworth Place)	
*Whitworth Parade	21 A4
(off Saint Patrick's Road)	
Whitworth Place	21 A4[17]
Whitworth Road	21 A4
*Whitworth Terrace	36 E1
(off Russell Ave.)	
Whyteleaf Grove	12 D4
*Wicklow Lane	36 D3
(off Wicklow Street)	
Wicklow Street	36 D3
Wigan Road	21 A4
Wilderwood Grove	41 C4
Wilfield	37 A4[15]
Wilfield Park	37 A4
Wilfield Road	37 A4
Wilfrid Road	42 F1
Wilfrid Terrace	42 F1 [5]
Willbrook	42 F4
Willbrook Downs	50 F1
Willbrook Estate	50 F1
Willbrook Grove	42 F4 [1]
Willbrook Lawn	42 F4
Willbrook Park	42 F4
Willbrook Road	42 F4

STREET NAME	PAGE/GRID REFERENCE
Willbrook Street	42 F4
William Street North	36 E1
William Street South	36 D3
William's Lane	36 D2²⁷
William's Park	43 A1
*William's Place Lower (off Portland Place)	36 D1
William's Place South	36 D3 ⁶
William's Place Upper	36 D1²⁹
William's Row	36 D2³⁰
Willie Bermingham Place	35 B3³¹
Willie Nolan Road	13 A4
Willington Avenue	41 C3
Willington Cottages	41 C3³
Willington Court	41 C3
Willington Crescent	41 C3
Willington Drive	41 C3
Willington Green	41 C3
Willington Grove	41 C3
Willington Lawn	41 C3 ¹
Willington Park	41 C3
Willow Avenue	40 D2
Willow Bank	45 C4
Willow Bank Drive	50 E1
Willow Bank Park	50 E1
Willow Court	40 D2
Willow Drive	40 D2
Willow Grove	40 D2
Willow Grove	53 B3
Willow Grove	53 C1¹³
Willow Mews	44 E1
Willow Park	53 A2 ⁶
Willow Park Avenue	20 F1
Willow Park Close	20 F1
Willow Park Crescent	20 F1
Willow Park Drive	21 A1
Willow Park Grove	20 F1
Willow Park Lawn	20 F1
Willow Park Road	20 F1
Willow Place	44 F3
Willow Road (Dundrum)	51 B1
Willow Road (Fox & Geese)	41 A1
Willow Terrace	44 F2
Willow Vale	54 D4
Willow Wood Close	17 C2
Willow Wood Downs	17 C2 ¹
Willow Wood Green	17 C2
Willow Wood Grove	17 C2
Willow Wood Lawn	17 C2
Willow Wood Park	17 B2
Willow Wood Rise	17 C2
Willow Wood View	17 C2
Willow Wood Walk	17 C1
Willowbank	51 C1
Willowbank Drive	50 E1
Willowbank Park	50 E1
Willowbrook Grove	29 C3
Willowbrook Lawns	29 C3
Willowbrook Lodge	29 C3
Willowbrook Park	29 C3
Willowfield	37 B4
Willowfield Avenue	43 C4
Willowfield Park	43 C4
Willowmount	44 F3 ³
Willows Court	17 C2
Willows Drive	17 C2
Willows Green	17 C2
Willows Road	17 C2
Willsbrook Avenue	32 E2
Willsbrook Crescent	32 E2
Willsbrook Drive	32 F1
Willsbrook Gardens	32 E1
Willsbrook Green	32 E2
Willsbrook Grove	32 E1
Willsbrook Park	32 E2
Willsbrook Place	32 F2
Willsbrook View	32 E2
Willsbrook Way	32 E2
Wilmont Avenue	54 E1 ¹
Wilsbrook Way	32 E1
Wilson Crescent	44 D4
Wilson Road	44 E4
Wilson Terrace	35 C3⁴⁴
Wilson's Place	36 E3³⁵
Wilton Place	36 E4
Wilton Terrace	36 E4
Windele Road	21 A3¹²
Windermere	17 B2
Windgate Rise	26 D3
Windgate Road	26 D3
Windmill Avenue	1 C1
Windmill Avenue	42 D1
Windmill Crescent	42 D1²
Windmill Lands	1 C2
Windmill Lane	36 E2

STREET NAME	PAGE/GRID REFERENCE
Windmill Park	42 D1
Windmill Rise	1 C2
Windmill Road	42 D1
Windsor Avenue	21 C4
Windsor Court (Dun Laoghaire)	53 B1 ¹
Windsor Drive	53 B1
Windsor Park	45 B4
Windsor Place	36 E3³²
Windsor Road	43 B1
Windsor Terrace	3 B3
Windsor Terrace	36 D4
Windsor Terrace (Dun Laoghaire)	46 D4
Windsor Villas	21 C4 ³
Windy Arbour	43 C3
Winetavern Street	36 D2
Winton Avenue	43 A2
Winton Road	36 E4
Wogans Field	31 A1
Wolfe Tone Avenue	46 D4 ⁴
Wolfe Tone Quay	35 B2
Wolfe Tone Square East	57 C4
Wolfe Tone Square Middle	57 C4
Wolfe Tone Square North	57 C3
Wolfe Tone Square South	57 C4
Wolfe Tone Square West	57 C3
Wolfe Tone Street	36 D2¹²
Wolseley Street	35 C4²⁴
Wolverton Glen	54 E2
Wolverton Glen	54 E2
Wood Dale Close	49 C2
Wood Dale Drive	49 C2
Wood Dale Green	49 C2
Wood Dale Road	49 C2
Wood Dale View	49 C2
*Wood Lane (off Benburb Street)	35 C2
Wood Quay	36 D2
Wood Street	36 D3
Woodavens	33 A3
Woodbank Avenue	19 C2
Woodbank Drive	19 C2
Woodberry	18 E3
Woodbine Avenue	44 E2
Woodbine Close	23 A1
Woodbine Drive	23 A1
Woodbine Park (Booterstown)	44 E2
Woodbine Park (Raheny)	23 A1
Woodbine Road (Booterstown)	44 E2
Woodbine Road (Raheny)	23 A1
Woodbine Terrace (Dundrum)	43 C4 ²
Woodbrook Downs	56 E4
Woodbrook Glen	57 C1
Woodbrook Lawn	57 C4
Woodbrook Park	42 D4
Woodcliff Heights	26 E2
Woodfarm Avenue	33 C2
Woodfarm Drive	33 C2
Woodfield	50 D2
Woodfield Cottages	34 F3 ⁸
Woodfield Place	34 F3¹⁵
Woodford	52 E2
Woodford Avenue	40 F1
Woodford Close	40 F1
Woodford Court	40 F1
Woodford Crescent	40 E1
Woodford Downs	40 F1
Woodford Drive	40 F1
Woodford Garth	40 E1
Woodford Green	40 F1
Woodford Grove	40 F1
Woodford Heights	40 F1
Woodford Hill	40 F1
Woodford Lawn	40 F1
Woodford Meadow	40 E1
Woodford Oaks	40 E1
Woodford Parade	40 E1
Woodford Park	40 F1
Woodford Park Road	40 E1
Woodford Rise	40 F1
Woodford Road	40 E1
Woodford Terrace	40 F1
Woodford View	40 F1
Woodford Villas	40 E1
Woodford Walk	40 F1
Woodford Way	40 F1
Woodlands	12 F1
Woodlands	18 D1 ³
Woodlands	43 A2 ¹
Woodlands Avenue (Cornelscourt)	53 C3
Woodlands Avenue (Stillorgan)	44 E4
Woodlands Court	13 A1
Woodlands Drive (Johnstown Road)	53 C3
Woodlands Drive (Stillorgan)	44 E4

STREET NAME	PAGE/GRID REFERENCE
Woodlands Park (Johnstown Road)	53 C3
Woodlands Pk (Mount Merrion)	44 E4
Woodlands Road	53 C3
Woodlawn	10 F4
Woodlawn Avenue	10 F4
Woodlawn Close	10 F4
Woodlawn Court	10 F4
Woodlawn Crescent	10 F4
Woodlawn Crescent	43 B4
Woodlawn Drive	10 F4
Woodlawn Green	10 F4
Woodlawn Grove	10 F4
Woodlawn Grove	43 B4 ⁷
Woodlawn Park	10 F4
Woodlawn Park (Dun Laoghaire)	53 C1 ⁴
Woodlawn Park Avenue	49 B1
Woodlawn Park Drive(Firhouse)	49 C1
Woodlawn Park Grove	49 C2
Woodlawn Rise	10 F4
Woodlawn Terrace	43 B4 ²
Woodlawn View	10 F4
Woodlawn Walk	10 F4
Woodlawn Way	10 F4
Woodleigh	43 A2 ²
Woodley Park	52 D1
Woodley Road	54 D3
Woodpark (Ballinteer)	51 B2
Woodpark (Blanchardstown)	18 F2
Woodside	15 D4
Woodside	22 F4
Woodside	26 D2
Woodside	43 A3
Woodside Drive	43 A3
Woodside Grove	43 A3
Woodside Road	51 C3
Woodstock Gardens	43 B1 ²
Woodstock Park	50 D1
Woodthorpe	52 E1 ⁵
Woodvale Avenue	17 C1
Woodvale Crescent	17 C1
Woodvale Drive	17 C1
Woodvale Garth	17 C1
Woodvale Green	17 C1
Woodvale Grove	17 C1
Woodvale Park	17 C1
Woodvale Way	17 C1
Woodview	30 D2
Woodview	31 C2
Woodview	5 B3
Woodview (Celbridge)	30 D2
Woodview (Dunboyne)	5 B3
Woodview Close	23 A1
Woodview Cottages	42 F3 ¹
Woodview Court	52 F1 ¹
Woodview Drive	57 C4 ⁴
Woodview Grove	18 E2
Woodview Heights	31 C2
Woodview Park	19 A3
Woodview Park	23 A1
Woodville Avenue	32 E1
Woodville Close	32 E1
Woodville Court	22 E1
Woodville Green	32 E1
Woodville Grove	32 E1
Woodville Lawn	32 E1
Woodville Road	21 A4 ⁷
Woodville Walk	32 E1
*Wormwood Gate (off Bridge Street Lower)	35 C2
Wyattville Close	56 D1
Wyattville Hill	56 D1
Wyattville Park	56 D1
Wyattville Road	56 D1
Wyckham Park Road	51 B1
Wynberg Park	45 B4
Wyndham Park	57 C2
Wynnefield Park	43 A1²¹
Wynnefield Road	43 A1
Wynnsward Drive	43 C2
Wynnsward Park	43 C2
Wyvern Estate	54 E3

X	
XAVIER AVENUE	36 F1 ³

Y	
YALE	44 D3
Yankee Terrace	45 A4
*Yarnhall Street (off Bolton St.)	36 D2
Yellow Meadows Ave	40 F1
Yellow Meadows Drive	40 E1
Yellow Meadows Estate	40 F1

STREET NAME	PAGE/GRID REFERENCE
Yellow Meadows Grove	40 E1
Yellow Meadows Lawn	40 E1
Yellow Meadows Park	40 E1
Yellow Meadows Road	40 E1
Yellow Meadows Vale	40 E1
Yellow Road	21 C2
Yellow Walls	3 A2
Yellow Walls Road	3 A2
Yewlands Terrace	42 F2
York Avenue	43 A1
York Road (Dun Laoghaire)	45 C4
York Road (Rathmines)	43 A1
York Road (Ringsend)	37 A2
York Street	36 D3
York Terrace	45 C4 ⁴

Z	
ZION ROAD	43 A2
Zoo Road	35 A2
*Zuma Terrace (on Mount Drummond Ave)	35 C4

PAGE/GRID REFERENCE — STREET NAME

LIST OF STREETS NOT NAMED ON MAP BUT SHOWN BY SMALL NUMBERS

2 D2 1 St. Colulmcille's Crescent
2 Well Road

3 A2 1 Hillcrest

3 B2 1 Haven View

4 D4 1 Alder Court

5 B3 1 Congress Park

7 A4 1 Ashmount

9 C4 1 Termon Court

10 D4 1 Ard na Meala

11 A4 1 Newbury Terrace

11 B4 1 Clonshaugh Grove
2 Clonshaugh Rise

12 D4 1 Temple View Vale
2 Temple View Crescent
3 Clonmellon Grove
4 Beechbrooke Grove
5 Curraghcloe Drive
6 Grangemore Court

13 A4 1 Seapoint Avenue (Baldoyle)
2 Parochial Avenue
3 Back Lane (Baldoyle)
4 The Mall (Baldoyle)
5 Breffini Gardens
6 Brookstone Lane

17 C1 1 Meadow Dale
2 Oakview Grove
3 Pinebrook Way
4 Pinebrook Close

17 C2 1 Willow Wood Downs

18 D1 1 Huntstown Lawn
2 Briarswood Park
3 Woodlands
4 Briarwood Road

18 D2 1 Coolmine Mews
2 Kirkfield

18 E2 1 Coolmine Court

18 F2 1 Herbert Crescent

18 F3 1 The Crescent
2 Castleknock Court

18 F4 1 The Sand Holes

19 A3 1 Beech Park Crescent
2 Hadleigh Green

19 B3 1 Mill Lane

19 B4 1 Castleknock Gate

19 C4 1 Martin Savage Road
2 Baggott Terrace
3 Elm Grove Cottages

20 D1 1 Cardiffsbridge Grove

20 D2 1 Valley Park Avenue
2 Valeview Gardens
3 Mellowes Court
4 Mellowes Crescent
5 Ravens Court
6 Valeview Crescent
7 Church View

20 D4 1 Roosevelt Cottages
2 Convent View Cottages
3 Convent View Crescent
4 Lyndon Gate

20 E1 1 Georges Road
2 Gofton Hall

20 E2 1 Ballygall Place
2 Glenhill Villas
3 St. Helenas Court
4 Ballygall Parade
5 Johnstown Gardens
6 Collins Row
7 Glebe View

20 E4 1 Kilkieran Court
2 St. Finbarr's Court

20 F2 1 Drapier Green
2 Glasnamanna Place
3 Johnstown House

20 F3 1 Northland Grove
2 Northland Drive
3 Glasnevin Oaks
4 Bellevue Cottages
5 Cremore Villas

20 F4 1 St. Philomena's Road
2 Tower View Cottages
3 Delvin Road
4 Bengal Terrace
5 Fertullagh Road
6 Connaught Parade
7 Clareville Court

21 A1 1 Pinewood Grove
2 Shanliss Gardens
3 Oldtown Park

21 A2 1 Albert College Grove

21 A3 1 Claremont Avenue
2 Church Avenue (Glasnevin)
3 St. David's Terrace (Glasnevin)
4 Barron Place
5 Comyn Place
6 St. Ita's Road
7 St. Malachy's Road
8 St. Michael's Road
9 Addison Place
10 Addison Terrace
11 St. Mobhi Grove
12 Windele Road
13 O'Brien's Place, North
14 O'Neachtain Road
15 River Gardens
16 Mobhi Court
17 The Haven

21 A4 1 Millmount Villas
2 De Courcy Square
3 Enniskerry Road (Phibsborough)
4 Glendhu Villas
5 Prospect Square
6 Glendalough Road
7 Woodville Road
8 St. Teresa Road (Glasnevin)
9 St. Teresa Place
10 Botanic Villas
11 St. Alphonsus Avenue
12 St. Brendan's Road
13 St. Clement's Road
14 Botanic Park
15 O'Brien's Terrace
16 Royal Canal Bank
17 Whitworth Place
18 Devery's Lane

21 B1 1 Ailesbury

21 B2 1 Tourmakeady Road

21 B3 1 Clonturk Avenue
2 The Village
3 Clare Park Villas
4 Beaucourt

21 B4 1 Tom Clarke House
2 St. Joseph's Avenue (Ballybough)

3 Clonturk Gardens
4 Cian Park
5 Holycross Avenue
6 Robert Street
7 Robert Place
8 College Manor
9 Victoria Lane
10 Edgewood
11 College Mews
12 Kingston Lodge

21 C2 1 Dromnanane Road
2 Dromnanane Park
3 Thorndale Court
4 Laragh (Flats)

21 C3 1 Torlogh Parade
2 Morrogh Terrace
3 Calderwood Grove
4 Croydon Terrace
5 Sion Hill Court
6 Collins Court
7 St. Vincent's Court

21 C4 1 Annadale Avenue
2 Shelmartin Terrace
3 Windsor Villas
4 St. Joseph's Terrace (Fairview)
5 St. Declan's Terrace
6 St. Aidan's Park
7 Fairview Green
8 Torlogh Gardens
9 Marino Mart
10 Fairview Passage
11 Fairview Terrace
12 Caragh Court
13 Marino Court
14 Fairview Court
15 Bushfield Square

22 D1 1 Kilbarron Court

22 D3 1 Cherrymount Crescent
2 Cherrymount Grove

22 D4 1 Brighton Avenue (Clontarf)
2 Hollybrook Court Drive
3 Hollybrook Court
4 Strandville House
5 Brooklawn (Clontarf)
6 Crescent House
7 Kilronan Court

22 E1 1 Lismeen Grove
2 Brookville Crescent

22 E2 1 Maryfield Avenue
2 Artane Cottages Lower
3 Artane Cottages Upper

22 E3 1 St. Brigid's Drive (Killester)
2 St. Brigid's Court
3 Quarry Cottages

22 E4 1 Warrenpoint
2 St. John's Wood
3 Lambourne Village
4 Knight's Bridge
5 St. David's Court

22 F1 1 Elton Court
2 Ayrefield Park

22 F2 1 Gorsefield Court

23 A1 1 Elton Walk
2 Glentworth Park
3 Invermore Grove
4 Kilmorony Close
5 Laracor Gardens
6 Gables

23 A3 1 Watermill Lawn
2 St.Anne's Court

23 A4 1 Seafield Grove
2 St. Gabriel's Court

23 B1 1 Howth Junction Cottages
2 Swan's Nest Court
3 Swan's Nest Avenue

23 B2 1 Thornville Terrace
2 Greendale Court

23 B3 1 The Grove
2 The Court

23 C1 1 Pacelli Avenue

23 C2 1 Hillside View
2 Del Val Court

24 D1 1 Sutton Court
2 Seafield Court

24 E1 1 James McCormack Gardens
2 St. Catherine's Terrace
3 Radcliffe

25 B1 1 Corrbridge Terrace
2 Avalo (Apts)

25 B3 1 Shielmartin Park
2 Martello Terrace

26 D1 1 Dunbo Terrace
2 Evora Terrace
3 Dunbo Cottages
4 Dunbo Hill
5 Howth Terrace
6 Harbour View

26 D2 1 St. Lawrence's Terrace
2 Seaview Terrace (Howth)
3 St. Mary's Road (Howth)
4 St. Mary's Place (Howth)
5 St. Nessan's Terrace
6 The Haggard (Howth)
7 Hillside Terrace
8 Dungriffan Villas
9 St.Nessan's Close

26 E2 1 Cannon Rock View
2 Upper Cliff Road

29 C3 1 The Deanery

30 D3 1 Larkfield Mews
2 Castletown Court
3 Cherrywood

30 D4 1 Balfe Gardens

32 D1 1 Sarsfield Terrace
2 Vesey Terrace
3 Hanbury Lane (Lucan)
4 Sarsfield Court
5 The Square
6 Dispensary Lane
7 Village Weir
8 Brookvale
9 Mount Gandon

33 A3 1 Collinstown Crescent

33 A4 1 Ballymanagin Lane
2 Moorfield Close
3 Neilstown Cottages

33 C1 1 The Covert
2 Glenside Villas
3 Clarkeville Terrace
4 Red Cow Cottages
5 St. Fintan's Terrace

33 C2 1 Culmore Park
2 Glenaulin Green

33 C4 1 Gallanstown Way

34 D3 1 Le Fanu Drive

34 E2 1 Park Lane
2 Maidens Row
3 Hibernian Terrace

PAGE/GRID REFERENCE	STREET NAME
	4 St. Laurence Grove
	5 St. Mary's Terrace
	6 Isolde Gardens
	7 Liffey Terrace
	8 Clayton Terrace
	9 St. Laurence Terrace
	10 Mullingar Terrace
34 E3	1 O'Hogan Road
	2 Lynch's Lane
34 E4	1 Old Naas Road Cottages
	2 Millrose Estate
34 F3	1 Park Street
	2 Phoenix Street
	3 Inchicore Terrace, North
	4 Murray's Cottages
	5 Partridge Terrace
	6 Tyrconnell Street
	7 Tyrconnell Villas
	8 Woodfield Cottages
	9 St. Patrick's Terrace (Inchicore)
	10 Abercorn Terrace
	11 Granite Terrace
	12 Ring Street
	13 Inchicore Square
	14 Oblate Drive
	15 Woodfield Place
	16 Hampton Court
	17 St. Jamee's Place
	18 St. George's Villas
	19 Abercorn Square
34 F4	1 Muirfield Drive
	2 Bernard Curtis House
	3 La Touche Court
35 A2	1 Islandbridge Court
	2 Hospital Lane
	3 Sarah Place
	4 Park Place
35 A3	1 Hybreasal
	2 Turvey Avenue
	3 Connolly Gardens
	4 Goldenbridge Gardens
	5 Goldenbridge Terrace
	6 Camac Close
	7 Kearn's Place
	8 St. Michael's Estate
	9 Memorial Road
	10 Camac Court
	11 Heuston Square
	12 Tyrone Place
	13 Lady's Lane
	14 Prospect Terrace (Kilmainham)
	15 Carrickfoyle Terrace
	16 Goldenbridge Walk
	17 The Belfry
	18 Beaconsfield Court
	19 Rosemount Court
	20 Rowerstown Lane
	21 Myra Cottages
	22 Harcourt Lodge
	23 Ashmount Court
35 B1	1 Glenmore Road
	2 Glencar Road
	3 Everton Avenue
	4 Ardmore Avenue
	5 Glenard Avenue
	6 Doon Avenue
	7 St. David's Terrace (Blackhorse Avenue)
	8 Aughrim Place
	9 Carnew Street
	10 Ashford Street
	11 Dunard Road
	12 Aughrim Villas
	13 Arklow Street
	14 Drumalee Court
	15 Phoenix Court
35 B2	1 Thor Place
	2 Halliday Square
	3 Sullivan Street
	4 Kinahan Street
	5 Montpelier Gardens
	6 Arbour Terrace
	7 Temple Street, West
	8 Swords Street
	9 Black Street
	10 Findlater Street
	11 Niall Street
	12 Finn Street
	13 Park Avenue West
	14 De Burgh Road
	15 Brodin Row
	16 Temple Court
	17 Phoenix Court
35 B3	1 Irwin Street
	2 Kennedy's Villas
	3 Cromwell's Quarters
	4 Shannon Terrace
	5 Cameron Square
	6 St. Maignenn's Terrace
	7 Donnellan Avenue
	8 McDowell Avenue
	9 O'Reilly Avenue
	10 Madison Road
	11 Mayfield Road (Kilmainham)
	12 Ewington Lane
	13 Glenmalure Park
	14 Rialto Buildings
	15 Herberton Park
	16 Clarke Terrace
	17 Mallin Avenue
	18 Ave Maria Road
	19 Morning Star Road
	20 Emerald Square
	21 St. James's Avenue (James's Street)
	22 Church Avenue South (Dolphin's Barn)
	23 Fatima Mansions
	24 Irwin Court
	25 McCarthy Terrace
	26 Almeida Avenue
	27 Almeida Terrace
	28 St. John's Cottages
	29 Carrick Terrace
	30 Vauxhall Avenue
	31 Willie Bermingham Place
	32 Brandon Terrace
	33 St. John's Terrace (Mount Brown)
	34 Knocknarrow Terrace
	35 Millbrook Court
	36 Prior Hall
	37 Camac Terrace
	38 South View Terrace
35 B4	1 Dolphin House
	2 St. James's Terrace (Dolphin's Barn)
	3 Rialto Drive
	4 Moracrete Cottages
	5 Dolphin Park
	6 Reillys Avenue
35 C1	1 Aughrim Lane
	2 Annamoe Parade
	3 Cherrymount Park
	4 Rosemount Road
	5 Fingal Place
	6 Phibsborough Avenue
	7 Leslie's Buildings
	8 Great Western Square
	9 Great Western Villas
	10 Kirwan Street Cottages
	11 Norton's Avenue
	12 Royal Canal Terrace
	13 Marne Villas
	14 St. Elizabeth's Court
	15 St. Joseph's Place
	16 St. Joseph's Court
	17 Castle Terrace
	18 Great Western Avenue
	19 King's Court
	20 Rathdown Square
	21 Aughrim Court
	22 Phibsboro
35 C2	1 Ostman Place
	2 Stanhope Street
	3 George's Lane
	4 Blackhall Parade
	5 Brown Street, North
	6 Friary Avenue
	7 Nicholas Avenue
	8 Sarsfield Quay
	9 Hendrick Place
	10 Arran Quay Terrace
	11 Church Street, New
	12 Marshalsea Lane
	13 Blackhall Street
	14 Morgan Place
	15 Phoenix Street West
	16 Stable Lane
	17 Aran St. West
	18 Burgess Lane
	19 Liffey Street West
	20 Thundercut Alley
	21 Oxmantown Lane
	22 Catherine Lane North
	23 Fitzwilliam Place North
	24 Morning Star Avenue
	25 Church Avenue West
	26 Father Matthew Square
	27 Ard Righ Place
	28 Houghton Terrace
	29 Rosemount Terrace
	30 Murtagh Road
	31 Sigurd Road
	32 Viking Road
	33 Olaf Road
	34 St. Mary's Terrace
	35 Slade Row
	36 Paul Street
	37 Smithfield Terrace
	38 Ellis Court
35 C3	1 Marshal Lane
	2 Grand Canal Place
	3 Rainsford Avenue
	4 Market Street, South
	5 Long's Place
	6 Park Terrace (Coombe)
	7 St. Margaret's Terrace
	8 Huxley Crescent
	9 Darley's Terrace
	10 Maxwell Street
	11 Fingal Street
	12 Pimlico Cottages
	13 Taylor's Lane (Pimlico)
	14 St. Catherine's Lane, West
	15 Allingham Street
	16 Meath Market
	17 Brabazon Street
	18 Brabazon Row
	19 Molyneux Yard
	20 Vicar Street
	21 Garden Lane
	22 Mark's Alley West
	23 Oscar Square
	24 Cow Parlour
	25 Newmarket Street
	26 Mill Lane (Newmarket)
	27 Warrenmount
	28 Warrenmount Place
	29 O'Carolan Road
	30 Geoffrey Keating Road
	31 Madden Road
	32 New Row Square
	33 Weaver's Close
	34 Ardee Row
	35 Brabazon Place
	36 Sweeney's Terrace
	37 Weaver's Square
	38 Poole Street
	39 St. John's Avenue
	40 Brabazon Square
	41 Gray Square
	42 Meath Square
	43 Reginald Square
	44 Wilson Terrace
	45 Catherine Street
	46 Spitalfields
	47 Hanover Street West
	48 Brickfield Lane
	49 Thomas Davis Street South
	50 John's Lane West
	51 Swan Alley
	52 Old Mill Court
	53 Ebenezer Terrace
	54 Harman Street
	55 Donore Terrace
	56 Hammond Street
	57 St. Michael's Terrace
	58 St. John Street
	59 Marion Villas
	60 Pyro Villas
	61 Ivy Terrace
	62 Coombe Court
	63 Emerald Terrace
	64 Thirlestane Terrace
	65 Thomas St. West
35 C4	1 Hamilton Street
	2 Ingram Road
	3 Rehoboth Avenue
	4 Priestfield Cottages
	5 St. Anne's Road South
	6 Lullymore Terrace
	7 Wesley Place
	8 Arbutus Avenue
	9 Greenmount Avenue
	10 Emmet Street (Harold's Cross)
	11 Greenville Avenue
	12 Gilbert Road
	13 Parnell Court
	14 Greenmount Square
	15 Hatter's Lane
	16 Limekiln Lane
	17 Clanbrassil Close
	18 Harold's Cross Cottages
	19 Greenmount Court
	20 Saint Clare's Avenue
	21 Donovan Lane
	22 Griffith Square
	23 Briansboro Terrace
	24 Wolseley Street
	25 Merton Avenue
	26 Rutledge Terrace
	27 Merton Park
	28 Priestfield Drive
	29 Western Road
	30 Mount Drummond Court
	31 Boyne Court
36 D1	1 Phibsborough Place
	2 Lynch's Place
	3 White's Lane, North
	4 St. Vincent Street, North
	5 Sarsfield Street (Phibsborough)
	6 O'Connell Avenue
	7 St. Mary's Avenue, North (Mountjoy Street)
	8 Palmerstown Place
	9 Mountjoy Street, Middle
	10 St. Mary's Terrace (Mountjoy Street)
	11 Belvidere Court
	12 Hardwicke Place
	13 Graham Court
	14 Frederick Lane, North
	15 Grenville Lane
	16 Parnell Place
	17 St. Ignatius Avenue
	18 Cowley Place Upper
	19 De Valera Place
	20 Eccles Court
	21 Cavendish Row
	22 Kelly's Lane
	23 Myrtle Street
	24 Leo Avenue
	25 Josephine Avenue
	26 Synnott Row
	27 St. Joseph Street
	28 Sherrard Avenue
	29 William's Place Upper
	30 Killarney Parade
	31 Kenmare Parade
	32 Muckross Parade
	33 Derrynane Parade
	34 Valentia Parade
	35 St. Benedicts Gardens
	36 Arranmore Avenue
	37 Cowley Place Lower
	38 Peter's Court
	39 Weaver Lane
	40 Gardiner Row
	41 Temple Lane North

PAGE/GRID REFERENCE	STREET NAME
42	Bath Lane
43	George's Place
44	Nerney's Court
45	Hardwicke Lane
46	Frederick Court
47	Britain Place
48	St. Mary's Place North
49	Long Lane
50	Wellington Place North
51	St. Michael's Place
52	Maunsell Place
53	Blessington Lane
54	Graham's Row
55	Berkeley Avenue
56	Blessington Court
57	Berkeley Place
58	Bethesda Place
59	St. Joseph's Place
60	Temple Building
61	Library View Terrace

36 D2

1	Linenhall Terrace
2	Lisburn Street
3	Lurgan Street
4	Linenhall Parade
5	Anne Street, North
6	George's Hill
7	Anglesea Row
8	Green Street, Little
9	Ryder's Row
10	Jervis Lane, Upper
11	Jervis Lane, Lower
12	Wolfe Tone Street
13	Chapel Lane (Parnell Street)
14	Sampson's Lane
15	Moore Lane
16	Henry Place
17	Thomas Lane
18	Cathedral Street
19	Earl Place
20	Prince's Street, North
21	Sycamore Street
22	Cope Street
23	Ball's Lane
24	Sackville Place
25	Findlater Place
26	O'Rahilly Parade
27	William's Lane
28	Proby's Lane
29	Hotel Yard
30	William's Row
31	Byrne's Lane (Jervis St)
32	Mary Street Little
33	Meetinghouse Lane
34	Campbell's Court
35	Dominick Lane
36	Strand Street Little
37	Ormond Square
38	Foster Place (College Green)
39	Aston Place
40	Crampton Quay
41	Church Lane
42	Dame Lane
43	Abbey Cottages
44	St. Michan's Street

36 D3

1	Hanover Lane
2	St. Nicholas Place
3	Castle Street (Cork Hill)
4	Iveagh Buildings
5	Cathedral Lane
6	William's Place, South
7	Dame Lane
8	Longford Street, Great
9	Longford Street, Little
10	Aungier Place
11	Redmond's Hill
12	Protestant Row
13	Montague Lane
14	O'Neill's Buildings
15	Pleasants Lane
16	Dame Court
17	Harry Street
18	Clonmel Street
19	Stable Lane
20	Liberty Lane
21	Pleasants Place
22	Camden Villas

PAGE/GRID REFERENCE	STREET NAME
23	Aungier Lane
24	Proud's Lane
25	Montague Court
26	Montague Place
27	Stokes Place
28	Glovers Alley
29	Balfe Street
30	Johnson's Court
31	Lemon Street
32	Duke Lane Upper
33	Anne's Lane
34	Coppinger Row
35	Chatham Row
36	Johnson Place
37	Bow Lane East
38	Digges Lane
39	Fade Street
40	John Field Road
41	Whitefriar Street
42	Whitefriar Place
43	Cathedral View Court
44	Cathedral View Walk
45	Longford Lane
46	Malpas Terrace
47	Hanover Square
48	Saint Francis Square
49	Coolevin Lane
50	Malpas Court
51	Christchurch Square
52	John's Lane East

36 D4

1	Fitzgerald Street
2	Desmond Street
3	St. Kevin's Road
4	Kingsland Park Avenue
5	Kingsland Parade
6	Portobello Harbour
7	Richmond Row
8	Blackberry Lane
9	Bessborough Parade
10	Richmond Place (Rathmines)
11	Ontario Terrace
12	Athlumney Villas
13	Cheltenham Place
14	Harcourt Lane
15	Albert Place, West
16	Tom Kelly Road
17	Florence Street
18	Albert Terrace
19	Peter Place
20	Charlemont Gardens
21	St. Ultan's Flats
22	Richmond Villas
23	Gordon Place
24	Synge Place
25	Synge Lane
26	Avenue Road
27	McMahon Street
28	Camden Market
29	St. Kevin's Cottages
30	Camden Buildings
31	Camden Court
32	Charlotte Way
33	Walworth Road
34	Martin Street
35	Warren Street
36	Portobello Place
37	Walker's Cottages
38	Walker's Court
39	Mountpleasant Parade
40	Mountpleasant Terrace
41	Bannaville
42	Garden View
43	Richmond Mews
44	Richmond Place South
45	Alexandra Terrace (Portobello)
46	Bloomfield Park
47	Grove Avenue
48	Spencer Street South
49	Bloomfield Cottages
50	Oakfield Place
51	Arbutus Place
52	St. Kevin's Parade
53	Lissenfield
54	Charlotte Way

36 E1

1	O'Sullivan Avenue
2	Sackville Gardens

PAGE/GRID REFERENCE	STREET NAME
3	Ardilaun Road
4	Ballybough Lane
5	Charlemont Parade
6	Clonmore Terrace
7	Clinch's Court
8	Richmond Crescent
9	Richmond Cottages (Summerhill)
10	Richmond Parade
11	Bailey's Row
12	Buckingham Place
13	Killarney Avenue
14	Preston Street
15	Shamrock Place
16	Shamrock Terrace
17	Aldborough Parade
18	Drumcondra Park
19	Belvidere Avenue
20	Richmond Lane
21	Fitzgibbon Lane
22	Mountjoy Place
23	Langrishe Place
24	Gloucester Place, Upper
25	Gloucester Place
26	Summerhill Place
27	Bella Street
28	Matt Talbot Court
29	Newcomen Court
30	Gilford Place
31	Shamrock Cottages
32	Wellesley Place
33	Brendan Behan Court
34	St. Margaret's Avenue North
35	St. Joseph's Terrace
36	Mountjoy Parade
37	Richmond Cottages North
38	St. Joseph's Villas
39	Clonmore Villas
40	Whitworth Avenue
41	Foster Place North
42	Ballybough Avenue
43	Ballybough Court
44	Trinity Terrace
45	Tyrrell Place
46	Summer Place
47	Sean O'Casey Avenue
48	Rutland Place North
49	Thompson's Cottages
50	Portland Close
51	Beaver Close
52	Gloucester Diamond
53	Gloucester Place Lower
54	Gloucester Place
55	Rutland Cottages
56	Buckingham Terrace
57	Duke Row
58	Ulster Terrace (North Strand)
59	Seville Terrace

36 E2

1	Pearse House
2	Erne Place Lower
3	Magennis Place
4	Mark's Lane
5	Deverell Place
6	Talbot Lane
7	Marlborough Place
8	Northumberland Square
9	Beresford Lane
10	Shaw Street
11	Park Lane, East
12	Prince's Street, South
13	Cards Lane
14	Spring Garden Lane
15	Dowlings Court
16	Peterson's Court
17	Mabbot Lane
18	Harbour Court
19	Abbey Street Old
20	Frenchman's Lane
21	Moland Place
22	Spencer Row
23	Emerald Place
24	Corn Exchange Place
25	Luke Street
26	Mark Street
27	Rath Row
28	Bracken's Lane
29	Magenis Square

PAGE/GRID REFERENCE	STREET NAME
30	Brunswick Villas
31	Leland Place
32	Champions Avenue
33	Lombard Court
34	St. Lawrence's Mansions
35	Trinity Square

36 E3

1	Cumberland Street, South
2	Boyne Lane
3	Bass Place
4	Erne Place, Little
5	Grant's Row
6	Meade's Terrace
7	Holles Row
8	Merrion Place
9	Baggot Court
10	Frederick Lane, South
11	Nassau Place
12	Schoolhouse Lane
13	Leinster Lane
14	Clare Lane
15	Roger's Lane
16	Leeson Lane
17	Duke Lane Lower
18	Dawson Lane
19	College Lane
20	Erne Terrace Front
21	Erne Terrace Rere
22	Devlin's Place
23	Harmony Row
24	Molesworth Place
25	Kildare Place
26	Merrion Close
27	Merrion Street Lower
28	Baggotrath Place
29	Little Fitzwilliam Place
30	Bell's Lane
31	Ely Place Upper
32	Windsor Place
33	Mackies Place
34	Holles Place
35	Wilson's Place
36	Stephen's Place
37	Stable Lane (Leeson Street Lower)
38	Fitzwilliam Court
39	Hagan's Court
40	Convent Close
41	Herbert Lane
42	Royal Hibernian Way

36 E4

1	Leeson Close
2	Hatch Lane
3	Leeson Place
4	Dartmouth Place
5	Dartmouth Terrace
6	Dartmouth Lane
7	Cambridge Terrace (Ranelagh)
8	Chelmsford Avenue
9	Old Mountpleasant
10	Mander's Terrace
11	Sussex Terrace
12	Convent Place
13	Hatch Place
14	Dartmouth Square North
15	Dartmouth Square South
16	Dartmouth Square East
17	Dartmouth Square West
18	Warner's Lane
19	Leeson Walk
20	Northbrook Lane
21	Selskar Terrace
22	Mountpleasant Place
23	Swan Grove
24	Orchard Lane
25	Berystede
26	Temple Place
27	Warwick Terrace
28	Sibthorpe Lane
29	Dexter Terrace
30	Leeson Village
31	Swan Place
32	Pembroke Place (Pembroke Street Upper)
33	Burlington Gardens
34	Burleigh Court

36 F1

1	Northbrook Terrace
2	Stoney Road (East Wall)

PAGE/GRID REFERENCE	STREET NAME
	3 Xavier Avenue
	4 Strandville Avenue
	5 Hibernian Avenue (North Strand)
	6 Gaelic Street
	7 Hyacinth Street
	8 Courtney Place
	9 Annesley Avenue
	10 Enaville Road
	11 Crescent Gardens
	12 St. Barnabas Gardens
	13 Boolavogue Road
	14 Russell Avenue, East
	15 Taaffe's Place
	16 St. Patrick's Avenue
	17 St. Mura's Terrace
	18 Malachi Place
	19 Strandville Place
	20 James's Street North
	21 Leinster Street East
	22 Oriel Place
	23 Austin's Cottages
	24 St. Brigid's Cottages
36 F2	1 Emerald Street
	2 Spencer Avenue
	3 First Avenue (Seville Place)
	4 Blythe Avenue
	5 Laurence Place East
	6 Second Avenue (Seville Place)
	7 Third Avenue (Seville Place)
	8 Fourth Avenue (Seville Place)
	9 Carbury Terrace
	10 Irvine Cottages
	11 Alexander Terrace (North Wall)
	12 St. Brigid's Gardens
	13 Bellman's Walk
	14 Ferryman's Crossing
36 F3	1 Clarence Place, Great
	2 Eblana Villas (Lr. Grand Canal Street)
	3 Island Villa
	4 Carlingford Parade
	5 Hastings Street
	6 Penrose Street
	7 Ormeau Street
	8 Somerset Street
	9 Gerald Street
	10 Bath Avenue Place
	11 Margaret Place
	12 Malone Gardens
	13 Shaw's Lane
	14 Albert Place East
	15 Love Lane, East
	16 Estate Cottages (Northumberland Road)
	17 St. Mary's Lane
	18 Haddington Place
	19 Cranmer Lane
	20 Landsdowne Lane
	21 Erne Place
	22 Brunswick Place
	23 Conway Court
	24 South Dock Road
	25 Rostrevor Terrace
	26 Greenore Terrace
	27 Hogan Avenue
	28 Grattan Court East
	29 Grattan Place
	30 Albert Court East
	31 Macken villa
	32 Mount Street Crescent
	33 Leitrim Place
	34 Emerald Cottages
	35 South Dock Place
	36 Berkeley Terrace
	37 Lansdowne Terrace
	38 Pearse Grove
	39 Camden Lock
	40 Clanwilliam Terrace
	41 Clanwilliam Square
	42 Northumberland Place
	43 Lansdowne Crescent
	44 Lansdowne Villas

PAGE/GRID REFERENCE	STREET NAME
36 F4	1 Eastmoreland Place
	2 Eastmoreland Lane
	3 Shelbourne Lane
	4 Herbert Cottages
	5 Shelbourne Avenue
	6 Carlton Villas
	7 Lansdowne Gardens
	8 Beatty's Avenue
	9 Dodder View Cottages
	10 Granite Place
	11 Morehampton Square
	12 Morehampton Mews
	13 Estate Cottages
	14 Ballsbridge Terrace
	15 Pembroke Place (Ballsbridge)
37 A2	1 Fisherman's Wharf
37 A3	1 Cambridge Street
	2 Fitzwilliam Street (Ringsend)
	3 St. Patrick's Villas
	4 Seapoint Terrace
	5 The Square (Irishtown)
	6 St. Brendan's Cottages
	7 Cambridge Avenue
	8 Tritonville Avenue
	9 Tritonville Crescent
	10 Seafort Gardens
	11 Leukos Road
	12 Clonlara Road
	13 Kyle-Clare Road
	14 Parkview Place
	15 Canon Mooney Gardens
	16 Caroline Row
	17 Havelock Terrace
	18 Dodder Terrace
	19 Ennis Grove
	20 Londonbridge Drive
	21 Strasburg Terrace
	22 Tritonville Close
	23 St. James' Terrace
	24 Cambridge Court
	25 Lansdowne Hall
	26 Sandymount Court
37 A4	1 Sandymount Green
	2 Sandymount Castle Road
	3 Sandymount Castle Drive
	4 Sydenham Road (Ballsbridge)
	5 Sandymount Castle
	6 Churchill Terrace
	7 Prince of Wales Terrace
	8 Railway Cottages
	9 Martin White Chalets
	10 Gilford Court
	11 Homelee
	12 Lynton Court
	13 Spafield Terrace
	14 Adair
	15 Wilfield
	16 Park Court (Sandymount)
	17 Dromard Terrace
	18 Seafort Cottages
	19 Seafort Terrace
	20 Seafort Villas
	21 Claremont Court
	22 The Sweepstakes
	23 Ballsbridge Park
	24 Lansdowne Square
37 B1	1 Alverno
	2 Haddon Court
37 B2	1 Breakwater Road North
37 B3	1 Prospect Terrace (Sandymount)
37 B4	1 Gilford Terrace
	2 Sandymount Castle Park
	3 Martello View
	4 Bethany House
	5 Hempenstall Terrace
	6 Martello Wood
37 C1	1 Churchgate Avenue
	2 St. Joseph's Square

PAGE/GRID REFERENCE	STREET NAME
	3 Vernon Court
39 C1	1 Bawnogue Cottages
	2 Nangor Crescent
40 D1	1 St. Patrick's Avenue (Clondalkin)
	2 Leinster Terrace
	3 Beech Row
40 D2	1 Church View (Clondalkin)
	2 Green Isle Court
40 E1	1 St. Killian's Park
	2 Monastery Heights
	3 Bettysford
	4 Castle Crescent
	5 Friar's Walk
40 E2	1 St. Brigid's Park
40 F1	1 Knockmitten Close
	2 Knockmitten Lane North
40 F3	1 Pinetree Grove
	2 Belgard Close
40 F4	1 Pinetree Crescent
41 A3	1 Parkhill Heights
	2 Parkview
41 B2	1 Tibradden Close
41 B3	1 Three Rock Close
41 B4	1 Tymon North Court
	2 Tymon North Place
41 C1	1 Field Avenue
	2 Wallace Road
	3 Percy French Road
	4 O'Dwyer Road
	5 Esposito Road
	6 The Valley
	7 Somerville Park
41 C2	1 St. Peter's Terrace
41 C3	1 Willington Lawn
	2 Glenmurry Park
	3 Willington Cottages
42 D1	1 Sunville Green
	2 Windmill Crescent
42 D2	1 Muckross Drive
	2 Lorcan O'Toole Court
	3 Stannaway Court
	4 Beechfield Mews
	5 Wellington Court
42 D3	1 Wellington Road (Templeogue)
42 E1	1 Tonguefield Road
	2 Cloyne Road
	3 Faughart Road
	4 Clonmacnoise Grove
	5 Bedford Court
42 E2	1 Riversdale Grove
	2 Hazel Park
	3 Kimmage Court
	4 Rathland Drive
	5 Brookfield Green
	6 Brookfield Court
42 E3	1 Templeville Park
	2 Fortfield Court
42 F1	1 Mount Harold Terrace
	2 Le Bas Terrace
	3 Mountain View Avenue
	4 Manor Villas
	5 Wilfrid Terrace
	6 Fitzpatrick's Cottages
	7 Ryan's Cottages (Harolds Cross)
	8 Parkview Court

PAGE/GRID REFERENCE	STREET NAME
	9 Gandon Close
42 F2	1 Ashdale Park
	2 Westhampton Place
	3 Terenure Place
	4 Eagle Hill Avenue
	5 Victoria Villas (Rathgar)
	6 Maple Drive
	7 Victoria Village
	8 Frankfort Court
	9 Frankfort Flats
	10 Rathdown Court
42 F3	1 Woodview Cottages
	2 St. Agnes Terrace (Rathfarnham)
	3 Dodder Park Drive
42 F4	1 Willbrook Grove
	2 Tara Hill Grove
	3 Beaufort Villas
	4 Glenann
	5 St. Mary's Terrace (Rathfarnham)
	6 Village Court
	7 The Park Lands
	8 The Lakelands
	9 The Woodlands
	10 Beaufort Court
	11 The Castlelands
43 A1	1 Rathmines Park
	2 Leinster Square
	3 Prince Arthur Terrace
	4 Swanville Place
	5 Castlewood Terrace
	6 Castlewood Place
	7 Grosvenor Park
	8 Grosvenor Lane
	9 Turrets Flats
	10 Purser Gardens
	11 Esker Villas
	12 Parker Hill
	13 Alma Terrace
	14 Observatory Lane
	15 Belgrave Place
	16 Cambridge Villas
	17 Salem Court
	18 Maxwell Court
	19 The Mews
	20 Roland Court
	21 Wynnefield Park
	22 Mount Anthony's Flats
43 A2	1 Woodlands
	2 Woodleigh
	3 Highfield Court
	4 Cowper Mews
43 A3	1 The Willows
	2 Stirling Park
	3 Orwell Court
	4 Millmount Terrace (Dundrum)
	5 Newtown Court
	6 Riverbank
	7 Orwell Bank
	8 Crannagh Way
43 A4	1 Castle Court
	2 Nutgrove Court
43 B1	1 Sallymount Gardens
	2 Woodstock Gardens
	3 Collier's Avenue
	4 Westmoreland Park
	5 Field's Terrace
	6 Rugby Villas
	7 Beechwood Park (Rathmines)
	8 Bushfield Avenue
	9 Charleston Court Flats
	10 Oakley Court Flats
	11 Cullenswood Road
	12 Moran's Cottages
	13 Mountain View Cottages (Ranelagh)
	14 Sallymount Terrace
	15 Chelmsford Lane
	16 Belgrave Villas

PAGE/GRID REFERENCE	STREET NAME
	17 Bushfield Place
	18 Smith's Cottages (Donnybrook)
	19 Beechdale Mews
	20 Oakley Square
43 B2	1 Dartry Cottages
	2 Strand Terrace
	3 St. Luke's Crescent
	4 Balnagowan
	5 Temple Square
	6 Milltown Grove
	7 Milltown Hill
	8 Thorncliff
43 B3	1 St. Columbanus Place
	2 St. Gall Gardens, North
	3 St. Gall Gardens, South
	4 Milltown Terrace (Dundrum)
43 B4	1 Glenbower Park
	2 Woodlawn Terrace
	3 Beaumont Close
	4 Briarly Court
	5 St. Nathy's House
	6 Ardtona Avenue
	7 Woodlawn Grove
	8 Henley Court
	9 Weston Terrace
	10 Frankfort
	11 Rosemount Terrace (Dundrum)
	12 Waldemar Terrace
	13 Airfield Drive
	14 Nutgrove Avenue
	15 Sweetmount Avenue
43 C1	1 St. Broc's Cottages
	2 Pembroke Cottages (Donnybrook)
	3 Belmont Park
	4 The Crescent (Donnybrook)
	5 Harmony Avenue
	6 Vergemount Park
	7 Norwood Park
	8 Brookvale Road (Donnybrook)
	9 Vergemount Hall
	10 Sandford Gardens
	11 Auburn Road
	12 Vergemount
	13 Eglinton Square
	14 Mount Sandford
	15 Rowan Hall
	16 Cedar Hall
	17 Millbrook Village
	18 Simmonscourt Terrace
	19 Brookfield
	20 Harmony Court
	21 Riverside Walk
43 C2	1 Prospect Lane
	2 Beech Hill Villas
	3 Beech Hill Crescent
	4 Beech Hill Terrace
	5 Palmerston Grove
	6 Clonskeagh Drive
	7 Clonskeagh Square
	8 St. Bridget's Flats
	9 Crannagh
43 C3	1 Annaville Grove
	2 Olivemount Grove
	3 Friarsland Avenue
	4 Harlech Villas
	5 Gledeswood Drive
	6 Olivemount Terrace
	7 Glenard Hall
	8 Belfield Close
43 C4	1 Ophaly Court
	2 Woodbine Terrace
	3 Alexandra Terrace
	4 Roseville Terrace
	5 Pembroke Cottages
	6 Pembroke Terrace
	7 Claremont Terrace
	8 Glenville Terrace
44 D1	1 Merrion View Avenue
	2 Simmonscourt Avenue
	3 Simmon's Court
44 D2	1 Nutley Square
	2 Donnybrook Close
44 E1	1 Merrion Court
	2 Merrion Gates
	3 Simmon's Court
	4 Strand Lane
44 E2	1 Seafield Park
	2 Bellevue Court
44 E3	1 The Stables
44 E4	1 Greygates
	2 Beaufield Mews
	3 Ashurst
44 F2	1 St. Helier's Copse
44 F3	1 Martello Terrace (Booterstown)
	2 Pembroke Cottages (Booterstown)
	3 Willowmount
	4 Cherbury Mews
44 F4	1 St. Helier's Copse
	2 Orpen Dale
	3 Park Villas
	4 Cedar Square
45 A3	1 Newtown Villas
	2 Maretimo Road
	3 Ben Inagh Park
	4 Maretimo Gardens, West
	5 Craigmore Gardens
	6 George's Place (Blackrock)
	7 St. Anne's Square (Blackrock)
	8 Bath Place
	9 Rockwell Cove
	10 Westfield Terrace
	11 Idrone Mews
	12 Brusna Cottages
	13 Collins Court
	14 Patrick's Row
	15 Eagle Hill
	16 Maretimo Terrace
	17 Maretimo Place
	18 Maretimo Villas
	19 Whelan's Terrace
	20 Carbury Place
45 A4	1 Avondale Park
	2 Prince Edward Terrace Lower
	3 Prince Edward Terrace Upper
	4 Lindenvale
	5 Twin Cottages
	6 Fieldview Cottages
	7 Cullen's Cottages
	8 Webster's Cottages
	9 Rockville Estate
45 B3	1 Ardenza Terrace
	2 Tobernea Terrace
	3 Ardenza Park
	4 Seapoint Terrace (Blackrock)
45 B4	1 Montpelier Place
	2 Montpelier Manor
	3 The Willows
	4 The Maples
	5 The Cedars
	6 The Alders
	7 The Poplars
	8 Stradbrook Gardens
	9 Brighton Terrace
	10 Belgrave Place
	11 Belgrave Terrace
	12 Brooklawn Avenue
	13 Brooklawn Wood
	14 Rockford Terrace
45 C4	1 Rosary Gardens, West
	2 Barrett Street
	3 Smith's Villas
	4 York Terrace
	5 St. Mary's Street
	6 Crofton Terrace
	7 Oakwood
	8 Harbour Terrace
	9 Grosvenor Terrace (Dun Laoghaire)
	10 Clifton Lane
	11 Clifton Avenue
	12 Clarence Street
	13 Clifton Terrace
	14 Alma Place
	15 Seaview Terrace
	16 Synnott Terrace
	17 Bentley Villas
	18 St. Michael's Terrace
	19 St. Brendan's Terrace
	20 Northcote Terrace
	21 Knapton Court
	22 Knapton Lawn
	23 Northcote Place
	24 Cambridge Terrace
	25 Primrose Hill
	26 Mountown Cottages
	27 Knapton Terrace
	28 Pakenham
46 D4	1 Wellington Street (Dun Laoghaire)
	2 Rosary Gardens, East
	3 Desmond Avenue
	4 Wolfe Tone Avenue
	5 Charlemont Avenue
	6 Summerhill Parade
	7 Haddington Terrace
	8 Victoria Terrace (Dun Laoghaire)
	9 Marine Terrace
	10 Northumberland Place
	11 Northumberland Park
	12 Dungar Terrace
	13 Stoneview Place
	14 Martello Avenue
	15 Crosthwaite Terrace
	16 Sussex Street
	17 Roby Place
	18 Charlemont Terrace
	19 Mill Street (Dun Laoghaire)
	20 Anglesea Lane
46 E4	1 Mornington Avenue
	2 Martello Terrace (Dun Laoghaire)
48 D2	1 Dromcarra Green
49 A1	1 St. Maelruan's Park
49 A2	1 Summerfield
	2 The Close (Tallaght)
	3 Allenton Crescent
49 B1	1 Bolbrook Drive
	2 Glenview Drive
	3 Bolbrook Avenue
	4 Bolbrook Close
	5 Avonmore Avenue
49 B2	1 Allenton Road
	2 Oldcourt Lawn
49 C1	1 Brookmount Lawn
	2 Knocklyon Mews
50 D1	1 Coolamber Court
	2 Pine Grove
	3 Ballyroan Court
50 D2	1 Orlagh Meadows
50 E1	1 Orchardton
50 E2	1 Beechview Court
	2 Cypress Avenue
	3 Larch Drive
	4 Beech Walk
	5 Walnut View
50 F1	1 Sarah Curran Road
	2 St. Gatien Road
	3 Fonthill Abbey
	4 Whitechurch Abbey
	5 Edenbrook Court
50 F2	1 Kingston Court
	2 Highfield Avenue
	3 Highfield Drive
	4 Manor Park (Ballinteer)
	5 The Dell
51 A1	1 Marley Villas
	2 Meadow Villas
51 A2	1 Priory Court
	2 The Cherries
51 B1	1 Meadow Avenue
	2 Hawthorn Drive
	3 Mount Albion Road
	4 Sycamore Drive
51 B2	1 The Crescent (Ballinteer)
	2 Ballinteer Court
51 C1	1 Westerton Rise
	2 Ashgrove Terrace
	3 Eagle Terrace
	4 Dundrum Court
	5 McGrane Court
	6 Ballyolaf Manor
	7 Dundrum Castle
51 C2	1 Clonlea Wood
	2 Ballinteer Park
52 D1	1 Drummartin Crescent
	2 Carrick Lawn
	3 The Pines
52 D2	1 Balally Terrace
	2 Moreen Lawn
	3 Blackthorn Grove
	4 Blackthorn Court
	5 Rathdown Terrace
	6 Blackthorn Green
52 D3	1 Lamb's Brook
52 E1	1 Dale Close
	2 Stillorgan Court
	3 Stillorgan Heath
	4 Convent Court
	5 Woodthorpe
52 E3	1 Glencairn Garth
	2 Glencairn Heath
52 F1	1 Woodview Court
	2 Ard Lorcain Villas
	3 Grange Cottages
	4 Ulster Terrace (Stilloran Grove)
52 F2	1 Leopardstown Court
	2 Leopardstown Lawn
	3 Silverpines
	4 Ellesmere
53 A1	1 Orchard Cottages
	2 Red Brick Terrace
	3 Moore's Cottages
	4 Hawthorn Manor
	5 Rosehill
	6 Ardagh Close
53 A2	1 Knocksinna Grove
	2 Knocksinna Court
	3 New Park Lodge
	4 Foxrock Mount
	5 Chestnut Park
	6 Willow Park
	7 Sycamore Grove
	8 Whitethorn Walk
	9 Birch Dale
53 A3	1 Brighton Cottages
	2 Kilteragh Pines

PAGE/GRID REFERENCE	STREET NAME
53 B1	1 Windsor Court
	2 Grange Grove
	3 Oliver Plunkett Villas
	4 Stradbrook Hill
	5 Springhill Cottages
	6 Grange Cottages
	7 Abbey Court
	8 Abbey Road
	9 Faber Grove
	10 Deans Court
	11 Devon Close
53 B3	1 Kerrymount Close
	2 Hainault Grove
	3 Hainault Lawn
	4 Monaloe Crescent
	5 Clonkeen Lawn
	6 Monaloe Court
53 C1	1 Oliver Plunkett Square
	2 Patrician Park
	3 Mounttown Park
	4 Woodlawn Park (Dun Laoghaire)
	5 Oliver Plunkett Terrace
	6 Fitzgerald Park
	7 St. Patrick's Terrace (Kill o' the Grange)
	8 Dunedin Drive
	9 St. Patrick's Close
	10 Highthorn Woods
	11 Aspen Park
	12 Birch Dale
	13 Willow Grove
53 C2	1 Hillview Cottages
	2 Whitethorn Walk
	3 Sycamore Court
	4 Hazel Lawn
53 C3	1 Little Meadow
	2 Cabinteely Park
	3 O'Shea's Cottages
	4 Cabinteely Court
53 C4	1 Kilbogget Villas
54 D1	1 O'Donnell Gardens
	2 Royal Terrace, North
	3 Myrtle Avenue
	4 Emmet Street (Sallynoggin)
	5 Eden Villas
	6 Laurel Hill
	7 Granite Hall
	8 Magenta Place
	9 Marlborough Park
	10 Royal Terrace Lane
	11 Beechwood Grove
	12 Rollins Court
	13 Seven Houses
	14 The Glen
	15 Glengara Close
	16 Silchester Wood
54 D2	1 Honey Park
	2 Thomastown Crescent
	3 Pearse Close
54 D3	1 Auburn Road
	2 Granville Crescent
54 D4	1 Annabeg
	2 Meadow Court
	3 Oakton Green
54 E1	1 Wilmont Avenue
	2 Congress Gardens
	3 Albert Park
	4 Claremont Villas
	5 St. Paul's Terrace
	6 St. Peter's Terrace (Dun Laoghaire)
	7 Findlater Street (Dun Laoghaire)
	8 Devitt Villas
	9 Dixon Villas
	10 Glen Terrace
	11 Glasthule Buildings
	12 Hastings Terrace
	13 Brighton Terrace
	14 Lawson Terrace
	15 Killiney Terrace
	16 Munster Terrace
	17 Neptune Terrace
	18 Cliff Terrace
	19 Beaufort
	20 Ballygihen Villas
	21 Seabank Court
	22 St. Helen's
	23 Chester Square
	24 Dundela Haven
	25 Arkendale Woods
	26 Arkendale Court
	27 Adelaide Villas
	28 Adelaide Terrace
54 E2	1 Barnhill Lawn
	2 Killiney Towers
	3 Barnhill Park
	4 Kilcolman Court
	5 Edwin Court
	6 Fairlawns
	7 Urney Grove
54 E3	1 Hill Cottages
	2 Mount Auburn
	3 Talbot Road
54 E4	1 Oakton Court
	2 Dale View Park
	3 Mountain Villa
	4 The Nurseries
	5 Mountain View Road
	6 Rainsford Lane
	7 Killiney Avenue
	8 Firgrove
54 F1	1 Carysfort Drive
	2 Ormeau Drive
	3 The Paddocks
	4 South Winds
	5 Ulverton Close
	6 Rocklands
	7 Bayswater Terrace
	8 Bullock Steps
	9 Liscanor
	10 White's Villas
	11 Mayville Terrace
	12 Castlelands Grove
	13 Ulverton Court
	14 Pilot View
	15 Bailey View
	16 Castlelands
54 F2	1 St. Patrick's Avenue (Dalkey)
	2 Railway Road
	3 Anastasia Lane
	4 St. Patrick's Square
	5 Cats Ladder
	6 Dalkey Grove
	7 Barnhill Grove
	8 St. Patrick's Road (Dalkey)
	9 Monte Vella
	10 Summerfield Close
	11 Victoria Terrace (Dalkey)
	12 Sorrento Drive
	13 Sorrento Lawn
	14 Coliemore Villas
	15 Seafield Terrace
	16 Temple Terrace
	17 Grosvenor Terrace (Dalkey)
	18 Charlotte Terrace
	19 Heany Avenue
	20 Desmond Cottages
	21 Ardbrugh Villas
	22 Burmah Close
	23 Dalkey Court
	24 Kilbegnet Close
	25 Sorrento Close
	26 Craiglands
	27 Ullardmor
	28 Sorrento Mews
	29 Sorrento Court
	30 Sorrento Heights
	31 Ardbrugh Close
	32 Castle Cove
	33 Torca View
56 D1	1 The Oaks
	2 Cherry Court
	3 Cois Coillte
	4 Holly Court
56 E1	1 Killiney Court
	2 Killiney Oaks
	3 The Sycamores
	4 The Elms
	5 St. Aubyn's Court
	6 Ennel Court
	7 Sheelin Grove
	8 Glencarr Court
	9 Domville Grove
	10 Streamville Court
	11 Glen Druid
	12 Bayview Glade
	13 Sheelin Hill
	14 Sheelin Walk
	15 Sheelin Drive
56 E2	1 River Lane (Loughlinstown)
	2 Clonasleigh
	3 Beechfield Haven
	4 Athgoe Drive
56 E3	1 Guilford Terrace
	2 Stonebridge Close
56 E4	1 Kiltuck Park
57 A4	1 Ballywaltrim Cottages
57 B1	1 Raverty Villas
	2 St. Peter's Terrace
57 B2	1 Myrtle Grove
	2 Arbutus Grove
	3 Thornhill Grove
	4 Ashley Heights
	5 Dargle Crescent
	6 Copper Beech Grove
	7 St. Patrick's Square
	8 St. Cronan's Road
	9 Sutton Road
	10 Dargan Street
	11 Fair Green Road
	12 Pearse Road
	13 Mountpleasant Villas
	14 Fairgreen Terrace
	15 Diamond Terrace
	16 Parkview Terrace
	17 Sutton Villas
	18 Esmonde Terrace
	19 Old Ravenswell Row
	20 New Ravenswell Row
	21 Vale View
	22 Old Rathmore Terrace
	23 New Rathmore Terrace
	24 St. Brigid's Terrace
	25 Gertrude Terrace
	26 Herbert View
	27 Auburn Villas
	28 Glenburgh Terrace
57 B3	1 Ballynoe Court
	2 Rathclaren
	3 St. Clair's Terrace
57 B4	1 Kingscourt
57 C2	1 Sidmonton Square
	2 Aravon Court
	3 Eglinton Road
	4 Rosslyn Grove
	5 James Connolly Square
	6 Sidmonton Place
	7 Novara Park
	8 Brennans Parade
	9 Cill Manntan Park
	10 Kilmantain Place
	11 Father Colohan Terrace
	12 Royal Marine Terrace
	13 Milton Terrace
	14 St. Kevin's Terrace
	15 Darley Cottages
	16 Brabazon cottages
	17 St. Laurence's Terrace
	18 St. Columcille's Terrace
	19 Marine Terrace
	20 Seapoint Villas
	21 Dunbur Terrace
	22 Elmgrove Terrace
	23 St. Aidan's Terrace
	24 Seapoint Terrace
	25 Goldsmith Terrace
	26 Prince of Wales Terrace
	27 Novara Terrace
	28 Waverley Terrace (Bray)
	29 Westview Terrace
	30 Augustine Villas
	31 Trafalgar Terrace
	32 Claremount Terrace
	33 Warburton Terrace
	34 Richmond Terrace
	35 Milward Terrace
	36 Fitzwilliam Terrace
	37 Marlborough Terrace
	38 Martello Terrace
	39 Florence Terrace
	40 Florence Villas
	41 Carlton Terrace
	42 Carlton Villas
	43 Alexandra Terrace
	44 Belton Terrace
	45 Church Terrace
	46 Old Brighton Terrace
	47 New Brighton Terrace
	48 Killarney Villas
	49 Market Square
57 C3	1 Sydenham Villas
	2 Sidmonton Park
	3 Loretto Avenue
	4 Loretto Terrace
	5 Sidmonton Gardens
	6 Rosslyn
	7 New Grange Park
	8 Newcourt Villas
	9 O'Byrne Villas
	10 Stoneylea Terrace
	11 Mountain View Apartments
	12 Loretto Villas
	13 Marie Villas
	14 Putland Villas
	15 Oldcourt Terrace
	16 Lauderdale Terrace
	17 Mayfield Terrace
	18 Vevay Villas
	19 Orchard Terrace
	20 Bray Head Terrace
57 C4	1 Cherry Tree Drive
	2 Roselawn Park
	3 Bentley Avenue
	4 Woodview Drive
	5 Kennedy Park
	6 St. Mary's Terrace
58 D2	1 Trosyrafon Terrace
	2 Montebello Terrace
	3 Esplanade Terrace
	4 Brennans Terrace
58 D3	1 Raheen Lawn
	2 Meretimo Villas
	3 Grosvonor Avenue
	4 Brookfield Avenue
	5 Sidmonton Court
	6 Mount Norris Villas

ADELAIDE (Peter Street)..	**36** D3
BEAUMONT HOSPITAL..	**22** D1
BLACKROCK CLINIC...	**44** F3
BLOOMFIELD MENTAL HOSPITAL (Donnybrook).............	**43** B1
BON SECOURS (Private) ST. JOSEPH'S (Glasnevin)............	**21** A3
CENTRAL MENTAL HOSPITAL (Dundrum)......................	**43** C3
CHEEVERSTOWN (Templeogue).................................	**42** D4
CHERRY ORCHARD (Ballyfermot)...............................	**33** C3
CHILDREN'S HOSPITAL (Temple Street).......................	**36** D1
CHILDREN'S NATIONAL HOSPITAL (Harcourt Street).......	**36** D3
CITY OF DUBLIN SKIN & CANCER (Hume Street).............	**36** E3
CLONSKEAGH, VERGEMOUNT..................................	**43** C2
CLUAIN MHUIRE (Newtown Park Avenue)....................	**44** B4
COOMBE HOSPITAL (Dolphin's Barn)..........................	**35** C4
DENTAL, DUBLIN (Lincoln Place)...............................	**36** E3
EYE & EAR (Royal Victoria, Adelaide Road)...................	**36** E4
GASCOIGNE HOME (Camden Row).............................	**36** D4
HAMSTEAD MENTAL (Glasnevin)...............................	**21** A2
HIGHFIELD (Private Mental, Drumcondra).....................	**21** B3
JAMES CONNOLLY MEMORIAL HOSPITAL (Blanchardstown)	**18** F1
LEOPARDSTOWN PARK (M.O.H.)..............................	**52** E3
LINDEN CONVALESCENT HOME (Blackrock)..................	**44** F4
MATER MISERICORDIAE (Eccles Street).......................	**36** D1
MEATH (Heytesbury Street).......................................	**36** D3
MOUNT CARMEL (Braemor Park)...............................	**43** A3
NATIONAL MATERNITY (Holles Street)........................	**36** E3
ORTHOPAEDIC HOSPITAL OF IRELAND (Clontarf).........	**22** E4
OUR LADY'S HOSPITAL FOR SICK CHILDREN (Crumlin)....	**42** D1
OUR LADY'S HOSPICE (Harold's Cross)........................	**35** C4
OUR LADY OF LOURDES HOSPITAL (Dun Laoghaire).......	**53** C2
PEMBROKE PRIVATE (Pembroke Street, Lower)...............	**36** E3
ROTUNDA (Maternity)...	**36** D1
ROYAL CITY OF DUBLIN (Baggot Street).....................	**36** F4
ROYAL HOSPITAL (Donnybrook)...............................	**43** B1
ST. ANNE'S SKIN & CANCER (Northbrook Road).............	**36** E4
ST. ANTHONY'S HOSPITAL & REHABILITATION CENTRE...	**44** E2
ST. BRENDAN'S HOSPITAL.......................................	**35** C1
ST. BRICIN'S MILITARY (Infirmary Road).....................	**35** B2
ST. BRIGID'S HOSPITAL (Crooksling).........................	**47** A4
ST. CLARE'S (Ballymun)..	**21** A2
ST. GABRIEL'S (Cabinteely)......................................	**53** C3
ST. JAMES'S HOSPITAL (Kilmainham).........................	**35** B3
ST. JOHN OF GOD (Stillorgan).................................	**52** F1
ST. JOSEPH'S (Clonsilla)...	**17** B2
ST. JOSEPH'S (Raheny)...	**23** A2
ST. LOMAN'S HOSPITAL (Palmerston)........................	**33** A1
ST. LUKE'S (Oakland, Highfield Road).........................	**43** A2
ST. MARY'S ORTHOPAEDIC (Cappagh).......................	**19** C1
ST. MARY'S ORTHOPAEDIC (Baldoyle).......................	**13** A4
ST. MARY'S HOSPITAL (Phoenix Park)........................	**34** E2
ST. MICHAEL'S HOSPITAL (Dun Laoghaire)..................	**46** D4
ST. MICHAEL'S NURSING HOME (Dun Laoghaire)...........	**46** D4
ST. PATRICK'S (James's Street).................................	**35** B3
ST. PAUL'S (Beaumont)...	**21** C1
ST. VINCENT'S (Elm Park, Merrion Road)....................	**44** E1
ST. VINCENT'S (Richmond Road)...............................	**21** B4
SIMPSON'S HOSPITAL (Dundrum)..............................	**51** B2
STEWART'S HOSPITAL (Palmerston)...........................	**33** C1
TALBOT LODGE CONVALESCENT HOME (Blackrock).......	**44** E4
TALLAGHT HOSPITAL (under construction)...................	**48** F1
VERVILLE RETREAT (Vernon Avenue).........................	**22** E4